ADVANCE PRAISE

"With the accuracy of a historian, the insight of a scholar, and the heart of a Christian leader, Kate Bowler explores an influential phenomenon within Christianity in this challenge to today's church leaders. Readers of Bowler's previous books will not be disappointed."
—**PHIL AND DEBBIE WALDREP**, founders of the *Women of Joy* ministry

"Filled with vivid human portraits, *The Preacher's Wife* is an absolute joy to read. Kate Bowler's account demonstrates, with great insight, the difficult balance megachurch women must constantly maintain, stepping into the limelight but never appearing to monopolize it. The book advances our understanding of evangelicalism and women's role in modern American religion."
—**MARGARET BENDROTH**, author of *The Last Puritans: Mainline Protestants and the Power of the Past*

"Kate Bowler provides an extraordinarily rich portrait of Christian female celebrities who are breaking church barriers on women's roles even as they uphold a carefully crafted stance of holy obedience. With generosity, perceptiveness, and wit, Bowler analyzes these women in all their intricacy as they manage beauty, sexuality, family life, and money on a public stage. A truly splendid book."
—**R. MARIE GRIFFITH**, author of *Moral Combat: How Sex Divided American Christians and Fractured American Politics*

"Fascinating, insightful, and utterly illuminating, this book shows why historians need to be involved in all of our theological conversations. Kate Bowler throws the lights on, bringing us a desperately needed perspective on the invisible rules governing how, when, and which women lead in the religious marketplace. As a woman in public ministry, I'm grateful for the clarity and challenge of Bowler's findings as well as her kindness, camaraderie, and wisdom. I won't see my work the same way again."
—**SARAH BESSEY**, author of *Jesus Feminist* and *Miracles and Other Reasonable Things*

THE
PREACHER'S
WIFE

THE PREACHER'S WIFE

The Precarious
Power of Evangelical
Women Celebrities

KATE BOWLER

PRINCETON UNIVERSITY PRESS

PRINCETON AND OXFORD

Requests for permission to reproduce material from this work
should be sent to permissions@press.princeton.edu

Published by Princeton University Press
41 William Street, Princeton, New Jersey 08540
6 Oxford Street, Woodstock, Oxfordshire OX20 1TR

press.princeton.edu

Library of Congress Cataloging-in-Publication Data

Names: Bowler, Kate, author.
Title: The preacher's wife : the precarious power of evangelical women
    celebrities / Kate Bowler.
Description: Princeton, NJ : Princeton University Press, 2019. | Includes
    bibliographical references and index.
Identifiers: LCCN 2019016248 | ISBN 9780691179612 (hardcover)
Subjects: LCSH: Evangelicalism. | Spouses of clergy—United States—
    Biography. | Women in Christianity—Biography.
Classification: LCC BR1643.A1 B69 2019 | DDC 277.3/083082—dc23
    LC record available at https://lccn.loc.gov/2019016248
ISBN (e-book): 9780691185972

British Library Cataloging-in-Publication Data is available

Editorial: Fred Appel, Jenny Tan
Production Editorial: Terri O'Prey
Text Design: Leslie Flis
Jacket/Cover Design: Amanda Weiss
Production: Erin Suydam
Publicity: Kathryn Stevens

Jacket image: iStock

This book has been composed in Minion Pro with Franklin Gothic Extra
Condensed display

Printed on acid-free paper. ∞

Printed in the United States of America

10 9 8 7 6 5 4 3 2 1

For Dad
who dusted me off and sent me back up the mountain
after I fell all the way down.

CONTENTS

A PERSONAL NOTE

In my experience, evangelical girls learn the limits of their own spiritual authority as an accounting of small details, little moments of encouragement or discouragement that nudge them toward a sense of being acceptable. I doubt that my own encounter with these expectations was terribly unusual, though few likely included a sit-down with a gentle giant named Merv in the mess hall of a Mennonite bible camp. My attempts to understand just what my counselors meant by "male headship" led to (by camp standards) an infamous tête-à-tête. To the naked eye, it looked like a fourteen-year-old girl demanding that a kindly thirty-something man account for what words like "submission" meant in the context of his marriage to the camp nurse. In what spheres of life must she ask for his permission? Was she allowed to make medical decisions without his say-so? Was it possible that she possessed special spiritual gifts that did not require his oversight?

Those are the only questions I remember asking at the time, but I spent the next three summers learning the complicated math involved in assigning male and female roles in the bare liturgical world of campfires and sing-alongs. Only men preached at nightly gatherings, baptized the occasional staff member, and served communion for Parents' Day. I have photographic evidence that even the fifteen-year-old boy in the novelty T-shirt with a naked Homer Simpson on the back (a boy who would one day be my husband) would be permitted this sacred office. Women sang the songs, prayed most of the time, shared stories, led bible studies before mixed audiences, and spoke informally from the pulpit. They taught any camp skill, from waterskiing to rock climbing to crafts, but if they were assigned maintenance duty they were never allowed to drive the truck to the dump, which had the added bonus of seeing the bears eat garbage. I was very disappointed about the bears. And about being relegated to picking up sticks when the teenage boys were given chain saws to clear the brush.

Nevertheless, my Mennonite bible camp was the touchstone of my adolescent spirituality and I found it difficult to stay angry. I left camp that final summer with some loud declarations about how I would come

This Mennonite evangelical summer camp encouraged women to play music. The author (left) was less than enthusiastic about this option.

back as a speaker and be a "lady James Dobson," having glimpsed stacks of James Dobson's *Focus on the Family* magazines in the bathrooms of Baptist homes. A decade later, when I received my Ph.D., I knew for a variety of reasons that I would never be a camp speaker or a lady James Dobson. However, my first act of theological service would be to return to rural Manitoba to answer the camp's need for someone to revise their morning bible studies. In a calculus that only evangelicals can understand, I would never be allowed to preach from their wooden pulpit in the chapel—but I could speak directly to the entire camp daily on theological matters, as long as I wrote down what I said.

Writing history is one of those things that evangelical women are allowed to do, and—for as long as I can remember—it suited me completely. I relished the opportunity to transform questions like "Why is that man on television preaching about money?" into long, satisfying years of research and writing. I wrote the first comprehensive history of the American prosperity gospel in my early 30s and then, in hopes of achieving tenure at Duke University, I began working on a new book centered on the questions I once had as a camper: "How do women learn their spiritual roles? What parts are they allowed to play?" I began to travel the country to attend the largest Christian conferences, which, I had already learned, were almost exclusively led by wildly charismatic women drawn from evangelical and pentecostal Protestant traditions. Their lives seemed loud and public, buoyed by social media tricks and trends, and utterly audacious. Housed in Christian traditions that refused to recognize women as spiritual oracles, how had they seemed to become them anyway?

I expected to write this book on my ascent into scholarly glory, securing for myself a place in academic Valhalla. Instead, I wrote these pages in the corridors of Duke Hospital, a short walk away from my quiet office, where I had first learned the news that I had Stage IV cancer. Tumors that bloomed in my colon and liver had, in a moment, disappeared every cheerful ambition and casual plan. And all I could see was my husband—that boy I met in bible camp as a teenager—and my toddler, Zach, who loves me more than tractors. But in that early chaos, I remembered someone I had recently interviewed. Her name is Margaret Feinberg, and she is a popular Christian speaker at major evangelical conferences who had written about her own experience with cancer. I liked her on sight. In an evangelical women's world of glossy flowing hair and promotional photos of laughing families, she has a short, brown pixie cut and an author photo where she looks like she is sharing a joke with her dog. Hours after receiving my diagnosis, I found myself dialing her number.

"Margaret, it's Kate. From last month. I just got diagnosed with Stage IV cancer." And then I used some unladylike words.

"Oh, Kate," she said. And then she also said something unladylike. She was perfect; pastoral, wise, quiet as I poured out my confusion and rage. In the months that followed, Margaret kept nudging me, encouraging me to treat my work like it too could live on. I resumed interviewing, researching, and writing with an urgency that surprised even me. With only a slim chance of surviving until tenure, I frantically wrote two manuscripts with the desire to make sense of a life turned sideways; the first was a memoir called *Everything Happens for a Reason (and Other Lies I've Loved)* about how having cancer made me recognize my own "prosperity gospel," and the second was this volume, which I wrote in the months leading up to a rather dramatic surgery. By then, I had come to appreciate many of the women in these pages. I can see now that it might have been a little unusual for Sandra Stanley, whose husband leads a church of forty thousand, to pop by Emory Hospital at my request to answer questions about living in the public eye while I sat in my chemotherapy chair, clipboard in hand. Sandra brought homemade bread and answered my questions with candor, and I was beginning to understand the role that anthropologist Ruth Behar calls "the vulnerable observer."[1] As I was so obviously struggling against my own limitations, I discovered that most people were quite willing to admit their own. Together we spent hundreds of hours discussing the narrow and precarious paths of power that women tread.

You might imagine that having written a history of Christian women celebrities would have made the flurry of publicity around my own memoir and podcast that much easier. I had learned a great deal from watching these women navigate the Christian marketplace, but I had never personally felt the weight of public expectations or the sting of criticism, both private and public. I was nervously pacing backstage at my first public event about the memoir when another speaker sidled up. "So you're only famous because you're dying, right?" she said coolly, as if it were a normal question. "Actually, it's because I have something to say," I shot back, but she had touched a nerve. In this world of Christian celebrity, a tragedy could be an opportunity for a new brand, a wider platform, and a new set of credentials, and it took me a full minute of glaring at her to remind myself that this was simply the dark logic of the marketplace. The capitalist ethos of this limited spiritual economy would make competitors out of friends and resentment a natural response to meeting a woman with Stage IV cancer.

Celebrity Christian women must live in the ambiguity of competing claims on their lives. Spiritually, they are called to transcend worldly concerns and even their own desires to clothe themselves with divine knowledge, paradigmatic virtue, and the gospel's story of the redemption of the world. But with their feet planted on this side of heaven, they are also products of institutional and cultural expectations with long-standing customs and prescriptions as well as a marketplace propelled by an exacting pragmatism that presses them toward results-driven metrics and messages. They understand that "celebrity" is inherently unstable, wonderfully generative but compromised by the endless demand for disclosure. Our world is full of such familiar strangers.[2] Country musicians, catwalk mannequins, heiresses to hotel fortunes, and social media influencers appear before us momentarily, only to be replaced in our attention by a *Bachelor* villain, porn star, mass shooter, or diet guru. With its own annual Forbes 100 List, the title of "celebrity" is as alluring as it is ephemeral, affixed not only to those who are famous but also to the process of becoming so. A celebrity is one who actively chases the public eye, wooing the media and cultivating a network of supporting agencies and fellow stars that manufactures mass recognition. Celebrities are by no means creatures of nature; they are, in the words of Chris Rojek, "cultural fabrications," the products of a host of intermediaries: "agents, publicists, marketing personnel, promoters, photographers, fitness trainers, wardrobe staff, cosmetics experts and personal assistants."[3] Celebrities are both producers and products, willing to manage the "backstage" of their personal lives to create an effortless "on-stage" performance.

In many ways, the celebrity Christian women in these pages are simply the latest commodities of a religious marketplace that has thrived for at least the past thousand years. In the Middle Ages, the proclamation of the gospel gave birth to the pilgrimage industry, rival theological masters vying for students, a brisk trade in saints' relics, church art and architecture, and the sale of indulgences, candles, holy water, and votive images. When Protestantism sought to put an end to such commerce, merchants soon found there were buyers eager for vernacular Bibles, martyrologies, and collections of sermons. The nineteenth century saw the rise of lucrative speaking tours by religious orators and the sale of religious sheet music and songbooks. From Billy Sunday to Aimee Semple McPherson to Billy Graham, the twentieth century was studded with charismatic stars who assembled astronomic followerships as they conducted evangelism over the radio, under canvas tents, and in arenas. The modern religious marketplace was made in the image of evangelicalism and developed in order to meet the desires of a Protestant subculture that wanted to remain distinct but not isolated, privy to the same music, television, radio, books, and goods that the wider culture enjoyed—but with a sanctified twist. The female luminaries of contemporary ministry sold memoirs, albums, videos, tickets, and every-thing from T-shirts to hats that read: "Bless This Mess." They were sales-women and preachers, depending on the moment.

By the end of my research, I had traveled across the United States and Canada to watch women compete in the evangelical marketplace. I visited thirty megachurches, attended fifteen of the largest women's conferences, and interviewed over a hundred Christian celebrities and supporting industry leaders. I had asked vestment makers about how clothing confers power, megachurch builders about the politics of church office space for pastors' wives, and conference organizers about whether it was a liability to have fat women on stage. I systematically tracked women in conference advertisements and on the staffs of the largest churches in North America, and once, out of boredom, made a spread-sheet which suggested that the chances of a famous woman dying her hair blonde was incredibly high if her husband's church had over ten thousand members. What I discovered is what I had learned long ago at bible camp: the visible and invisible rules that govern the lives of evan-gelical women can be mastered and occasionally subverted by those will-ing to play a difficult long game with handsome rewards and harsh penalties.

GLOSSARY OF IMPORTANT TERMS

Brand: The over-arching public image that a celebrity, product, or institution wishes to project. The shaping of this image is essential to establishing a place in the market and, once shaped, it must be carefully maintained.

Celebrity: Refers to both a high level of public recognition and the act of continually seeking and nurturing an image. A celebrity is both a person and a product, and the effort it requires is typically disguised and sustained by a cluster of behind-the-scenes staff.

Charismatic: After World War II, pentecostalism began to spread beyond its denominational boundaries (e.g., Assemblies of God) and appeal to middle-class, white audiences across Catholic and Protestant traditions. In the 1960s and 1970s, the charismatic movement was known for its ecumenical and playful emphasis on spiritual gifts. The Vineyard Church and Calvary Chapel are later examples of charismatic (not strictly pentecostal) churches.

Complementarianism: The belief, contrary to egalitarianism, that God assigned men the role of headship over the family and the church. It holds that although both men and women bear the image of God, the sexes have separate gifts.

Conservative: (See "liberal") I use this term narrowly to describe the scriptural literalism, right-wing politics, and "pro-family" framing of evangelical and pentecostal traditions and, in particular, their hierarchical view of women in ministry.

Evangelical: This hotly debated term describes a tradition dating back to England in the 1700s. In these pages, I refer exclusively to the modern American iteration that emerged from the fundamentalist-modern controversy of the early twentieth century. Evangelicals are known for their emphasis on scripture, conversion, revivalism, and, later, a subculture that defines their place over and against the wider American culture. Occasionally this book (as in its subtitle) follows the wider custom of referring to "evangelicalism" as an umbrella term that includes pentecostalism.

Gender: A term differentiated from "sex" when referring to the male and female human, especially as it regards cultural and social rather than merely biological differences.

Historic Black Denominations: The omnipresence of American racism and legal segregation spurred the development of separate black denominations. Some of the largest historic black denominations include the African Methodist Episcopal Church, the African Methodist Episcopal Zion Church, and the National Baptist Convention. The term is used here as a kind of shorthand for the African American counterpart to the traditionally white "mainline" denominations, for both share liturgical and theological similarities and a preference for an educated clergy.

Liberal: I use this term narrowly to describe the theological progressivism, left-wing politics, and social justice leanings of mainline Protestant denominations and, in particular, their supportive attitudes toward women in the pulpit.

Mainline: Largely white Protestant denominations such as the United Methodists, the Evangelical Lutheran Church in America, the Presbyterian Church USA, American Baptist Churches USA, the United Church of Christ, Disciples of Christ, and the Episcopalian Church, which until the mid-twentieth century comprised the majority of American Protestants.

Market: The demand for a good or service. The particular market I am referring to is the evangelical commodities and industries that boomed from the 1970s onward. Postwar evangelicalism created a subculture with a tremendous appetite for products that enabled them to participate in consumer culture without feeling tainted by it. It is best imagined as a tangled series of industries including television, radio, books, magazines, speaking tours, and endless value-signaling products from T-shirts to license plates.

Megachurch: The accepted definition of a megachurch is a Protestant congregation with two-thousand-plus regular attendees, including both adults and children at its weekly worship services.

Megaministry: A term I use to describe the overlapping major Christian industries in the United States, including megachurches, parachurches, television networks, music labels, and publishing houses. Although Catholicism can adopt some aspects of megaministry, it is overwhelmingly Protestant in general and evangelical and pentecostal in particular.

Parachurch: A parachurch is a ministerial organization with evangelistic aims (which might include relief and justice work), but is not primarily defined by liturgical functions. It does not typically serve communion, baptize believers, or keep membership as its primary goals. It has a high degree of specialization (women's ministry, college ministry, etc.). Examples include Focus on the Family and InterVarsity Christian Fellowship.

Pentecostalism: A movement that began in the early twentieth century and asserted that the spiritual gifts visited upon the early church (speaking in tongues, words of knowledge, supernatural healing, etc.) were available to contemporary believers. These beliefs coalesced into denominations such as the Church of God in Christ (African American), the Assemblies of God (white), and the Pentecostal Assemblies of the World (African American). The early years of the movement were marked by racial segregation and Trinitarian schisms.

Pentecostalized Historic Black: In the 1970s and 1980s, African American churches had their own version of the charismatic movement with a renewed emphasis on spiritual gifts. The result was that many of the fastest growing churches and church associations were pentecostalized versions of African American Methodist and Baptist traditions. See, for example, the Full Gospel Baptist Church Fellowship (est. 1992) and its leadership who double as megachurch pastors.

Prosperity Gospel: After World War II, many pentecostal leaders began to tout financial miracles and a new language of faith as spiritual power. In the 1970s, spread largely through television and a network of bible colleges and churches, this theology taught that God rewarded the faithful with health and wealth.

Subculture: A group inside a larger culture, with distinguishable values. These differences can be ethnic, aesthetic, religious, ideological, etc. In this work, the term most often refers to the separate theological (and overwhelmingly white) culture that evangelicals created in the years following World War II.

ACKNOWLEDGMENTS

I am the child of academics, which is to say that I know what it is like to have a full bookshelf in the family bathroom. This, even now, seems profoundly unsanitary. But it does mean that I have two parents who love to see ideas follow you everywhere. My mom, Karen, is like Anne of Green Gables, if she had a Ph.D. in music: a playful faith that knows how to make life sing. And my dad is a grizzly bear. A grizzly bear with a Ph.D. in Tudor history, a voracious appetite for editing my work, and a soft tummy for hugging. I would say that last part is incidental, but it is not. This was a banner year for hugs. One of the great discoveries of adulthood is that you realize your parents are people. And what a joy to discover that they are some of the best people in the world.

I have always suspected that weddings and funerals are where families and friends rally together or combust, and mine rallied like nothing I have ever seen. They somehow knew that this book gave me purpose and a place to go for a while every day so I did not have to sit around being professionally cancerous. My husband, Toban, took on this book as our shared family ambition, giving me every bit of the love and time I needed to make this project a reality. My sisters, Amy and Maria, brought love into my world of needles and chemotherapy. My in-laws, Ken and Els, built me things, ran after my toddler, and took me to the hospital. They love me as if I am theirs. My sister-in-law stayed up nights with me, nursing me back to health, literally, because she is both an actual nurse and an incredible human being. She and my brothers-in-law are dearer to me than I can express. And my besties Carolyn, Chelsea, Katherine, and Kori are my other selves, the keepers of my jokes and my insecurities.

I have so many people to thank because this book was an act of hope, and these people taught me to hope. Keith and Brenda Brodie did not yet know me when they signed on to support the travel for this book with a generous gift. It was the greatest compliment for a person who no longer believed she would ever be able to get back to work, and I am so deeply grateful for their example and for their humanity. Thank you to Don Richter, Edwin David Aponte, and the Louisville Institute for generously providing support for a sabbatical. Not only did they make arrangements to accommodate my sudden medical leave, but also sent gifts and prayers to bless me.

My academic community was my lifeline. Duke Divinity School—you Methodist sweethearts—brought me food and moved my research and medical leave time around so that I would have time to heal and to write. When you heard the news, you gathered the entire community in prayer throughout my surgery. You are my home.

My guild of American religious scholars filled me up with kindness and secondary sources. They read my work, encouraged my every step, and understood how good work reconstitutes you. My Young Scholars of American religion cohort walked with me through it all. When we thought I would die in a few months, they lovingly fortified every effort with wine, dancing, and debate. Thank you especially to Laurie Maffly-Kipp, Marie Griffith, Leigh Schmidt, and the Danforth Center at Washington University for generously reading and critiquing this manuscript.

Thanks are due to all the people who helped me think this through, gathered material, and saved me from error: Phil Goff, Doug Winiarski, Dana Robert, Luke Bretherton, Stephen Chapman, Mark Chaves, Grant Wacker, Thomas Tweed, Matthew Sutton, Glenda Goodson, Joey Morningstar, Mark Roberts, Darin Rodgers, Laceye Warner, Dan Vaca, Phil Sinitiere, Wayne Warner, Lauren Winner, Mandy McMichael, and Molly Worthen. And, of course, to my students at Duke Divinity School who agree to take my classes called things like "Big Hair, Big Jesus" and who improve my thinking. Judith Heyhoe, as ever, was a generous editor. Chris Destigter was a wonderful footnote chaser, and Eliza Griffith a life-changing photo wrangler. This book was much improved also by the insights of my two doctoral students, Aaron Griffith and Joshua Young. Aaron lent me his insights and expert pen for the last push of this book as a senior researcher. And Joshua Young not only helped me map out this complicated world but showed himself to be the most diligent researcher I know. Thank you for being my shared brain these many years.

I could not have made it over the finish line without a few other special people: Jim Heynen (whose wisdom would be painful if he weren't so kind), Kurt Berends and Sara Hohnstein of the Issachar Fund, Greg Jones (my visionary dean), Zoë Pagnamenta (my agent), and Fred Appel (my editor and fellow Winnipegger). You are better than I deserve. Dave Odom from Leadership Education at Duke Divinity was a sage, supporter, and a saint. His unflagging support helped me finish this project when it did not seem humanly possible.

Many thanks also to the people who lent their experience and expertise by word or by example: Alli Worthington, Amy Lynn and Benji Kelley, Angie Hong, Anita Renfroe, Annie Downs, Barbara Brown Taylor, Barbara O'Chester, Gail Song Bantum, Beth Moore, Candi Finch, Carol Bechtel, Carol Johnson, Chris Adams, Christena Cleveland, Christine Caine, Christy Nockels, Cynthia Hale, Debbie and Phil Waldrep, Denise George, Donna Miller, Ed Bahler, Elizabeth Eaton, Frank Reid, Glennon Doyle, Grace Ji-Sun Kim, Jeanne Stevens, Jenni Catron, Jennifer Knapp, Jonathan Merritt, Harriett Olson, Hayley Morgan, Jo Hudson, Julie Pennington-Russell, Julie Rodgers, Katherine and Jay Wolf, Kathy Khang, Ken Carter, Lisa Cotter, Lisa Harper, Liz Curtis Higgs, Lori Wilhite, Lysa TerKeurst, Mandy Arioto, Margaret Feinberg, Mark Driscoll, Meighan Stone, Mickey Maudlin, Monique Moultrie, Morgan Lee, Nadia Bolz-Weber, Nancy Wilson, Patsy Willimon, Patty Fitzpatrick, Paula Williams, Paul McCain, Rachel Held Evans, Rebekah Lyons, Rick Dunn, Sandra McCracken, Sara Harlow, Scott Jones, September Vaudrey, Sharon Thompson, Soong-Chan Rah, Stephen Fendler, Susie Hawkins, Susan Gillies, Tammy Dunahoo, Tom Cox, Tracy Higley, Warren Bird, and Wes Granberg-Michaelson. And to Jessica Richie, the best project director on the planet, and proof that ex-cheerleaders will out-work, out-plan, and out-smart us all.

My profound gratitude goes out to the many women in this book who let me into their worlds so we could talk about how we all try to spin the straw of our lives into gold. Or at least into nicer straw.

THE PREACHER'S WIFE

Introduction

The female part of every congregation have, in general, an
influence which, while it cannot be defined, cannot, at the
same time, be resisted.

Samuel Miller, *Letters on Clerical Manners and Habits*, 1827[1]

If there was one universal law of Christian megaministry, it was found
in the book of Genesis: "It is not good for the man to be alone. I will
make a helper suitable for him."[2] He should not be alone. She will do
him some good.

In almost every spiritual empire, there was a "she."

She may be the one on the main stage, smiling into the spotlight, telling a lightly worn anecdote as she sets her dog-eared Bible on the po-
dium. She might be seated in the darkened first row, a wide-brimmed
Sunday hat nodding up and down, or behind the stage in the green room
clucking at her kids to mind their business. She could be the mother,
silvered but stately, the matriarch of a charismatic son and the symbol
of her bygone generation. She might be the daughter singing an extra
solo with the choir, avoiding the curious gazes of those who suspect that,
if there is no son, she would inherit her father's mantle. A few upstarts
would take to social media to stoke a cause or take an institution to task,
swatting away questions about whether there was a *he* who supported
what *she* does. But most often, she was the slender wife at his side, their
fingers lightly interlaced as he calls her his "better half" and his sweet-
heart again, this and every Sunday morning. This was the presumed
order of Christian megaministry, the yin and the yang.

These women lived with many forms of power. They populated network television lineups, megachurch main stages, SiriusXM radio stations, Barnes & Noble bookshelves, and stadium events in every major
city. They went by many names: pastors, co-pastors, bible teachers, authors, speakers, executive directors, or, more commonly, pastors' wives,
and they pitched their expertise in any number of ways, from women's
ministry directors to teachers, preachers, singers, bloggers, advocates,
nutritionists, parenting experts, sex therapists, prophetesses, life coaches,

and television hosts. The biggest stars topped the *New York Times* best-seller list and garnered some of the highest rates of Christian television viewership in the world. Some grew so famous that they, like Oprah, need only one name. Beth. Joyce. Victoria. Jen. Their stars had risen so high that almost any churchgoing woman in America would call them celebrities.

The heights of spiritual superstardom in America—what I call "megaministry" (see Glossary)—was a tangled series of networks of the largest evangelical and pentecostal churches, denominations, parachurch organizations, Christian publishing companies, record labels, and television and radio networks. Megaministry was an overwhelmingly conservative Protestant phenomenon (which I often, imperfectly, simply call "evangelical" in character). Size was the most dominant feature of this modern ministry. There were more large churches than ever before: the number of churches with more than two thousand members (called megachurches) has grown by 3,000 percent since 1970.[3] Christian television programming measured its potential broadcast audiences by the billions.[4] Secular media conglomerates owned and acquired evangelical imprints to launch their own Christian nonfiction titles onto the bestseller lists.[5]

Christian celebrity was a tricky category to define because, to the average American, its stars were almost invisible. Though there were megachurches and leaders in almost every state,[6] most of the largest crowds and organizations made their home in the urban sunbelt. The industry of megaministry seemed more like NASCAR than the NBA, a regional and specialized market with millions of devoted followers, but not a national and omnipresent attraction. I use the term "celebrities" here with an asterisk, a wink that says you must know where to look to find them. Jen Hatmaker, whose career soared so high that she starred in her own Target commercial, playfully referred to herself as only "low-grade Christian famous," not an A-list celebrity but "D-minus level, enough to get recognized in airports, but not enough to really have any true advantages."[7] These were not household names in the same way as those of a politician, actress, or athlete might be. But in evangelical and pentecostal Christian subcultures, these women garner the level of adoration (and scrutiny) and more often are associated with the entertainment industry.[8] They must hire assistants to help them navigate gawking crowds or keep book signings from becoming therapy sessions as fans turned to them as gurus on marriage, parenting, miscarriage, singlehood, and faith.[9] Whatever they are called, they are not to be underestimated. Politicians court them as powerful brokers of public trust, and retail giants like Walmart, Costco, and Target kept their books in stock. Forbes recently appraised the collective income of America's pastor-personalities at an eye-popping $8.5 billion a year.[10]

Women like Victoria Osteen live their entire ministerial careers in megaministry's bright spotlight. To America's largest church, the forty-thousand-member Lakewood Church, she is the statuesque blonde beside her leading man who spearheaded their megachurch's ministry for women and preached weekly sermonettes about the divine good life.[11] To the seven million weekly viewers of their television show, she is a celebrity, a life-coach, and the author of such spiritual chick-lit as her *New York Times* bestselling *Love Your Life*. If she fell, she fell hard. Her Lakewood message that churchgoers obey God for the sake of their own happiness ignited a media firestorm, as did the 2005 accusation—later ruled false—that Victoria had assaulted a Continental Airlines flight attendant over a stain on her first-class armrest.[12] Blogs debated everything from her likability to the height of her heels. When she sat down for an interview with Oprah in the Osteen family's Texas mansion, there was little doubt that, loved or hated, she was a new kind of pastor's wife. She lived a world away from the plain face in the front pew expected of evangelicals a generation ago.[13] Tucked into Joel's arm, she rules as one of megaministry's first ladies.

At first glance, the celebrity of women in megaministry was completely baffling. After all, most of the largest denominations in the country did not consider women fit to be pastors. The Southern Baptist Convention, the largest Protestant denomination in the country,[14] waged fierce wars in the 1980s against women's spiritual leadership—and won. Female pastors in the denomination were kicked out or driven away as Southern Baptist leaders drew a hard line. Looking at the fifteen hundred or so megachurches dotting the country as a whole,[15] it becomes apparent that most congregations were not only opposed to women's pastoral leadership in theory but also in practice. (See Appendix V for a fuller account of this phenomenon.) The largest megaministries usually grew from

Victoria and Joel Osteen, who lead the country's largest church, are an iconic pastoral couple and an example of the heights to which a pastor's wife can climb. Forsythe Fotography/Crown Media United States, LLC.

conservative traditions[16] that did not ordain women or, if they did, rarely promoted them.

However, the success of women in megaministry showed how women—especially conservative women—had negotiated places for themselves and re-made popular religion into a woman's playground. One of the most famous Christian women in America sprang from the hard soil of Southern Baptist life. Her name is Beth Moore, and she routinely outsold and outperformed her fellow evangelists[17] as the singular attraction of one of North America's largest spiritual conferences.[18] What we see in her career is what we find in so many others, that her popularity began as a delicate dance between professed submission to men and implicit independence from them.[19] She promised that she was under the authority of male pastors and that she sought to be a leader only of other women, but her constant presence on television made it impossible for her to maintain the appearance of teaching an all-female audience.[20] Her power could never lie in the wooden pulpit of a brick-and-mortar church. Instead, she was a traveling evangelist whose products—books, speaking tours, and bible studies—were among the largest money-makers for LifeWay, the publishing arm of the Southern Baptist Convention.[21] Without a church, she ruled a theological kingdom.

This book is an exploration of the public lives of America's Christian female celebrities. It tells the story of women's search for spiritual authority in an era of jumbotrons and searing stage lights. Using abundant materials drawn directly from megachurches, parachurches,[22] publishers, television networks, and music producers—as well as over a hundred personal interviews with Christian celebrities and industry veterans—I show how the women of megaministry carved places for themselves out of the hardwood of American complementarianism. Their successes prompt us to ask two simple questions: What kinds of roles are they permitted? What do these women gain and lose in order to be market-ready?

The central narrative of this book shows how, alongside the rise of megaministry in the 1970s,[23] a cluster of unlikely women became stars of American Christianity. They were theologically conservative, far less equipped and encouraged than their liberal counterparts, and confined to a small number of eclectic roles that largely rested on the fame and institutions of others. Boxed in by high expectations of modern Christian womanhood, these women both broke the rules and played their parts, winning wide recognition as the spiritual go-tos for millions of Americans. In effect, conservative women were driven into the marketplace because of the restricted organizational roles they could occupy in their home churches.

The public lives of Christian women were shaped in large part by two powerful forces: first, the complementarian theologies that prescribed a limited set of feminine virtues and capacities; and, second, the industries that sustained their careers, which had their own rules about leading women. These two forces occasionally collided. For instance, as we see in a later chapter, female preaching was often renamed "bible teaching"

TODAY'S CHRISTIAN

REAL STORIES • REAL ISSUES • REAL FAITH

woman

SEPTEMBER/OCTOBER 2005

Bible study teacher
BETH MOORE
Catch her PASSION
for God's Word. PAGE 30

9 Ways to
Help Your Child
THRIVE in
Public School

TOUGH LOVE
Learning to forgive someone
who doesn't say "I'm sorry"

6 WAYS
to find more
time for prayer

DISCOVER
God's Gift of Rest
(It's waiting for you NOW)

FLEX APPEAL!
LIFTING WEIGHTS IS
GOOD FOR YOUR
BODY *AND* SOUL

NEVER SAY NEV...
A coma survivor's
take on FAITH and
END-OF-LIFE DECISIONS

$3.95 Canada $5.50
todaysChristianWoman.com

Beth Moore is the most famous leader in contemporary Southern Baptist life, despite having no formal denominational role. Reprinted with permission from *Christianity Today*, www.christianitytoday.com.

owing to the enormous market for it. Or consider the pressures a woman on stage might feel to have a facelift, despite the fact that there was nothing terribly virtuous about it. Again and again, theology and capitalism came to some kind of understanding, and the women in this business were often proof of it.

The women who ruled, first ruled the market. No matter how faithful a celebrity might be—and most of the women I interviewed were deeply altruistic—popular ministry was governed by the whims of a fickle marketplace, which might lavish praise one moment and cold opprobrium another. The shrewd learned to treat audiences as customers, anticipating their needs and predicting their hungers as trends evolved. They inured themselves to the breathless pace of the self-promotion: the turnstile of speaking engagements, bible studies, video series, and all of the accompanying products to keep revenues hovering above costs. They made bargains with their loved ones about when to be on the road or burn the midnight oil meeting deadlines and launching new products. Though the saintly among them hoped that the industry was a benign medium by which theological goods were delivered, almost everyone I interviewed acknowledged her unease with how (and to whom) the Christian industry meted out rewards.

There was no smooth path to God's house for a Christian woman celebrity, no steady march to equality or easy gains. Rather, there were a few common roles that women adopted and adapted to achieve a place of prominence. As each chapter follows the evolution of a particular role—preacher, mother, performer, counselor, beauty—we see that there was nothing particularly stable about them. These roles were perches—sometimes narrow, sometimes wide—on which to rest the weight of female authority. At first blush, these roles seem unflinchingly subservient to the dominant patriarchal evangelical subculture. Serita Jakes, the first lady of the country's largest African American church, claimed only to complement her husband's ministry with her vast debutante program and her books with titles like *Beside Every Good Man*. In the same city, Debbie Morris led the women's ministry for her husband's twenty-eight-thousand-member Dallas megachurch under the banner of "Pink," dedicated to helping women steward their influences as wives and mothers.[24] However, these gentle performances of docility often masked a nuanced negotiation with the categories they were given.

There are two other subplots that must be noted from the start. The first centers on race. The dominant account of women in megaministry in these pages is that of white women, not only because they were typically the best-known stars, but also because there has always been a much larger print industry to promote them and a marketplace to reward them.

The narrative largely reflects the statistical breakdown of the races of the megachurches profiled in this study: white (67 percent), black (23 percent), Latino/a (2 percent), Asian (1 percent). As each chapter will show, this book is also an account of how African American (and, to a lesser extent, Latina and Asian American) women in megaministry embodied the same roles as white women, but with different constraints. While white women, for instance, eventually wriggled out of the expectation that they constantly announce their submission to their husbands, black women did not. They bore the additional burden of modeling womanhood in a society that denigrated them. Long after it fell out of fashion in the white middle class, they would embody God's divine order for the black family in American life.

This book's analysis of the women *on* stage—the women whom the market rewards—must be viewed while keeping a keen eye toward those who are *off* stage. Though there are many women of color who are notable pastors, scholars, activists, and speakers, there was nothing like a megaministry "pipeline" to develop and support new and existing talent among ethnic minorities. Having studied hundreds of conference advertisements from the 1970s to the present, I identified a few consistent trends: evangelical stages remained overwhelmingly white, while pentecostal stages were platforms for black, white, and (to a lesser extent) Latina women, though typically they appeared before segregated audiences.[25] Indigenous women almost never found inroads into the industries that marketed Christian women, and whose own complicated relationship with being evangelized had to grapple with the burdened inheritance of colonialism.

Women of color spoke frankly about how difficult it was to gain national exposure when there were so few opportunities. "If we are going to get invited by a white woman to join her stage, it feels like there is always room for just one of us," said Kathy Khang, whose book, *Raise Your Voice,* argued for the need for a more diverse cast of theological voices.[26] The almost uniform whiteness on national platforms was tied to the twisted racial logics of a marketplace calibrated to the desires of largely segregated churches. The particular reasons for this were inextricable from the histories of each community. Kathy aptly summarized the distinct set of obstacles Asian American women faced breaking into the celebrity circuit.

We aren't white but the myth of being the model minority also comes into play. We are both exotic and assimilated, in part, because some of our cultural norms do not emphasize standing out as individuals and seeking fame for ourselves. And in the United States, there isn't a strong sense of what the Asian American church and its voice *is* in comparison to the white evangelical church or the black church and I think that sort of distinction is required in a celebrity world.[27]

In the marketplace, women of color found themselves locked into a narrow set of racial roles and, as a result, often locked out of the market itself.

Further, there were many ethnic-minority megachurches—Chinese, Korean, and Spanish-speaking in particular—that were unlikely to encourage female celebrity. There might be several explanations. First, as outlined in Appendix II, there was a very close connection between famous wives being called into leadership and the congregations' relationship to the marketplace. First-generation immigrant pastors and their wives were likely to be focused inward, on the needs of the community, rather than on building their national platforms.[28] Second, some interviewees noted that first-generation immigrant megachurches (particularly Korean American churches) were strongly hierarchical and placed constraints on elevating women into leadership.[29] Third, as Pastor Gail Song Bantum observed, second-generation Asian American women who succeeded in megaministry had already left the immigrant church and married non-Asians, thus becoming bridging figures in white or multiethnic contexts. Their leadership in first-generation churches was constrained not only by patriarchy, but also by the essentializing immigrant identity of churchgoers fearful of losing their connections to their homelands.[30] On the whole, the mere existence of ethnic-minority megachurches did not elevate women of color to leadership positions.

A second significant subplot follows the status of women in the Protestant mainline denominations. This book begins with a short, broad history of women seeking institutional power in American churches as leaders of the missionary enterprise and, later, as pastors and priests. After World War II, women in the cluster of denominations that comprise the mainline (or what academics often offhandedly call "liberal" or "progressive" denominations),[31] challenged their exclusion from

Pastor Gail Song Bantum, Executive Pastor of Quest Church, is one of the only Asian American women who serve in senior leadership at an American megachurch. Image courtesy of Gail Song Bantum.

ordained leadership and re-made these denominations into some of the largest religious bodies with both sexes in the pulpit and behind the altar. At one level, their success in ordained ministry was suggestive of re-markable gains since the first American woman was ordained more than a hundred and fifty years ago.[32] But as their experiences will show, very few of the women in any spiritual orbit were scripturally, doctrinally, and ecclesiastically supported in their ambitions. There were always caveats, and a vast gap remained between having rules in place that support the ordination of women and actually putting them in pulpits, particularly important ones.[33] Drawing on fresh interviews with many of the leaders of mainline megachurches and entire denominations, I show how these women's careers became a wedge issue and a convenient way of testing agreement on questions as lofty as scriptural inerrancy and as practical as skirt hemlines. Christian ministry was still overwhelmingly a man's world.

THE PREACHER'S WIFE

Under the church's website banner, Ed and Lisa Young were smiling at the camera in matching denim, her hand lightly touching his chest and his arm around her back. "For just a moment, forget everything you've ever thought of when it comes to church," reads the caption beside them. "Imagine a home for all who are looking for hope. This is Fellowship Church!"[34] Though in their mid-fifties they looked a cool decade younger, which did not hurt sales for *Sexperiment*, their *New York Times* best-selling guide to sex that had the couple spending twenty-four live-streamed hours in a staged bed on the roof of their church. She was the founder of "Flavour," the women's ministry for their twenty-five-thousand-person congregation, and the author of a few books on marriage, beauty, children, and a cookbook, *A Dash of Flavour.*[35] Together, they were the branded image of the largest Southern Baptist church in the country, which met at seven different locations throughout Texas and Florida or via the streaming of Ed Young's "Fifty Shades of THEY" on Netflix.[36] Everywhere one looked for Fellowship Church, the two of them were pictured smiling and inviting all to join them next Sunday for the latest sermon series like "Shark Weak" or "Espresso Yourself."[37]

In the world of modern megaministry, a pastor's wife was the welcome mat. She was the smile, the open arms, and the "Hello! Won't you come in?" to a church experience with a dizzying array of ways to participate. With multiple services and a half dozen campuses, a pastor's wife like Lisa Young could not simply stand by the door handing out bulletins and greet people as they entered. The country's largest churches had outgrown any leader's capacity to know the majority of their congregants. Every megachurch wife I spoke to described what it was like to look out over a flood of attendees and not recognize a soul. Although she may not always know them, they know her; somewhere in the sea of digital and in-person experiences of a single ecclesial community, the pastor and his wife were anchoring figures. If there was a billboard on the side of the highway advertising a church, she would be there, leaning over her husband's shoulder or slipped under his protective arm. And on megachurch websites, a photograph of the pastor and his wife was the most common advertisement for the church.

The omnipresence of women's images was matched only by the dearth of substantive information about them. Most churches wanted to make it clear that the pastor's wife had no actual position on staff or, in any case, that her importance was relative to his. This made introductions into a linguistic obstacle course, because as women were presented they almost instantly disappeared. An eight-thousand-member Arkansas megachurch introduced its senior pastor, Rick Bezet, to online audiences in a very typical way. Next to an image of him beside his wife Michelle, were the words:

Rick & Michelle Bezet // LEAD PASTOR[38]

Rick Bezet is the founder and lead pastor of New Life Church of Arkansas. Since starting [New Life Church] Conway in 2001, New Life has grown to include ten churches in nine cities with 20+ services, and two online services. . . . Rick and his lovely wife, Michelle, have been married for over 20 years and they have four children. They live in Conway, Arkansas.

Michelle appeared next to a title she did not possess as part of the branding for a church that may or may not employ her. In the Christian public's mind's eye, a famous wife was a block of marble chiseled mostly by the imagination. She might be the neck that turned her husband's head, the Salome that turned his heart, or the Ruth that laid herself at his feet. Her defining qualities and acts in shaping the ministry must be interpreted in gestures and shadows. Did she stand tucked behind him or sit quietly in the front row? Was she alone on stage explaining how she would give up ministry in a heartbeat if her husband simply told her to? Perhaps she sat beside him as the cameras filmed their television show, but when the credits rolled the show was in *his* name only. Sometimes I wondered if the fastest way to identify a woman's role in megaministry was to interview all of the lighting technicians on every mainstage in the country. Who would the spotlight fall on when the lights went down? Did the crowd know her face? Her role was a curious one. Whether she eclipsed everyone in the room or was an unseen partner to her husband's ministry, her mere existence sparked with power.

Assessing questions of significance and power were further complicated, as I discovered, by the ambiguity with which most public women in ministry narrated their own significance. Almost all women in the largest churches, parachurches, and on other platforms went to great lengths to hide their importance as a way of shielding themselves from criticism.

The self-presentation of Proverbs 31 founder Lysa TerKeurst was a study in deflected significance. Though she ran a multi-million-dollar organization that reached hundreds of thousands of women every day, making her one of the most powerful women in modern evangelical circuits, she described her success as being able to: "get through the day having spent time with the Lord, exercised in some way, had a laugh with one of my kids, had clean underwear in my husband's drawer when he needed them and made a friend smile."[39] Before their marital woes became public knowledge,[40] Lysa described her husband as a loving leader and a longsuffering man, who, once a month, "simply puts up with me and my bout of the Princess Must Scream syndrome."[41] While no one expected Oprah to keep her partner Stedman's underwear drawer stocked, these audiences were keenly attuned to indications that Ter-Keurst grounded her identity in relationship, motherhood, and wifehood. Superstar Beth Moore was quick to assure audiences that her husband, Keith, wore the Wranglers in their relationship, while televangelist Joyce Meyer continually invoked her husband Dave's benevolent approval of her media empire. As icons of the middle class, these women were expected to embody its trials and triumphs. They must be hard-working but not competitive, polished but not fussy, wholesome but not perfect. And as famous women, they must do what all famous women do and pretend to be average, subject to the acid test of "relatability." Their stories should be peppered with mishaps—they broke the eggs bagging their own groceries, put their shirts on inside-out, and ruined their children's Halloween costumes.

Some of these women were particularly formidable given that most cobbled their skills together on their own, without men in ministry's equivalent pastoral education. As we will discuss in Chapters One and Four, women had rarely been expected or encouraged to be theologically credentialed. As a result, most never sat in classes to learn systematic theology, scriptural exegesis, counseling, Christian history, or preaching. Instead, they assigned their own reading, honed their own preaching skills (often before female audiences), and earned their place in the Christian industry without the benefit of formal training. They were queens of self-mastery.

Or not. Some women earned their place in the sun and others simply basked in the reflected glow of others. While most women fought to be worthy of their status, it was possible to find megaministry women happy to float on the credentials of their mates, offering what skills they already had with mixed results. Like any inherited job, women may assume a church position as an entitlement and a perk. A megachurch wife might cheerfully list "shopping" as her primary hobby, knowing that her massive church salary and limited obligations give her plenty of money and time for it.[42]

Regardless of whether she craved the public eye or longed for anonymity, she must pick her place. A famous Christian woman could be many things—ambitious or deferential, canny or naive, intuitive or clueless, sweet or with a dash of salty language. But, whoever she was, she lived in front of many audiences.

Though not all famous Christian women were pastors' wives—and in fact, many of the most widely recognized were not—the most common role for a woman in megaministry was that of the preacher's wife. (See Appendix II for a full account of how this phenomenon was tracked.) Like Whitney Houston's famous movie character, the preacher's wife was married to the ministry and her talents were inexorably drawn into the life of the church. This should come as no surprise: the complementarian theologies that governed the largest Protestant churches installed hundreds of men at the helm of institutions and pressed their willing (and sometimes unwilling) wives into service. Further, many of the leading women in itinerant or parachurch ministry were also married to men in ministry. For this reason, a famous megaministry woman found that her power maintained the appearance of being borrowed. Regardless of her own credentials, she drew fame from the familial role she held as a mother, sister, daughter, or, most often, wife of an important godly man. It was seen in almost every small gesture like her Twitter handle or the way the conference host announced her onstage: Taffi was Creflo Dollar's wife. Dodie was Joel Osteen's mom. Priscilla was Tony Evans's daughter. Though there were some scrappy women who built their ministries from scratch it was hard and lonely work. Most women built on the poured foundation of marriage and family.

The woman who professionalized her role as wife or family member could build a career of her own. It was a convenient arrangement for both churches that affirmed women in ministry and those that did not, because audiences presumed that a wife's actions were subject to her husband's approval and therefore sanctioned. She could likewise benefit from the administrative staff, publicity, in-house audiences, and personal

LOIS I. EVANS AND
VONETTE Z. BRIGHT —
CONFERENCE CO-HOSTS

JOEL & VICTORIA OSTEEN
LAKEWOOD CHURCH
HOUSTON, TEXAS

T.D. & SERITA JAKES
THE POTTER'S HOUSE
DALLAS, TEXAS

TIM & BEVERLY LAHAYE
CONCERNED WOMEN FOR AMERICA
RANCHO MIRAGE, CALIFORNIA

JOHN & DIANA HAGEE
CORNERSTONE CHURCH
SAN ANTONIO, TEXAS

STUART & JILL BRISCOE
BRISCOE MINISTRIES
BROOKFIELD, WISCONSIN

GARY & NORMA SMALLEY
SMALLEY RELATIONSHIP CENTER
BRANSON, MISSOURI

KAY ARTHUR
PRECEPT MINISTRIES INTL.
CHATTANOOGA, TENNESSEE

BRIAN & BOBBIE HOUSTON
HILLSONG CHURCH
SYDNEY, AUSTRALIA

LARRY & MELANIE STOCKSTILL
BETHANY WORLD PRAYER CENTER
BAKER, LOUISIANA

TED & GAYLE HAGGARD
NEW LIFE CHURCH
COLORADO SPRINGS, COLORADO

KENNETH & TOGETTA ULMER
FAITHFUL CENTRAL BIBLE CHURCH
INGLEWOOD, CALIFORNIA

WENDELL & GINI SMITH
THE CITY CHURCH
KIRKLAND, WASHINGTON

ADRIAN & JOYCE ROGERS
BELLEVUE BAPTIST CHURCH
CORDOVA, TENNESSEE

ROBERT & CHERYL RECCORD
NORTH AMERICAN
MISSION BOARD
ALPHARETTA, GEORGIA

JACK & ANNA HAYFORD
CHURCH OF THE WAY
VAN NUYS, CALIFORNIA

TOM & DONNA MULLINS
CHRIST FELLOWSHIP CHURCH
PALM BEACH GARDENS, FL

JOEL & BECKY HUNTER
NORTHLAND: A CHURCH
DISTRIBUTED, LONGWOOD, FLORIDA

BILLY JOE & SHARON DAUGHTERY
VICTORY CHRISTIAN CENTER
TULSA, OKLAHOMA

This 2004 "Free to Soar" Pastors' Wives conference showed how indispensable a wife was to public ministry. Their titles varied wildly depending on the wives' theological tradition, ranging from "co-pastor" (prosperity theology) to untitled helpers (evangelical). Kay Arthur bucked the trend by simply being stand-alone famous. Reprinted with permission from Charisma Media, www.charismamedia.com.

and professional relationships that floated his career. In the pages that follow, the preacher's wife serves as an embodied argument for the twin forces—complementarianism and capitalism—that steered the careers of evangelical women celebrities. The preacher's wife was the safest woman in ministry: authorized to exercise her gifts by her husband's pastoral oversight and shielded from the worst excesses of the market-place. Most women's careers in ministry depended on borrowed insti-tutions, a guest spot on a television program, or a women's conference in someone else's church. Certainly, women without famous husbands *could* build a career on their own with a skeleton staff, but their livelihoods hung on a delicate web of relationships and connections. They depended on each other to keep their content and their brand in circulation and to find that sweet spot between irrelevance and controversy.

For women, this is an era of *almost*—almost feminist, almost patriarchal, almost progressive, and almost regressive—and in these pages we hold the prism of their experiences up to the light. The lives of public women invite us to ask again what Americans expect from women in the spotlight; and whether they will ever grow used to women's presence in the main seats of power, in the pulpit, in the corner office, or in the White House. The women of megaministry are exceptional, but they are not simply exceptions. They are religious reflections of almost-mythic American ideals of women as wives and mothers, pillars and martyrs, in a culture divided over whether women should *lean in* or opt out.[43]

THE GENDERED NATURE OF WHO'S WHO

To understand the public lives of these women requires a brief explanation of megaministry itself and the role that gender plays in building name-recognition. If this were a history of men in megaministry, this account would be far more straightforward. We would not have to piece together a far-flung network of traveling ministries, for most men did not endure the hazards of itinerancy in order to earn a paycheck. We could simply examine a list of the fifteen hundred or so churches in America, past and present, that earned the title "megachurch" for their claim that two thousand or more people attend worship there each Sunday. The names of its senior pastors would leave readers with a sense of familiarity—Rick Warren, T. D. Jakes, Joel Osteen, Jeremiah Wright, Andy Stanley—not only because the largest churches typically broadcast their services on television, but also because of their relationship with the media. When journalists need a comment from a Protestant leader on anything from an invasion to an earthquake, they typically ask a man because he is the leader of a megachurch or of a handful of politically tinged parachurch organizations such as James Dobson's Focus on the Family. A man is at the helm of an institution that validates his authority and employs a staff who knows his schedule and his talking-points.

As reporter Elizabeth Dias told me, "It is so hard to quote a woman in this world. All of the infrastructure is set up to put a man on the phone, and if I do find a woman to talk to then no one at the magazine has heard of her."[44] She would know. Her reporting put the first female preacher on the cover in *Time* magazine's history.[45] Since recognition breeds more recognition, senior pastors hold a significant institutional advantage when it comes to building and maintaining a national platform.

Women who aspired to leadership had a much more complicated relationship with Christian institutions. Roman Catholicism, with sixty-five million adherents in the United States, was the largest Christian tradition in the country, double the size of the nearest Protestant denomination, and its position against women in the priesthood was absolute.[46] Though this narrative is dominated by Protestants, we will see that even a cloistered nun can have a national following if she leaves the sacred offices and the sacraments alone. Mother Angelica, an owl-eyed Franciscan sister from Alabama, became one of the best-known Catholics in America for two decades when she founded EWTN, her Eternal Word Television Network, and broadcasted her unique style of no-nonsense televangelism, which was said to have a reach of 264 million households around the world.[47]

Women's success in leadership was predicated on whether they could find institutions *to* lead. To paint a rather grim portrait, it was much more common for a woman to gain a major pulpit through the death of her husband than through a promotion.[48] This was because many megachurches (especially pentecostal and prosperity megachurches) tapped husbands and wives as "co-pastors." An early widowing thrust the wife into solo leadership, and provided one of her only opportunities for a promotion. In almost every case where a woman was permitted to lead a large church without the spiritual oversight of a man, she had founded the congregation herself and stayed single. Only a handful of women have ever led a megachurch in American history and their authority has been brittle. (See Appendix V for a list of the many women who fell from power during the brief period of this research.) As a result, most women in megaministry have found either a position of indirect institutional power in a congregation (as, say, a co-pastor or women's ministry director) or they have founded or occupied a position in an organization not officially designated a "church." The reasoning goes: she is not a pastor

Kathy Khang got her start in public ministry as a campus ministry leader for InterVarsity Christian Fellowship. Image courtesy of Kathy Khang.

if her audience is not a church. In practice, these distinctions become rather blurry. Many of the women in this book (particularly Asian women) got their start preaching to college kids in Protestant or Catholic campus ministries, which, despite the fact that they perform most of the functions of a congregation, are not technically considered churches. Likewise, female televangelists were usually exempt from criticism because the studio audience was not a local congregation, though in scuffles with the Internal Revenue Service over tax-exempt status some television studios have declared that they are.[49]

Because this book is focused on the role of women—and each chapter tells the history of women as preachers, homemakers, performers, counselors, and beauties—I have chosen to scatter the discussion of the various megaministry industries in which they operated throughout the book. Since the 1970s, many branches of the popular religious marketplace have been dominated by evangelicals and pentecostals. These include book publishing (e.g., Zondervan, Thomas Nelson, WaterBrook

Multnomah, Revell, Bethany House, Chosen, Harrison House, InterVarsity Press, Kregel, LifeWay, Moody, Tyndale, Crossway); music production (e.g., Capitol Christian Music Group, Hillsong Music, Motown Gospel, Maranatha Music, RCA Inspiration); retail marketing (e.g., Hobby Lobby, Family Christian, LifeWay Christian Resources); magazine publishing (e.g., *Brio, Charisma, Relevant, Christianity Today, Christian Marketplace, Virtue, Today's Christian Woman*); movie studios (e.g., Affirm Films, Big Idea Entertainment, Lightworkers Media); television networks (e.g., Christian Broadcasting Network, Trinity Broadcasting Network, Praise the Lord Network, Eternal Word Television Network); radio networks (e.g., K-LOVE, Moody Radio, Salem Radio, United Christian Broadcasters); and a wide variety of other products and services, including award shows, film festivals, dating services, children's programing, music festivals, apparel lines, and an endless array of independent businesses. As we saw in the rise of Victoria Osteen at Lakewood Church, some megachurches grew so large that they housed multiple industries within them, doubling as concert venues, music studios, retail outlets, and television studios. Occupying a coveted pulpit for Sunday morning's sermon was not the only way to have a ministry.

Pentecostal evangelist Daisy Osborn once observed that if the pulpit is the man's Holy of Holies, then the parachurch was like the temple's outer courts, where the women were allowed.[50] But women like Daisy knew the power of these external organizations. Their talents were largely hidden by the seeming insignificance of parachurch organizations, but this hidden-in-plain-sight quality often worked in women's favor, allowing female-led organizations to thrive in a culture ambivalent about women in ministry. Some of the most successful were sprawling enterprises. Let us look again at Lysa TerKeurst, who, as I mentioned, was the founder and president of Proverbs 31 Ministries, based in Charlotte, North Carolina. Hers was a parachurch organization with a paid staff of almost fifty people tasked with finance and operations, donor development, digital media, communications, customer service, marketing, and, of course, the endless stream of content sent to five hundred thousand subscribers.[51] The organization was not simply an online bible study, but a platform for Lysa's brand, the place where readers could go to buy her *New York Times* bestseller, hear from her staff daily on theological topics, or find out the dates for her latest speaking tour or upcoming writer's conference. It also made her the gatekeeper of other women's successes, as she could choose which other speakers and authors to endorse.[52] At best, institutions like Lysa's parachurch ministry mirrored most of the advantages of a megachurch and offered similar resources, but they also shared the restrictions of the megachurch. While, in theory, the organizations could be focused on any topic (justice, the environment, political advocacy, etc.), most essentially followed the megachurches' "separate spheres"[53] model of women's ministries, restricting women to speaking only to women. And while this women-only focus was market gold, it rarely earned these women the national brand recognition that male senior pastors could achieve simply by being male senior pastors.

As we will see in these pages, the presence of women in megaministry reflected the advantages of power—effectively inventing roles ideally suited to the women at the helm—or subjecting them to the whims of theological communities with capitalist logics. For instance, scripture tells women to be modest,[54] and the American fashion industry reminds them to be spectacularly beautiful, so women on stage must look flawless in a tea-length skirt. Church tradition says women are subject to their husbands, and American culture privileges egalitarianism, so women should be on stage, but a step behind their husbands. There were endless variations on this theme, as women publicly negotiated the freedoms and constraints each context afforded them. And, of course, as in any market, only the very lucky, clever, or stubborn would endure.

Chapter One

THE PREACHER

But I suffer not a woman to teach, nor to usurp authority
over the man, but to be in silence.
—1 Timothy 2:12[1]

Ten thousand women were crammed into Norfolk's biggest arena with
heavy Bibles on their laps and a thick brochure for the Living Proof Live
Event in their hands detailing the schedule for the April 2016 weekend.
Almost every hotel room around the city had been booked for months
as women drove in from across the southeast and down the eastern
seaboard to hear Beth Moore, the Texas dynamo whose bible studies
had been bestsellers for almost two decades. Beth was the biggest name
in evangelicalism, as far as women were concerned, with 880,000 Twitter
followers, a packed annual speaking circuit, and the constant promotion of her material by the largest Protestant denomination's publishing
house, the Southern Baptist LifeWay.[2] When she entered the arena, the
women around me strained their necks to see the top of her blond head
across the dark expanse and murmured about how Beth raised her hands
in worship, how she sang along with the opening band, and how she
might address them tonight.

Beth hopped up on stage with open arms and a loud welcome, assuring the audience that even after nineteen years in ministry she had
prepared a word for them tonight that came from her fervent prayer and
diligent study.

"Tell your neighbor, 'I am a student!'" she called out.[3]

"I am a student," echoed the crowd, thumbing through their Bibles
for the correct verses. Beth was a bouncy and cheerful narrator who
loved to jump immediately into the reading of a Bible passage and its
slow exegesis. She was known for the way that she read a verse and then
retold it, sinking into the details to draw out the texture and emotion of

Beth Moore preaches a dynamic lesson to a sold-out Norfolk, Virginia, crowd. David Lowe Photography–davidlowephotos.

the story as she acted out the parts of the characters. Luke's gospel account of Jesus's healing of the Roman centurion's servant was her text that night, and she pulled her listeners into a verse-by-verse elucidation of its meaning. The centurion had told Jesus not to come to his house but to heal the servant with only a word, and Jesus had been amazed at the man's faith.

"What kind of faith is this that Jesus *marveled, marveled*. He marveled. There are two times—and there may be translations that use the word more than this—but most [Bibles] use the word concerning Christ himself two different times in the gospels . . . the other is in Mark 6:6

and I want you to go there for a quick second . . . where are you? Mark 6? Tell me one more time."

"Mark 6," repeated the crowd.

"And it says: 'He could do no mighty work there, except that he laid his hands on a few sick people and healed them.'"[4] She read the words carefully with the slow voice a teacher might use when giving instructions to a classroom. Then she quickly looked up and quipped: "Now I'm gonna tell you something: I would consider *that* a good day. Anybody?"

The audience laughed as if they had been holding their breath, exhaling relief as they moved out of the moral gravity of the scriptures and back into Beth's peppy chatter.

"I'd be going WHOOOOOOOO!" she exclaimed. "If He could do that tonight in this place, I'd consider that a mighty, mighty fabulous evening." They laughed again, but before the sound died down Beth was back to the text, explaining little bits of Jewish custom, pretending to be a biblical character, or parsing a Greek verb. Beth had once been an aerobics teacher, and there was little sign that she had given up her ability to keep a crowd following along as she taught for over an hour. She rarely spoke about her personal life or gave interviews, and when she made references to her own shortcomings that night she demurred, "I don't want to trip anyone else up by telling you about it." Instead, she wanted audiences to know her as a teacher of the Bible. And with over eleven million of her products sold, Beth's name was virtually synonymous with women's bible studies.[5]

While Beth bounced across the stage, Ana Maldonado marched. In Miami's American Airlines Arena, Maldonado was like a military officer on the stage of her annual *Conferencia Apostólica y Profética* (Apostolic and Prophetic Conference) commanding a crowd of ten thousand to hear a message straight from God. She and her husband Guillermo's church, *Ministerio Internacional El Rey Jesús* (King Jesus International Ministries), had grown into one of the largest Spanish-speaking congregations in the country since its founding in 1996,[6] and Maldonado had earned the title of *profeta* (prophetess) for her claims of divine intercession. She was a star of Latin American pentecostalism and its transnational network, as well as a visionary figure who claimed to have a special message from God.

"God said, 'Pray Isaiah 60 . . . intercede Isaiah 60 . . . pray it for the entire month of December, because certainly the word that I have for *Ministerio Internacional El Rey Jesús* is Isaiah 60,'" she shouted in rapid fire, her English translator struggling to keep up.[7] "*Levántate porque la gloria de Jehová ha nacido sobre ti!*" ("Arise because the glory of Jehovah has been born upon you!").[8] She pumped her fist in the sky and stomped her heels into the ground to hammer home every word. Isaiah's message concerning the rebuilding of Jerusalem became a prophecy, a foretelling of the greater growth of their church and the prospering of its people. The crowds clapped and cheered as she delivered the news, jumping to their feet when she paused to brag that she was keeping the devil on the run.

In St. Louis, the convention center was packed with more than twenty-seven thousand women eager to see Joyce Meyer take the stage at her largest annual event.[9] Joyce was one of the world's most famous pentecostals, a televangelist whose program *Enjoying Everyday Life* was one of the most-watched Christian television programs with an estimated (potential) audience of 2.3 billion,[10] a Twitter following of six million,[11] and more than a hundred books in print by her thirty-fifth year in ministry.[12] She was a prosperity preacher through and through, but a woman so powerful that famous evangelicals who normally criticized this theology showed little compunction in headlining her conferences. When she took the stage on the opening evening, laying her Bible on the glass lectern and clearing her throat to speak, the applause from the crowd was so deafening that it took her ribbing humor to quiet them down. Her messages were almost always the same—a few verses sprinkled into an earthy and personal message about individual victory—but that did little to deter the crowds.

In the world of megaministry, women rallied massive Christian audiences all the time—but the significance of a woman speaking was the subject of considerable debate. She exhorted. She testified. She sang. She taught. She prayed. She preached. She shared. She prophesied. Defining the nature of her theological speech was, however, inherently slippery. To avoid the appearance of disobeying scriptural injunctions, women who were obviously preaching scripture—women like Kay Arthur, Jill Briscoe, and, later, Beth Moore—made a habit of calling themselves "bible teachers" instead. This was a perennial issue, one that commentators on

Joyce Meyer, a divorced middle-aged woman from the Midwest, was an unlikely celebrity with an incredible knack for staying relevant. Reprinted with permission from Charisma Media, www.charismamedia.com.

American Christianity have long wrestled with. As the editor of *The Herald and Presbyter* in 1874 had opined, "She may teach in the Sunday-school, hold her Bible classes, composed perhaps of hundreds or even thousands of both sexes, lead the congregation in the service of song, etc.; in these things we are all agreed. She may not be a bishop; in that we are nearly or quite unanimous. But where the 'lecturing' ends . . . and the sermon begins, is not so plain."[13]

This chapter begins with a short account of the question of women's power in the church in order to shed light on a peculiar pattern—conservative women with unlikely power and, as we shall see, liberal women with unlikely weakness. In order to understand the surprising dominance of evangelical and pentecostal women over the modern Christian marketplace, we must first draw lessons from what sociologist Mark Chaves called the "loose coupling" between the rules granting full clergy rights to women and the implementation of them: restrictive rules did not necessarily prevent women from taking roles assigned to men, and affirming rules did not always create the conditions for male and female equality.[14] Conservative women—which is to say here, women in traditions that formally restrict female leadership (see Glossary)—had once built Christian institutions of tremendous strength. We will see how nineteenth-century American Protestant women, through lessons learned in the battles for the abolition of slavery, improved social and working conditions, and the right to vote, achieved real influence through their control of the international missionary movement. Presaging conservative Christian women today, this earlier generation exerted a great deal of public influence through their adherence to traditional, domestic gender norms. The woman's sphere was circumscribed, but it was nonetheless one of influence. But as women chalked up further institutional gains, their sphere contracted. We will see how they lost their position of preeminence and found themselves largely locked out of the education and credentialing that would afford them parity with clergymen.

Liberal women—defined for our purposes as those in traditions that officially affirmed female leadership (see Glossary)—fought for denominational policies that gave them standing in the pulpit. Yet, a measure of denominational authority did not win them influence in the largest congregations or in the wider marketplace. In the past few decades, mainline Protestant denominations have slowly adopted the feminist mantle and opened doors to women in ordained leadership, whether as pastors in churches or as denominational executives. Despite this openness and celebration of women in positions that had previously been held by men, there were few progressive female megaministry celebrities. As we will see, ordained progressive women secured some degree of institutional sway, but they lacked the popularity and the cultural capital of their conservative counterparts. To overstate the case only a little, we might say that conservative women gained considerable influence without institutional power, while liberal women gained institutional power without considerable influence.[15]

INSTITUTIONAL POWER

What is the proper role for women in the Christian church? Since this is a book about women and power in the church, let us pause and consider for a moment how very vexing this question has been in Western societies for centuries. Some passages in the New Testament seem to provide clear instruction in the matter, as when Paul wrote to the believers at Corinth: "Let your women keep silence in the churches: for it is not permitted unto them to speak; but they are commanded to be under obedience as also saith the law. And if they will learn anything, let them ask their husbands at home: for it is a shame for women to speak in the church." This theme of female subordination continues in the first letter to Timothy, where Paul says, "Let the woman learn in silence with all subjection. But I suffer not a woman to teach, nor to usurp authority over the man, but to be in silence. For Adam was first formed, then Eve. And Adam was not deceived, but the woman being deceived was in the transgression. Notwithstanding she shall be saved in childbearing, if they continue in faith and charity and holiness with sobriety."[16]

Despite these words, Paul also recognized a leading role for women in the early churches that he visited or communicated with. Junias is hailed as a fellow-prisoner and apostle (Romans 16:7); Phoebe is called a deacon (Romans 16:1–2); Prisca and her husband Aquila are treated as fellow missionaries (Acts 18; Romans 16); other women such as Syntyche, Mary, Julia, Tryphena, Tryphosa, and Eudoia are recognized as among those who support the work of spreading the gospel (Romans 16; Philippians 4). Recent scholarship has suggested that women played a large part in church worship and leadership before the church moved against such practices. According to some scholars, women served as deacons, presbyters, stewards, bishops, and teachers; they sang, prophesied, preached, oversaw congregations, and administered the sacraments.[17]

Though some suggest that women once held priestly roles, the prohibition against women preaching or teaching was observed over the centuries almost universally in all branches of the Christian church. In fact, female leadership was in itself a mark of heresy, as one can see in the examples of the Montanists and early-modern radical Protestant sects. By the fourth century, when the church became a legal entity and was no longer subject to persecution, early examples of female leadership seem to have been forgotten and Christian institutions set on the path of an all-male priesthood. Throughout the Middle Ages, women's ecclesiastical service was restricted largely to the convent from which, occasionally, exceptional women arose whose writings were widely read or whose prophetic or mystical voices were heeded by a larger audience. Hroswitha of Gandersheim, Hildegard von Bingen, Catherine of Siena, Julian of Norwich, and many others made their mark on their societies, but they did not challenge, much less overturn, the patriarchal order of the medieval church. Nor did the great religious reformations of the sixteenth and seventeenth centuries do much to allow women to achieve positions of eminence in Christian organizations or assemblies—the fates of upstarts such as Anne Hutchinson, Eleanor Davies, and Madame Guyon show what happened when women attempted to speak with authority in, or to, the church.

The revolutionary movements of the late eighteenth century in America and Europe enunciated bold assertions about inalienable human rights, and though men such as Thomas Jefferson, Thomas Paine, and Maximilien Robespierre meant these ringing phrases to apply only to white males, it was inevitable that others would claim that these rights were not only self-evident, but universal. Black men in Haiti and European women like Olympe de Gouges, Théroigne de Méricourt, and Mary Wollstonecraft used the language found in the Declaration of Independence and the Declaration of the Rights of Man and of the Citizen to push for greater freedoms for all. Toussaint de l'Ouverture died in chains but helped to create an independent slave-free republic; de Méricourt died mad, de Gouges was guillotined, and Wollstonecroft became a social pariah, but they sparked a fiery debate about women's social position that lasted into the nineteenth century.

The political and legal position of American women in the nineteenth century was indeed a perilous one. In the eyes of the law they were an inferior form of humanity, on a par with children and the mentally disabled; all of their property, including any wages they brought home, was deemed to belong to their husbands. They had no right to the custody of their children, could not sign contracts, devise a will, or vote. When they went to church, they would hear sermons enforcing their restricted status and on their obligations to obey. Overwhelmingly, society saw the role of women as being confined to the home; Charles Butler's *The American Lady*, first published in 1836, opined that domestic duties were "to be regarded as ever imperative and inevitable; and the paramount objects of female pursuit to be the attainment of perfection in the characters of a wife, a mother, and a Christian."[18] Any attempts to participate politically would prove disastrous. Having no idea what their votes might mean, they would be, said opponents of their emancipation, "the corruptest, most unmanageable voters in the world."[19] A woman's place was in the home, using her natural gifts to support a husband, guide the servants, and raise the children.

Nonetheless, many determined women continued to press for greater legal, social, and political freedoms, and their struggle sparked intense debates about the proper roles for women's energies and lives. Throughout the nineteenth century, women played a significant part in many reform movements, the first of which was to block the forced removal of Southeast native tribes beyond the Mississippi, a cornerstone piece of Andrew Jackson's legislative plans. Catharine Beecher and Lydia Sigourney organized the first national women's petition campaign. They besieged Congress with their demands and, though their actions were in vain, they laid the foundations for American women's greater participation in national discourse.[20] Some historians have termed this to be a feature of "republican motherhood"—an attitude that women, though denied the vote, might fight in the public sphere for issues that required a particularly female voice, one that promoted public virtue and sympathy for the needy.[21] Many who were involved in this campaign would go on to take part in the antislavery movement.

Questions about the freeing of slaves inevitably raised questions about the oppression of women, an uncomfortable mirroring of concerns. Public debates over women's claim to the universal rights broke out in the 1830s, with the work of the Grimké sisters for the American Anti-Slavery Society. Born in South Carolina, Angelina and Sarah Grimké abandoned their wealthy family's slaveholding ways and became prominent abolitionists. They went on speaking tours, addressing both women's groups and mixed audiences. Angelina wrote *An Appeal to the Christian Women of the South* (1836) and was the first woman to testify before an American legislative body when she gave evidence on slavery abuses to a Massachusetts state committee.[22] The boldness and taboo-breaking of the Grimkés drew criticism not only from supporters of slavery, but from women inside the abolitionist camp as well, those who thought the female role should be a circumscribed one. Though women were enormously effective in the movement, gathering signatures, distributing tracts, giving lectures, raising funds, and generating support for the cause through their writings (most notably Harriet Beecher Stowe's *Uncle Tom's Cabin*), they were continually discouraged from assuming leadership roles. When Lucretia Mott, the tireless leader of the Philadelphia Female Anti-Slavery Society, was sent as one of five American delegates to an international abolitionist congress in London, she was not allowed to participate and was compelled (along with all the other women delegates) to watch the proceedings from the gallery.[23] Exasperated with the many obstacles that men put in their way, middle-class white women began to compare their situation with that of those they were trying to liberate. "The slavery of sex," as they phrased it, led some women to appeal to the abstract universal rights enunciated in revolutionary times.[24] "We hold these truths to be self-evident: that all men and women are created equal," trumpeted the crusaders of the first women's rights gathering in Seneca Falls, New York, in 1848.[25] The frustrations they had suffered in the antislavery movement had led directly to demands for their own suffrage and fuller participation in the political life of the nation.

Success in winning the vote would lie many decades in the future. For the rest of the nineteenth century, and well into the twentieth, American women struggled with competing notions of their place in society. Debate centered around two divergent gender ideals—that of the "true woman" and that of the "new woman." The ideology of "true woman-hood" was born out of the early republic and held sway throughout the nineteenth century. It was a theology of sacred domesticity that would become the foundation for a constellation of societal values. A true woman found her worth in the home as a model of purity, piety, and wifely submission orbiting around her husband and family. She was simultaneously elevated and subordinated, assumed to possess innate moral superiority and yet confined to a narrow set of roles: childrearing, housekeeping, and building her home into a refuge for her husband from the world of work. The spiritualization of the home reflected a new geography of marriage, brought about by the urbanization and industrialization that had pulled men outside the home to labor in cities. Where once women and men had worked side by side on the farm, in cottage industries, or in small shops, the new economy effectively separated men's work from women's work. For white, middle-class women, marriage became synonymous with domesticity and economic dependence[26]; enslaved women, unmarried women, and poor women could only aspire to such gentility as they routinely worked both inside and outside the home. In the American popular imagination, there were newly baptized "separate spheres" of work and home, public and private.

The figure of the "new woman" emerged in the latter half of the nineteenth-century to describe the woman who stepped outside her assigned space and sought a public role. This did not necessarily mean adopting a radical or subversive posture. Often, what women chose to do meant quite the opposite: many women justified their actions as an extension of accepted ideas on motherhood and moral responsibilities. This can be most easily seen in the battle against the evils of the alcohol trade, and it is here that American women increased their involvement in public life. It occurred to some that as women were the victims of alcohol, they could also be the cure: and thus in 1874 the Woman's Christian Temperance Union (WCTU) was formed. Prompted by religious impulses and by a belief that women could influence society for the better,[27] the WCTU and other such social organizations acted in what has been called the "public female sphere."[28] Ideals of womanhood empow-

ered middle-class women and justified their entry into both social reform and politics, but those same ideals also restricted their activities
and kept activist women from challenging gender stereotypes.[29] The fight
against the alcohol trade shows how conservative women, whose deepest values were focused on home and church, might transfer these values to a broader stage and thus change the social and political policy of
the state.[30] The Women's Christian Temperance Union was the largest-
ever American women's group. Under the leadership of Frances Willard
(1879–1898), who said she "could move fifty thousand women as she
moved her right arm," the WCTU famously led the fight for the prohibition of alcohol sales and became involved in a host of other reforms
as well: from day nurseries to homes for unwed mothers, Sabbath ob-
servance, and women's suffrage.[31] Willard coined the motto "The Ballot
for Home Protection" to indicate that exercising the franchise was but
an extension of woman's role as the guardian of the home into the public sphere.[32] However, Willard's boldness was not always appreciated by
large sections of the female population for whom public roles were
deemed unseemly. Many of these women also found the radical positions of some of suffrage advocates, such as Elizabeth Stanton or Victoria Woodhull, a serious barrier to joining the movement.[33]

Two developments combined to provide a space for such women: the
emergence of the notion of a "female public sphere"[34] and the increasing importance of women in Christian missionary movements. Under
the banner of "Woman's Work for Woman," the categories of "true" and
"new" womanhood grew closer, drawing together moral conservatism,
a high view of superior female virtue, and an interest in causes requiring social activism. Middle-class women participated in sex-segregated
efforts and built female institutions: women's clubs, women's colleges,
settlement houses, and above all, women's missionary societies.

Nineteenth-century missionary societies were among the earliest and
most popular gatherings of women in an age of revival and reform.
Women had long been moved to take up the cause of evangelism. Jarena Lee, the first woman authorized to preach by the African Methodist Episcopal Church said: "If the man may preach, because the Savior
died for him, why not the woman, seeing he died for her also? Is he not
a whole Savior, instead of half of one?" She, and other itinerant female
preachers of the Great Awakening, covered thousands of miles in cir-

cuits that aimed at bringing the gospel into untouched rural and frontier areas.[35] Motivated by the desire to rescue the unsaved and thus transform the world, the volunteer work of these women became the driving
force behind a wide array of missionary causes. As the historian Dana
Robert has shown, this work included domestic and foreign efforts that
typically centered on education, medicine, and evangelism to women
and children.[36] In the name of missions, women prayed, raised money
and supplies, rallied support, and, as the century wore on, built ecumenical and denominational organizations that spanned towns, cities, and
states to finance the work of men and women in the field. These sex-
segregated missionary societies became one of the most important
avenues for collective, public action. After the Civil War, missionary
societies grew to national prominence in an atmosphere of rapidly expanding possibilities for education, employment, and social reform.[37]

The ideal of true womanhood was in full flower, and women's strong
support for missions was assumed to be a natural demonstration of their
motherly concern and sense of Christian duty. Their industry only reinforced the popular consensus that women were inherently spiritual
and a conscience for the church, a coinciding of feminine and Christian
ideals. "Sometimes I feel," wrote one female missionary, "as if a woman
could comprehend the Christ, this utter sacrifice of self as no man can."[38]
The women's missionary societies' acts of public charity were widely publicized and encouraged women—mostly white, middle-class women—
to channel their efforts toward large-scale moral reform and, in doing
so, blurred the division between new woman and true woman.[39] Though
justified as a bastion of feminine piety, the societies were a source of tremendous public authority outside the domestic sphere. Motherhood
was becoming a public act. "The natural mother of little children is also
the natural mother of nations," argued Rev. Antoinette Brown Blackwell,
the second woman ordained in the United States.[40] As women cajoled
politicians, spoke in public forums, led meetings, fostered national
networks, and, increasingly, held the keys to burgeoning treasuries, missionary societies provided a stage for the expanded role for women in
society. Knowingly or not, they had taken the advice of the famous social
reformer Susan B. Anthony: "Take the *world* for your *Pastoral Charge*."[41]

For a woman seeking a life of missionary service, the first role available was that of wife.[42] Soon after the founding of the American Board

of Commissioners for Foreign Mission in 1810, the organization came to see the wisdom in commissioning a married man, as a wife would save him from loneliness and the impropriety of evangelizing foreign women. And so women with their hearts set on this calling agreed to marry men, sometimes men they hardly knew, in order to serve on the frontier or abroad as "helpmeets" and "assistant missionaries" to their husbands. Barred from preaching and ordination, they nonetheless inhabited many roles as the century progressed: Bible translator, evangelist, nurse, social worker, and physician. The most common role, however, was that of teacher.

Women's missionary societies grew exponentially, and by 1900 forty separate societies could boast more than three million members.[43] The first wave of women's missionary auxiliaries took shape in the 1870s: Methodist (1869), Congregationalist (1869), Presbyterian (1870), Episcopalian (1871), American Baptist (1871), African Methodist Episcopal (1874), Christians (1874), Dutch Reformed Church (1875), and the Lutheran Church (1879). In the 1880s, a second wave of non-denominational mission boards followed, whose commitments to evangelism included the willingness to send unmarried women into the fray. With the infusion of single women to the American missionary force, by 1900 the total number of Protestant missionaries tripled to six thousand, approximately two-thirds of whom were women.[44] In 1909, the women's missionary movement had much to celebrate on their fiftieth anniversary. Sixty percent of all American missionaries were women, and they ran an impressive number of institutions: twenty-three hundred schools, eighty hospitals, and eighty-two dispensaries. One in ten were doctors at a time when women could not get employment as physicians in the United States.[45] The country's first women's college, Mount Holyoke Female Seminary, earned its nickname "the Protestant nunnery" for its education of mostly unmarried women for the work of missions and its bold motto: "Go where no one else will go, do what no one else will do."[46]

The significance of women's participation in the missionary movement cannot be overstated. Unlike their roles in the drives for abolition, prohibition, and suffrage, their work in world evangelism gave them real influence *inside* their churches—the same churches that most often put up barriers that barred females from achieving institutional power

through ordination, preaching, or serving as elders. In missionary auxiliaries at home or in the mission field, on the frontier or abroad, women
were responsible for large sums of money, directing schools and colleges,
and occupying teaching roles and positions of authority that were denied them in their home churches. In the Presbyterian Church, for
example, no woman could sit on a Session, be a commissioner to the General Assembly, or be an ordained minister, yet women operated national
denominational mission boards and wielded enormous unofficial influence through their lobbying and fundraising.[47] Denied official ordination in the United States, many women missionaries discovered that
overseas they could take on all the roles of a male clergyman. Said Amanda
Berry Smith, the African American Holiness preacher who achieved
her fame as an overseas missionary, "I am satisfied with the ordination
that the Lord has given me."[48] When Anna Howard Shaw, a women's suffrage movement leader and one of the first ordained Methodist women,
protested the Methodist Episcopal Church's refusal to ordain women,
she pointed out that the bulk of foreign and home missions lay in the
hands of "God-ordained [women] even though refused ordination by
man."[49] The power enjoyed by women in the foreign mission fields only
made good sense. They served as teachers and doctors where insuffi-
cient numbers of men could be found for these jobs; they served as an
effective way to reach local women and children; they served alongside
husbands where a church plant was required. And they had done so
since the earliest days of the mission movement.[50]

But their public roles had to be jealously guarded for they were easily
lost. Take, for instance, the case of Iva Durham Vennard, who founded
the Epworth Evangelistic Institute (a training school for deaconesses in
St. Louis). In the spring of 1909, she returned to work after giving birth
to a baby boy only to discover that a male-led coup had taken place in
her absence. Women faculty teaching bible and theology courses had
been replaced by clergymen; her school's charter had been rewritten; and
instruction in Christian education had replaced evangelism courses in
the curriculum.[51] This would not be the last time that women would find
themselves ousted from their hard-won places in missionary organizations. In fact, the influence they wielded there did not, in the end,
give women a greater say in church affairs, nor would it last long into

Anna Howard Shaw was a physician, women's suffrage
advocate, and one of the first Methodist women to be
ordained.

the twentieth century; a constellation of forces would result in men taking
control of the institutions of the missionary empire that women had built.

In 1909 the United Brethren Church's women's board of missions lost
its separate identity in a merger.[52] The next year the Methodist Episcopal Church consolidated home and foreign women's work, stripped
women of power for missionary appointments, and discontinued its line
of women's missionary periodicals. Over the next few decades, the
women's missionary boards and auxiliaries of the Disciples of Christ,

the Presbyterian Church, the Congregationalist Church, and the Methodist Episcopal Church were absorbed into male-dominated organizations, and in 1932 the Federation of Woman's Boards of Foreign Missions itself merged with the Foreign Missions Conference. The reasons for this trend were many. The First World War had created new movements to attract women: ecumenism, peace education, social justice, and higher education for women. The achievement of female suffrage had attenuated the strength of gender solidarity; women's desire to be integrated into the broader mainstream mission work of churches as equals brought an end to separate spheres of mission work. "Woman's Work for Woman" seemed a rather dusty and antiquated credo in an age grasping at equality. The law of unintended consequences played a role. Women's groups interested in child welfare had long pressed for the professionalization of social work, but the new professional class that emerged ended up dictating that mothers stay closely tied to the home and diminish their role in outside activities.[53] Inevitably, the debate over the proper role of women in public space played a part. The Fundamentalist-Modernist controversy that raged during these decades evoked critiques by fundamentalists of the failings of the feminized "heart religion" of the late nineteenth century—and the realms of female mission organizations and female missionaries were viewed as natural enemies of God's plan for the right ordering of human society.[54]

For a brief moment, American women had possessed direct power in their churches, commanding large budgets, directing thousands of agents, and winning the admiration of a large segment of the population. By the middle of the twentieth century that power had evaporated. Where were women to look for opportunities for meaningful service and leading roles in the modern church? For many, the issue now was whether a female could be an ordained member of the clergy, a question that had been debated, in fits and starts, since the beginning of a nation.

ORDINATION: A BRIEF HISTORY
(SEE APPENDIX VI FOR A TIMELINE)

The history of women's ordination in American churches begins in the early republic, with Clarissa Danforth of the Free Will Baptist Church becoming in 1815 the first woman ordained by a denomination in the United States but it initially proceeded only sporadically. In 1853, Antoinette Brown Blackwell was ordained by a Congregationalist church, but her ordination was not recognized by the denomination, so she eventually left and joined the Unitarians who recognized her ordination in 1878. (The Unitarians would go on to become the first major denomination in the United States with a majority clergy being female.)[55] Women were ordained in the nineteenth century by the Salvation Army, the Christian Church (General Convention), the Church of God (Anderson, IN), the Pentecostal Holiness Church, and the African Methodist Episcopal Zion Church. The struggles for female suffrage, the participation of women in various social reform movements, and their admission to post-secondary education and academic professions such as pharmacy, medicine, and dentistry, added growing weight to arguments that they should not be barred because of their sex from leadership in the church.[56]

By the early twentieth century, the churches that we would now call the Protestant "mainline"—Episcopalians, Lutherans, Presbyterians, Northern Baptists, Congregationalists, and Methodists—resisted female ordination, while many churches from the part of the religious spectrum today termed "conservative"—pentecostal and holiness denominations, both black and white—were open to females in the pulpit. In Ida B. Robinson and Aimee Semple McPherson, we see women founding their own denominations (Mount Sinai Holy Church of America and the International Church of the Foursquare Gospel, respectively), much as Mary Baker Eddy and Ellen White had earlier pioneered Christian Science and Seventh Day Adventism. However, as time went on, even some of the churches that had traditionally been open to women in the pulpit began to pull back. In the Nazarene Church, for example, women were 20 percent of the clergy in 1908, 6 percent in 1973, and 1 percent in 1989. In the Church of God the numbers were 15 percent in 1992, down from 32 percent in 1925.[57] These declines are said to reflect a move from a prophetic to a priestly view of the clergy, as well as to increased professionalization and a demand for seminary training.[58]

It was not until after the Second World War that mainline churches began to change their minds. Methodists in the northern states had allowed women as lay preachers in the 1920s, but were not agreeable to female ordination until 1956. Northern Presbyterians ordained female

Antoinette Brown Blackwell was a leader in the women's rights movement and one of the first women to be ordained in mainline Protestantism. Reprinted with permission from Andover-Harvard Theological Library, Unitarian Universalist Association. Minister files, 1825-2010 (bMS 1446).

ministers in 1954; their southern counterparts waited another decade to follow suit. Some Lutheran denominations (but not the Missouri Synod) opened their pulpits in 1970. It took an irregular ordination of eleven women in 1974, with three dissenting bishops claiming "obedience to the Spirit," to prod Episcopalians to accept female priests two years later.[59]

The "woman question," as it was often called in evangelical circles, was becoming inseparable from the causes of feminism in both the church and the wider American culture (which we will return to again in Chapter Two). In her history of Southern Baptist women, Elizabeth Flowers observed that the debate over women's ordination began to serve as a litmus test in Protestantism's largest denomination for a range of other issues, particularly biblical inerrancy, and became a defining controversy for their leadership from the 1980s onward.[60] Southern Baptists, who had earlier allowed women to be ordained, began to regulate women's roles and behaviors more stringently in light of the rise of feminism and the movement's demands for gender equality. By 1984, though Southern Baptist churches had ordained two hundred women, the Southern Baptist Convention was roiled by controversy (and national media outrage) over a denominational resolution that argued women were unsuitable for ordained leadership "because man was first in creation and woman was first in the Edenic fall."[61] This decision reflected a hardline conservative position within the denomination that led to spates of schism and disfellowshipping.

Evangelicals were not alone in making women's ordination a defining issue of conservatism. In the 1970s, the "Shepherding movement" signaled a growing pentecostal interest in upholding male ecclesiastical hierarchies. A national clergy network led by five prominent ministers— Don Basham, Ern Baxter, Bob Mumford, Derek Prince, and Charles Simpson—emerged out of Christian Growth Ministries based in Fort Lauderdale, Florida. Its flagship publication, *New Wine*, and its leaders' near constant presence on national platforms and Christian television carried their message of submission and authority clear across the country. The Fort Lauderdale Five, as they became known, advocated a form of discipleship in which believers as "sheep" submitted to a "shepherd," a leader who provided spiritual authority and "covering" for them. Critics quickly dubbed it an exercise in empire building that placed the five leaders at the top of a financial and doctrinal pyramid, and rumors of its authoritarian abuses, by 1975, had made the movement into one of the most controversial doctrines circulating in the charismatic movement. What received less attention, however, was how the movement's emphasis on male leadership was remaking pentecostalism in its own image.

Shepherding leaders argued that the church suffered under effeminate men and overreaching women, and that women ought to cede positions of church leadership to godly men who governed the church and ruled the home. *New Wine* regularly taught that the home was the "covenantal prototype of the entire church" and "the first unit of government in God's social order."[62] The family became the first link in a long chain of male headship, men over women, each a new level of authority from pastors to elders to executive leaders on up. The larger charismatic movement (see Glossary), as a rather nebulous ecumenical network, continued to exercise doctrinal flexibility around women's ordination. However, as the impact of the Shepherding movement began to be felt, pentecostal women in ministry staggered under the blow. Divine healer Kathryn Kuhlman, arguably one of the most famous evangelists of her time, began to complain that her donations were drying up and, to fight back, she began to refuse to share a stage with the Shepherding movement's leaders.[63] Even the Foursquare Church, founded by Aimee Semple Macpherson, made it difficult for women to get a hearing.[64] The number of female candidates for ministry shrank significantly. Theological emphasis on God's divine order trumped the deep language of spiritual equality that had animated the charismatic movement in the first place.

Despite these restrictive shifts in the Southern Baptist Convention and charismatic circles, throughout the last two decades of the twentieth century the number of women seeking clerical ordination grew. By 1994, American Protestants were 25 percent more likely to be in a church served by female clergy than they were in 1981.[65] A full half of all American denominations ordained women.[66] However, their late-twentieth-century success in achieving ordination did not bring about a golden age for female clergy. The term "stained-glass ceiling" was coined to describe the ghettoization of female clergy in churches that ordained women and, more remarkably, even in those churches where some women had achieved the status of bishop or denominational leader.[67] It remained a widespread phenomenon that while mainline denominations expressed a willingness to ordain women, they were less likely to encourage them to seek leadership, provide them a supportive seminary experience, place them in charge of thriving churches, or pay them as well as their male counterparts. In the National Congregation Study, a massive study of American congregations, Mark Chaves found that fewer than 12 percent of local churches were headed by a woman.[68] At the turn of the twenty-first century, almost no women were leading a congregation with a membership of over one thousand. On the whole, women were slower to receive pastoral calls and more likely to be placed in nontraditional clergy roles.[69] Others have noted the paucity of women in denominational leadership; in 2016, the Episcopal Church, for example, had only twenty female bishops out of a total of 239, while the United Methodist Church had but seventeen.[70]

There were a number of reasons for this, most of them institutional. Seminaries are the gatekeepers to the clerical profession and attitudes in these institutions have, in many cases, not been conducive to the development of a cadre of female clergy. According to one survey, seminaries have fostered "role incongruity," which means that women are discouraged from aspiring to leadership positions because "the stereotypical role of being female is seen as incompatible with the stereotypical role of leader."[71] Women are presumed to be more nurturing and submissive, while leadership is deemed to demand assertion and dominance. In these seminaries, male students aim at higher status positions in their denominations, while females express a desire to go into smaller, lower-status jobs in the ministry.[72] These attitudes are congruent with the complaints of female seminary graduates that their educational experiences were marked by resistance or hostility.[73] After graduation, women clergy report feeling marginalized in their careers and note that they were slower to receive pastoral posts and were often pushed into non-preaching positions.[74] It was very often the case that while the head offices of denominations were agreeable to the ordination of women, the local congregations that were responsible for hiring their own pastors were far less willing to hire a woman for a leadership role in their own churches[75]—"God calls but the church stalls."[76] Some research also suggested that there was an informal, though not real, limit to how much female penetration of the profession denominations were willing to tolerate. A study of Episcopal and Unitarian-Universalist clergy reported that when women reached 30 percent of the ministeriate a backlash set in.[77] Some have attributed the reluctance of local churches to hire women to a male opposition to feminist theology and a presumed support from female clergy for more radical doctrine and social justice issues. Female clergy, perhaps because of a sense of marginalization, have reported a greater sense of identification with African Americans and immigrants in their ministry than male clergy and have expressed a level of support for liberation theology, inclusive language, marriage equality, and abortion rights that was higher than that of men clergy.[78]

A 2014 statement commemorating the fortieth anniversary of the "Philadelphia 11"—the irregular ordination of eleven women that eventually moved the Episcopal Church to allow female clergy—bemoaned this state of affairs:

> We rejoice that the last forty years have seen the growth of women's ordained ministry throughout the Church. Women's ordination has transformed the Church, not only in the gender of those in ordained ministry but in how all people understand and perform their ministry.
>
> At the same time as we celebrate the change in the Episcopal Church, we are mindful of the continuing challenges facing women in ordained ministry. As recent studies have shown, women continue to lag significantly behind their male colleagues in terms of income and church leadership. Women serve disproportionately in smaller, less well off parishes. In many places, ordained women remain a novelty. Female bishops are few. Women of color and LGBT women continue to face rejection and exclusion. We have much to celebrate, but also injustices and misunderstandings to face.[79]

In the early years of the twenty-first century, the election of women to the highest offices in the Protestant mainline became a powerful symbol of spiritual egalitarianism and a defining marker of whether a tradition could consider itself "progressive." Of the seven denominations that comprised the Protestant mainline, every one had elected women to lead the church within a decade: Disciples of Christ (Sharon Watkins, 2005), United Methodist Church (Janice Huie, 2005), Episcopal Church (Katharine Jefferts Schori, 2006), Evangelical Lutheran Church (Elizabeth Eaton, 2013), American Baptist Churches (Susan Gillies, 2015), Presbyterian Church, USA (Denise Anderson and Jan Edmiston, 2016). And among historic African American denominations—the African Methodist Episcopal Church, African Methodist Episcopal Zion Church, and Christian Methodist Episcopal—all appointed women as bishops in the same period.[80] Even

On July 29, 1974, at the Church of the Advocate in Philadelphia, eleven women were ordained as the first women priests in the Episcopal Church. This was highly controversial at a time when the church did not endorse female priests. Used with permission of *Philadelphia Inquirer.* Copyright © 2018. All rights reserved.

the Assemblies of God, one of the flagship pentecostal denominations, elected its first woman general secretary in 2018.[81] On mainline denominational websites, the celebration of "firsts" became a significant aspect of historical reflection and a special point of pride as old churches tried to present a fresh face to the culture. However, just as studies of major corporations reveal that appointing the first women to positions of power rarely leads to consistent appointments of *more* women to power—a practice often referred to as tokenism[82]—so too in Protestant denominations the appointment of women at the top has not paved the way for women in the profession.

With the debate over gay, lesbian, and transgender Christians in the clergy looming large over the church, denominations now seemed keen to demonstrate their commitment to heterosexual women, as the standards of what constituted "liberal" were changing. For roughly forty years only a small handful of American denominations (including the United Church of Christ, Unitarian Universalists, Metropolitan Community

Churches) had passed resolutions that permitted the ordination of openly gay or transgender clergy, and the ordination and appointment of LGBTQ+ pastors in other traditions had to be arranged at great personal and professional cost to all involved.[83] There were rare positions of authority open to women like Nancy Wilson, who grew up United Methodist in the 1950s and 60s and, seeing no visible women in leadership, quickly intuited that there were even fewer opportunities for her as a lesbian. She joined the Metropolitan Community Church when the denomination was only four years old in 1972 and saw the denomination transform from one primarily shaped by the experiences of gay men and the leadership of its charismatic founder, Troy Perry, to an ecumenical organization specializing in global justice work for gays, lesbians, bisexuals, and, later, transgender people. She led for eleven years until her retirement as the first openly gay woman to lead an American denomination.

In the half century since women began to be ordained in most mainline denominations, ecclesial garments for clergywomen remained a visual reminder of the male template for the figure of the pastor. "In the denominations that have traditionally worn pulpit robes, the big robe suppliers were just modifying a man's robe by making the shoulders smaller and other minor decorative additions," explained Patty Fitzpatrick, who founded WomenSpirit, her own line of women's robes in 1995.[84] Patty had noticed that men's garments did not work well on women's bodies: "There were no pockets—only slits for pockets—because men always have pockets in their pants. They are straight cut garments that were belted in with a cincture. One Episcopal priest that I talked to early on said she looked like a sack of flour with a rope around it." Affordable robes were typically wide and blisteringly hot in the summer, unaccommodating to a woman's changing body in pregnancy, nursing, or simple weight gain. Stoles—those decorative strips of fabric draped over the shoulders—often looked absurdly oversized on slim or short women. "I am not ashamed of the Gospel, but I am chagrined in how it makes me look in swaths of polyester," joked United Methodist Pastor Mandy Sloan McDow, using it as her tagline on her Twitter page.[85] Small clothing lines of "clergy couture" popped up to address the needs of fashion-conscious female pastors, but for the most part women were stuck making adjustments to garments designed for the male frame.[86]

"Clergy couture" like this knit dress, made by WomenSpirit, radically changed the fit of sacred garments for women. Image courtesy of *Women-Spirit*, www.womenspirit.com.

"It's very hard to offer variety with such small numbers of buyers," lamented one traditional robe supplier. "But we are introducing a nursing blouse for women soon," he added hopefully.[87]

In mainline seminaries, congregations, and denominational headquarters, there were many small attempts to make allowances for women; but it was difficult work when the fabric of mainline Protestant life was largely cut around the figure of the male pastor.

THE MAINLINE AND THE MARKET

Susan Gillies didn't mind admitting that she was a "tough old bird."[88] At the age of seventy-two, she had recently retired as the first woman to head the American Baptist Churches (ABCUSA), a mainline Baptist denomination of 1.3 million members, over fifty-two hundred local congregations, and roughly eight thousand pastors and church leaders of various kinds.[89] Just two years before Susan Gillies was named interim general secretary, only 10 percent of paid clergy positions were held by women.[90] Susan had felt a call to ministry as a teenager in the 1960s, even though she had never seen a female pastor in her denomination before, so when she got to college she majored in the only thing she had seen women do in the church: Christian Education (teaching children). She dropped her major after a semester and went on to work in public radio. "I thought I'd grow up, have babies, and maybe publish a women's magazine," she remembered. Instead, she wound up divorced and without children. She returned to the denomination to work with laity around questions of faith in the workplace, slowly climbing in the ranks to become deputy executive director of the American Baptist Home Mission Societies, then called National Ministries, and later served as executive minister of the American Baptist Churches in Nebraska before the top position opened. As she contemplated her options, she understood that there were "four strikes" against her: she was a woman, divorced, not ordained, and an outsider to the region where Northern Baptists are most concentrated (Indiana, Ohio, West Virginia, and Pennsylvania).

"I put my name in and I was told that there would be a courtesy interview," she told me. "That 'courtesy' interview lasted seven whole hours and I stood the whole time. They kept asking me if I wanted to sit but I said no. Something in me realized that I had to have presence, so I stood. I don't know why I didn't take off as they questioned me about every small thing, except that I believed that it was the intention of the Holy Spirit to allow them to struggle with who I am. I told them that they would have to decide if they can live with the fact that I'm a woman. But that I understood their concerns about me not being ordained." The final vote on Susan's candidacy was split, and though many people advised her not to accept the position, she took it regardless. A decade later, she told me with a laugh what one of pastors who had voted against her said: "You know, I don't believe in women in leadership, but it's been great having you. You've done a good job." The job, as it turned out, was an especially complicated one, for the denomination had a congregational polity of loosely connected churches with radically different theological, regional, political, and racial demographics. "We recently lost almost an entire region, California, over debates about same-sex unions," she said. "We refused to kick churches out if they were for gay marriage or against—it's a Baptist thing—because our policies only govern the office of the secretary general and staff."

"Wait," I said, scrambling to keep up. "Are you saying that you are the only person who has to follow the policies of the denomination? Just you." While Southern Baptist Convention had taken a firmer grip over the practices of local congregations from the 1980s onward, the Northern Baptist Convention (renamed the American Baptist Churches) maintained a commitment to the autonomy of local congregations and the freedom of the individual believer's conscience, a hallmark of Baptist theology.

"Yes, the church governance is only set up to offer recommendations."

"You have the most unusual kind of authority," I replied. "You are the most important symbol of a far-flung denomination filled with churches that don't have to listen to you. Plus, you have to embody sole faithfulness to your own tradition's policies."

"I haven't had very much attention," she laughed. "The only big difference now is that when I go to conferences the denomination pays to let me get my own hotel room. No more sharing!"

"Why don't you try and get more attention? There is an enormous market for female Christian celebrities, but there are so few liberal women trying to compete for it," I asked. As the first woman to lead her historic denomination since 1921, Susan would be a natural choice.[91] She had the institutional platform and the Baptist network through which to circulate her brand with seeming ease. As we talked, however, Susan identified one of the primary barriers preventing liberal women from entering the Christian marketplace, a barrier that I heard echoed in other interviews: self-promotion.

"The mainline church is known, unfairly, for being boring," she reflected. "A lot of our attempts to author books have been boring, but for them to sell, you've got to get out there and sell yourself. I have written books, but when I'm out there in Pumpkin Creek [fictitious town], I can't bring myself to do it. I end up selling my books for less than I paid for them. I don't have that self-promoter instinct." Denominational leadership required a great deal of administrative skill, but her position did not require or necessarily reward a self-promotional approach to leadership. It was a consequence of the professionalization of the clergy[92] that the criteria for positions like Susan's were based on education and a set of learned organizational and ministerial capacities. As Brooks Holifield has argued in his history of American pastors, postwar mainline Protestantism was united in its vision of the clergy as a highly learned figure with a "rational authority," rather than a person with charismatic authority centered on special gifts and personal talents.[93] These priorities were echoed in mainline seminary coursework, which typically emphasized the study of scripture, theology, history, and pastoral care of the laity rather than the kinds of skills that engendered the entrepreneurship that was second nature to evangelicalism's culture of Christian celebrity. And, at times, conservatives and progressives operated in separate markets altogether: conservatives appealing to the wider popular culture, whose products were largely defined by the appetites of the evangelical subculture, while progressives were tethered to the prestige economy of the university and the chattering classes. Progressives trafficked in the less visible (though no less financially driven) market of religious products steered by public intellectuals who made the concept of "celebrity" seem a tad garish.

Indeed, mainline seminaries had become very rarely a pathway to popular power. The strongest female voices of progressive faith did not typically have theological degrees but had learned their craft in the evangelical-dominated marketplace. The late Rachel Held Evans, *New York Times* bestselling author, for instance, penned four popular books about abandoning biblical literalism as she moved away from her evangelical roots and toward Episcopalianism. Likewise, blogger-turned-bestselling author Glennon Doyle created an empire of readers and activists supporting the *Together Rising* nonprofit. Neither paused for a seminary degree or considered one a prerequisite for ministry, both because their traditions (Episcopal and United Church of Christ, respectively) have a strong practice of lay ministry and also, perhaps, because there would be little credibility, influence, or practical skills to be gained by such credentials. "One of my biggest insecurities is that I write about faith but don't have a seminary degree," confessed Rachel Held Evans. "Of all the criticisms I receive, that one stings the most. . . . That said, I've come to see how a background in literature and journalism helps me bring out shades and contours from the biblical text that pastors and theologians might miss. We need artists engaging faith just as much as we need trained ministers. An Episcopal bishop from Virginia once said to me, 'You know we'd welcome you to any Episcopal seminary in the country, but I hope you don't do it; I'm afraid it might ruin you.' I took that comment as vote of confidence and remind myself of it when I start to doubt myself again."[94]

Further, convincing scholars and pastors to take up the bold publicity campaigns that the popular marketplace requires (and abandon the indirect and institution-focused self-promotion of the chattering classes) created a significant barrier. Graduates of theological higher education were simply less inclined to promote themselves as their evangelical counterparts did. "Mainline seminaries fail to foster creative strategies for the renewal of the church, particularly when it comes to finding a place for healthy marketing and self-promotion," said Laceye Warner, who served as the associate dean of Duke Divinity School, a United Methodist institution.[95] In the world of mainline Protestantism and its culture of gentility, bald marketing was gauche. "If I tried to splash my picture on everything, I think it would go sour," summarized Susan Gillies, "and that's a big problem. There is an enormous appetite for good religious reading and so little to read by progressive authors. And part of the problem is the resentment around anyone with a little *chutzpah* who becomes a star."[96]

It has been difficult, however, for mainline denominational publishing houses to find a star. Mainline denominations had been staples of religious television until the Federal Communications Commission (FCC) in 1960 changed the rules that subsidized their airtime, after which they were outbid by entrepreneurial conservatives willing to pay.[97]

By the 1970s, new FCC policies further strengthened conservatives' hold on television by allowing religious broadcasters to purchase not only airtime but also new stations and channels (opportunities again snapped up by enterprising evangelicals). As we will discuss in Chapter Three, this led to the omnipresence of the narrow cast of conservative personalities who acted as gatekeepers of the airwaves and the result was a chilling of the relationship between the mainline and televangelism. Mainline denominations were also reluctant to adopt the sex-segregated model of women's conference circuits, women's magazines, and women's books that were making conservative women into household names in the 1970s (as we will see in Chapter Two). It was common wisdom among book publishers that the majority of their readers were women, and yet progressive denominations were reluctant to market directly to women in overtly gendered ways.

When I spoke to two senior staff at Cokesbury, the retail division of the 12.8-million-member United Methodist Church, I asked why they seemed to intentionally veer away from merchandizing catering specifically to women, particularly given the success of Bibles with feminine flourishes, like pink glitter, fuchsia accents, or floral flourishes.[98]

"What prevents you from going the hyper-feminine route when marketing to women? Why won't I ever see any butterflies on your books?" I jokingly asked Cokesbury's Associate Publisher Susan Salley.[99]

"It's disrespectful to women," she said with a smile, "but I'm laughing because we did market one of our authors with a lot of butterflies because her book was about change and metamorphosis. But it was in browns and deep teals and blues. It wasn't pink."

"Women's Bibles are a fairly large segment of the Bible market," piped in Chief Ministry Officer Justin Coleman. "In 2016, we released a women's bible that we are quite proud of. We believe it is very different than any other on the market. The commentary is usually quite conservative and written by men, so we set out to create a Bible filled with female scholars and female senior pastors. No male contributors. But when it came time to pick the cover—this probably speaks to our gut intuition—we were worried because it came back from the printer too light. We didn't want to do the stereotypical thing . . . ," he tapered off sheepishly.

"We had to send it back because it was too pink," finished Susan, chuckling.

"What is a better color for a mainline woman?" I asked.

"Oxblood. Burgundy. Bricky red," she replied firmly.

Mainline women who veered outside of their roles as contributors to the denomination and to their home churches would likely find that, as Susan argued, "it would mess up their reputation, whether in leadership or in academia." Since women in the mainline still fought to gain entry to the center of denominational life, focusing on the women's sphere and specializing in their needs seemed regressive (even though women were the primary popular audience). The benefit of ordination has also been its burden: female pastors have spent the vast majority of their time tending to their institutions, and only churches with multiple staff could afford to have their pastors divert much energy into writing, traveling, and platform-building.[100] Further, the megachurches that have been the pride of their denominations rarely had a woman at the helm. The United Methodist Church, for instance, had not a single woman leading any of its several dozen megachurches, and so its official publisher, Abingdon Press, largely produced books by its megachurch star Adam Hamilton. For publishers, book agents, conference centers, and other talent scouts, it meant that the pool of available speakers with recognizable names remained miniscule.

To make matters worse, the size of mainline denominational audiences was small in comparison to their conservative counterparts. The American Baptist Churches, for example, were only one tenth the size of those in the Southern Baptist Convention.[101] Further, it was difficult for publishers to target readers loyal to their denomination's products when, almost by definition, mainliners considered themselves cosmopolitan in nature. In fact, part of the scholarly difficulty in defining "the Protestant Mainline" was its outward-looking nature, focus on interdenominational cooperation, and its porous boundaries, such that historian David Hollinger argued that the term should be simply replaced with "ecumenical Protestants."[102] Mainline publishing houses could not necessarily count on the exclusive loyalty of readers to their denominational brand and found themselves competing, often unsuccessfully, with the imprints of major publishing conglomerates targeted to readers like theirs. HarperOne, an imprint of HarperCollins, was founded in 1977 in San Francisco to symbolize the California counterculture who sought alternative spiritual wisdom more focused on "health, personal growth, [and] social change" than narrow theological allegiances.[103] In 2007, when the United Church of Christ sought a partner to publish the New Revised Standard Version of the Bible, the denomination chose HarperOne.[104]

The failure of mainline Protestants to produce female leaders with a large public platform might also have had theological roots in their lack of interest in the mass proselytism that marked evangelical denominations. Why bother seeking a presence on television, bestseller lists, or in arena conferences without an evangelistic purpose? In a recent Barna survey, 100 percent of evangelicals surveyed agreed with the statement that "I, personally, have a responsibility to tell other people my religious beliefs," while about only half of mainline churchgoers agreed. Sixty-nine percent of evangelicals reported having explained their faith in the past twelve months to someone who had different beliefs, in hope they might accept Jesus Christ as their Savior (as opposed to 42 percent of mainline Protestants and 33 percent of Catholics).[105] There were platforms for mainline messages—like Oprah's Super Soul Sunday, which featured Episcopal priest Barbara Brown Taylor—but these opportunities were rare. The progressive issues of social justice, anti-racism, and environmentalism that informed the mainline language of mission had yet to find a robust audience under the banner of Christian publishing, possibly because they seemed to many to be indistinguishable from similar "secular" progressive causes.[106] A mainline woman who wanted to become a celebrity would find few available rungs to climb on her way up.

A final obstacle to consider in the alienation of the mainline from the marketplace was the problem that loomed over all megachurches: succession. Women could assume leadership of the largest North American churches if there were senior pastors willing to concede their power to them. We can see the role that gender expectations played in megachurch succession in the ministry of the Reverend Dr. Jo Hudson. Jo was one of the few women to ever take over a megachurch, but, all things considered, it was not a typical church. Cathedral of Hope in Dallas, Texas, claimed to be the largest gay congregation in the United States, a towering forty-three-hundred-member church and a symbol of gay pride planted in the heart of the Bible Belt.[107] She inherited the church from her predecessor, Michael Piazza, who had been a champion of hers when she had been outed as a lesbian while serving as a United Methodist pastor (a denomination that forbade noncelibate gay clergy). Jo had had to start her ministerial career over again, eventually joining the LGBTQ+-affirming United Church of Christ denomination. She was asked to join the staff of Cathedral of Hope shortly after a moment of crisis in 2003: Michael Piazza was at war with the denomination, the church voted to leave their Metropolitan Community Church denomination altogether, and almost all the ordained staff had walked out. Jo joined the clergy staff in 2004 and within six months was elected senior pastor, while Michael stayed on as her mentor for several years.[108]

She had become the only openly lesbian senior pastor in the history of megachurches, but, even so, she felt her role was often prescribed by her gender. She was the leader of a predominantly gay male church, which put her in a minority position within her own congregation: "Frankly," she said, "I didn't get invited to certain events because I wasn't a gay man."[109] The Board of Directors "treated me differently as a female leader from the time I began to the time when I left. There were clear feelings that I recognized as misogyny." Like many women chosen to steer powerful institutions through troubled waters, a phenomenon known as the "glass cliff," Jo entered a position with a high risk of failure and found that her success did not necessarily mean smooth sailing. Once the church was on stable footing, Jo began to feel that her predecessor was regretting his retirement even though he was hardly retired, often serving as a preacher and still a powerful figure in the gay community. "He marched for causes. He spoke out against things. He was very prophetic at a time when it was dangerous to do so," Jo explained, "but when I came, he began to describe himself as a prophet and me as a pastor. I know he didn't intend it, but it clearly implied 'I'm the man, you're the woman.' It meant that I did the nice things and he did the edgy, dangerous things. I cared for the congregation and he challenged them." And the more Jo took over the reins of the church, she observed, the more their relationship suffered. She went on to lead the church for nearly nine years before, one Sunday, she resigned with only a few words. The *Dallas News* reported a chippy quote from her church board's vice chairman about how "she just made her statement and left," but Jo never replied to media calls for a statement.[110] She wanted to move on.

Women in the mainline struggled to find an easy relationship with institutions that had the capacity to reach into the marketplace. As the case of American Baptist general secretary Susan Gillies showed, the path to denominational leadership was rocky even among progressive traditions that affirmed women in ministry. And once there, mainline leaders like her found that the boundaries around their authority were narrowly drawn in ways that kept them from expanding their public platforms. So too in mainline megachurches, the example of Jo Hudson demonstrates how difficult it remained for women to simply inherit prominent congregations. Almost every large church in America had been built around the charismatic authority of its (often founding) leading man. Mainline women seeking a national ministry would discover that they had to build their fame largely outside of the institutions they had fought to lead.

THE EXCEPTION THAT PROVES THE RULE

"I am as puzzled as anyone else about how this happened," said Nadia Bolz-Weber, the founding pastor of a congregation in the Evangelical Lutheran Church in America, the fifth-largest American Protestant denomination with 3.7 million baptized members. While Garrison Keillor had made the Midwest famous for the faith that sparked the Reformation—("We're Lutheran people. Even the Catholics up here are Lutheran"[111])—Nadia was becoming the denomination's most sought-after speaker for her reputation as more "cranky and sarcastic" than Minnesota nice. "I don't look like a pastor," said the *New York Times* bestselling author of *Pastrix* and *Accidental Saints*. "I'm very heavily tattooed. I have sleeve tattoos, basically, and very short hair, and I'm like 6-foot-1-inch [tall]. I don't actually act like a pastor either."[112] Nadia was the fresh face of a denomination recently shaken by the 2009 schism over same-sex unions (and the dwindling of mainline attendance in general); the congregation she founded in Denver, Colorado, called the House of All Sinners and Saints, was the kind of home for LGBTQ+ people that cast her liturgical tradition as edgy and relevant.

In order to keep Nadia inside the fold, the Evangelical Lutheran Church in America had made some accommodations. Nadia described

Pastor Nadia Bolz-Weber's sharp wit and comfort with controversy brought a little spice to Lutheranism's bland reputation. Image courtesy of Nadia Bolz-Weber.

how leaders had allowed her the flexibility to plant and keep her own congregation despite policies dictating that new pastors be trained in other churches first.[113] Nadia recalled telling her bishop sardonically: "You could put me in some church in the suburbs or in the country, but you and I know that would be ugly for everyone involved."[114] So the leadership made exceptions for their unusual ordinand, a former stand-up comic with a history of alcohol abuse whose call to ministry had come from the experience of delivering the eulogy at a friend's funeral. She founded her church as a place where the LGBTQ+ community and people with addictions would feel welcome and in the process discovered places within the rigid constraints of her tradition that made the arrangement work. Her church did not require membership or even baptism as a qualification for its participants to serve in leadership roles or vote at the annual meeting—both of which were mandatory in every ELCA constitution. They wrote new bylaws instead, effectively including anyone except, in Nadia's words, "those who couldn't cast their own reflection and fog a mirror, so that vampires and zombies cannot attend the meeting. We don't name vampires and zombies—because that felt xenophobic—but we implied it," she said wryly.[115]

Taken as a whole, the Evangelical Lutheran Church of America was not instrumental in creating Nadia's stardom. The denomination had certainly boosted her reputation with a few coveted platforms, including their mammoth annual youth conference once held in the New Orleans Superdome (dubbed the "LutherDome"). However, it was the small but densely connected network of progressive evangelicals embodied in *Sojourners* magazine and its founder Jim Wallis that first launched her onto the national stage. The magazine started to publish her sermons, progressive Christian stars began to reach out as mentors and advisors,[116] and Nadia sought out other Christian celebrities to answer her questions: "Who could I call up and say, should I do this?"[117] She decided that she would say a firm "No!" to reality television and an enthusiastic "Yes!" to events outside of mainline Christianity, because it was "more gratifying than being the darling of two hundred Presbyterians in North Carolina."[118] She mastered the mainline Protestant speaking circuit—select youth conferences, preaching festivals, university chapel services, and historic downtown church events—which lay outside of the conservative Christian world that filled arenas, megachurches, television studios, and most online broadcasts. She chatted on mainstream media outlets like NPR[119] and, with progressive evangelical favorite Rachel Held Evans, started a conference dubbed the "Why Christian? Conference."[120] The twelve-hundred-person conference was known for featuring lesser-known mainline female, ethnic minority, or queer talent who would otherwise likely be without popular platforms.

Nadia thrived in a small but vital corner of the American Christian popular marketplace. However, the successes of its leaders paralleled much of the fragility that marked the vocations of conservative women, whose careers, as the following chapters will trace, also depended on touchstones of fame. Their primary institutions and denominations were not seedbeds for their message—the work of celebrity was done through personal connection, branding, social media, and a sustainable number of paid invitations to speak to keep their names in the media. Unlike a megachurch pastor whose message was kept burnished by a deep bench of staff, progressive women—such as any woman without a famous husband or a large church of her own—scratched out their reputations with few advantages. The experience of women in mainline churches had shown how difficult it was for them to transform denominational gains into widespread influence.

CONSERVATIVE SEMINARIES

It was not only difficult for mainline women to find a pulpit with a platform: it was a Herculean task for any woman. (See Appendix V for an overview of how women in megachurch leadership have fared poorly.) A quick overview of the largest evangelical seminaries and the largest churches in the country shows that they were not well-suited to place talented women in positions of ecclesiastical authority. Take, for instance, the degrees and continuing education programs available to women at Southern Baptist seminaries, which number among the largest theological education institutions in the United States. For women, Southwestern Baptist Seminary offers a Master of Divinity and a Master of Arts in Christian Education with concentrations in women's ministry and homemaking. Until recently, women's degrees in Southern Baptist seminaries were part of a larger debate about a woman's rightful place with courses like "How to Pack Your Husband's Suitcase" and "How to Can Green Beans."[121] Though curriculum has been updated with coursework on church planting for women and the how-tos of coordinating women's ministries, barriers to women's enrollment in these programs are still high.

The Southern Baptist women who did persist in seeking seminary training found limited opportunities available after graduation. Some worked overseas, where they found, like the missionary women before them, that there were less stringent restrictions. On American soil, their options narrowed. If they worked at a local church, they would typically be required to submit to male oversight of some kind; for instance, a female youth worker would need a male youth worker supervising her. (This would be essential for ministry work with teenagers, as some traditions held that this was the age of manhood and therefore the cut-off for any woman to teach them.) Since, according to the National Congregations Study, the average American church held eighty people and could only afford a small staff, this put women at a significant disadvantage.[122] A church would need a larger staff and budget to hire a woman, because they would always be required to hire for her a male superior. Jobs in women's ministry were scarcer still, as family members of pastors or volunteers were usually tapped to lead women's and children's ministries with no degree required. Only the largest churches could afford a paid staff person to run a women's ministry, which was in any case not always a staple in congregational life. Further academic work could also seem out of reach. In fact, Southern Baptist female seminary graduates with a doctorate were so hard to come by that, on occasion, Southeastern Baptist Seminary had to call men to teach classes in its Biblical Women's Institute.[123]

The largest evangelical seminaries in the country exhibited similar restrictions in how they employed women to teach. Historian Joshua Young and I examined websites and publications of the largest evangelical seminaries in North America and found that the women numbered from 3 percent to 14 percent of the overall faculty, and that their positions were concentrated in several traditionally gendered fields: counseling, Christian education, women's ministry, and music (see Figure 1).[124]

In Southern Baptist Seminaries—which were the most restrictive when it came to women's issues—it was not unusual to find that the only woman employed was the librarian. It must not be supposed that women being trained in "Biblical Studies" were being trained as future theologians or pulpiteers. Rather, they were typically being channeled into using that knowledge to teach other women and children. As complementarian megachurch pastor John Piper put it, "The issue is not whether women should attend seminary in one of its programs and get the best biblical grounding possible. The issue is whether women should be models, mentors, and teachers for those preparing for a role that is biblically designed for spiritual men." And his answer to the latter question was negative: "In seeking to justify women teacher-mentors for aspiring pastors, one will be hard put to stress that they're not in the same category as pastors, and thus, as we believe, out of step with the Scriptures."[125]

The silos in which women found themselves in seminaries were the same silos they found themselves hired into after graduation, whether

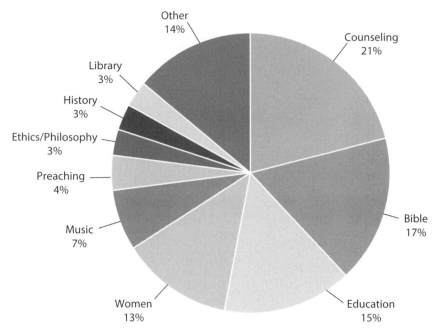

Figure 1. In evangelical seminaries, women were hired to teach in a wider variety of subfields.

they were liberal or conservative. When Joshua Young and I examined the status of women in both the largest megachurches in the country and the largest congregation in every respective denomination, we found a similar pattern: women were overwhelmingly hired in these same categories: counseling, women's and children's education, worship, and the arts, as well as various administrative roles (see Figure 2). (See Appendix V for how this research was done.) Whether or not the congregation affirmed women in ministry, the preaching and teaching (dubbed "executive ministry") were overwhelmingly left to the men. On the whole, megachurches were not hiring women for any significant teaching position, and the implications for future church leadership were obvious—the largest churches in America were not poised to hand their churches over to a woman on staff. Very few leadership roles for women in ministry—either evangelical or mainline—had the appearance of being in a line of succession.

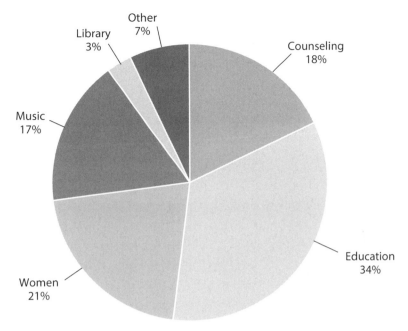

Figure 2. Southern Baptist seminaries had the most restrictive roles for academic women: counseling, Christian education (teaching children), and women's ministry.

In 2018, fewer than 1 percent of American megachurches were led by a female senior pastor. This lack of women in formal leadership in megachurches, however, should come as no surprise. As we have seen, there was a long history of theological objection to women preaching and teaching. Even where women were enrolled in seminaries, structural and cultural expectations steered them away from the pulpit and, in turn, away from access to traditional institutional power. Discouragement in seminaries and home churches led to a lack of mentorship and experience. Most of the women I interviewed who specialized in scripture and were widely known as "bible teachers" reported that they had not been encouraged to attend seminary for formal training; they had taken it upon themselves to research and self-teach biblical studies, theology, and even biblical languages. They created their own curriculum and methods for inductive bible study to be taught to women, first in their home churches, then reaching global audiences of women who also wanted to study the Bible in depth but did not have the expertise. These women built their careers without the educational and institutional advantages of their male counterparts. Diplomas did little to change that. They would have to rely almost entirely on their personal connections or an authority based on charisma, a recognition of special gifts by those with audacity to believe that they were called.

THE RELUCTANT CELEBRITY

Barbara Brown Taylor had served as a progressive Christian polestar for over two decades. A popular author and preacher, she was perhaps the closest thing big-steeple liberal Protestantism had to a celebrity like Beth Moore or Joyce Meyer. She had made the *New York Times* bestseller lists and sat across from Oprah on Super Soul Sunday to talk about communing with the divine. She was an ordained Episcopal priest beloved by theological progressives and a spiritual muse to academics and fellow mainline preachers alike. But she remembered her rise to fame as "the moment that my preaching life took a turn for the worse." *Time* magazine had reported the results of a 1996 survey by Baylor University on the twelve "most effective" preachers in the English-speaking world, and she had been the only woman on the list. At first, she told me, it was fun. Her husband teased that it was like being declared badminton champion of the world. But when newcomers began to flock to her tiny rural church, even going so far as to take flash photos during the service, she began to feel herself being pulled into a dizzying cycle of performance, evaluation, and "the specter of competitive preaching." She found it more and more difficult to ignore the applause and concentrate on the ministry. Of course, Barbara said with a laugh, she wanted an *audience* but the logic of branding, publicity, and marketing made her uncomfortable. She resigned her post the following year.

Under the hot lights of megaministry, women like Beth Moore and Joyce Meyer showed just how brightly conservative women could shine. They garnered massive returns from television and radio appearances, podcasts and books, and sold-out arena conferences. They were the unlikely celebrities of a theological world that found little use for a woman at the helm of a megachurch or holding a theological degree in her hand.

Barbara Brown Taylor is the closest thing that mainline Protestants have to a celebrity, but she (and her audience) is troubled by the category of celebrity itself.

They learned how to reach millions of eager consumers using theological language and marketing tools sensitive to the spiritual mood and cultural moment, and in doing so vastly overshadowed the mainline market. The long history of women's struggle for ordination and an institutional expression of spiritual equality had left most women in the precarious position of seeking permission for the authority to teach. And most would find that denominations, megachurches, and seminaries were slippery paths to leadership. A select few who sought authorization to teach with authority moved outside of existing institutions and into the marketplace, choosing to master the self-conscious work of religious celebrity. As we shall see in subsequent chapters, these women would have to manage the simultaneous performance of motherhood, showmanship, vulnerability, and sexuality. It was a turn toward public scrutiny that would prove too much for preachers like Barbara, whose ambivalence about her own fame mirrored many of mainline Protestantism's concerns about the spiritual marketplace as a whole. "Christian celebrity is an especially troublesome oxymoron," she explained, "since being Christian calls for a certain self-forgetfulness that celebrity makes difficult to achieve. . . . We all have good days and bad days. From dust we came and to dust we shall return. On with the show." [126]

THE HOMEMAKER

Every wise woman builds her house . . .
—Proverbs 14:1, NIV

No one left the Horner Homemaking House without a token of Southern hospitality, a toasted coconut bar carefully wrapped in wax paper, or a shortbread cookie tucked into an envelope and sealed with Horner's signature gold foil labels. It was the delicious culmination of a tour through this spacious home on the edge of Southwestern Baptist Theological Seminary's campus, each room tastefully appointed in heavy dark woods and thick tapestries and dedicated to the memory of a particular patroness and commemorated with her portrait, a woman whose virtues had embodied the paradigmatic Proverbs 31 wife.[1] In the parlor, we ran our hands along the baby grand piano where one lady would entertain her husband's guests, and in the sewing room we learned how to monogram our own handkerchiefs with two state-of-the-art machines named "Ruth" and "Naomi" after the Old Testament heroines. Students of the seminary's homemaking concentration could learn to design and create their own outfits there; photos papering the walls showed girls in homemade T-shirts, long tunics, tea-length skirts and wide pants, each modest and well made. The laundry room was dubbed the "ministry room," because it was Christian service and not simply labor that happened there. But the kitchen was the heart of this home, an enormous workspace stocked with stoves, fridges, pantries, and sinks with recipes like "Mom's Meatloaf" printed on tiles set into the stonework above. There, in our cookie-icing demonstration, we learned to "taste the sweetness of God" in the fellowship of cooking and eating. The young tour guide, her hands clasped before her chest, explained how homemaking was a "lost art." She had learned that her home was her calling, the place where her love as wife and mother would someday bloom when she

Dorothy Patterson, in one her trademark hats, speaks to an audience of pastors' wives. Jeff Westcott Photography.

found a husband. In the meantime, a home was an expression of female resourcefulness, the bits of creativity that any woman could channel into decorating for the seasons or blessing others with her service by cooking, laundering, and cleaning. The home was also the mission field, a place where Christian discipleship could be fostered with a hot meal. This conference, appropriately dubbed "The Art of Homemaking," had made these points again and again: your house is not simply a home. It is a showpiece of Christian womanhood.[2]

The Art of Homemaking conference was made in the image of Mrs. Dorothy Patterson, wife of President Paige Patterson, both key players in a theological civil war in the Southern Baptist denomination that was fought in no small part over the role of women in the church.[3] The conservatives won, and the war is now remembered as the conservative "resurgence" or "takeover," depending on which side you were on, but, almost twenty years later, the conference serves as a time capsule for its defining issues.[4] Mrs. Patterson, as she liked to be called, was still a model of extravagant deference to her husband: she was billed as a "homemaker" despite her doctoral degree, was almost always seen in wide church hats that she wore as a symbol of her living "under the authority" of her husband, and was a fixture in the front row, where she declined to introduce even her own Art of Homemaking conference in the presence of men. Paige Patterson did the honors. He paced the stage beforehand, giving commands in a deep drawl to the duck-tolling retriever he brought as a nod to the love of hunting shared between himself and the evening's honored speakers from the hit A&E show *Duck Dynasty*. It also served as a punch line to his joke that his dog, not his wife, had already learned to obey him.

It was well known that Paige Patterson kept among his trophies of safari animals a stuffed baboon posed reading Darwin's *Origin of the Species*, a perfect symbol of his stance as a heresy hunter on matters of scriptural inerrancy, creationism, and complementarianism.[5] To the Pattersons and many others, the authority of men over women was a matter of sound doctrine rooted in scripture. For as the Apostle Paul wrote in Ephesians 5: "Wives, submit to your own husbands as you do to the Lord. For the husband is the head of the wife as Christ is the head of the church, his body, of which he is the Savior."[6] But theological arguments for women in the home were perhaps better seen in every detail of Dorothy's handiwork. Her conference was designed to be the model of old-fashioned Southern hospitality, where homemaking was a deliberately political and theological act. From the breakout sessions called "The Heart of the Christian Hostess" to the linen and floral centerpieces on elaborately set tables where women could sip oolong tea with the editor of *Tea Time* magazine, all was done in the interest of teaching a woman how to be a lady. She could also learn to be a Christian voice in the political arena. Speakers reminded audiences familiar with the names of Simone de Beauvoir and Betty Friedan that they lived in a counter-Christian world confused about the proper roles for men and women.[7] In the makeshift marketplace in the lobby, women sold homemade crafts, jewelry, and jams to bolster their stay-at-home income and got brochures from the Concerned Women for America about how to lobby from their kitchen tables. And while many of the attendees' long homemade skirts would have seemed a bit dated in the wider world of evangelical women, their iron-clad anti-feminism was where most women's ministries had begun. Indeed, it had launched the careers of many women who were primarily known for their own art of homemaking.

This chapter takes us back to the start of "women's ministries." In the 1970s, conservative Christian women became caught up in a much larger debate in American culture about women's work. In the wider social and political maelstrom that surrounded women's pay, voting, reproductive rights, and ability to divorce, many Christians protested that these freedoms eroded their traditional roles as wives and mothers. In the heat of these culture wars, a significant shift in leadership roles for women took place. Mainline women renewed their attempts to break into the ranks of ordained leadership, while conservatives redoubled their efforts to make the Christian family the bulwark against changing cultural forces. The result was unexpected. Conservatives would become key players in a growing industry—books, magazines, conferences, and even new church and parachurch organizations—catering to Christian women. The ones who truly became stars from the 1970s onward trumpeted the virtues of Christian wifehood and motherhood, but tangled expectations would create complications. They had professionalized their domestic life, making their home into a showpiece and their marriage into a business.

THE FEMINIST CHALLENGE

Elisabeth Elliot lived many lives. She had become a widow in 1956 at the age of twenty-seven, when her husband, Jim, and four others were infamously murdered by the South American tribe they had tried to convert. Pregnant and bereaved, she poured her grief into words with a best-selling theological memoir, *Through the Gates of Splendor*, explaining how his death was a sacrifice used for the glory of God. "I believe," she said, "with all my heart that God's Story has a happy ending. But not yet, not necessarily yet. It takes faith to hold on to that in the face of the great burden of expectation. What God means by happiness and goodness is a far higher thing than we can conceive."[8] She began her life again, resolved to follow in her husband's footsteps, with their young daughter and the sister of another slain missionary in tow, to evangelize the very people in remote Ecuador who had killed their loved ones. The stories

Elisabeth Elliot returned with her young daughter to the mission field in Ecuador after her husband's death. She is a study in contrasts: a widowed missionary evangelist and symbol of female submission. Photo from the Billy Graham Center Archives, Collection 278 Papers of Elisabeth Elliot, courtesy of Lars Gren.

of her loss and hard insights as a missionary to that tribe and others catapulted her to evangelical stardom, a Protestant Mother Teresa of sorts who brought recognition to post-World War II conservative Christian culture and its missionaries' dreams of evangelizing the world.[9] But by the 1970s, American conservatives were not as engrossed in the stories of missionary martyrdom that sent single women out into the jungle to preach. The Christian home was under siege, and the stars of the decade would be evangelical and pentecostal women who declared that they were called on to defend it.

The social revolution known as second-wave feminism was propelled by the force of hundreds of thousands of frustrated, well-educated, and energetic women discontented with a host of demeaning attitudes and legal disabilities that seemed constricting and outdated. The inability to open a checking account in one's own name, or obtain independent bank credit, or start a business; the obligatory use of "Mrs." and one's husband's surname; patronizing advertising; the ubiquity of sexist humor; a seeming indifference to spousal abuse; professional barriers to hiring or advancement—every woman could have named a dozen ways in which age-old attitudes had diminished her sense of self-respect.

For black women, the challenges were even more pronounced, as they faced the dual threats of gender discrimination and racism. The "women's liberation movement" took dead aim not only at "male-chauvinist pigs" but at the entire way of life that undergirded the American middle class. For the well-publicized radicals at the cutting edge of the phenomenon, age-old institutions had to go: like romantic love, like marriage. "A woman needs a man like a fish needs a bicycle," quipped Gloria Steinem, who also observed that "marriage was the model for slavery law in this country."[10] Black feminists, eventually dubbed "womanists," zeroed in on the oppression not only of masculinized American culture, but also on the arrogance of white feminists who had often ignored their voices and contributions to the struggle for equality and liberation.[11]

In 1972 and 1973, Supreme Court decisions legalized first birth control, and then abortion for all women.[12] Motherhood was a choice for the first time and, naturally, this raised questions about the necessity of childrearing and homemaking. "Motherhood: Who Needs It?" asked journalist Betty Rollins in a popular newsmagazine.[13] Childlessness soon became a common scenario for sitcom families on American television[14] and the independence of young women was the theme song of the *Mary Tyler Moore Show*, which posed, and answered, the musical question: "How will you make it on your own?"[15] It was an era of radical questioning. "All men have oppressed women. . . . We do not need to change ourselves, but to change men," read the "Redstockings Manifesto," a 1969 New York tract that appeared in the bible of the women's liberation movement, *Sisterhood Is Powerful*.[16]

Christian academics were not immune to many of the complaints raised by the women's liberation movement. A number of female theologians at elite universities responded warmly to the call for raised consciousness and, in doing so, opened up a new academic field: feminist theology. At Boston College (a Jesuit-founded institution) Mary Daly fashioned a long career attacking androcentrism in religion and the oppression she saw visited on women by the church. Her 1973 book *Beyond God the Father* used Marxism, psychology, anthropology, Friedrich Nietzsche, Martin Buber, and medieval Catholic thinkers to denounce phallocentric morality and patriarchy.[17] Rosemary Radford Ruether, author of books like *Sexism and God-Talk*, and Elisabeth Schüssler Fiorenza, founder of the *Journal of Feminist Studies in*

Religion and author of *In Memory of Her: A Feminist Theological Reconstruction of Christian Origins,* worked to advance feminism in biblical interpretation and theology in the Catholic tradition. Among their Protestant counterparts were Sallie McFague at Vanderbilt Divinity School and Letty Russell at Yale Divinity School, who became one of the first women ordained in the United Presbyterian Church.[18] In those Protestant denominations that had resisted female clergy, women pressed for ordination, a goal achieved by Lutherans in 1970,[19] Episcopalians in 1976,[20] and the Reformed Church in America in 1979.[21]

Evangelical women theologians were also willing to take up the feminist challenge but, unlike their mainline and Catholic counterparts, they rejected the titles "radical" or "pioneering." They tried to demonstrate that a more literal biblical hermeneutic could also be egalitarian. In 1969, Nancy Hardesty of Trinity Evangelical Divinity School and writer Letha Scanzoni decided to collaborate on a book that would examine the drive for increased women's rights through the lens of evangelicalism. The result was *All We're Meant to Be,* a bestseller that "helped show evangelical women around the United States that they could be both evangelicals and feminists."[22] This book, the magazine *Daughters of Sarah*, and a coalition of social activists called the Evangelical Women's Caucus were at the center of an attempt to come to grips with the mid-century ferment in politics, race relations, and religion. Their 1973 discussion paper, for instance, was illustrative of the movement's fundamental concerns:

> All persons, male and female, are created in God's image and are thus equal.
>
> All persons are given equal responsibility by God for the propagation of the human species and for the preservation of the earth.
>
> Thus, women must be treated equally with men. In the church women should be allowed to exercise fully whatever gifts the Holy Spirit has endowed them with, including public leadership in worship and administration on both local and national levels.
>
> In the home, women should exercise equal rights and responsibilities with their husbands in the marital relationship and in regard to any children. A woman's homemaking should be considered of equal value with other work outside the home and compensated accordingly.

In the business world, women should be given equal pay and equal benefits commensurate with their training and experience without regard to sex or marital status. This includes so-called "Christian" organizations.

In education, women should be given equal opportunity to pursue their goals without discrimination in admission, course offerings, financial aid, athletic facilities, faculty appointments, promotions, etc.[23]

Evangelical accommodation to these changing constellations of work and family were written into the titles of publications like *The Dual-Earner Marriage*, a manual for husbands and wives learning to share domestic responsibilities with topics on "Just for wives: surviving the 'Second Shift.' Just for husbands: 'the inadequate provider' and 'reluctant homemaker' syndrome."[24] Then, of course, came a rash of budgeting and time management books like *The 25-Hour Woman* to help women squeeze the expectations of full-time employment and full-time motherhood into her life with a spiritual gloss. The cover showed a stiff woman posed as the big hand of a ticking clock and the promotional promise that special techniques would help them "avoid feeling victimized by conflicting demands." It was obvious, however, that the evangelical authors knew that women's many roles within the family, marriage, workplace, church, and community were often at odds.[25] How-to books for women took great care to explain that women must be competent but not ambitious, attractive but not alluring, confident but mild-mannered. The stated goals of Joanne Wallace's handbook for *The Working Woman* was a study in these paradoxes. It promised help with:

- Quick and easy recipes
- Speaking in front of people
- Setting and reaching goals
- Preventing procrastination
- Efficient time management
- Cultivating winning attitudes
- Building personal influence on the job
- Self-defense and sex discrimination
- Using color seasons to enhance attractiveness
- Handling job stress[26]

A smiling Phyllis Schlafly leads a demonstration of women against the Equal Rights Amendment in front of the White House in Washington, D.C. Photo by Warren Leffler, courtesy of Library of Congress, Prints & Photographs Division, *U.S. News & World Report* Magazine Collection, LC-DIG-ds-00757.

For others, the challenge had to be met with direct political confrontation and a re-sacralization of the home. The roles of wife and mother took on a decidedly populist tone in Christian circles with the campaign to stop the Equal Rights Amendment (ERA). In 1970, the National Organization for Women (NOW), founded by Betty Friedan, stepped up public pressure to amend the American constitution to include a ban on sex discrimination. Within two years the House of Representatives and the Senate had adopted an amendment that then had to be ratified by thirty-eight states. But by the mid-1970s, a vocal and well-organized STOP ERA effort effectively made celebrities out of two women who professionalized their roles as politically savvy mothers. Phyllis Schlafly, a lawyer and Catholic mother of six, founded the Eagle Forum, and Beverly LaHaye, mother of four and wife of famous pastor Tim LaHaye, launched the Concerned Women for America, which, by 1984, crowed that their 365,000 membership was a third larger than NOW's.[27] Women's liberation, Schlafly said, "deliberately degrades the homemaker and hacks away at her sense of self-worth and pride and pleasure

Pastor's wife Beverly LaHaye founded Concerned Women for America as a guardian of family values in an era of emerging feminism. Reprinted with permission from Charisma Media, www.charismamedia.com.

in being female."[28] Religious women responded to the call to action in droves, so enthusiastically that 98 percent of the ERA's opponents claimed church membership while less than half of its opponents did.[29] LaHaye credited part of the success of her movement to the enormous reach of famous evangelical wives. "I've been a minister's wife for 30 years, so I have a quicker access to church women," she said.[30] With a $2 million budget, organizations like hers were one sign of the audience and industry that were growing up around conservative women.

THE EVANGELICAL MARKET OF THE 1970S AND 1980S

The trumpet blasts of the regiment of liberated women coincided with a growing realization in the world of media producers that evangelicalism was a rich target for their products. Journalists and pollsters discovered that tens of millions of Americans claimed to be "born again" and that these conservative Christians were avid consumers of literature. Indeed, as the historian Daniel Vaca has argued, evangelicalism with its array of disparate denominations and theologies was as much a phenomenon shaped inside churches as it was a shared culture produced by the books people bought and read.[31] It was a boom time in religious retailing, with Christian bookstores and their revenues climbing steadily over the course of the 1970s. One hundred publishing houses churned out religious titles, making this one of the fasting growing segments in the industry and a financial bonanza for the evangelical bookstores that were its largest distributors. By 1980, bookstore sales alone had hit $770 million.[32] It was an exciting time for Christian publishers, who found that they could provide content eagerly sought by many women at a moment when changes in the secular sphere were challenging their deeply held beliefs. "We need women speaking to women," argued Helene Ashaker, a national leader in college campus ministry, begging her all-female audience to volunteer immediately to join her in combating the "braless college chicks" and their women's lib philosophy.[33] "Women are looking to other women for leadership. Armies are building on both sides, and ours [had] better be bigger."[34]

Creating this bigger army was also the work of a number of new Christian women's magazines, such as *Virtue* and *Today's Christian*

Woman, founded in 1978 as a sister publication to *Christianity Today*.[35] "We were unhappy with the drift of secular women's magazines. They were pro-choice and pro-consumerism," said the first editor of *Today's Christian Woman*.[36] The periodical was pitched to the "new traditional woman," a term coined by their advertising agency to define the magazine's non-denominational audience and its appeal to both a modern style and traditional ethos.[37] These magazines claimed audiences in the hundreds of thousands, while Christian book publishers could point to millions of their products sold. One author estimated that publishers for an evangelical audience produced one-third of all commercial book sales in the United States in the 1970s.[38] Marabel Morgan, Anita Bryant, Beverly LaHaye, and Dale Evans Rogers proved to be bestselling authors and newly minted celebrities.[39] These were women speaking to women about the domestic sphere where conservative Christianity had already crowned them queen.

The explosion of Christian television was also making pastors' wives into famous televangelists, with women like Tammy Faye Bakker and Jan Crouch gracing the stage as hosts, along with a carousel of female talent—speakers, authors, but usually singers—performing before audiences of several million.[40] Books and television were providing new opportunities for conference speakers, but it was largely celebrity wives who made the most of the opportunities before them.

Consider, for instance, the popular pentecostalism of this period. Pentecostal preachers like Oral Roberts, John Osteen, and John Gimenez drew thousands into stadiums or into their own auditoriums to host national conferences. In the 1980s, there were hundreds of these conferences each year, though only the most famous earned national headlines, an advertisement in *Charisma* magazine, and throngs of attendees. It was a regular feature of these national conferences to have a "women's section," on the assumption that families traveled to these events and wives might need something to do. Since the focus was male senior pastors, the offerings for women were limited; the 1985 National Leadership Conference starred three famous men with the following choices for women's seminars:

- Color coordination
- Makeup
- Nutrition

Dodie Osteen

invites you to the Second Annual

LAKEWOOD INTERNATIONAL

LADIES CONVENTION

FEATURING SPECIAL GUESTS

Anne Gimenez   Billye Brim   Gloria Copeland

FOUR WORD-PACKED DAYS

September 27th-30th

LAKEWOOD INTERNATIONAL OUTREACH CHURCH
7400 E. Houston Road, Houston, TX 77228

The 1984 Ladies Convention at Lakewood International Outreach Church is sure to be an exciting time in the Lord. Each day will bring manifestations of God's Spirit, as well as fresh revelation in the Word. You'll be blessed and edified during this time of refreshing.

Services begin Thursday, September 27th at 7:30 PM, and continue 3 times daily through Sunday night, September 30th.

Dodie Osteen, wife of megachurch pastor John Osteen, hosted some of the era's most successful women's conferences. Reprinted with permission from Charisma Media, www.charismamedia.com.

- Gracious hostess and etiquette
- Praise in the dance
- On being a pastor's wife
- And more exciting topics![41]

Soon the wives of famous pentecostal evangelists seized the reins and decided to host their own conferences. Now advertising themselves as "liberated women" (or as Daisy Osborn billed her followers, "Women

Who Win!"[42]), they created national organizations for Christian women leaders (defining "leader," of course, in a variety of ways). The 1987 conference of the newly formed "International Women in Leadership" not only advertised the accomplishments of Anne Gimenez, its founder, and a host of female leaders in church and government, including Elizabeth Dole, a US senator highly ranked in the Reagan and Bush administrations, it offered opportunities for both speakers and participants to hone their skills. Sessions included:

> Management training . . . Leaders are Born, Managers are Made.
> Every Vocation a Calling . . . Biblical Reasoning in All Areas of Life.

Its splashy pink advertisements listed the dozens of members of its advisory board, which read like a Who's Who of almost every famous pentecostal megachurch and parachurch wife in the country. The best of both worlds fell to women like Anne Gimenez, who alongside her husband, John Gimenez, co-founded Rock Church; Dodie Osteen, wife of Lakewood Church's founding pastor John Osteen; and charismatic televangelist Marilyn Hickey, who could play the part of speaker *and* host of their own megachurch conferences in the massive auditoriums of their home churches. There were perks to being Mrs. Minister.

MRS. MINISTER

It is little wonder that the biggest celebrities of the decade, male and female, were those who made the Christian family the last line of defense against changing cultural norms. Psychologist James Dobson founded Focus on the Family in 1977 for "nurturing and defending the God-ordained institution of the family and promoting biblical truths worldwide,"[43] and his books, such as his bestselling *Dare to Discipline*, quickly became *the* ubiquitous go-to guides for childrearing, with instructions so specific that, for example, he told parents to spank their kids with a wooden spoon. It was a comforting mix of parenting advice and evangelical mores that promised to shore up families in a permissive and backslidden culture. As historian Seth Dowland has demonstrated, "family values" were the order of the day and included a constellation of issues related to school textbooks, homeschooling, public prayer, abortion, and godly government. Pastor Jerry Falwell's Moral Majority was founded in 1979 as a "pro-life, pro-family, pro-moral, and pro-America" organization that would consolidate tremendous political energy around the defense of the monogamous, heterosexual family.[44] The women who rose to fame in this period were not topical experts like James Dobson or institution builders like Jerry Falwell, whose megachurch, Thomas Road Baptist Church, and fledgling Liberty University, acted as conservative political platforms. Instead, they were one of two kinds of wives—women like Phyllis Schlafly, who billed themselves as mothers and housewives at the same time as they led causes outside the home, and women like Beverly LaHaye, the spouses of famous pastors who parlayed their fame into a new kind of career: the professional wife. The most formidable conservative female opponents of the feminist cause would say that they were nothing special, only a wife and a mother. But this language had taken on extraordinary power, particularly when it applied to a woman who knew how to stand by her man.

For the greater part of the 1970s and 1980s, bestsellers by famous wives helped articulate a language of female submission in sharp contrast to the emergent causes espoused by 1970s feminism: abortion, Title IX, no-fault divorce, workplace advancement, and the Equal Rights Amendment. These wives became some of the strongest proponents of "traditional" households, because they were already in a career called "the minister's wife" that demanded it. During most of the twentieth century (and even after women's ordination began to break the mold), it was usually assumed that the role of the minister was a two-person career. He was the man of God and she must learn to be a "minister's wife." It was a decidedly middle-class profession, and, like the wives of professors, lawyers, army officers, politicians, and business executives, the job came with a few perquisites.[45] A minister's wife was afforded respect and status borrowed from her husband and from God, and, if she were lucky, perhaps a parsonage. But the role was so conventional that it was practically a cliché. Ministerial handbooks cautioned wives not to "pour ourselves into the stereotype—like gelatin into a ring-mold salad."[46]

Minister's wives were, for the most part, expected to play their parts quietly. *The Minister's Wife* advice manual warned that women must not usurp their husbands for "our career is not *clergywoman* but *homemaker*."[47] Some books recommended avoiding leadership of any kind in the church so as not to rival the pastor-husband's power, and—even if she were a better speaker—she should certainly stay out of the pulpit.[48] As mainstream culture pondered questions of women's liberation, evangelical readers wanted to know whether the most conservative kind of woman—a wife and a preacher's wife no less—could ever be as happy. "The bras are burning, the flags are waving, and pins and bumper stickers burgeoning to announce the dissatisfaction of women . . . . The libbers are upon us and we must come to terms with them—and ourselves," said one pastor's wife.[49] A whole genre of pastoral spouse literature answered with a well-publicized yes.[50]

Wives of famous pastors were in an ideal position to combat the primary accusations of feminists: that housewives were trapped and unsatisfied.[51] Ruth Peale's 1971 *The Adventure of Being a Wife* was penned under the name "Mrs. Norman Vincent Peale," which summarized much of her message: that her greatest achievements have come from being conformed to the image of her husband. Almost every famous preacher's wife tried her hand at it. There was *His Darling Wife, Evelyn* about the wife of Oral Roberts and *Woman: Be All You Can Be* by Dale Evans Rogers, wife and co-star of singing cowboy Roy Rogers. Other family members got into the game with books such as *They Call Me Mother Graham*, a celebration of the significance of Billy Graham's mother "in a day when the bonds that hold families together are unraveling as never before."[52] The mother of famous 1970s televangelist Rex Humbard weighed in on the decline of modern faith with *Give Me That Old-Time Religion*, and the daughter of 1980s televangelist Robert Schuller wrote separate books about both her famous parents.[53]

The appetite for stories of their lives soon translated into books like *Living Cameos,* featuring famous wives such as Edith Schaeffer, Shirley Dobson, Macel Falwell, Beverly LaHaye, and Rexella Van Impe.[54] Even Rita Bennett, the wife of the Episcopalian priest who had helped kick off the charismatic movement in mainline Protestantism, became a star: *I'm Glad You Asked That* showed her looking like a beautiful bohemian, wearing a homemade floral dress and ultra-long hair, ready to answer intimate questions about husbands and wives.[55] Colleen Townsend Evans, whose book *A New Joy* had sold a quarter of a million copies, published reflections about her marriage and her famous husband—she had abandoned a thriving Hollywood acting career to wed Presbyterian luminary, the Rev. Louis H. Evans Jr. She revealed that he was not only

Ruth Peale made being "Mrs. Norman Vincent Peale" into a long career, which included overseeing *Guideposts*, their successful positive-thinking magazine. Reprinted with permission from *Christianity Today*, www.christianitytoday.com.

her spiritual guide but also her friend. This was not a shocking revelation, but that was precisely the point: there was remarkable consensus about the importance of a woman's submission. Each woman had her own brand of submission: Beverly LaHaye's was political; Anita Bryant's was bubbly; and Elisabeth Elliot's was poetic as ever, even in the way she called the sexes "gloriously and radically unequal."[56]

The three major topics these women addressed were the true meaning of liberation, the acceptance of innate sexual differences, and the

Singer Anita Bryant was one of the most popular conservative figures of the 1970s, known as much for her singing as her activism against gay rights. Courtesy of History Miami Museum, 1995-277-11260.

spiritual importance of femininity as a marker of the Christian counterculture. In the 1972 memoir *One Woman's Liberation* by Shirley Boone, wife of 1950s chart-topper Pat Boone, "liberation" centered on her struggle for a happy marriage to a husband who battled the temptations of Hollywood while she struggled with loneliness and jealousy. The story wanders through the private rooms of their famous lives, giving readers a tantalizing peek at the ordinary dinner conversations and glamorous soirées, but it culminates with her discovery that the age's "new morality" was a threat to her family and to the divine order of creation. Pat's accepting responsibility as the spiritual leader of their family restored Shirley emotionally and spiritually, and so the story ends with frank chastisements of women who will not accept their place. She fretted that "women's libbers militantly object to the place in society God has ordained for their sex, but by doing so, they lose much precious liberty the Lord intended them to have."[57] The hard-won ease of their marriage came from a loving husband who "frees his helpmeet . . . by being head of the house and protecting her" and being a submissive wife who "relieved of a lot of the hard, emotion-taxing decision making."[58] A wife under her husband's authority would not resort to nagging or counterproductive independent action. Freedom came from letting herself fall into the deep grooves of God's divine roadmap for men and women.

Though the rhetoric made much of their inequality, it simultaneously elevated such women to one of the most powerful titles of all, that of wife. This was odd, given that most evangelical and pentecostal women were not only wives and mothers, but had joined the workforce in the 1970s.[59] (African American and Hispanic women simply remained in the workforce, having never experienced a similar golden age of single-earner households.) But when white evangelical and pentecostal women looked for paid employment, they clung to the ideal of wifedom far longer than the American mainstream. The wider society had already begun to valorize the working woman, and this trend gained cultural recognition by the 1980s in everything from Madonna's power suits to the rash of Wall Street comedies like *Nine to Five* and *Working Girl*, proving women could make it to the corner office. By the 1990s, evangelical women were still critically considering their place in relationship to second-wave feminism and its various causes as a third wave crested in the 1990s. Though difficult to precisely define, third-wave feminism was typically characterized by sex-positivity and heightened awareness of the ways gender intersected with class and race to shape (and limit) women's agency.[60] At least on the surface, the stars of the Christian industry seemed entirely undisturbed by the vast economic changes that had turned most women out of the house. They had instead become the greatest public defenders of private domestic life, and would soon do so from church offices with their names on the door.

THE RISE OF WOMEN'S MINISTRY

For a century, there had been a power-broker in church life who was not *the* wife. In fact, she was often not *anyone's* wife—she was the head of the women's missionary auxiliary. She might be spindly like Southern Baptist Women's Missionary Union president Alma Hunt, or energetic like Mother Lillian Coffey, Church of God in Christ's national director for women and a fearsome woman indeed. She was the face of an army of volunteer women pouring labor, lives, and money into their denominations for domestic and international church planting, relief work, school building, and other uncounted acts of mercy. As we saw in Chapter One, since the late nineteenth century this had been the chief area in which Protestant women could wield genuine influence in their churches and have a real impact around the globe. Three million women in forty different societies worked at home to raise tens of millions of dollars to support thousands of foreign and frontier evangelists (60 percent of whom were women), who would educate local women and children, staff hospitals, schools, and orphanages, and simply preach.[61] At a time when American Christian women could not occupy pulpits in their own churches, sit on governance committees, or serve as delegates to conferences, they operated mission boards with amazing energy and efficiency. For decades, these auxiliaries fought off efforts to subordinate them to local clergy and yield control of their funds, but gradually as the twentieth century wore on they would lose their influence. By the 1970s and 1980s, when the pastor's wife emerged on the national scene as a different kind of hero, female missionary societies—for so long the domain of independent and, often husbandless, women—had been gutted as an ecclesiastical force. Mass volunteerism was becoming less economically viable as women were being called into the workforce and consequently had less availability for time-intensive causes outside work and family. For economic reasons, cultural reasons, and ideological reasons, white women were leaving the home and taking on different identities as wage earners, careerists, and independents with newly public lives.

The popular Christian response to these seismic shifts can be seen, in part, by comparing the celebration of the single missionary heroine, that hardy and cause-driven warrior, to that of the megachurch wife. If the missionary woman's life was public, hers was private. It was reinforced again and again that her first ministry was to her home. In fact, the more public her work, the more stridently she defended her place at home. Consider the career of Nina Bronner, the wife of Bishop Dale Bronner and worship leader of an African American prosperity megachurch in Atlanta. After a lengthy account of her public service, her biography reads:

> All who meet her are drawn to her instantly. Although she wears many hats, she realizes that her first ministry is to her husband and children. Dr. Nina home-schooled her children. She firmly believes, as her father-in-law, the late Nathaniel H. Bronner, Sr., always taught, that no amount of success can compensate for failure at home.[62]

Missionary women had abandoned their rightful place at home while megachurch wives lived as embodiments of it. (We will see shortly how difficult this was, ideologically, for the families of American revivalist preachers, whose itinerancy complicated their defense of domestic life.) Missionary nonfiction of the era like *The Top of the World* ("They joyfully left the comforts of the south to become missionaries in their own country, braving cold and isolation . . . in Canada's Frozen North"[63]) testified to a tough breed of missionary women. These were the portraits of sacrificial women, brave pioneers, and modern-day martyrs who loved their families but loved God more. It was a grand love story of the church, slowly eclipsed by a portrait of God's love expressed through the family, as "the home" became the theological centerpiece of evangelicalism.

If the missionary woman was scrappy and resourceful, the ministry wife was a more delicate and feminine creature. Popular paperbacks about missionary adventurers typically showed a photo spread of the author in the mission field, too busy to worry about fashion in her homemade dress, silvering hair, and spectacles.[64] Megachurch wives, by contrast, were portraits of femininity, cued in to the secrets to flattering makeup and coloring that they did not mind sharing at the next women's ministry conference.

Though single women missionaries were lauded for their heroism, they were also privately accused of insubordination, independence, and lesbianism.[65] Ministry wives, on the other hand, embodied an idealized domestic arrangement with the man as head. The wife on stage was an advertisement for any number of things: her natural subordination; his fidelity in leading the family (this would be very important after the televangelism scandals in the late 1980s when sexual misconduct shook public perceptions of the ministry); and the sense that the domestic sphere for women had been reborn in an American culture that had muddied divine roles for husband and wife.

The response of the Southern Baptist Convention to the rise of women's ministries was telling of this wider turn. A group of famous megachurch wives began to create new resources and experiences for women apart from the Women's Missionary Union. In the early 1970s, a woman named Barbara O'Chester, wife of megachurch pastor Harold O'Chester, began a series of women's retreats with four staple sessions that captured the hot topics for women.[66] The first was a direct confrontation with claims of feminist freedom with a session (riffing off the scintillating bestseller *The Joy of Sex*) called "The Joy of Submission."[67] The second was called "The Spirit-Filled Life," which responded to the charismatic movement's emphasis on the Holy Spirit with teachings about how women could experience the direction and leading of God in their daily lives. The third, "You and Your Child," spoke to women's anxious desires to find community and purpose in childrearing. ("We used to listen to *Focus on the Family* every day and talk about it with each other," enthused one Southern Baptist megachurch wife. "Other than Dr. Spock, there was almost nothing available to help young moms raise their families."[68]) And, lastly, "The Act of Marriage," which was the biggest draw. Named (with permission) after the scintillating sex manual of the same name by Tim and Beverly LaHaye, the session encouraged women to enjoy their sexuality within marriage in the experimental era of feminist guides like *Our Bodies, Ourselves*.[69] This tall demure woman would embolden her readers to make sex a regular feature of their married lives and, if they couldn't afford lingerie, she had an easy fix. Every time she ran this seminar, she would give an unsuspecting attendee a gift in front of her giggling friends, a man's T-shirt with two strategically placed holes cut out of the front. It was a showstopper.

When I spoke to Barbara O'Chester, now in her eighties, about her work on the forefront of this shift from missions to women's ministries, she described how exciting it was to feel as if pastors' wives were on the cusp of something new for women. Her small retreats for her own church swelled into gatherings of six thousand, as "places where we could meet the questions posed by the culture head-on."[70] Susie Hawkins, wife of O. S. Hawkins, the former pastor of First Baptist in Dallas, had been one of Barbara's retreat attendees and one of the first of this cast of megachurch wives volunteering to lead women's ministries in her own congregation (though almost always without pay). "It was exciting that there was nothing old-fashioned about it. We had women leaders who everyone respected—and that's the word, *respected*—and we didn't feel so out-of-step with culture after all. It was empowering. It was! We learned to get a theological grasp on *why* we believed what we did. Suddenly we even had theological permission to seduce your own husband, it was great!" She laughed. "It was a lot more fun than talking about missions, that's for sure. Those poor missionary societies. They never stood a chance."[71]

One of the leading megachurches that shaped the character and direction of women's ministry in the Southern Baptist denomination was Bellevue Baptist Church in Memphis, Tennessee, with its charismatic leader, Adrian Rogers. Adrian had been recently elected president of the SBC, and it seemed that whatever he and his wife, Joyce, did, Southern Baptists followed. As historian Elizabeth Flowers has chronicled, the energy once invested in their missionary enterprise was later channeled into the new anti-feminist cause as "women's ministry."[72] In 1980, Joyce Rogers hosted four thousand women at Bellevue to, as her co-organizer summarized, "encourage women in fulfilling their traditional roles as wives and mothers as well as challenge women to become involved in promoting moral virtue and traditional family values in our society."[73] The conference theme was "A Wise Woman Builds," and headliners drawn from across the evangelical women's world included names such as Elisabeth Elliot, Beverly LaHaye, and Vonette Bright (wife of Campus Crusade for Christ founder Bill Bright). It heralded the move away from the Women's Missionary Union (WMU), the historic hub of women's activity in church life, and toward women's ministry. Soon after, Bellevue became the first Southern Baptist megachurch to launch a women's ministry, quietly letting go of the WMU in the process. Many megachurches would soon follow.

With the rise of evangelical megaministry and the post-1960s decline of liberal mainline churches, contemporary women with national platforms no longer explicitly tied Christian womanhood to missionary activism. This shift in evangelical women's work from foreign to domestic missions, and from "out-reach" to the community to "in-reach" to the church's internal constituency, became a broad pattern across denominations. In the Church of God in Christ, the largest African American denomination, a similar generational shift moved the focus away from missions to women's ministry and to the type of woman who would lead it. Beginning in the 1970s, a new kind of woman began to dominate the Women's Department, which had been the thriving center of all women's missionary and churchly activity. Past leaders like Mother Lillian Coffey had directed thousands of women in dozens of auxiliary programs, where they earned an experiential authority that allowed them to stand shoulder to shoulder with the bishop as female proxies to his power. The new leaders were more feminized and less civically minded, argued historian Anthea Butler, and power in the denomination was moving away from those who had earned their credentials in volunteering for the Women's Department and toward the conferred status of bishop's wives and first ladies.[74] The ministerial biography of First Lady LaVette Gibson, one of the stars of the reality TV show *Preachers of LA*, was a study in this transformation. For two decades, she helped found Life Church of God in Christ in Riverside, California, with her husband, serving as its chief administrator, curriculum developer, missionary coordinator, and women's ministry director. At the same time, she served in her denomination's Women's Department in a number of capacities and received her evangelist missionary license. But when her own star rose, as her biography tells it, "the Lord directed Sister LaVette to release this, and other positions in the Jurisdiction, to focus more on the ministry of Life Church."[75] She would henceforth be known as First Lady for her church and a speaker at Church of God in Christ women's conferences. Across denominations, a broad generational shift seemed to be taking place. Even the Assemblies of God renamed their Women's Missionary Council as "Women's Ministries" and retitled their missionary magazine *Woman's Touch*. A Southern Baptist women's ministry leader explained to me: "The missionary auxiliaries were starting to feel like our mother's thing. Women's ministries felt like it was for us."[76]

Wives were not simply national figures, they were becoming congregational leaders as well. One of the most obvious reasons was that the incredible increase in the scope of congregations was posing new opportunities and challenges. Who would coordinate the church's ambitious plans to develop a women's ministry? These organizations were no small matter. Instead of coffee and casual bible study, women's ministries were becoming vast and complex institutions in their own right, with staff members, large budgets, local and national conference hosts, and generators of new curriculum. So, when a church needed a leader and a branded image for their work with women, the megachurch pastor's wife was a natural choice. And she, in turn, would benefit from the organizational, managerial, and ministerial skills she gained from learning to grow her own empire.

Women's ministries were fast becoming an important and defining feature of Christian subcultures, sometimes simply within denominations, sometimes in pan-denominational and non-denominational expressions (which would become the prevailing trend through the 1980s and 1990s). A look at the names of some of these megachurch women's ministries showed how they thought of themselves as a sorority ("Girlfriends," "Girlfriends Unlimited," "Women2Women," "SISTERHOOD"), a feminine necessity ("Pink Promise," "ChickChat"), and a maternal flourish ("Feathering the Nest").

The romantic view of women missionaries that had caused audiences to rush out to hear Elisabeth Elliot, the lone widow winning over the Huaorani people, faded as conservatives came to believe that men's leadership over the family and the church should include the mission field as well. Over the remainder of Elliot's life, the figure of the missionary hero would grow less and less a possibility for women. Even the remainder of Elliot's life reflected the shift, as she became arguably better known for her writing and speaking on matters related to domesticity, sex, and dating than for her past missionary activities. By the 1980s, one of the largest North American missionary organizations, the Southern Baptist Foreign Mission Board, began to take measures to restrict women missionaries to "their biblical role of Christian homemakers."[77] Aspiring

Elisabeth Elliots would have to retreat ever deeper into their husbands' shadows.

CO-PASTOR

Women's congregational leadership did not begin and end with the women's ministry. By the 1980s, a number of women in the prosperity gospel movement[78] began to call themselves something new: co-pastor. Female leadership in the prosperity gospel had grown in number and stature since the giants of the movement had founded educational institutions (Oral Roberts University in 1963, Gordon Lindsay's Christ for the Nations in 1970, and Kenneth Hagin's Rhema Bible Training Center in 1974) that accredited and ordained them. What had once been a handful of women was now a small army of female leaders who claimed top billing on the largest stages. The American viewing public tuned in to see the familiar faces of wives like Marilyn Hickey, Vicki Jamison Peterson, Tammy Faye Bakker, Jan Crouch, Evelyn Roberts, Freda Lindsay, Gloria Copeland, Dodie Osteen, Sandy Brown, and Marte Tilton— up-and-coming evangelists hoping to capitalize on the growing women's ministry industry that specialized in the needs of the Christian wife and mother. Wendy Treat, co-pastor of the Christian Faith Center in Seattle, made her early reputation as a theological expert on the demands of harried women ("The roles of today's woman can seem overwhelming: wife, mother, single woman . . . can one woman do it all?").[79] Kenneth Hagin's protégés David and Roxanne Swann got their start as child-rearing coaches in the principles of prosperity theology with books titled *Guarantee Your Child's Success.* By the time Kenneth Hagin wrote *The Woman Question* to explain how it was "usually best" to keep gifted men at the helm of churches while women must endeavor to "be content with whatever place the Lord opens," his female graduates were already calling themselves co-pastors at some of the fastest growing churches in the nation.[80]

Inside of prosperity circles and far beyond them, even the most hierarchical complementarian could agree that there was something about a husband's presence that sanctified his wife's pastoral work. For Don Basham, a leader in the charismatic movement and a strong opponent

Word of Faith Christian Center was one of the first prosperity megachurches in the country. The prosperity movement was important in popularizing the "co-pastor" model. Each of the speakers seen here typically traveled with their spouse. Reprinted with permission from Charisma Media, www.charismamedia.com.

of women in ministry, the lives of Aquila and Priscilla in the Book of Acts (who shared the burdens of ministry in the early church) made some manner of partnership acceptable: "Women can minister in the company of and subject to the authority of their husbands," argued Basham, as long as each woman was physically in her husband's presence and thus in "the protected, subordinate role God intends for her."[81] Yet not every tradition agreed on precisely what that shared ministry should entail. Many evangelicals, particularly Reformed believers and post-conservative resurgence Southern Baptists, typically forbade women from addressing men and so the formation of these newly public church roles for women was a step too far.

The symbolic importance of the woman beside her man remained one of the most common images of megachurch life. In the entrance foyer of Lakewood Church, the country's largest congregation, there was a bronze statue of John and Dodie Osteen, co-founders of the congregation and the charismatic predecessors of Joel and Victoria Osteen.

The way they stood together as a couple was so familiar that it was entirely unremarkable. He was in a handsome suit, a step forward as he raised his Bible in the air with an inviting smile. She stood a little behind him in a pencil skirt and blazer, both hands clinging to his arm and a wide smile lighting her face like his. Her ability to perfectly mirror him—even in the way the eye skips over her presence—was one of her most skillful public acts. "Co-pastor" became not simply an ecclesial designation but a regular performance for women across theological traditions regardless of title. Her primary act was one of relationship, the ability to humanize her husband's role. The scandal-plagued televangelist Robert Tilton needed the validating presence of Marte Tilton. The cover of his book *Dare to Be a Success* showed the happy couple at what appeared to be the set of their television show, their hands entwined, their tanned faces pulled into wide smiles. His salmon blazer picked up the pink of her silk camisole, while her blue blazer matched his tie. There was not a hair out of place with this beautiful couple who seemed perfectly in sync, down to the way their heads tilted slightly toward each other. The implicit argument was that she *knows* him, so her reaction to him offers us clues about his true character. A husband without a wife lived without the affective advantages of his wife's presence. Macel Falwell, wife of Jerry Falwell, knew the power of a woman's presence,

This statue of John and Dodie Osteen at Lakewood Church depicts Dodie as the ideal pastor's wife in the shadows of the man who wields the Word. Image courtesy of Phil Sinitiere.

The trial of Jim Bakker became a national obsession and television spectacle. Throughout the proceedings, Tammy Faye expressed her unflagging trust in her husband and their ministry. North Carolina Collection, University of North Carolina Library at Chapel Hill.

complaining that her husband's tough public image came from the media's refusal to portray him with his family.[82]

After the televangelism scandals of the late 1980s and early 1990s, the figure of the celebrity preacher had lost credibility. Oral Roberts, Jim and Tammy Faye Bakker, Jimmy Swaggart, and Robert Tilton had each been caught up in a public relations crisis that soured widespread support for popular ministries. Television audiences dropped from 15.1 million in 1986 to under 10 million by the 1990s.[83] Sexual misconduct had toppled the ministries of Jim and Tammy Faye Bakker and Jimmy Swaggart, cementing an equation between adultery and Christian celebrity. One solution came by promoting wives to the actual title of co-pastor or a similar role, thus placing the family at the center of the ministry. There would no longer be any competition between the church and the family, because the church *was* the family.

Long after the specter of the scandals faded, the husband and wife brand prevailed. In my examination of megachurch wives' web presence (see Appendixes I and II), almost every senior pastor of the largest American megachurches mentioned his wife and children on his church website, but around one-fifth swapped out their own photo for one with their wife and children. The men's profile pictures looked like Christmas cards, perhaps a sea of matching denim as a family perches on a hay bale or staggered up a grand staircase, dressed in red and white, grinning children tilting their faces toward the camera. These earnest photographs were posed with the appearance of ease, and their affective work was immediate: their presence communicates love, sincerity, and wholeness. An additional one-fifth of them feature an entirely separate profile for his wife, regardless of whether she has an official title or is employed by the church. These separate profiles heap praise on their leading women, listing her every accomplishment and paying tribute to her character, but they typically end with a maternal flourish that places her work in a domestic context. The profile for Mia Wright, co-pastor of the largest African American Southern Baptist congregation (though, officially, the Southern Baptists recognize no such title for women), ends with the following: "Beyond her impressive academic background and professional accomplishments, the highlights of her life are her family—three gifted sons, and her husband, Pastor Remus Wright."[84]

The overwhelming majority of female speakers, authors, and pastors' wives introduced themselves much like Lisa Young, pastor's wife of the twenty-five-thousand-person Fellowship Church in Grapevine, Texas: "Wife, Mother, Woman After God's Heart." Within a megachurch context, regardless of church governance, the presence of the minister's wife gave the church the appearance of a family, an image that churches were quick to market. If the church was the home, then they were the parents, masculine and feminine was built into the founding myth. It was a deeply compelling account repeated in word and image across megachurches. Victoria Osteen was lauded as a "supportive wife" who represented the "feminine heart" at Lakewood.[85] Her marriage was a metaphor and an example. LaWanda Cherry's church biographer described her place in her seven-thousand-member Maryland congregation as follows:

> Rev. Cherry believes her life and her marriage are to be an example to
> the church and the Body of Christ, and she takes this assignment from

God very seriously. She considers it a privilege to be used by God to assist her husband in ministry and to serve the congregation of From the Heart Church Ministries®.[86]

The common trope of church as family became exaggerated in this heavily charismatic model that placed such great weight on its founding families.

The rise of the co-pastor model in pentecostalism only increased the visibility of woman as the yin to his yang. Though only 5 percent of modern megachurches, according to the latest study by Warren Bird of the Leadership Network,[87] actually used the title of co-pastor, it became a common one in the top tier of American megachurches, owing, in no small part, to the heavy presence of prosperity churches among them. Prosperity megachurches comprise 40 percent of churches over ten thousand, and almost all have co-pastors, making them a highly visible model. The model of co-pastor was also popular where pentecostalism had made inroads among historic black churches. Non-denominational and prosperity-leaning black churches often appointed pastors' wives to be co-pastors and not "first ladies." It was such a pervasive trend, in fact, that even the largest black Southern Baptist church, Fountain of Praise, openly touted Mia Wright as "co-pastor" and "partner in ministry and church leadership," making clear that she was more likely to be seen as the host of prosperity-owned TBN's *Praise the Lord* than speaking at the Southern Baptist Convention's ladies' lunch. By the 2000s, the creation of a "co-pastor" position had become so common in pentecostalized historic black denominations that the National Baptist Convention posted on their website an official answer to the question: "Can the pastor appoint his wife a co-pastor without church input? Is there such a position?" The response: "The answers to your questions are simple: No and No."[88] But, of course, it was never that simple.

Denominations that balked at the term "co-pastor" found it hard to prevent women from taking up the title "co-founder." After all, the history of most successful megachurches was an account of how the church began with only a handful of people in the pastor's home. This story of humble beginnings offered indirect praise to the founding pastor, who grew the ministry to epic proportions, but it also, inadvertently, made possible a new title for his wife. Church plants usually began as family businesses where every member played many roles. The husband might be the only one preaching, but everyone was cleaning, setting up chairs, corralling children, setting out food, handing out fliers, and running errands. A home church fell under the umbrella of the domestic, where all her actions seemed authorized, so she led and sang and rearranged the furniture. In short, she became the church's first staff member. In the last decade, megaministry women have begun to claim that title of co-founder. Even when their denominations explicitly forbade women's senior leadership, the title managed to maintain the appearance of propriety. Despite the Southern Baptist prohibition of women in leadership, in the last ten years Kay Warren began to claim her role in the co-founding of one of the most successfully branded churches in the world, Saddleback Church in Lake Forest, California. Her husband, Rick, authored the runaway bestseller, *The Purpose-Driven Life*, and, despite the fact that Kay was nowhere on the church's organizational chart, the two have been the public face of the church since its beginning. As long as the banner of wife was flown, women could more easily find various kinds of duties and institutional platforms.

There was of course a central incongruity of these domestic metaphors. Jesus was a celibate, single man, and scriptural references already identified his bride as the Church itself. But the family image with its subtle countercultural suggestion was too powerful to ignore. The result would be an almost endless portrayal of women like First Lady Pamela Hawkins, the vice president of product management at the Bank of America, posed like a beautiful car model beside her bishop husband with outreached arms in an expansive gesture of welcome and a tribute to "the calling on her life which is to educate and motivate children, glorify the Lord, support her husband, and the [Voices of Faith church] family to fulfill God's purpose."[89] Even the church needed a better half.

THE INDISPENSABLE WIFE

"Taking an interest in your husband's work is just one more way of making yourself indispensable to him," advised Ruth Peale.[90] She had come to the firm opinion that she would not be left out of her husband's fast-paced life and advised other women to follow her rather elaborate plan.

First, she must make a study of him. What are his strengths? What tasks does he always leave to the last minute? How much does he need to process his emotions at the end of the day? She concluded that she must know him better than he knows himself. This was a wife's duty and as a woman she had an advantage, for her natural intuition would allow her to discern his problems and find the remedy. Second, she must conform herself to the needs of her man. This would be no small task, and Ruth offered her own life as proof of it. She had learned how spotless Norman liked the house and scuttled about tidying every nook and cranny. She had found ways to draw out his feelings, particularly his deep insecurities after giving a speech, and fed him encouragement as he needed it. She had realized that his national fame as the pastor of Marble Collegiate Church, with some four thousand souls in its heyday,[91] only exacerbated his disorganization, and that he would need a steady administrative right hand. So, she set to work learning the skills and people involved in the business side of Norman's life, going to committee meetings, giving reports, learning accounting, and even memorizing Robert's Rules of Order to run the meetings herself.

"A woman may also find, if she forces herself to take an interest in her husband's work, that she has more aptitude for business than she thinks," she said, marveling a little at her own capacity for this line of work.[92] By the time she was listed in *Who's Who in America*, it was for her own merits. She helped establish and run the Peale Center, cofounded *Guideposts* magazine with a circulation of 2.5 million, and became the first woman president of the National Board of North American Missions of the Reformed Church in America. She was the New York State Mother of the Year in 1963 and the Religious Heritage of America's Churchwoman of the Year in 1969. Ruth became the cornerstone of Norman's entire life, which built her both a satisfying marriage and satisfying career.

Many of the earliest televangelists and megachurch founders had relied on their wives as their administrators, organizers, and business managers. This had been a well-worn role for those whose careers were born in revivalism, which was as much a lifestyle as it was a ministry. It called for a flurry of endless travel, promotion, and negotiation with local partners, the press, and the public that required what early-twentieth-century preacher Billy Sunday used to call "good horse sense."[93] His wife,

Nell, had it in spades, running his evangelistic campaigns with ruthless efficiency. As the itinerant pentecostal revivalists who had ruled the 1940s and 1950s settled into established ministries—many would join the first wave of televangelists—some found that their new headquarters were well suited to the talents of their spouses. Freda Lindsay, wife of Texas revivalist Gordon Lindsay, took on an administrative role at their fledgling Bible school and later took full command after her husband's death. Rex Humbard, another old-time evangelist, ran one of the largest television ministries of the 1970s in partnership with his wife, Maude Aimee, known as "Old Battle-Ax" for her heavy hand.[94] She was a woman so prepared for revivalist ministry that her mother had named her after the great Aimee Semple McPherson. Their Cathedral of Tomorrow in Akron, Ohio, would become the first church to put television cameras in their five-thousand-seat auditorium and broadcast across the nation. Women took charge of any number of organizational forms, from parachurches to television ministries to Bible schools—almost anything dedicated to "outreach," so long as it was not to the local congregation itself. Even Ruth Peale was not the administrator of Marble Collegiate, but rather the head of *Guideposts*.

In practice, however, it was difficult to run a ministry together when the rhythms of childrearing and ministry were so rarely in sync. In the early days of almost every ministry, there was a time of role reversal when the young wife paid the bills and the husband either went to seminary or started his career with paltry wages. "Ours is the masculine role—that of the provider. The husband on the other hand, goes to class. His role is as the one provided for—the feminine role," lamented *The Minister's Wife* handbook.[95] There were plenty of examples of first wives who would be replaced by another, more intellectually or temperamentally suited to the life of ministry. Richard Roberts's first wife, Patti, found that being daughter-in-law to the Oral Roberts family business of ministry was a too heavy a burden to shoulder. Her tell-all memoir *Ashes to Gold* revealed embarrassing secrets about the jet-set lifestyle enjoyed inside what was supposed to be a healing ministry.[96]

Advice manuals warned how "the tragic beginnings of an outgrown wife may be recognized."[97] It was particularly difficult to find balance when pregnancy and young children were not conducive to the harried travel schedule that characterized most ministries. Billy Graham's wife,

Maude Aimee Humbard was one of the first women to convert a worship service into a television show. She and her husband, Rex, transformed their massive church, The Cathedral of Tomorrow, into a studio. Reprinted with permission of the *Akron Beacon Journal* and Ohio.com.

REV. REX AND MAUDE AIMEE HUMBARD
...pastor and his wife

Ruth, simply abdicated her place by his side and moved the kids to the mountains of North Carolina, where she could raise the children of the world's most famous evangelist in peace. Billy would not be present for four of his five children's births. In most of the interviews I conducted for this book, it was the age of the pastoral family's children that determined the wife's role in ministry more than anything. Megachurch wives

Ruth Graham, seen here with her husband, Billy, receiving the Templeton Prize in 1982, avoided the spotlight in favor of a private life with her family. Copyright© 2018 Religion News Service LLC. Republished with permission of Religion News Service LLC, all rights reserved.

usually abdicated responsibilities in the infant years, developed children's programming during the school years, and took on larger roles once the children were in high school or college.

Other women simply shoehorned their children into the rhythm of ministry. Frances and Jimmy Swaggart's schedule was so hectic that even when their young son fell ill, they would feel compelled to press on to the next meeting. "Jimmy and I wouldn't speak," remembered Frances, "we felt so guilty about raising him that way. We never had another child."[98] What Ruth had promised as a path forward together was also a warning for wives who could not keep up. "[If] she fails to satisfy him," she cautioned, "it will be very hard in the long run for him to give her the affection, admiration, and loyalty that she needs and wants from him too."[99] She followed this story with a long account of a woman whose husband found comfort in the arms of another, and the lesson was clear: a woman without a husband stands to lose everything.

THE S WORD

The apportionment of power between husband and wife was not simply a private matter, either. In the 1970s and 1980s, submission had become something akin to dogma as conservative Christianity reacted to economic and social challenges that had pulled many wives out of the house and into paid employment. Over half of the readership of *Today's Christian Woman*, to take a sample of an evangelical readership, had entered the workforce.[100] In this new dispensation, it had become increasingly difficult to assume what women's work was—she might work longer hours or earn more than he did. He may have heeded the call to assume more of the housework. Those church leaders uneasy about such a situation began to emphasize that there was a natural order to things—in families, in churches, and in nations—and that God had ordained the superiority of men and a life of submission for women. Defenses of the Christian patriarchy were everywhere, from bestsellers like Larry Christenson's *The Christian Family*, seminars like Bill Gothard's,[101] parachurch ministries like Focus on the Family, and entire movements, like the Shepherding controversy (see Chapter One).

The ambiguity around what constituted modern women's work created great shows of deference from conservative Christian women who were beginning to be offered other choices. Books like *Being #1 at Being #2* encouraged women to accept their husbands' place as number one ("Do you find yourself in the role of supporting cast rather than the star?").[102] However, submission was as much a performance as it was a teaching, something to be seen and believed. A 1968 how-to manual for Christian wifedom offers clues about how such submission was meant to be performed. Submission, the author contended, was like a divine drama with God playing the part of producer, husband playing the part of Jesus, and wife playing the part of the church. A wife's "script" is submission, but it is not treated as an established fact but an ongoing series of gestures. She puts out the nice china for him with a little comment about how "I've been asking the Lord to help me be a better wife." Her "hearty and joyous" lovemaking demonstrates "the *quality* of her submission" in the most powerful manner.[103] The wife is even given a script and props for his enthronement as she "voluntarily dethrones her will to make him her lord," a coronation ceremony that requires that she cut out a paper crown for him.[104]

The most vocal defenders of submission understood that subservience must be enacted. Dorothy Patterson regularly made mention of the fact that, despite her own onerous teaching and speaking schedule, she was Paige's enthusiastic helpmeet. "I enjoy teaching, I enjoy traveling, I enjoy speaking to women, but I don't enjoy anything as much as being the wife of Paige Patterson," she happily told one reporter, while also mentioning her willingness to iron their pillowcases and sixteen of Paige's shirts *before* turning to her own work. "I had an appointment at 10 a.m. and a speaking engagement that night, so I started at 6:30 a.m.," she said. "I just couldn't go another day without having all those shirts in order."[105] Though both had doctoral degrees in theology, he takes his rightful place and she takes hers. Likewise, the cover of the evangelical women's book *A Woman's Privilege* shows a housewife with a cape draped over her apron using a scepter as a scrub brush. The message is clear: she is still royalty at the kitchen sink.[106] Submission was always much easier to *see* than to defend. A photograph series in *Upon This Rock*, a tribute to Anne and John Gimenez's Virginia megachurch, shows its entirely unremarkable body language. The caption reads: "Pat Robertson interviewing the Gimenezes." The illustration shows a sunny day and Pat Robertson and John Gimenez are turned toward each other, chatting into their respective microphones. A step behind her husband, Anne clasps her empty hands in front of her, smiling though no one is looking at her.[107]

Talking about submission was a complicated act, for it was difficult for men to discuss without reinforcing their reputations as dominating and primary beneficiaries of this teaching. So, for the most part, submission was played out with the lightest touch.[108] The most popular defenders of the doctrine of submission were usually women, who could put audiences' minds at ease that their husbands exercise benevolent leadership rather than a cold dictatorship. "Woman is the feminine of man. We are not only created to be man's helper, but also his complement," wrote cowgirl Dale Evans Rogers of her co-star and husband.[109] In fact, the stronger the public teaching against women in ministry, the stronger the woman on the stage had to be. Take, for instance, the opening of the Art of Homemaking conference, where President Paige Patterson's quip comparing his wife's obedience to a dog. Audiences would have flinched if Dorothy Patterson were not a steel magnolia herself, who, in closing that evening, flatly told her husband to sit down so someone else—someone who knows what they are doing—could make the announcements. Her books were careful studies in how to submit to your husband but, in public, they seemed to relish their parts in this Punch and Judy show. The famous couple was almost expected to fight or tease or put each other in their place in a culture preoccupied so much with talk of power, dominance, and submission.

If a famous pastor was married to a shrinking violet, the pageantry of respect around her only increased. Take, for instance, the bombastic Jerry Falwell, primary architect of the Religious Right, whose rhetorical fireballs were lobbed at almost every target—single parenthood, homosexuality, divorce, abortion, drugs, public schools, secular politicians, and even fellow televangelists. His wife, Macel, was rarely seen on stage, preferring the privacy of family life, and so much had to be said *about* her as a formidable woman. "My wife and I have been married twenty-eight years. . . . And I want to tell you in twenty-eight years we've had some knock-down and drag-outs. [Laughter] I've lost every one of them. [Laughter] I tell you, men, the best thing you can do is quickly raise your hands and unconditionally surrender because you're gonna lose."[110]

It was a hard doctrine disguised as a joke, a playful show of weakness by men and strength by women. The role reversal—his submission, her dominance—was meant to calm fears about men lording their power over their wives. It was a twinkle in the eye that told the audience, *it's okay.* When asked in a rare interview whether she was "the power behind the Jerry Falwell throne," she demurred, "a lot of people say that I do fit that role."[111] In truth, legitimating the inequality between men and women—while allowing both parties to be heroes—was the most difficult aspect of these public partnerships. Ministries longed to strike that note celebrated in the tagline of one California megachurch's women's ministry: "Confident heart. Surrendered soul."[112]

Over time, the doctrine of submission took two different paths as megaministry proliferated and diversified. White evangelicalism, for the most part, softened in its public stance on the subject. David Platt, a young star of the Southern Baptist denomination and president of their mission board, was the embodiment of the undemanding patriarch with his boy-next-door image, calling female audiences "sisters" in a soft, imploring tone and making goofy jokes about how ineptly he courted his wife. Evangelicalism was still a standard image bearer of Christian families but submission was less discussed than occasionally alluded to. When Beth Moore, the most famous Southern Baptist evangelist, spoke to ten thousand women in Norfolk, Virginia, in 2016, she devoted only a minute to the denomination's teachings on the matter by saying: "Some women think they can do *anything* in the church," a sentiment that was initially met by cheers until the audiences collectively realized that she was beginning a critique and fell silent. "I'm not looking to take a *man's* place . . . I'm just looking for *my* place," she continued, and audiences warmed the silence with applause.[113]

"Women don't talk a lot about the s-word anymore," another megachurch wife told me.

"What's the s-word?" I asked.

"It's the word no one says. Submission."[114]

Black churches, on the other hand, largely adhered to a rich pageantry of submission, particularly when it came to the First Lady. The most deference in women's biographies in the four hundred largest churches in the countries fell to African American women of almost all theological persuasions (ranging from historic black denominations to nondenominational and pentecostal churches). A First Lady was not simply a woman but an icon in three respects. She was dutiful wife, first and foremost. Second, she was the church's paragon of womanhood. And, lastly, she was an ambassador to the community. In this last respect, the role departed significantly from white women of similar denominational stripes. White women would not be called on to serve on the board of a city council's literacy initiative, for instance, but, rather, she might write a book called *The Princess Within*. As we shall see throughout the book, black women had to be both a public symbol of the church and the family with a stronger performance of submission.

The presentation of all wives, however, could be so deeply respectful that it masked the intensity of the massive family-run industries that surrounded them and of which they were often a part. Let us restrict ourselves for a moment to the unseen connections and interactions between the subjects of the 1987 inspirational book, *Christian Wives: Women Behind Evangelists Reveal Their Faith in Modern Marriage*, seven intimate interviews with wives of famous evangelists about their highs and lows in marriage and ministry: Tammy Faye (Jim Bakker), Macel (Jerry Falwell), Ruth (Billy Graham), Maude Aimee (Rex Humbard), Evelyn (Oral Roberts), Arvella (Robert Schuller), and Frances (Jimmy Swaggart). These women and their families represented many of the largest ministerial empires in the country, the greater part of twenty-four-hour Christian television programming, enormous crusades, a half-dozen megachurches, a handful of bestselling paperbacks, and the founding of two universities. So, naturally, a host of endorsements, friendships, rivalries, in-fighting, and even scandals lay between them. Macel's husband, Jerry, led a hostile takeover of Tammy Faye and her husband Jim's television network and theme park within the year after Jim's financial and sexual scandals came to light. Evelyn's husband benefited enormously from the blessing of Ruth's husband, Billy Graham, in the dedication of Oral Robert's fledgling university. Maude Aimee *and* her husband Rex served as encouragers and mentors to the Roberts, Swaggarts, and Falwells in their television ministries. Arvella spent much of her interview thanking Mrs. and Mr. Norman Vincent Peale (author of *The Power of Positive Thinking*) for all their support, when Mrs. Peale had, in fact, cornered Robert Schuller in her kitchen and told him to stop using the term "positive thinking" because the term belonged to her husband.[115] And Frances, nicknamed the "Dragon Lady" by her own ministry staff, doggedly pursued evidence of Jim Bakker's sexual indiscretions—even going so far as to send someone to spy on the Bakkers—only to later discover her own husband was sleeping with prostitutes.[116]

Though committed to a private ethic of submitted wifehood, the public lives of megaministry women could lead them in many directions, as champions, partners, allies, accomplices, or even fools for their husband's ambitions. In practice, the doctrine of submission seemed more like theological taffy than quick cement, an unusual kind of freedom that pulled in many directions.

MARTHAS

"We're not co-anything," Donna Miller said emphatically. "As much as I can, I've been my own person."[117]

Donna, the pastor's wife of one of the largest churches in North Carolina, was explaining her job to me. In her thirty-eight years in ministry, she chose not to serve as the women's ministry director and was rarely found on stage. "I'm an extrovert but I'm not the at-the-front kind of person. Come over to my house. I'll meet you for coffee. Bring your kids. That's more me," she said, "but it wasn't that easy at first." When the couple started at Westover Church, they were taking over from a much-loved pastor and his wife who had been incredibly active with the women at the church. Donna initially tried to fill her predecessor's place, until her husband, Don, confronted her about it: "Why would you think you have to do this? Don't! It's making you miserable." She stopped, and, over the years, she tried her hand at other things. She was a "mentor mom" with their church's chapter of Mothers of Preschoolers (MOPS) and taught Sunday school sometimes.

"People on staff tell me you're not the kind of person to chase the spotlight," I told her.

"I was trying to figure out how to explain to you what my life is like, and I thought of this . . ." Donna reached into her purse and pulled out a crumpled Sunday bulletin and smoothed it out on the table between us. The margins were filled with names and she started explaining each one. The sanctuary of their church seated three thousand, but it was clearer and clearer to me that Donna was the kind of person who walked the aisles introducing herself to strangers, taking down prayer requests and putting people in touch with the right staff. And that, at some point during the week, she took some people out for coffee or scribbled a card to them to let them know she was praying for them. She was an old-fashioned pastor's wife in a church so large that no one could possibly expect it.

Though she was not on stage, there was nothing private about Donna's life. "There are so many people involved in our lives," she said candidly. Her husband was the public face of a church with a dozen pastors and a board of elders who, in good Presbyterian fashion, governed the church. That, coupled with the church's large congregation, meant that she could never go unseen to the grocery store in her sweatpants. But she had found freedom in the bustle, because it meant that a strong governing body at the church, ultimately, safeguarded her family.

"I'm thankful to be in a ministry that doesn't depend solely on Don or me. You know, someone once criticized him for not being a strong leader and when he told me I immediately said, 'Thank you! Thank you for *not* being a strong leader!'"

"If he were the typical solo megachurch pastor making all the decisions, it would require a lot from both of you," I ventured.

"It is part of why our church doesn't allow husbands and wives to be on staff together. I think it's been a great thing because it prevents too much power from being concentrated in one place. It's also our rule that only one person from every family can be on staff, so a son can't be on the same board as his father, for instance." Many of the largest non-denominational churches, especially from prosperity gospel traditions, did not have strong governing institutions outside of the pastoral family, and, as Donna observed, this polity asked a great deal from both husband and wife.

"Well, you would have made a great professional megachurch wife and celebrity on the women's ministry circuit. You're well-spoken and annoyingly pretty," I said with a mock sigh. Even on the cusp of retirement, Donna had an unfussy beauty. It would be easy to assume that with her outgoing personality she would be a natural.

"Oops! Right! I have two books. I forgot to tell you that," she laughed. "I did the women's ministry circuit for a while, but I completely stumbled into it. I wanted to teach my girls when they were little about what we believe, so I started writing down topics and I would throw them in a box. An actual box. When we started at Westover, I was asked if I would share on the topic of children and faith so I fished out the box. The women liked what I had to say and asked me to write it up, so I did. Eventually a writer who worked at Moody Publishing got her hands on one from a neighbor and she called me up. I thought it was a prank call from my friend Ronda," she shook her head. Donna published *Growing Little Women* and a sequel for younger children, which received the Silver Medallion in Christian publishing.[118] She said that last bit as an afterthought as we were packing up to leave.

"What happened? You had it made," I wondered aloud.

"Oh, I decided it wasn't for me. I hope you don't think I'm a simple person . . . It's only that I've loved my simple life."

There was an elegance to the division of labor that keeps one person free from church life. He embodied public life and she private life. He

It was almost impossible for Sandra Stanley, wife of the pastor of one of the largest congregations in the country, to lead a private life. Nevertheless, she tried to stay out of the spotlight to focus on special projects and issues around foster care. Image courtesy of Sandra Stanley.

was the church and she was the home. But, as Donna's example showed, there was no pure private life in the world of megaministry. Wives had to make their peace with the expectations that plagued them and the constant blurriness between home and a church too big to ignore. And even when Donna kept her ideas in a box (both metaphorical and wonderfully literal), forces conspired to press her talents into service, moving her toward being the celebrity she studiously avoided.

Her ability to choose a quieter life was reminiscent of the experience of another stay-at-home wife, Sandra Stanley. Her husband, Andy, led North Point Church in Atlanta, Georgia, the second largest church in America, with a sprawling series of campuses. When Sandra and I chatted about how she had determined her role inside the church, she neatly summarized the many types of consent—marital, personal, and ecclesiological—that a woman needed to avoid the professionalization of her wifehood. First, she needed to come to an understanding with her husband. Many celebrity pastors expect their wives to be on stage beside them, so there needed to be an amiable understanding between them that her absence was not a deterrent to their collective happiness. Second, she needed a strong sense of self-awareness to avoid being steered by the church's expectations and the wider Christian culture. Sandra preferred to focus her efforts on issues like fostering—being a foster parent herself—rather than the wider role of women's ministry and co-pastoring. And third, ecclesiologically, church governance could not hang on their marriage, such that she had to be drawn ceaselessly in polity and politics. But there was a fourth factor, less a matter of consent and more one of necessity that I would not have noticed if Sandra had not pointed it out. "When North Point church was founded," she observed, "there were already strong women on staff to run programs like the women's ministry. They didn't need me."[119] In the evangelical megachurch world, the work of children, women, and family was imagined as women's work requiring a woman's touch. But Sandra was right. It didn't have to be hers.

THE WORKING MEGACHURCH WIFE

The professionalization of the megaministry wife exacerbated the age-old problem of compensation. From the highest to the lowest levels, a ministry wife was rarely paid, and it has long been the case that churches and synagogues who hired a man expected to get a two-for-one deal. Whoever she was, she would learn to lead bible studies, host luncheons, sing in the choir, and know every attendee by name. "Whenever we were called to a new church, I would bake forty chocolate pies and have every church member, over group by group," recalled Patsy Willimon, wife of Bishop Will Willimon, one of United Methodism's only household names.[120] In historic black churches, the expectations for first ladies could be even more demanding, becoming more of a formal office than a role. As the female representative of one of the most significant social institutions in black communities, she must be the paragon of virtue and diplomacy. A few churches even insisted on an official job application being submitted by the spouse of every ministerial candidate to ensure that her unremunerated talents matched the expectations of the congregation.[121]

The larger the church, the more difficult it became for a wife to keep her own profession.[122] In the handful of Korean American megachurches, pastors' wives were expected to so tirelessly support their husbands by staying at their sides that it was nearly impossible to do anything else.[123] It was such a common conundrum that, in 1974, the United Presbyterian Church had even called for a "Bill of Rights for Ministers' Spouses," to enshrine the right *not* to be a professional pastor's wife.[124] But, nonetheless, the visibility of this role made it very difficult for any woman—no matter what her theological tradition—to maintain a separate career. In all churches with over ten thousand members, only two women were publicly known to be career women, medical doctors who chose different paths. Before her divorce, Lucretia Noble was the rarely seen pastor's wife of one of the largest Southern Baptist churches in the country, NewSpring, but she gave up her practice because she felt God calling her to support her husband more fully;[125] Stephaine Walker, on the other hand, kept her position at Vanderbilt University Hospital, despite significant pressure to set this aside to more fully embrace her role as First Lady. She was stepping into a weighty role, for her husband was not only a Nashville megachurch pastor but the presiding bishop of the Full Gospel Baptist Church Fellowship, a network of pentecostalized black Baptist churches with a powerful coterie of megachurch pastors at the helm. In their book, *Becoming a Couple of Destiny*, they trade his-and-her accounts of the awkwardness surrounding her separate career, particularly when one of the first questions she fielded from other First Ladies was always: "How long have you been in ministry?"[126] "In a marriage like this," she wrote, "it's critical to have a very strong sense of self" and not lose her individuality "behind his mammoth image."[127] But though she did not join him on staff, she joined him in the spotlight as the woman at his side, appearing in advertisements for the church's upcoming conferences and penning a feature for their church magazine, "From the Desk of the First Lady." The larger the ministerial enterprise became, the more it could demand any talents that a wife could offer.

THE MINISTRY WIDOW

I have heard an old saying repeated by megachurch pastors and staff time and again that goes something like this: Every pastor has two women in his life—the church and his wife. There are only so many hours in a day, it seems to suggest, and a man must always choose between the bottomless needs of his congregation and the bottomless needs of his wife and family. And, of course, it hints at the unquestioned assumption that women are jealous and competitive by nature, resentful of each other and the demands that pull their husbands away. But the adage astutely pointed to the hidden economy within each church embodied by the pastoral family and the price its members are willing to pay for the privilege of ministry. No matter what, someone will be playing the mistress.

Not every wife flourishes in her husband's shadow. Sharon Ries, the pastor's wife in the twelve-thousand-member Calvary Chapel in Costa Mesa, openly wrestled with the loneliness of her marriage. In the 1980s, her husband, Raul, was a rising star who made a splash in a denomination keen to reach California's youth culture. His remarkable conversion became a made-for-television movie, *Fury to Freedom* (1985).[128] It was pitched as an inspiring true story of Raul, the martial arts champion, as the film's tagline read, "Tormented by Anger. Saved by Grace." In the movie and in her autobiography, which she penned soon after the movie came out, Sharon bounces through the narrative as a cheerleader, homecoming queen, and beautiful all-American with a lot of intermittent roller-skating, aerobics, and Kung-Fu demonstrations. Much like *The Karate Kid* released a year earlier to box-office gold, Raul finds an inner peace through his discipline, but, with an evangelical twist, he converts his *sensei* and uses his martial arts as a platform for his testimony. In the movie's climax, the lead character, Raul, rights his life by abandoning his cheating ways (signaled by Sharon now accompanying him to Kung-Fu) and connecting with the spiritual needs of violent and misled young people trapped in the same heavy yoke of anger. But Sharon's account continues long after the movie ends. Despite its pink cover and bubbly font, her book, *My Husband, My Maker*, is a rather dark spiritual autobiography, framed as a love story to a husband who was not faithful and who was never fully hers. Chapters of praise to a faithful God likewise chronicle the slow erosion of her persistent dream to be the center of her husband's world. As she chronicled her life, she was the homecoming queen he left waiting, the young bride he slammed in the head with the telephone receiver, and the faithful wife he cheated on with other women. The climax of the story seems like it should be Raul's sudden about-face when he is converted in a moment of incoherent rage when he planned to murder his wife and children. Raul is saved and, ostensibly, so is their marriage. But the book is setting the stage for Sharon's second test of faith—that of feeling abandoned to his new bride, the church, after Raul devoted his life to the ministry. Sharon began to replace her desire for a loving husband with an even greater romance with the "Master Lover" that is, God:

> My Maker, the Lord of all creation, is my Husband! On my wedding day I had verbally said my vows to God. . . . Now the picture became even more clear. Even though I was married to Raul, the studio and the ministry occupied from five to six days and evenings a week. I was a widow—a widow chosen by God. He would care for me as my Husband. He was calling me to cleave to Him, to depend upon Him.[129]

Christian publishing was filled with stories of unexpected pregnancy, an orphaned child, or a family crisis. *Fury to Freedom* itself had been a monument to evangelicalism's ability to anticipate hot topics and offer a timely response. But when it came to the topic of spousal abuse or "battered wife syndrome," which was gaining attention throughout the 1970s, conservative Christians were silent at first.[130] Many Christian organizations worked with abused women and, like the National Association of Christians in Social Work, argued that there should be no Christian justification for abuse: "Neither party must be allowed to continue to believe that there is a biblical basis for the husband's violent behavior or the wife's endurance of it."[131] Feminists made the critique that evangelicalism's cherished doctrine of submission legitimized subordination and therefore sanctioned abuse.[132] This attack put conservative Christians on the defensive. Women's retreats in the 1970s and 1980s regularly heard confessions of abuse, but there was little consensus on the solution. Modern readers might cringe at Sharon, a victim of spousal abuse, joking that "I had been taking Kung-Fu lessons so I could spend a little extra time with Raul. I took a beating three nights a week to be with this guy!"[133] By the late 1980s, evangelical presses and others would have more to say; Christian men's movements like Promise Keepers would frame a benevolent patriarchy around greater limits on men, and churches issued pastoral care policies on the subject of violent abuse.[134]

But it was fair for a wife to wonder, in a culture of submission, to what extent should ministry hurt? One megachurch wife, who asked to remain anonymous, spoke of the degradation of being married to a man who did not see her as a separate person but as an extension of his own needs.[135] For many years, she had been the perfect ministry wife, deeply involved in the church and raising their children. "The image we presented that we were this amazing spiritual family full of God," she said, though her husband never prayed, read scripture, or spoke of faith in the home. She had grown up in the context of molestation, abandonment, and abuse, and had married a minister she hoped would be a respite from the pain of her past. She had worked hard to become an accomplished career professional but noticed how easily she had slipped into the invisibility of her role as wife of her charismatic husband.

Two decades into her married adult life, she had begun to feel herself start to come alive, to laugh more easily, inhabit her own body, and feel freer. But as she was finding her voice, she explained, he was losing his. Her newfound confidence had come at a time of increasing insecurity for her husband, who was faltering in his larger-than-life ministerial role, and his behavior toward her turned darker and darker. He belittled her accomplishments and discouraged her from returning to work. He began to grow increasingly predatory about his sexual desires, ignoring her pleas not to perform certain acts and pretending, afterward, that she was not devastated and shaking. He stopped trying to get consent "and sex is something he did to me," she said quietly. When she found the strength to leave him, she looked back on the making of the man, minister, and the father of her children who, during the course of their marriage, could somehow both lead a massive congregation in worship and rationalize raping his wife. "I've asked myself a million times whether the job ruined him or revealed who he was, and the answer I always arrive at is that it was probably a little bit of both."

The term "ministry widow" was used to describe women who lived lonely lives married to a pastor. And Sharon's story seems to suggest that, other than turning to God, there was no remedy for it: "[Raul's] absence become another nail, one that gnawed at me every day. Its wound continues to feed my branches."[136] Eventually she succumbed to having a greater role in the church and described her decision to participate in his ministry in terms one might use for preparing to be a missionary. She relinquished her own desires and refocused on "an eternity shared with my Maker, the Lover of my soul."[137] The church had become Raul's wife and her husband.

In megaministry, where so much depended on the perfection of pastoral families to anchor multi-million dollar institutions, it could be a pressure cooker. In 2014, megachurch pastor Isaac Hunter was found dead from an apparent suicide. He had resigned after admitting to an affair with a staff member and his wife had filed a domestic-violence petition against him.[138] The moral failings of leading men created an enormous burden for families to shoulder. This was particularly true when it came to the problem of succession. While pastors usually rose to fame because they were charismatic, tireless, and had a strong sense of being chosen for this work, families often struggled to feel quite so *called*. In the last few decades, aging prosperity pastors were the most likely to attempt to secure their megachurches as personal legacies by promoting their sons (and rarely daughters) to leadership. Fred Price chose Fred Price Jr.; Robert Schuller picked Robert Schuller Jr. then Sheila Schuller; Marilyn Hickey tapped Sarah Hickey, and so on. Of course, the most famous example was Joel Osteen, whose dimpled smile and cheerful sermons multiplied his father's congregation almost six times over to make Lakewood Church into America's largest church. But not everyone had a Joel Osteen in the wings, and not every husband or wife liked being the ministerial plus one. When the church was a family business, a failing family was a failing business. Even so, pastors accused of moral failing rarely changed course. Even after televangelist Zachary Tims was divorced by his co-pastor and wife, Riva, for a year-long affair with an exotic dancer, his billboards still featured his image with the byline: "A Family Church Meeting Family Needs."[139]

Ruth Peale had once warned women that a wife's ability to pattern herself on her husband could be a form of power, and she was not wrong. But it was a fickle kind of authority, dependent on her ability to shoulder every burden, eliminate any obstacle, and meet any need. "Sometimes I think the best epitaph a wife could hope for would be just six words: 'She was a wonderful shock absorber,'" she said in sum.[140] It was a tremendous responsibility for any woman, and it could work as long as she could maintain her image as the keeper of her man and their home, the inviolable sanctuary.

The icons of domesticity held strong long after much of the industry around women's ministry dwindled. In the new millennium, magazines like *Today's Christian Woman* started to feel dated and the large-group congregational model of women's ministry faltered. Where there had once been Ladies' Teas with themed tables and road-trips to see itinerant ministries like Women of Faith, Women of Joy, or Extraordinary Women, now there were new efforts to attract a digital and less-churched generation. Bible studies dropped their focus on homework and moved to quick online devotionals that catered to the frenetic pace of modern motherhood. In the 2000s, a new cast of celebrity "mommy bloggers" wrote about finding God in laundry, friendship, and ordinary suburbia. Readers wanted to hear about creatives who feathered their nests as the nostalgic turn in American culture breathed new life into homemaking. The hard antifeminism of the 1970s was out of date, but the old-fashioned skills of gardening, sewing, and crafting were part of a harkening back to simpler times. Christian lifestyle magazines like *Life: Beautiful* popped up, papered in images of red strawberries, heavy blooms, and frosted cupcakes. With peppy articles and lush photos, magazines—and the host of webzines like them—were a variation on an old theme.[141] Home was a sacred retreat from a busy world, a place of comfort and safety, birthday parties, and meaning-making. The strongest argument from the home and its homemaker turned from the performative to the aesthetic.

Women launching new ministries understood that their work was equal part word and image, with a side of Christian Etsy culture (which we will turn to again in Chapter Five). Its newest stars were Home and Garden Television Network reality show rehabbers like Joanna Gaines and Jen Hatmaker (women literally building Christian homes), or Shauna Niequist, daughter of Bill Hybels, whose latest bestseller asked women to be *Present Over Perfect*, eschewing the stress of work for more time at home. Mormon mommy bloggers' gorgeous photos of their children in matching chambray and bowties looked roughly the same as evangelical and pentecostal authors' "About Me" section. The family was her primary advertisement, her expertise, and, often, the reason for her start in ministry, all disguised in three simple words: "Wife and Mom."

Chapter Three

THE TALENT

As each has received a gift, use it to serve one another . . .
—1 Peter 4:10[1]

Tammy Faye Bakker looked like a scoop of pink sherbet in her matching rose dress and heels, parading down a busy street bopping her blonde
head to the beat of her television show's theme song.[2] It was *The Tammy
Faye Show*, her own feature on the Praise the Lord Network (PTL) that
she founded with her husband, Jim, and whose twenty-four-hour programming saw her living out much of her married life on camera.
Though she was an Assemblies of God pentecostal, born and bred, there
was little evidence that the cast, crew, or audience wanted to see her
take the microphone and preach. Instead, viewers seemed to like her
for all the unusual behaviors that songwriter Gary Paxton of "Monster
Mash" fame had managed to squeeze into her opening song. The cameras rolled as Tammy slapped the desk in a loud guffaw or dabbed a
Kleenex to her eye, keeping her trademark mascara from smudging, as
the lyrics rhymed about how she was like a kid but still a real woman.
She was Tammy, a "double whammy," sharing her Christian love.[3]

By the time Tammy had hit the stage for her live program, audiences
had been visually reminded of all the parts that she played. She was the
goofy woman-child who spoke with a squeaky voice through her famous puppets; she was the musician at the piano hammering out from
memory some old hymns for the crowd; she was the warm hug that de-
lighted elderly audiences of Heritage Park USA, Jim and Tammy's
South Carolina Christian theme park and television studio; and she was
the wife at Jim's side, dressed in anything from a gingham babydoll dress
to a sultry gown. From her contagious smile to her heavy makeup to her
try-anything antics, she was a television natural. She was utterly trans-
parent, unpretentious, and chipper, but best of all she was a born

performer. Precisely what she did was hard to say. She bounced between television programs on the network and she struggled to find her place.[4] But she was, without a doubt, the main draw. As the wife of one PTL singer explained, "Tammy's the one ingredient they have to have. She's the person who captivates and intrigues people. She's the laughter, the 'movie star,' she's the exciting somebody that they all want to see."[5]

In song, dance, and entertainment, women like Tammy Faye have been in the big business of ornamenting the stage. In the early years of megaministry, many women earned their fame as backup musicians for their husbands and, as their ministries settled into institutions, the producers and orchestrators of such talent. As televangelism, arena conferences, and megachurches came into their own, women became an indelible part of Christian worship and entertainment as performers and producers of all kinds. Music and entertainment has long been the significant exemption from the mores of "promiscuous assemblies," allowing women to hold forth before mixed gender audiences because in song or storytelling or dance they were not *technically* teaching. The power that became theirs was episodic by nature, a bit of magic stirred up from their words or songs or bodies on a borrowed stage. But magic it was.

FROM BACKUP TO MAINSTAGE

Much of the talent of early megaministry was nurtured on the sawdust trail, the tent revivals of the postwar era that pulled tens of thousands of Americans into canvas cathedrals to hear a message about the power of God. Men like Oral Roberts, T. L. Osborn, A. A. Allen, and Gordon Lindsay made headlines as evangelists of a great revival of prophecy, healing, and, by the late 1950s, prosperity that they believed would change the world and usher in the End of Days. But it was a grueling existence for families who labored under a punishing campaign schedule and a ruthless itinerancy. Wives and children had to do their part, living on a shoestring budget and moving town to town, setting up yet another tent with another piano and rows of chairs to fill with eager believers. When these upstart revivalists fell in love, they seemed to realize that their marriages had certain musical prerequisites. Evelyn

Roberts, wife of Oral Roberts, observed of their courtship: "Old practical Oral. He was not going to marry someone who could not play the
piano."[6] It was a common tale. Jerry Falwell fell in love with his wife,
Macel, at the piano. Jimmy Swaggart fell head-over-heels when he saw
Frances in the choir. Paul and Jan Crouch, someday founders of the largest Christian television network in the world, spent their first date singing for a pentecostal crowd.[7] It was a love story that not only made
church audiences swoon but made good business sense. Many of the stars
of the 1960s and 1970s—the formative years of televangelism and the
Christian entertainment industry—used their wives as backup musicians
and producers of the backdrop to their message.

It was 1948 when the young Robert Schuller, the successor to Norman Vincent Peale and his power of positive thinking, walked into a
small Iowa church as the visiting minister and found a young woman
named Arvella at the church organ. After their first date, the story goes,
he told his best friend he had found the girl he was going to marry. Early
in their marriage, he bought her a two-manual organ with his meager
salary, but the investment in her talent would always pay off. When the
young couple was invited by the Reformed Church in America denomination to establish a "mission church" in Garden Grove, California, they
could not find a suitable space, so Robert settled for a drive-in movie
theatre. He preached every sermon perched on top of the snack bar while
Arvella accompanied him on the organ, which they towed into place
with their small trailer.[8] Music would remain an integral part of the
Schuller ministry's success, and its penchant for the spectacular. Their
much-hyped Crystal Cathedral was a glittering monument and the largest glass building in the world, housing one of the largest pipe organs.
Their Sunday services were repackaged as *The Hour of Power* telecast for
national broadcast, which evolved into one of the most watched programs in the country with five million viewers in 1987 and Arvella as
the executive producer.[9]

"I was always in the music area of the church," remembered Arvella.
"I knew worship; I didn't know television. My husband just said to me,
'Honey, I need you because I'm still a pastor . . . and I have my message
each week. Would you take over the rest of the program? You know wor-
ship, you know me, and you know our people and our audience.'"[10]
Arvella soon oversaw a twenty-five-member production staff, selecting

Arvella Schuller was the behind-the-scenes manager of both her husband, Robert, and the rise of their positive-thinking empire. Copyright © 1988. *Los Angeles Times.* Used with permission.

everything from the scripture, solos and choir pieces, staging, camera positions, and weekly full rehearsal.[11] It was said that Arvella, in keeping with her husband's theology of positive thinking, would strike out any negative words that cropped up in the choir's music, words like "saved a *wretch* like me" in the classic hymn "Amazing Grace."[12] She was a stickler for the details and relished her role as the silent orchestrator of the television program that made her husband a star and her church into an icon of Christian entertainment. She even took to rewriting his books, which went on to hit the bestseller lists.[13] "My career is my husband," Arvella Schuller told the *LA Times* in no uncertain terms.[14]

While Arvella's talents took her offstage—her staff jokingly called her position "The Man Upstairs" for her omnipresent perch in the cathedral broadcast center—other women found ways to be both star and producer. Maude Aimee was married to Rex Humbard, one of the world's first televangelists, but she was also one of the stars of his pioneering television program, which by the mid-1970s boasted twenty-five million viewers. She had been a gospel singer since she was a child, and the two had spent their early married years on the road as revivalists and gospel performers able to fill the largest crusade tents. When they settled down in Akron, Ohio, they founded one of the country's first megachurches, the Cathedral of Tomorrow.[15] By 1970, their broadcast of the same name appeared on more television stations than any other American program, making such a name for themselves in gospel music that even Elvis Presley considered himself a fan (Rex would preside over the King of Rock and Roll's 1977 funeral). The multimillion-dollar church was the first designed to double as a television studio with a 5,400-seat auditorium with stage lighting, sound, and video, that broadcast to more than 650 television station worldwide.[16] Their growing family would go on to tour as the Humbard Family Singers and produced numerous records like "Rex Humbard Family Singers Sing The Family of God," with album jacket covers posing the lot of them along a grand staircase, oldest to youngest, like the Von Trapp family. The family was in the business of keeping people entertained and running the ministry, and by the late 1980s almost all their grown children and their spouses had taken a job at Rex Humbard Ministries, which Maude Aimee ran like a Texan Margaret Thatcher. "She's breathed the fear of God in every employee," said her daughter Elizabeth.[17] Or as Maude Aimee said of her approach, "If you're doing anything for the Lord, if you're not going to do it right, then don't make a mess. . . . My mother and brother used to say, 'It's a good thing you married her, Rex, because only you and God could live with her.'"[18] All audiences knew was the woman on stage and they loved her.

With twenty-five million viewers by the mid-1980s, televangelism was a career-changing platform for many women to showcase their talents. Three major networks—the Bakkers' Praise the Lord (PTL), Jan and Paul Crouch's Trinity Broadcasting Network (TBN), and Pat Robertson's Christian Broadcasting Network (CBN)—were pumping out religious programming twenty-four hours a day, seven days a week by the early 1980s. It was a borrowed stage where thousands of eager performers sang, danced, and shared testimonies, usually with a book or an album tucked under their arm to sell. The details varied according to the host and the show, but the television stage was *the* most coveted place to be seen in the Christian industry and, for women, one of the few places to perform and be interviewed without the appearance of impropriety.

Most Christian television kept the spotlight on the men who founded the network, and their flagship programs mimicked the talk shows of

Jan Crouch, co-founder of one of the largest Christian television networks in the world, was known for her sweet, high voice and wildly ornate hairdos. Copyright © 1988. *Los Angeles Times* and Mark Boster. Used with permission.

secular television. CBN had *The 700 Club,* PTL had *The PTL* Club, and TBN had *Praise the Lord,* each with an anchor's desk at which would sit the male founder doing his best to look like Johnny Carson. But though it was a clear imitation of mainstream television right down to the unseen announcer crowing "Heeeeeeeere's Jim Bakker," the Christian talk show was a powerful gatekeeper and career-maker. The desk was his and the guest-couch his also to share.

Few women could single-handedly command a large religious television audience. One who shone was Kathryn Kuhlman, dubbed "the world's most famous woman evangelist" and "The Miracle Lady." Kuhlman had survived an ill-advised marriage and scandalous divorce to create a powerful preaching ministry that eventually took to the airwaves. Her program, *I Believe in Miracles,* which attracted a viewership in the millions, featured this single woman in an elaborate gown welcoming guests who had experienced a supernatural healing. Kuhlman required no male counterpart to share the spotlight; she dominated the screen as much as she towered over the running of her evangelistic foundation.[19]

Perhaps the single greatest success in claiming a television network as an entirely feminine enterprise came in the form of a brass-tacks

Ohioan named Rita Rizzo, better known to audiences as Mother Angelica. She was a study in contrasts, a cloistered Catholic nun who, by 1990, could be seen twenty-four hours a day on her own television network. Broadcasting from Our Lady of the Angels, a Franciscan monastery in the heart of the deep south, she managed a staff of ninety-five made up mostly of nuns and volunteers she had won over with her unvarnished truth-telling and an off-beat sense of humor.[20] She had been born into poverty, a sickly girl from a turbulent home, and though a series of visions of Jesus and miraculous healings confirmed her faith as a young woman, her heath was fragile all her life.[21] Nevertheless, she easily won over the Bakkers, Pat Robertson, and other proponents of faith healing who owned the other major Christian television networks. She was an unusual sight on pentecostal television in her black and white habit but a perfect guest with her breezy openness to the charismatic movement and playful lack of pretension. On one occasion as a guest on *PTL*, she exclaimed to Jim Bakker, "I am convinced God is looking for dodoes. He found one: me! God uses dodoes: people who are willing to look ridiculous so God can do the miraculous."[22] Bakker even sent his own set designers to build Mother Angelica her first studio, a reproduction of a living room with pictures of Jesus and the Pope hanging in the background and walls as powder blue as Bakker's trademark suits.

The American public tuned in to see her as the nun-next-door, who managed to come across as utterly unassuming and yet authoritative in her habit with an open Bible, gazing at the camera from a living room chair. She became a mainstay on national Christian talk shows and the face of her empire, a star whose celebrity even rubbed off on the nuns under her care, who cut their own musical album in Nashville. But her true strength came from her ability to keep her hands on the reins, a feat Mother Angelica accomplished through a web of extra-ecclesial relationships—those she forged outside of the hierarchy (and budgets) of the Roman Catholic church. Her first forays into public ministry had come from trying to keep her monastery afloat, and—with the help of a secondhand tape recorder, a dubbing machine, and one nun's willingness to forgo her sewing room—the sisters soon had a solvent business selling Mother Angelica's mini-books and cassette tapes. By the mid-1970s, the nuns had $100,000 worth of machinery printing thousands of books a day and distributing them through a network of volunteer

In a decade of televangelist excess, Mother Angelica was beloved as a straight-talker and an altruist. Reprinted with permission from Charisma Media, www .charismamedia.com.

"missionaries" spread out across the country.[23] The hand-drawn sign above the old sewing room door read: "THE MASTER'S PRINT SHOP. WE DON'T KNOW WHAT WE'RE DOING, BUT WE'RE GETTING GOOD AT IT."[24] It was a self-sufficiency that she had learned early on when, with costs running high and a budding national ministry, she wrote to every American bishop to offer them a free copy of her program for rebroadcasting and not one replied.[25] She founded the Eternal Word Television Network (EWTN) in 1981, swimming in debt and immediately imperiled by a travel ban issued by the Vatican overseers of monastic life, who ruled that Mother Angelica must abandon her long-standing practice of giving talks outside the cloister—talks that largely paid for the salaries of her network employees. Between debt collectors on one hand and the Roman Catholic authorities on the other, her network depended on her perpetual ingenuity in finding ways to stay commercially essential *and* ecclesially innocuous. EWTN was advertised as "a supplement to, not a substitute for, the Church,"[26] but she was fast becoming the most famous Catholic in America, a smiling face in a crisp white wimple, and a competitor to the official Catholic foray into television, the Catholic Telecommunications Network of America (CTNA). The nun with only a high school education was soon plunged into a long conflict with American bishops over Catholic cable and satellite programming, fending off unreasonable attempts to kick her out of broadcasting and swatting down the rather more reasonable accusation that EWTN was independent and lacking theological oversight. She lived donation to donation, filming her daily programs with the moral seriousness of an evangelist and the charm of a saleswoman who needed to pay the bills. She began every program with an encouragement to learn to be great saints and finished telethons with pitches like: "All right, cough it up, kids."[27]

Tales of Mother Angelica filming every show without a script, schedule, or plan—with nothing but a quick prayer beforehand—was the stuff of television legend, but it was also indicative of the kind of improvisation needed to turn raw talent into stardom. Running a network required a punishing filming schedule that demanded much from its leads, but it also guaranteed tremendous exposure for those who craved the spotlight. When Jan Crouch first started in broadcasting, she played every part from secretary, makeup artist, set decorator, and on-screen phone operator before cementing her fame as the cotton-candy-haired fixture at Paul's side, the first person to shout "Amen" or shed a confirming tear at his words.[28] Over the years, audiences came to expect her in every frame, unmissable with her mounds of pink-frosted blonde hair, easily double the height of her pretty face, and a vision in frilly and sparkly gowns. Likewise, Tammy Faye Bakker loved the attention that the cameras brought and produced numerous musical albums for her fans, including the 1987 record *We're Blest*. She was a natural in front of their massive studio audience, playful and entirely unfiltered, which always endeared her to both staff and viewers who felt that they knew her personally. Throughout the Bakker's marriage, they would film one show after another in a single day, changing costumes backstage and reemerging on a round robin of sets. Their telethons were grueling marathons that demanded wide-eyed attention from the crew to keep a perpetual live feed as well as a variety of performances, which typically included Tammy Faye belting out a signature number and joking with the crowd while Jim did the bulk of the fundraising and guest interviews.

Since each network could usually only produce a few hours of programming a day, the paucity of original footage created a tremendous market for other women with previously little stage presence. Before the price of airtime became too expensive by the late 1980s, the glut of Christian television flooding the airwaves made it seem like anyone with a little camera equipment could find themselves on the silver screen. *Jack Van Impe Presents!*, the television outreach ministry of apocalypticist Jack Van Impe and his chipper wife, Rexella, catapulted to success in the 1980s as one of these low-budget staples of late-night television. The show featured Jack "The Walking Bible" Van Impe interpreting the end-times' meaning of the daily headlines, while his fascinated wife and co-host, Rexella, peppered him with questions or sang a song or two. Women were welcome as long as they abided by the general rules of sports news casting: a main commentator describes the action and the personality at his side adds a splash of color.

Though televangelism was largely shaped in the image of the man behind the desk, it also recast the space as entertainment—the talk show, the stage—rather than church.[29] Instead of filled pews there were "studio audiences." Instead of worship there were "performances by a special guest." It was common for mostly men to preach on these programs, but

Dr. and Mrs. Jack Van Impe

"JACK VAN IMPE PRESENTS!"

The Fastest Half-Hour in Television

A WEEKLY NEWS ANALYSIS PROGRAM
700 Stations Including:

C A B L E			
Inspirational Network	**Trinity Broadcasting Network**	**Vision TV in Canada**	**Black Entertainment Television**
Saturday 10:00 p.m. EST	Wednesday 9:30 p.m. EST	Sunday 3:00 p.m. EST	Friday 7:30 a.m. EST
Monday 11:00 p.m. EST	Monday 1:00 a.m. EST	Saturday 7:30 p.m. EST	**WGN Super Station**
Tuesday 12 midnight EST	**Family Net**	Monday 1:30 a.m. EST	Friday 7:00 a.m. EST
	Thursday 6:30 p.m. EST		

JACK VAN IMPE MINISTRIES • BOX 7004 • TROY, MI 48007 • (313) 852-2244

Rexella Van Impe co-hosted a weekly news analysis program with her husband that was so wide-ranging that people could tune in to debates on everything from apocalyptic prophecies to whether cats have souls. Reprinted with permission from Charisma Media, www.charismamedia.com.

the real draw was the constant guests. These were regular opportunities for women to sing, dance, say their piece, or even flirt a little, behaving more like they were on the set of *The Lawrence Welk Show* than a church mainstage. Shows like *The PTL Club* became a regular stop for female talent, all-girl groups and family bands, churchy solos and a fat gospel ballad. It was a place for stars like southern gospel royalty Vestal Goodman, whose glittering gowns almost brought disco glamour to the South, and eleven-time Grammy winner Shirley Caesar, who would later found a megachurch of her own, to sing and bask in some well-earned applause. This variety show atmosphere was a perfect stage for gospel music and its lauded muses. For the most part, the soundtrack of 1980s televangelism was the white gospel music stylings of musicians like the Happy Goodmans, the Singing Rambos, and the Gaithers, family bands with formidable female voices who shared a love for hill-country harmonies and a brand associated with old-time music. Unless they were directly tied to television ministry, white gospel artists did not gain the kind of superstardom that later white female artists would achieve with the rise of contemporary Christian music. In the early years, it was black artists, whose songs only occasionally appeared on (mostly white) Christian television, who had the commercial industry and deep-bench of talent to make gospel music a coveted platform for women.

GOSPEL STARS

Though African American artists often sang their hearts out on these televised platforms, the industry that sustained gospel-singing women predated and outlasted the golden age of televangelism. In the early twentieth century, African American female singers had hit the "gospel highway," touring from churches to school auditoriums to small-town halls to denominational conventions, sleeping in cars, lunching on crackers and bologna ("gospel chicken"), and risking the violence and humiliations of travel in Jim Crow America. Their music had moved out of the church and into a performance mode, spread by radio, recordings, and gospel concerts. It was never an easy profession for women: touring females were often accused of a lewd lifestyle owing to the loose reputation of the male quartets, and many churchgoers would advise women to stay home and mind their families.[30] Nevertheless, a number of remarkable performers like Sister Rosetta Tharpe and Mahalia Jackson carved out careers as soloists, created the virtuoso approach that still marks the music, and showed that women gospel singers could be successful in the rapidly growing national industry of black music. By the 1950s and 1960s black gospel was enjoying a "golden age" with a newly professional sound, national radio play, and an emerging industry of musicians, marketers, distributors, retail outlets, and charting metrics to test the outcome. There was money to be made in old time religion. RCA Records signed the young Aretha Franklin, whose transition into "soul" music demonstrated the seemingly endless marketability of gospel into subgenres that were market gold.[31]

The golden age of black gospel music also fashioned a new idol, making the gospel singer one of the most powerful symbols of feminine spirituality inside and outside the black church. The 1972 cover of *Jet* shows this saintly embodiment well: Mahalia Jackson stands in a red choir robe, her eyes cast up and her hands lightly folded in prayer as she seems to sing to heaven alone.[32] Jackson was charismatic, improvisational, and soulful; her sound had a theatricality and physicality to it, sliding high and reaching deep. She conquered New York's Carnegie Hall, sang at Reverend Martin Luther King Jr.'s funeral, and recorded the first gospel album in history to sell a million copies.[33] The National Baptist Convention even crowned her their first official soloist. The Queen of Gospel Music brought international fame and an almost religious devotion to the figure of the woman who seemed to be able to call down the Holy Ghost with the sheer power of her voice.

By the early 1970s, a black female artist could hope to win not just a Grammy Award, but accolades from newly formed associations: a Dove Award by the Gospel Music Association or black gospel's prestigious Stellar Award (later honors included the Soul Train Music Awards and the BET Awards). By the early 1980s at-home viewers could even watch their favorite stars take home their awards on the Christian Broadcasting Network. The black gospel sound had been broken open into numerous genres—R&B, jazz, adult contemporary, hip hop—and a vast range of media was devoted to helping audiences get to know the real-life women behind the vocals.[34] Unlike performers in predominantly white branches of the Christian music industry,[35] African American artists did

Aretha Franklin, the "Queen of Soul," was reputed to be one of the greatest singers of all time and an example of the commercial viability of sacred music. Publicity photo of Aretha Franklin from *Billboard*, February 17, 1968.

not live inside the sheltered walls of religious subcultures haunted by the specter of secularity. Rather, they were the famous faces of an already distinct minority culture with a well-established parallel entertainment industry that folded gospel artists into coverage of African American politics, showbiz, business, and even church. Their wide-ranging significance had no white analogue. Mainstream audiences might briefly remember recording legend CeCe Winans sitting on Oprah's couch and singing at Whitney Houston's funeral, but black media made her so unforgettable that, no matter how long it had been since she produced an album, *Essence* magazine would wish her happy birthday.[36]

The role of the female gospel artist had tremendous commercial energy, but there was always the understanding that her voice was not simply a commodity but a spiritual gift. Gospel pioneer Marion Williams,

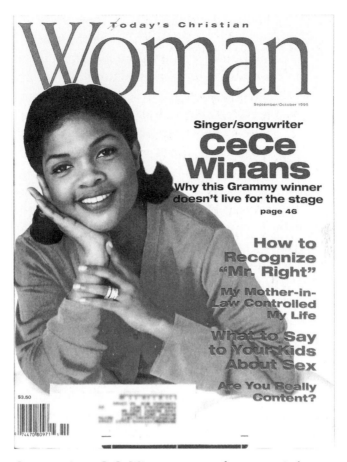

Grammy winner CeCe Winans was part of a great musical
dynasty. In the 1980s, she and her brother BeBe were regulars on
Jim and Tammy Faye Bakker's programs. Reprinted with
permission from *Christianity Today*, www.christianitytoday.com.

whose octave-jumping high notes were the envy of Little Richard himself, told the *New York Times*, "When I'm singing, I get inspired by God.
I call it 'the anointing.' It's an extra-special thing. When the inspiration
of God is missing, I just rely on talent."[37] It was a divine touch that people
came to expect from black gospel women in particular, though men like
Kirk Franklin continued to set the standard for blockbuster success in
the industry. Common beliefs about the raw power that singers were
thought to possess dated back to Holy Ghost religion and its emphasis
on cultivating God's presence through worship. Gospel lyrics were filled

with references to holiness and the pentecostal practices of dancing, shouting, speaking in tongues, or being "slain in the Spirit."[38] Indeed, much of the gospel performance itself—from foot stomping to kicking off high heels to run the aisle—followed the liturgical rhythms of pentecostalism. The singer was not simply a performer, then, but a vehicle for the Spirit who breathed a word from God in every note. It was a weighty task, for she was responsible for creating the spiritual atmosphere for a congregational encounter with God. The music held the key to any number of different kinds of encounters, from a soul-stirring piece that prepared the heart for confession to a "shout" song's driving tempo that pushed congregants into a holy dance. As gospel singer Lena Mae Perry explained: "When you sing a song slow, people sit and listen. Then the thoughts are rolling over and over in their mind. And things will pop up in their mind that they have experienced. . . . When you sing that song fast—now this is what I've experienced—all right, you got a beat, and all you try and do is keep up with the beat."[39] Fast or slow, hushed or full-throated, singers were expected to orchestrate the divine.

Central to gospel's self-definition was that it was first and foremost religious music, and so every artist began their promotional biography with an account of how their talent was not simply in the service of art, but was a consecrated act. The most common story told about CeCe Winans's upbringing in the famous Winans family, a Detroit gospel dynasty, was that, despite living in the heart of Motown, the kids listened to gospel alone. It was that musical diet that nourished the ten children's artistry and helped them grow into a Grammy-winning empire.[40] These mythic stories were echoed by other gospel singers like Grammy-winning Tramaine Hawkins, who recalled her mother went into labor with her while leading the church choir and shared how her first solo at the age of four was in her grandfather Bishop E. E. Cleveland's historic church.

Female artists, however, would continue to bear the burden of debates inside the industry over what constituted the bounds of religious music. Tramaine Hawkins, or Lady Tramaine, as she came to be known, was emblematic of the punishing highs and lows of failing to be seen as sufficiently religious. She was the famous soprano who hit the notoriously difficult high notes of the 1969 breakout hit "Oh Happy Day" but whose dancy *Billboard* hits of the 1980s earned her sharp criticism.[41] She would win back her critics with subsequent albums, but her rollercoaster of

Tramaine Hawkins is a Grammy winner and gospel singer whose musical roots are deep in the church. Reprinted with permission from *Christianity Today*, www .christianitytoday.com.

successes and failures made clear that talent alone could not guarantee the stability of a career.

The most durable careers were built on multiple platforms. Take, for instance, the fame of Mary Mary, the modern gospel duo of sisters Erica and Tina Campbell, who earned significant standing in the industry when their debut album, *Thankful*, went platinum. Before long they had won four Grammys, seen their subsequent albums hit the top spot on Billboard's Top Gospel Album chart, and filmed multiple seasons of their reality television show following their lives behind the scenes and on the stage. But their careers constantly reflected a raging debate over the purity of gospel music and the female bodies who performed it. The most persistent accusation was that their appeal was too worldly, a perennial charge that continued well into the twenty-first century. In 2008, their hip hop infused single "God in Me" featured cameos by a roster of stars.[42] Erica Campbell's later solo song "I Luh God" (a deliberate mispronunciation of "I Love God") caused waves by clearly mimicking the gritty sounds of "trap music" that memorialized the "trap" of drugs and poverty. National black media debated the question that *Vibe* magazine put starkly: Has "trap gospel" finally "taken gospel too far"?[43] Their sexual appeal was as readily debated. Much ink was spilled over the photo of herself in a tight white dress Erica posted on Facebook to announce her Grammy nomination for "A Little More Jesus,"[44] and the 2014 Stellar Awards audiences roared when Erica was teased about it onstage. But the key to their longevity lay in their ability to promote themselves across multiple streams of media. In addition to music and television, Erica Campbell took one of the most coveted syndicated spots with RadioOne as the host of her own program, *Get Up! Mornings with Erica Campbell*, making her one of the few black women on gospel radio.[45] Gossip sites buzzed about how the younger star had taken the show from the fifty-three-year-old Yolanda Adams, one of the most celebrated gospel artists of the 2000s,[46] but all that was certain was that celebrity was notoriously difficult to cement.

For female black gospel artists, expectations from the industry and the church were often at odds. The career of Dorinda Clark put these competing roles in stark relief. The Clark Sisters were the bestselling female gospel group in history and a point of special genealogical pride. The five women are the daughters of Mattie Moss-Clark, one of the

Erica and Tina Campbell are the sisters behind gospel duo Mary
Mary. Their Grammy-winning music is evidence of the
continued commercial viability of gospel music. Reprinted with
permission from *Christianity Today*, www.christianitytoday.com.

most famous choir directors in the 1960s heyday of mass choirs and a
jewel in the crown of the entire Church of God in Christ.[47] By the mid-
1990s, the Clark Sisters launched their own solo careers and won their
own individual awards with a family name so ubiquitously known that
they were regular guests on Christian talk shows and even subject to
their own unauthorized documentaries.[48] But this fame was anchored
in the church, where Dorinda was also a licensed Church of God in
Christ evangelist and a constant presence in black megachurches.[49]

When the audiences of the much-hyped reality show *The Preachers of Detroit* saw her introduced as one of its stars, her story began:

> I am evangelist Dorinda Clark-Cole. I am a minister at the Greater Emmanuel Institutional Church of God in Christ. I am called an evangelist because our church believes that it's not appropriate for a woman to be a bishop because of what the scripture says. I believe a woman has her place in the church, and I think a woman should be submissive. To me, men are better leaders.[50]

The industry built her into the kind of stand-alone star who would name a show after herself—TCT's *The Dorinda Show* aired throughout the Midwest—but her religious vocation repeatedly emphasized that somewhere in her hidden personal life was a man to whom she was subject.

The most comfortable arrangements put women's talents to use under close supervision, but it was a tricky endeavor. Shirley Caesar was one of the most famous women in gospel's history, an eleven-time Grammy winner with her own Hollywood star who had sung for every American president since Jimmy Carter. Her most beloved audience, however, was the congregation of the fifteen-hundred-member Mount Calvary Word of Faith Church in Raleigh, North Carolina, where she served as its singing pastor.[51] Her husband, Harold, before his passing, was the presiding bishop of the small Mount Calvary Holy Church denomination and was listed as the co-pastor of their church. He was a gentle man who did not seem to mind that his wife was the star.[52] Her church services were equal parts solemnity and over-the-top theatricality, for Shirley loved to hear the music swell and see other dignitaries hop on stage to help her act out a lesson.

Her famous story about an old man who joins a "dead" church (one that doesn't believe in dancing and speaking in tongues) was a beautiful spectacle. In the viral video of a performance of her classic piece "Hold My Mule," Pastor Shirley paces the sanctuary stage in a sweeping crimson gown, wiping sweat from her brow as she sings every word of the sermon. As she tells it, the old man dances around his lifeless church and church members scramble to hold down his limbs, but the Spirit is like fire shut up in his bones. At the word "fire," her growling voice jumped an octave while the cymbals crash and the guitar riffs skirt up and down the scale. When the church couldn't stop the old man, Shirley sang, they marched over to his house where they found an old mule. Shirley paused the story for a moment and pointed at several congregation members who scrambled onto the stage with her. By the time she began to describe how the old mule worked the plow, the men were assembled in a line on stage dancing like Motown singers. The audience clapped in time as the choir joined in, pretending to be the reluctant church members who discovered the real reason why the old man couldn't stop dancing in the first place: the old man and his old mule had somehow been blessed with abundant crops. This revelation kicked off a new song from the congregation to express their own thanksgiving and the camera panned the audience, resting on her husband, Harold, standing in the pews. The reigning Queen of Gospel could sing and dance and shout down heaven itself, but it helped that her husband was there with his big broad grin.[53]

POP PRINCESSES

By the 1980s, white evangelicalism had an adult contemporary soundtrack and a cast of natural beauties ready to hit the high notes. contemporary Christian music (CCM) had matured into a booming industry that, by 1995, was producing revenues of $750 million a year.[54] But no one represented the heights of CCM and its "crossover" potential like their own queen of pop, Amy Grant. The doe-eyed teenager from Nashville signed her first contract with Word Records while still in high school and, by her early twenties, she had won her first Grammy. She was the evangelical market's great hope for mainstream success, having earned the distinction of being the first CCM album ever to be certified platinum. But it was her personal life that made her irresistible to her fans. She was beautiful, warm, a showpiece of wholesome fame seen up close in her marriage to another industry darling, singer-songwriter and long-time collaborator, Gary Chapman. By the mid-1980s, she was a certified star in mainstream pop with a *Billboard* chart topper and a fan base that only increased with hits like "Baby Baby" and endless product lines. The press called it "Amymania." She was often accused by the Christian music industry of treading too close to the line of secularity, but the more than fifteen million albums she had sold by the mid-1990s[55] and constant coverage of her marriage and three children made her bulletproof. She was the most successful crossover artist of all time, and so when it was announced that she and Gary would be separating—and not long after that Amy would be marrying country music star Vince Gill—the Christian media exploded with accusations of infidelity. Amy and Vince vehemently denied the allegation and the two went on to have a long marriage and long careers, earning Amy a star on the Hollywood Walk of Fame and a place in the Gospel Music Hall of Fame. But no matter how many times she proved herself to be a willing voice for the Christian industry, both Amy and her albums always seemed to be on trial. In 2016, Southern Baptist LifeWay Christian Resources refused to carry her Christmas album, *Tennessee Christmas,* because it was allegedly not "Christian enough," a rejection made even more awkward because LifeWay was headquartered in her hometown of Nashville.[56] The fifty-six-year-old singer released a statement responding to the rather tired controversy, saying that she accepted the fact that her album did not meet their criteria but she wished the focus was on "what it means to live in faith and reflect love to the world around us."[57] It was an old adage that Amy had "sold-out," a battle ostensibly fought over her lyrics for decades but more likely about a fact about which she was too frank to prevaricate. When she had first skyrocketed to fame in the 1980s, she had said plainly: "I'm trying to look sexy to sell a record. But what is sexy? To me it's never been taking my shirt off or having my tongue sticking out. I feel that a Christian young woman in the '80s is very sexual."[58]

As CCM expanded and many of its major labels were bought up by secular conglomerates, the marketing of young starlets' sexuality remained one of the industry's thorniest issues. The late 1990s and 2000s saw the coming-of-age of pop princesses like Jessica Simpson, Britney Spears, and Christina Aguilera, the reigning triumvirate of blonde hair and low-rise jeans. Too much sex in Christian music and the artist was deemed vulgar. Pop star Jessica Simpson—whose award for Female Hottie of the Year at the 2000 Teen Choice Awards made her an uncommon abstinence advocate—explained how her looks kept her from a career on a Christian label: "They said I was too pretty to be singing Christian music. I was in overalls and a ponytail, and they were telling me I couldn't go out there and sing because it would make boys lust."[59] But there was no denying that a little sex sold even in a subculture with

A REVELL PUBLICATION   WINTER 1961-82 $2.95

Today's Christian

Woman

Getting the Better
Of Bitterness

Elisabeth Elliot
On Being a Woman

How Two Career
Couples Cope

BURN OUT—
It Could Happen to You

Unlock Your Creative Self

AMY & GLORIA GRANT
A Mother/Daughter Love Story

Until her divorce, Amy Grant was the darling of evangelicalism.
Reprinted with permission from *Christianity Today*, www
.christianitytoday.com.

strict parameters around the dip of V-neck shirts. That these artists were
more likely to be singing in an arena than in a church unmoored them
from some of the natural boundaries that gospel music and Christian
worship music enforced, and so artists were called on constantly to account for how they policed themselves and acted as role models for the
Christian community. Australia native Rebecca St. James was a natural.
She was evangelicalism's answer to Alanis Morissette, an angsty rocker
with long brown hair whose ultra-modest clothes and willingness to
champion conservative moral issues made her into a cherished role
model of young womanhood. Her concerts doubled as revivals, with

invitations to salvation, and each album was followed by a companion devotional book marketed as an intimate look at Rebecca's scribbled thoughts, scrapbook photos, and song lyrics.[60] Her song "Wait For Me" was one of the anthems of the "True Love Waits" national campaign for sexual abstinence that made even the Jonas Brothers into (temporary) converts, urging teens to sign pledge cards saying that they would wait until marriage and wearing a "purity ring" on their right ring finger to signal their own commitment.[61] Fans could follow Rebecca's abstinence teaching with her bestselling book, *Wait for Me: Rediscovering the Joy of Purity in Romance,* journal and subsequent study guide, or simply watch Rebecca's music video where she sings to a gorgeous stranger (ostensibly her future husband) who can't seem to find her in a public park while holding a treasure chest containing a gold heart necklace.[62] And with her follow-up, *SHE: The Woman You're Made to Be*, Rebecca's tribute to "a new definition of godly womanhood"—empowered, submitted, and pure—earned her media appearances on CNN and Fox News.[63] She was a portrait of ease inside evangelicalism's high walls, a pretty starlet who gave tips on layering T-shirts to "help our brothers with this whole lust battle" and sticking a shoe in the door to keep girls from being in a closed room with their boyfriends. Her very public private life was the best part of the show.[64]

It was a long road, though, from purity rings to adulthood. The industry buzzed about the young Jaci Velasquez, the Texan Latina whose debut album went platinum and whose bilingual hits and crossover appeal made her the face of a Target commercial and landed her on the Billy Graham crusade stage the same year.[65] One of the first questions in any interview with the beautiful teenager was about her sexual choices and any advice she might give to her fans.[66] By any standard, Jaci's career was a success with almost five million albums sold; she was one of the most successful Spanish-language crossover artists in the business, a Dove Award winner and a Latin Grammy nominee. She even starred in films like *Chasing Papi,* a Latino comedy with television star Sofia Vergara. But, as many a poster child for sanctified sex would discover, there was never an expiration date on public expectation. When she announced in 2005 that she had divorced her husband of less than two years, some speculated that it was the biggest divorce scandal since Amy Grant.[67] She would earn back audiences with a subsequent album, a media

Rebecca St. James was a 1990s singing sensation and a popular advocate for abstinence. Reprinted with permission from *Christianity Today*, www.christianitytoday
.com.

Jaci Velasquez was one of the few Latina celebrities of 1990s evangelicalism. Photo by Paul Morse, White House photographer.

blitz of contrition, and rebranding as "a ridiculously happy wife and mother of two precious children," such that *Christianity Today* called her a "diamond refined."[68] Famous men would apologize too when their marriages crumbled and their stardom turned to brass, but audiences, it seemed, did not weep over their lost virginity.

By the early 2000s, CCM was an industrial giant with $920 million in sales and a tremendous investment in young women like Jennifer Knapp, whose debut album *Kansas* sold five hundred thousand copies.[69] She was the Dove Award winner of 1999 for New Artist and a Grammy nominee the year after, a half-smiling face on the red carpet and an edgy style that made young fans forget that she was Christian-industry approved. But, as she explained to me, the work of becoming and remaining industry sanctioned was grueling. She had become a Christian in college after a dark season of alcoholism and abandonment, and she found herself both unnerved and a little desperate to meet the expectations that she encountered as a young artist with a host of industry professionals eager to market her. Her label gave her a stylist but she learned quickly that she could violate the unwritten rules of immodesty even by the way she bent down to pick up a guitar pick on stage. The cover of *Kansas* shows her standing in a simple long sleeve shirt, her hair loose around her face, a guitar strapped to her back—but there was talk about how the strap fell between her breasts. As a new Christian, she found the sexualized attention to these minutiae baffling.[70] She experienced two powerful articulations of who she was at the same moment: that she was called by God to use her voice to be a leader in the church, "but don't talk too long on stage. Don't show your arms and don't show your cleavage. It's like, 'Wait, what just happened?'"[71]

The power she felt on stage as the one calling the audience into a divine mediation was "a mystery." It was like crossing a sacred threshold and she found, almost by surprise, that she was able to command a room like few others. But it was a "dangerous" ability, she said reflectively. Alone on the stage, she was a powerhouse; but securing the stage was another matter. As a touring musician, she began to realize slowly that she needed to be vetted at every stop. "I couldn't go stay at a hotel by myself. I had to go stay with the pastor's family. Because everything was called a 'ministry' it meant that I had to be accountable and observed at all times. Every waking minute." Hers was a borrowed stage, and so she needed to secure "constant male permission. . . . When you get to speak, how long you get to speak, even down to men I had never met coming into my greenroom and praying for me before every concert. It wasn't framed as anything sexual, but it was really fucked up how many absolute strangers were given access to me." Her manager ("a lovely guy") helped her behind the scenes manage the almost endless number of gatekeepers who could open doors for venues, product placement, endorsements, and promotion, but she understood the importance of doing that herself too. "I had more confidence in knowing that there was a male counterpart [her manager] . . . but I think one of the reasons why I'm successful in CCM is because I went straight to the gatekeepers myself and I knew how to handle it." It was an unusual feature of this industry that from production to marketing to the actual display of her albums, almost every link in this industrial chain had an ideological element. Jennifer found herself persuading individual bookstore owners to like her, since Christian stores of the 1980s and 1990s were significant stakeholders.

The theological scrutiny only increased, though, with the rising momentum of the True Love Waits campaign. At first she acceded to bids to join other female stars in their battle against premarital sex.[72] "Early on, I got gigs because I would tell my testimony about how . . . God had saved me and now I'm this pure thing. That was fifty percent of why I ever got a stage in the beginning. But that schtick only lasted so long, because I grew up." She worried that promoting a message that implied that young women should be objects of shame. "Why is holiness a pass or fail situation?" she wondered. She later found out that a devotional book on sexual purity had been written and published with her name on the cover regardless. "They used my name," she said. "That was the script they needed. I was shocked." Her strong sense of idealism was breaking as she saw her identity—now her "brand"—filtered through the entrepreneurial interests of so many third parties. She fired her manager and began to manage herself in her last year performing, but there were questions about her sexuality that she could not address and that would be the key to her undoing.

In the last year before her sudden exit from Christian stardom, Jennifer was still not able to give an answer to a swirling industry rumor that became an outright accusation from her mentors and friends—that she was gay and that she was no longer a Bible-believing Christian because of it. "I was to be celibate, straight, and waiting for God to send me the perfect man. I had been celibate for ten years," she said candidly, "but, if God was sending me anyone, it was a woman."[73] In the lowest moments of her life, ensnared by addiction, she had turned to music to pull her out, but now she became convinced that she had to abandon it altogether. "All I could think about was the kind of humiliation awaiting me if my private spiritual crisis became known to the Christian public. I was more than aware of how intolerant the Christian industry can be of those who fall short of their standards."[74] She knew the financial blow to her career would be swift and lethal, and it was. She moved to Australia for a seven-year hiatus and what she thought was her permanent retirement. Years later, when she came out to the media, she became one of the first stars in the entire music industry to do so; in fact, her "coming out" revelation was initially bumped because Latin pop star Ricky Martin's had hit the news cycle first.

Jennifer was quite clear: she did not run away from the music industry because she was afraid of being found out as gay. "Sexual orientation was only one of many personal, theological and psychological issues that I felt had become distorted while trying to shape myself into the woman I was taught to be," she said.[75] She left the industry believing that the "message and marketing of *what* Christianity is and *who* it is was one that I could no longer endorse." There was little doubt in Jennifer's mind about why CCM ended their love affair with independent singer-songwriters like her. "In the nineties, there were a lot of artists that were creating a narrative of Christian music that was actually inspiring. The fallout of that was that some of us were gay. Some of us drank. Some of us were liberal—okay, *many* of us were liberal. [We] were giving people permission to have their own journey. Now you see the industry get sucked back into praise and worship," she said with a sigh. The singer-songwriter craze had catapulted many women to superstardom—something not quite imitable in the emerging Christian worship genre—and, as Jennifer observed, inherently destabilizing for an industry that wanted its stars to stay on script.

THE CHART-TOPPING CHURCH

Megachurches were some of the most coveted platforms in the Christian industry and fast became a revolution in Christian entertainment open to women's talents. From the 1960s onward, as we have seen, a new cast of supersized churches was making worship and worship leaders a significant aspect of their appeal. Megachurches, as an institutionalization of the crowd itself, favored preachers who could captivate audiences and experiences that could move them, and many churches began to take seriously the impact that music could have on attendance. As historian Wen Reagan and I have documented, many churches in the 1980s and 1990s began to craft a musical vision for their churches with in-house singer/songwriters or worship leaders who could attract attention. Of course, revivalism had always needed a soundtrack. Dwight Moody had Ira Sankey (the "Sweet Singer of Methodism"), Billy Graham had George Beverly Shea's strong baritone; and, of course, Aimee Semple McPherson preached, sang, and dramatized her sermons alongside her fleet of stagehands, sets, lights, and props, bringing Hollywood to pentecostalism. When megachurches brought worship leaders on as well-paid and well-publicized assets, it created new congregational positions for talented women. The global reputation of Australia's Hillsong Church reflected the partnership between pastor Brian Houston and worship leader Darlene Zschech. Lakewood Church had Joel Osteen and Dove Award winner Cindy Cruse-Ratcliff, known for her soaring vocals that pioneered the "Lakewood sound."[76]

Lakewood's discovery of their own "sound" was actually reflective of a wider transformation in Sunday morning worship. More and more megachurch pastors followed in the example of televangelism and devoted significant resources to production, equipment, lighting, and choreography. By the 1990s, prosperity megachurches were leading the charge to transform congregations into an avenue for arena rock. The "adult contemporary" piano and vocals gave way to a fuller, deeper sound, and the platform became a bona fide stage with synchronized lighting and trained staff; and, most striking was that a younger, edgier lead replaced venerable George Beverly Shea types. The house lights were dimmed and the stage lights cranked high and, as if overnight, the expectations for the musicians on stage skyrocketed. The worship leader was now a highly visible artist with crowds to please. From the pitch of her voice to the way she squeezed her eyes shut during a sustained pause, the performer's stagecraft was on full display. Unlike black gospel, there was little value on the physicality of their vocal performance. Cindy Cruse-Ratcliff's viral performance of "Majesty" was a perfect portrait of white megachurch worship's limited theatre.[77] Standing at the edge of the stage in a black blouse tied tightly at her neck without a hint of skin, Cindy stands immovable during the song's building emotional crescendo. She clutches the microphone with one hand while the other points to the sky and the crowd to punctuate every theological point and high note. When the choir behind her digs into the chorus and the band begins to let loose, Cindy throws her head back, walks a few paces, or jumps up and down a few times in place. Her performances will mostly be dictated by what she will never do. She will never heave her bosom or moan during the pauses; she will not linger too long on the high notes or dip down low to growl in a throaty alto. She does not carry a handkerchief to wipe sweat from her brow or look overly labored, like a female James Brown.[78] Though she performs in a church founded by card-carrying pentecostals with a profound delight in the unexpected movements of the Spirit, she will follow the dictates of other white women in megaministry and stay on her mark.

Many women came to fame as the beautiful frontwoman for megachurches and their new sound, a reflection of the churches' accommodations to modernity without compromising its gender dualism. These charismatic women—many of whom were married to a senior pastor— became the musical mirror of the senior pastor and the face of the church's emerging brand. Jennifer Crow was the worship leader of Victory Church, one of Oklahoma's largest, with her husband, Mark. Matt

Chandler, president of the Acts 29 Network, could hear his wife, Lauren, perform at The Village Church, where he served as senior pastor. Elizabeth De Jesus served as worship director and women's minister at one of the largest Latino megachurches in the country alongside her husband, Wilfredo, a social-justice-oriented pentecostal and religious advisor to President Obama. And Edwin McManus, an El Salvadorian American pastor in Los Angeles, featured his daughter Mariah's band at a megachurch that even the *New York Times* had to admit was "hip."[79]

Few could rival the musical juggernaut that was the annual Passion conferences, founded by Louie and Shelley Giglio.[80] The Passion conferences began in 1997 in Austin, Texas, as a national worship gathering of college students. By 2000 the Passion conference garnered forty thousand attendees and provided one of the most important platforms for talents like Chris Tomlin, Matt Redman, and Christy Nockels, who signed on to Louie and Shelley's subsequent music label, sixstepsrecords, founded the same year. Louie was considered the visionary of their musical enterprise, which came to encompass an upstart megachurch in Atlanta called Passion City Church, but Shelley was the chief strategist and the musical manager, as well as the head of "The Grove," the church's women's ministry. "My position in a conference is in the back row, it's in the front of the house, it's behind the scenes," she said.[81] But the background was where setlists were finalized, agreements were hashed out, and careers were launched, and Shelley became an important gatekeeper in the industry.

The Passion conferences were emblematic of the rising profile of contemporary worship music as a commercial powerhouse in the late 1990s. Singer-songwriters were finding new career prospects as more megachurches were able to afford their own in-house worship leader and their songs were generating more income through Christian Copyright Licensing International, which allowed local churches to easily purchase the rights to use their songs.[82] Women like Christy Nockels were stitching together long careers through multiple institutional platforms. The singer-songwriter got her start with her husband, Nathan, as worship leaders in their local church, writing songs together and producing their first album, *Holy Roar*. Louie and Shelley Giglio heard their work and invited them to Austin to sing in the first Passion conference, a collaboration that produced over a dozen live albums and made Christy the stand-out female face in Christian worship. Over the years, she and Nathan were the weekly worship leaders at various megachurches, from Houston's First Baptist Church to the Giglio's Passion City Church, while producing their albums as a duo called Watermark and then with Christy as a solo artist and Nathan as producer.

When I spoke to Christy in 2016,[83] she had recently released a live album entitled "Let It Be Jesus" with Shelley's sixstepsrecords and was touring with the Women of Joy conference as the worship leader for several thousand women at various stops across the urban south. I had seen Christy perform multiple times as a staple on the women's ministry circuit and had been struck by her ability to seemingly disappear, fading into the corporate worship, though she was the only silhouette visible on an otherwise darkened stage. Her stage presence seemed to be grounded in her deep interiority, and her songs held a mystical quality that was a bit unexpected in the pietistic (though rarely prophetic) mode of American evangelicalism. We started talking about the process of songwriting and how her songs, though rooted in her own life and experiences, could speak to people in very different situations. For Christy, it was a process that required that she set aside the glamour of celebrity to cultivate a rich spiritual intuition.

"I truly believe that a songwriter is like someone who dips into a stream," she told me.[84] "Honestly, we as songwriters sometimes will marvel at someone across the world releasing a song at the same time that is thematically similar. Like when the song 'Oceans' by Hillsong United came out. There was a storm or an anchor or an ocean theme for a while, and in all those songs released around the world at the same time, we all wrote them at the same time. I think it's that faithfulness to dip into that stream, because we have to believe that He's the one breathing them out. What do I [God] want to say to my church, and what do I want to comfort my people with?"

It was not an uncommon idea among artists of various kinds that inspiration existed "out there" but could be caught like fireflies in a bottle. But what Christy described was like swimming in a mystical crosscurrent, a divine flow she tapped into but also actively infused into her own songs, "sowing prayers" as she wrote. It was a moment of divine connection that many people called the anointing, though where the Spirit touched down was usually a mystery even to the songwriter. She had been praying more and more in secret, trying to learn how to render invisible truths visible, rather than center her identity in the moments where she stood in front of the crowd. Otherwise, she said, "I'm more likely to wonder, 'Do they know I have a new record out? Are they going to like this or are they going to wish Natalie Grant was here?'"

Natalie Grant, another women's ministry mainstay, had earned almost every accolade a worship artist could get, having once received the Gospel Music Association's Dove Award for Female Vocalist of the Year four years in a row and even starred in her own made-for-television movie on the Gospel Music Channel.[85] And I immediately warmed to Christy for the way she attempted to resist the overbearing demands of the marketplace and that she could admit to the insecurity that performance brings. One of the first things I learned interviewing women in megaministry is how rarely they will admit to being envious.

"This is a pretty shiny industry," I remarked to Christy. "I imagine you get a lot of input into what you wear and how you should position yourself compared with others."

"I'm trying to think . . . it was in 2002 after my son was born. I remember there was a moment when the Lord stilled my heart about striving and worrying about other female artists. They're doing this, and they are winning these awards, and they've got all these resources. Why don't I have that? The Lord showed me this picture of a damper pedal, and that I have to trust Him with the times that He closes the damper. I had to lay down my ambitions, my striving of the shiny thing. I think I was exhausting myself trying to keep pace with everyone else."

Sitting across from Christy, it would be natural to assume that her looks and her voice guaranteed her place in the nascent worship industry. The commercialization of worship music had led to speculation, at the very least, that all megachurch worship leaders had to be as beautiful and as charismatic as the professionals. When an Oregon church made headlines for its written ban against "excessive weight" in its worship leaders, Christian media was quick to disclaim what other blogs agreed was a practice many megachurches followed but were too sheepish to put in print.[86] Geoff Surratt, a former executive pastor at Saddleback Church, responded sharply that "no amount of lighting, fog or digital processing can manufacture genuine worship; real corporate worship is a mysterious, spiritual connection that flows from God through gifted leaders."[87] But since the difference was intangible, who could know the difference?

"It must be hard to ensure that your 'performance' is simultaneously worship," I remarked to Christy.

She nodded thoughtfully. "You have to become aware of yourself. You have to find your way back to your calling and the divine exchange, the promise that if you draw near to God that God will draw near to you. The only way to lead worship is when I can participate as well."

In the many women's conferences I attended, I witnessed singers orchestrate many of the significant moments of large gatherings. They sang the high notes that brought feelings of exaltation, the slow beats that invited confession, and spoke the short sermons between songs that pushed audiences toward themes and lessons that the invited speaker would hammer home. The distinction between gospel and song, exposition and reflection, blurred when a woman came to the stage to sing.

"As a songwriter, you are crafting music but also making a number of theological arguments about who God is," I said, fishing absentmindedly for the kind of rhetorical mode that singing belonged to.

"I think there are different songs for different seasons. There are songs of confession, songs of lament, or maybe songs like preaching that are proclamation too. A friend of mine always says that worship is like a megaphone. It's a proclamation of the gospel in all its forms."

"I wonder if you feel like a preacher sometimes."

She grinned. "I never thought of that before, but yes. I really do."

THE HARMONY

It was a widely accepted practice that as long as women were "the talent" they were given some leeway. After all, Tammy Faye's first hit was a children's show starring puppets she had made out of bubble bath containers.[88] Though there was nothing approximating an industry around other arts, there were places for women in ministry to serve as dramatists, comedians, sacred dancers, and spoken word artists, particularly when women's conferences became an arena mainstay in the 1990s and organizers needed females who could entertain and edify

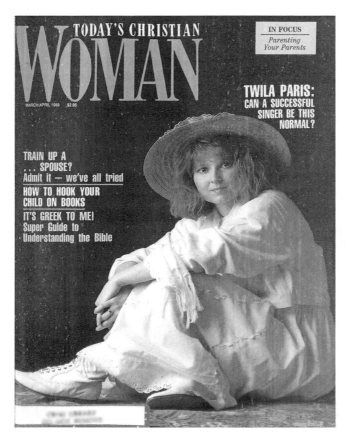

Like many contemporary Christian pop stars, Twila Paris
married her manager, cementing work and home. Reprinted with
permission from *Christianity Today*, www.christianitytoday.com.

the crowds.[89] With so many facets of megaministry devoted as much to
entertainment as to preaching, it made good business sense to have
performing women grace the stage. The commercial success of Christian
music had brought tremendous opportunity as well as endless scrutiny
to female performers. The spectacle of these songbirds on television
sets, arena stages, concert venues, and in sanctuaries alike had blurred
the lines of what constituted "Christian music," engendering even
greater debate about whether the women themselves lived up to sacred
standards. Singing women were asked to pass every test of modesty,
purity, propriety, and deference while they simultaneously entertained
the masses and mediated the divine. And since women rarely owned

their own stages, these performances—and the authority that came with it—were often episodic by nature.

Whether they were shaking the rafters with their voices or making a studio audience laugh, the women of megaministry's talents were usually on display. Except therein was the rub. What was the difference between, as Marion Williams had put it, her talent and her anointing? A talent could be managed, circumscribed, and squeezed into place for maximum effect and entertainment value: but what about a spiritual gift? It was, after all, a deeply-held Christian belief that spiritual gifts for the edification of the church were distributed to both men and women, and that, as St. Paul taught, "in everyone it is the same God at work."[90] If a woman were indeed anointed, gifted for a particular purpose, it would be hard to deny her power.

These two competing performances worked in tandem: a woman's anointed voice ushering in the unmediated presence of the divine and a moment that signaled that the woman herself was subject to an invisible spiritual hierarchy of men. From bookstore owners to managers and megachurch pastors, the gatekeepers were typically men who would grant an approval, a "spiritual covering" that allowed women to claim they were still "under the headship" of a male spiritual leader. It was, of course, always a little awkward that the itinerant character of a singing career meant that husbands were usually the support staff and everyone from Twila Paris to Debby Boone married their managers (or made managers out of their husbands). Nevertheless, the fundamental logic was complementarianism at heart. It seemed to hold that singing women appealed to the emotions, leaving the men with exclusive real estate over doctrine and the mind. A woman could inhabit a turnstile of endless nonpulpit roles, from pop princess to televangelist, so long as she was the sweet harmony to his strong melody.

Chapter Four

THE COUNSELOR

... power is made perfect in weakness.
   —2 Corinthians 12:9[1]

Texas bible teacher Kasey Van Norman was the first to tell audiences that she was a bit of a mess. "Not only have I been through cancer," she said, her hands outstretched as she counted tragedies with each finger. "I've been through rape. I've rebelled in just about every way you can think of. Been very sexually promiscuous. I've been through an extramarital affair. To receive healing and restoration . . . that He is using me. I mean, that's the beauty . . . I mean, I'm *broken*. I'm a *wreck*. I have so much junk."[2]

Kasey was a headliner on the Extraordinary Women tour of half a dozen southern cities, a tall brunette with a long face and a Julia Roberts smile. Though she was a licensed counselor, she seemed most comfortable sloughing off the role of tight-lipped therapist and unburdening herself before audiences, revealing everything from minor frustrations to major insights as she talked a mile-a-minute about God's interventions in her life. She liked to end her mix of confession and exhortation with the comforting reminder that God "uses the broken pieces" of people's lives; and thousands of women listened, nodded, jotted down a note, or responded to her invitation to approach the stage with a scrap of paper scrawled with their deepest shame and leave it there. When the lights went up, her audience squeezed into long lines that snaked around the stadium to get their picture taken with the woman who called herself a "hot mess" and "just a girl who struggles every day."[3]

In evangelical conversion narratives, there was a familiar story of befores and afters, past transgressions and present sanctification. It was traditionally an account that demonstrated the power of God's

Kasey Van Norman, licensed counselor and speaker, made vulnerability a hallmark of her ministry. Image courtesy of Kasey Van Norman.

surprising intervention into human lives, a miraculous rebirth that caused people to sing, as in the old hymn, of sinners who "lose all their guilty stains."[4]

But in the last twenty years, Christian women celebrities have not simply been recounting their past sins in exciting detail and claiming the power of God to change them. They have staked their reputations and their ministries on their imperfections, their "junk," their brokenness. Since the 1970s, popular Protestant preachers have adopted the same psychological language that seeped into popular culture to sell the benefits of Christianity to North American audiences.[5] For these evangelical and pentecostal women, that bore out a new opportunity. Instead of standing on their credentials, they began to justify their authority on the grounds that they stood on the ultimate foundation of psychological insight—experience. Female celebrities billed themselves as veterans of life itself.

By the 1990s, the most famous Christian women in ministry were famous not for what they had accomplished, but for what they had endured. They told and re-told the worst moments of their lives, picking through the litter of their dark pasts. And no matter how many times they recalled these memories, the effect was the same. They had lifted the veil to the past and allowed their histories to be heard, felt, discussed, and even analyzed. The audience had the sense that their true selves had been revealed. These revelations built bridges out of their experiences to their countless listeners, who found common ground between these life stories and their own. Millions of Americans turned to them as sympathizers who understood their troubled hearts and minds.

Very few women in Christian megaministry were credentialed counselors or therapists. But almost all acted as if they were. They gave advice on a wide range of topics, from self-esteem, healthy relationships, emotional management, and marital bliss to overcoming anxiety and depression. They boldly ventured into the dark recesses of the mind, crafting solutions for even the most severe mental illnesses that in fact required professional, medical intervention. More than this, they stood in front of thousands of listeners and unburdened their souls. And despite their posture as the counselor not the counseled, they whispered their deepest shames into the microphone.

If we scan the horizon of Christian megaministry, we see that what was once the occupation of priests and psychologists had become women's work. It was rather curious that these women were experts without formal credentials in the big business of confession and absolution, vulnerability, and disclosure. They covered the shelves of Barnes & Noble and filled up women's Kindles with books—half biography, half advice columns—about how truths from scripture calmed their own interior wrestling and helped them overcome major life obstacles. These stories kept women on primetime television and silenced audiences into the most hushed moments of major Christian conferences, raw stories like Kasey Van Norman's that pulsed with pain. "These wounds," she told audiences, "had been festering and getting deeper with each act of self-abuse, each experience of rejection, each unfulfilled longing to hear the words, *I love you*."[6]

The Christian marketplace was ruled by women who knew the power of redemption. The gospel was, after all, most powerfully witnessed in accounts of personal transformation, sins cast aside and new beginnings born afresh. But so often, women's careers were made and sustained by a cycle of confession and catharsis. Like the wheel that churned Hollywood's celebrity gossip industry, the relentless marketplace chewed through the stories and revelations of its stars at an unremitting pace.[7] Leading women learned the benefits of baring their souls at the risk of showing too much, earning the trust of audiences at the expense of their privacy. Therapeutic authority was as powerful as it was fleeting since audiences, once satisfied, could not help but reward these women by wanting more.

A WOMAN OF EXPERIENCE

To understand this odd combination of Christian testimony and amateur therapy we must first begin with an account of how American women became valued as counselors. As the role of the advice columnist and the psychologist began to blur, the women of megaministry would make the most of the authority granted to those who played the woman of experience. Women's counsel began to be a regular feature of nineteenth-century American public life in a new genre called the "advice column."[8] Though they were for a long time kept from reporting hard news, they earned the title of "agony aunts" or "sob sisters" who answered letters seeking help with emotionally charged problems of etiquette and relationships. At first, these female oracles often gave their advice pseudonymously since appearing in public under one's own name was deemed unladylike. In England, C. E. Humphry wrote as "Madge" for *Truth* magazine; in America, Elizabeth Meriwether Gilmer presented herself in print as "Dorothy Dix," Marie Manning was "Beatrice Fairfax," while "Nellie Bly" disguised Elizabeth Cochrane.[9] The readers who begged for their wisdom were often anonymous too, and the newspapers printed only the replies to their letters. In this collection of inquiries sent to *The Ladies' Home Journal*, advice columnist Ruth Ashmore's counsel was direct and far-reaching:

> BESSIE D.—For riding, a very short corset is usually recommended.
>
> H.D.P. AND OTHERS—Let your men visitors care for their own hats and walking sticks.
>
> MRS. H.W.—I would advise your bathing your feet in very hot water in which has been put a handful of borax.
>
> GRETCHEN—I do think it very improper of any young woman to allow a man to kiss her whenever he wishes.
>
> T.F.G. AND OTHERS—I cannot recommend any medicine to reduce the flesh. Care as to diet and regular exercise is the only healthy way to get rid of superfluous flesh.
>
> PAULINE—In writing to a man friend whom you are in the habit of calling by his Christian name, there would be no impropriety in beginning the letter "My Dear John." "My Dear Friend" is not considered good taste. (2) Massage is said to develop the arms.[10]

It was a peculiar kind of authority, sometimes subversive, usually conservative, upholding the unwritten rules of respectability that often kept women in their place. "Madge," for example, told her readers that the well-bred woman avoids physical contact on the train or bus while the "woman of the lower classes may spread her arms, lean up against her neighbor, or in other ways behave with a disagreeable familiarity; the gentlewoman never."[11] But, even so, these writers were seldom happy with the status quo that kept women in an inferior position. In reply to a question from a male reader about how to approach a girl, "Beatrice Fairfax" tartly replied:

> My dear friends . . . It is the proud prerogative of man to say what he thinks and to ask for what he wants, whether it happens to be a lady's affections or hot coffee. Only upon the clam, the oyster and woman is silence enjoined. Man may speak. Man may tell what he wants to call. Man may proclaim what he loves. Man may demand if he has a rival. Man may propose.
>
> Avail yourself of the glorious privilege of your sex, and ask for what you want. . . . Never think of adopting the silent methods of woman, who is speechless in great affairs, not because she wants to be but because she has to be. Her silence would be as troublesome to you as her involved draperies, and you would be as silly to adopt one as the other.[12]

Dorothy Dix Talks.

THE SELFISHNESS OF MEN.

A compliment in a ballroom—a brutal trampling under foot in a panic.

Whispered words of devotion in a scented boudoir—a cowardly desertion in times of danger.

Of the 300 women on board the ill-fated Bourgogne, which sunk at sea a few days ago, only one woman was saved. Of the 200 people who came out alive, only one was a woman. Survivors tell how women, struggling to reach the boats, were beaten down and trod upon, how those who those who succeeded in getting on rafts were pushed off and thrust under the water with boat hooks, how the little white hands of women and children, clinging to life lines, were hacked off with knives. It is a story of ferocious brutality that has but one parallel in modern times.

Dorothy Dix and her winsome column, "Dorothy Dix Talks," reached millions with its bits of advice and common wisdom. Illustrated 1898 column by Dorothy Dix, from *The Picayune*, New Orleans.

Elizabeth Meriwether Gilmer, known to readers as
Dorothy Dix, was the forerunner of the modern advice
columnist. Felix G. Woodward Library, Austin Peay State
University.

Their advice could roam quite freely, as certain topics were deemed
to benefit from a female perspective: domestic matters certainly, but also
questions of social reform and crime with a family or moral component.
Explaining why these emotionally laden areas should fall to writers of
her sex, the most widely read female journalist of her day, Dorothy Dix,
replied: "It is only the women whose eyes have been washed clear with
tears who get the broad vision that makes them little sisters to all the
world."[13] Her tears authenticated her connection to others and her right
to voice her "broad vision." The classic American sociological study *Middletown* would claim that Dix's columns, with a readership of roughly
sixty million, became the single most important agent in shaping Americans' opinions on marriage.[14]

What were the qualifications of these early women advice-givers? No formal training was required; it was assumed that a woman's life story was sufficient justification of the value of her counsel. The *New York Evening Journal* told its readers: "Miss Fairfax is a Virginian. She is a woman of experience. She has read and observed widely. She is young enough to sympathize with love's young dream. She will answer, to the best of her ability, all letters on subjects pertaining to the affections."[15] In popular culture, advice-giving was also seen as the role of the woman of experience: on the radio it might be the soap-opera star "Ma Perkins" ("America's Mother of the Air") and in the comics, "Apple Mary" or her successor, "Mary Worth." Their wisdom was inevitably described as "homespun"; that is, based on personal values and life history of the character. Their ability to relate to their listeners or readers was deemed more important than esoteric knowledge. Radio celebrity Ma Perkins was introduced as the ever-relatable "woman whose life is the same, whose problems are the same as those of thousands of other women in the world today."[16] The everywoman was an expert.

In the late nineteenth and early twentieth centuries, many female advice-givers began to adopt a new, slippery language of psychology and the study of the human mind that had begun to appear in popular culture. With the influence of Sigmund Freud and the consolidation of the academic study of psychology, a new kind of mental expert was born: the therapist. As Brooks Holifield has argued, the therapist began to displace the figure of the pastor as the final authority on people's mental worlds.[17] Many pastors, particularly in mainline Protestantism, started to cede authority over "mental health" to psychologists and their ilk (evangelicals and fundamentalists would wait until after World War II to follow). But, in truth, there was never a clean line between psychology and religion, and women's magazines were certainly proof of it with advice on everything from table-setting to mental telepathy.[18] A host of new Christian movements played with emergent ideas about the power of the mind—from mind cure, mesmerism, Christian Science, and its emergent successor called New Thought (a loose constellation of thinkers and denominations centered on a metaphysical belief in the power of thought)—and this endless talk of spirit and mind gave women license to downplay the significance of bodily distinctions like Man and Woman. The era saw teenage girls become celebrity spiritualists who were able to contact the other realm, while Mary Baker Eddy founded the Christian Science church and Emma Curtis Hopkins was one of the originators of New Thought, whose authors were filling the pages of the *Ladies Home Journal* with ways to change readers' lives by changing their minds.[19]

The figure of the psychological expert only grew with the horrors of World War I, which produced not only millions of physically maimed casualties but also masses of mentally damaged men, further legitimating Freudian and associated therapies that sought to repair those minds shattered by life in the trenches. "Shell-shock," or what we would now term post-traumatic stress disorder, which had been seen during the war (even by psychiatrists) as cowardice or a moral disorder, instead became the stuff of medical research, poetry, film, and government enquiries.[20] The psychological industry established itself as authoritative, throwing New Thought and other folk therapeutic techniques into the shade.[21] Ordinary citizens increasingly encountered psychology in testing by employers or schools.[22] Inevitably, however, the growing influence of psychiatry and psychology produced its own form of popular medical literature and began to appear in popular culture, in novels first, and then, after World War II, in film. The movies of Alfred Hitchcock, such as *Vertigo* and *Spellbound*, gave shape to this fascination with twisted psychology, as did the novels of Albert Camus (*The Stranger*) and J. D. Salinger (*Catcher in the Rye*). Women were worried about being thought to be suffering from psychological *malaise* and were proposed new remedies (here one thinks of Simone de Beauvoir and Betty Friedan).[23] Psychological jargon entered popular speech and middle-class American men and women began to consume psychoactive drugs to soothe the psychic troubles of modern life.[24]

Since its inception, American pastors had been trained using the insights of psychology to unravel the problems of "soul-sickness."[25] Churches like Emmanuel Church in Boston became seedbeds of healing therapies for alcoholism or the home of the spiritual ministrations of organizations like Alcoholics Anonymous. In mainline seminaries, these changes became established features of pastoral formation with programs like Clinical Pastoral Education—training would-be pastors in chaplaincy for the sick, dying, imprisoned, and those in crisis.[26] Similar training for lay people expanded with thousands of "Stephen Ministries" programs in churches across the country, training people to offer comfort and support to fellow members.[27] After World War II, evangelicals began to take stock of psychology, founding journals, degree programs, and credentialed institutes like the Fuller School of Psychology (1965) and Rosemead School of Psychology (1968).[28] The new popularity of blending Christian and psychological examinations of the inner state also coincided with a season of spiritual and ecumenical exploration for Catholic, mainline, and pentecostal denominations. A broader charismatic movement (as denominations began to incorporate beliefs and practices similar to those found within pentecostalism) brought a playful interest in the Holy Spirit to the baby boomer generation. Their Christian coffee houses, outdoor concerts, and barefoot guitar ballads showed that they were comfortable with the gospel not only as a message but a state of mind. A favorite of the charismatic movement, Agnes Sanford established herself as one of the leading healers of her generation with her widely read *The Healing Light*, which instructed readers on how to restore not only their bodies but their emotions and mental states.[29] The Agnes Sanford School of Pastoral Care, opened in 1958, continued this medley of psychological and spiritual training for clergy and laity.

The advent of the TV psychologist came in 1955 when twenty-eight-year-old psychologist Joyce Brothers appeared on the wildly popular quiz show "The $64,000 Question," whose tension-building musical theme and "isolation booth" became cultural clichés and where winning the ultimate prize made celebrities out of the contestants.[30] Her fame, which might have been expected to be ephemeral—how many other 1950s quiz show winners can you name?—became lasting when she was offered her own television program in 1958. On it she became the first TV psychologist, the forerunner of an entire new industry, one in which women would be leading performers.[31] From *Dear Abby* to Sally Jesse Raphael, famous advice givers were a confusing blend of professional and amateur counsel doled out away from traditional sources of prestige: the university, clinic, conference, or journals article. Rather than appear in her office, Joyce Brothers was more likely to be seen on *Hollywood Squares* or the late night talk show circuit.[32] Instead of the therapist's couch, there was the talk-show couch. There, not only were psychologists regularly featured on their programs, but average people were invited to confess their problems before a listening crowd. These drama-

Dr. Joyce Brothers became a fixture on television as a psychological expert. Photo by Phyllis Twachtman, courtesy of Library of Congress, Prints & Photographs Division, New York World-Telegram and the Sun Newspaper Photograph Collection, LC-USZ62-117953.

tized therapy sessions became a fixture of American television, and tearful revelations and public confession became a part of the journey toward recovery.[33] This classic "therapeutic dyad" between patient and therapist was expanded for television to include the patient, the audience, and the expert who diagnoses the problem and offers both solutions and entertainment for the masses. An enormously popular sub-genre of this type of program, dubbed "tabloid TV," featured a leering host determined to bring out the most lurid of revelations from hapless guests for the benefit of an audience howling out their condemnation or approbation of a new roster of television clichés: trailer-park moms, irresponsible baby-daddies, or defiant teen strippers.[34]

From the 1970s onward, the self-help era was in full flower with a wide assortment of hybrid religious and psychological solutions. Television critics complained that characters were starting to talk like therapists, psychologists fretted that women's magazines were "an encyclopedia of applied psychology," talk show psychotherapy became so prevalent that the American Psychological Association had to change its code of ethics to allow it.[35] Bookstores replaced cookbooks and home repair books with a rash of self-esteem aids like *I'm OK, You're OK, Games People Play,* or *I Ain't Much Baby—But I'm All I've Got.*[36] Acronyms were in the air: "TA" (Transactional Analysis), "TM" (Transcendental Meditation), and "est" (Erhard Seminars Training)—self-improvement guaranteed. An advertisement for *Do It Yourself Psychotherapy* (1973) modestly promised: "This book will save you thousands of dollars and give you control of your own life and your best self. No More Paid Advisors, Sex Hang-ups, Feelings of Inferiority, Psychosomatic Illness, Guilt. Enjoy More Personal Power, Boundless Sensual Pleasure, New Found Self-Reliance, Your Birthright of Health, New Life Styles."[37]

In 1966, Philip Rieff's prescient *The Triumph of the Therapeutic* had observed that the rise of novel "therapeutic elites" had made a new religion of saving a people from guilt, cultivating self-awareness, and replacing "I believe" with "I feel" as the beginning of wisdom.[38] Rieff had imagined the psychotherapist as king, but it would prove to be evangelical and pentecostal women who would claim the crown. If one glanced at a list of book titles released by the evangelical publisher Baker from the 1940s onward, one would see a clear shift in women's writing, beginning in the 1970s, toward heavy psychologically laden subjects (spousal abuse, abortion, molestation, sexual violence): books such as *Surviving the Secret, The Wounded Parent,* and *Helping Women Recover from Abortions.* But the Me Decade also pathologized sin, diagnosing a Christian's faults and foibles with new language. A woman lacking self-control needed to read *The Compulsive Woman,* and anyone needing a little hope or faith could find it in *Bible Therapy.* Charismatic movement leader Rita Bennett, author of *How to Pray for Inner Healing for Yourself and Others,* produced a number of prayer counseling manuals that suggested guided visualization, recovery of prenatal memories, and healing of emotional wounds while the pentecostal Women's Aglow Fellowship increasingly made reference to the Twelve Steps.[39] Common tropes of women's ministry were those of abasement, shame, and brokenness, and so salvation was to be found in vulnerability, transparency, and honesty. The term "authenticity"[40] became weighted by the implication that this person had aired her "brokenness" and was, if not healed from it, working with it. Pentecostal celebrity Sheila Walsh spoke often of her time in a psychiatric hospital and what she learned about transparency and authenticity from "the philosophy of Alcoholics Anonymous, where people introduce themselves in the most basic terms: 'I'm Simon, and I'm an alcoholic.' Surely that should be on our lips as the church: 'I'm Sheila, and I'm a sinner.'"[41]

In the early 1990s, conservative Christian women would begin to fashion a new blend of the religious and the therapeutic modes of confession for television audiences and readers in ways that would make them media stars. Realizing, as the author of *The Rise of the Therapeutic Society* observed, that "vulnerability characterizes contemporary selfhood and victimhood confers privileged status to those who claim it," evangelical and pentecostal women began digging into their own pasts to explain the spiritual virtues inherent in weakness.[42] Their opportunity came amidst the fall of male televangelism luminaries. One by one, Jimmy Swaggart, Oral Roberts, Jim Bakker, Bob Larson, Robert Tilton, and Peter Popoff brought their calling into disrepute for one reason or another. It was dubbed a crisis for the national disgrace it earned and, for the next decade, spurred a flood of books on integrity and mutual accountability among preachers who had proven that their ministries were beyond correction. Men who had asserted their own holiness and traded on their Christian integrity were revealed to be flawed and self-destructive. From Jimmy Swaggart's dalliances with prostitutes to Jim Bakker's hush money for affairs and indictment for fraud, this kind of idol was not going to be allowed worship anymore. In a world grown cynical from the hypocrisy of evangelical preachers, the answer was ministries that would highlight the failings of the speaker, rather than polish the tarnished brass covering of the feet of clay. The new saints of megaministry would prosper by confessing that they were never saints at all.

THE CONFESSION

Two thousand young women packed into the sold-out Moody Theatre in downtown Austin, Texas, for the 2016 annual conference of the "IF:Gathering," ready to hear a message from their favorite evangelical speaker and, hopefully, a word from God.[43] The most buzzed-about organization in women's ministry hosted an event that is the most beautiful of its kind, a tailor-made occasion with scattered peonies on the tables in the lobby and ethically sourced Cambodian totes sat on each chair filled with goodies for every participant. Everything about the experience felt *special,* curated, from the almond butter and apples in the wings for every healthy eater to the care with which the typical ugly conference badge was replaced by a swinging pewter pendant necklace. Everything and everyone was gorgeous, as each celebrity who took the stage seemed to have gotten the same memo: long, beach-tousled hair; a breezy, cropped dress; cowboy boots. It was Austin, after all. The fashion was up-to-the-minute, but the rhythms of its event were as old as American revivalism.[44] The day started with the welcome, moved to emotional worship and a hard-nosed message, and then dove into what would be the climax of the event: the confession. Traditionally, at the end of the first night of any old-fashioned camp meeting, after a rousing sermon, people who had not yet given themselves to Jesus would be asked to pray the Sinner's Prayer with a simple formula. Repent and be saved.

The conference founder Jennie Allen had a sweet, wide face framed by loose blonde waves and came across as a free spirit with a touch of revival fire. She led most of the conference, but the number of famous women who joined her onstage (or filmed additional segments backstage for the organization's later use) was what made this event so staggering. It became the Who's Who of women's ministry. HGTV star Jen Hatmaker kept the audience laughing with her goofy chatter, pentecostal evangelist Christine Caine shouted about the power of God, and author Ann Voskamp prayed in her low, throaty voice. But it was Jennie who ran the show.

"See, girls, you are enough," Jennie said firmly. She called us "girls" throughout, drawing us all into the same intimate sisterhood in this dark auditorium. "And you *have* enough. But only—and hear this clearly—because JESUS. IS. ENOUGH. We do not have to keep living this way . . . . Repent and believe."[45] She wanted to crack open the audience to experience the catharsis of admitting their sin and freeing themselves of shame. Shame was one of the most common words used at these conferences, and quotes from sociologist Brené Brown's TED talk on the subject always manage to worm their way into the conclusion.[46] Shame is a burden, undone by acts of public vulnerability like this confession. Jennie Allen volunteered to show the women how it is done, so she settled onto her stool, gripping and twisting her water bottle lid nervously.

"And now I'm going to do something *so* fun—I really can't wait—and now I'm going to confess my sin in front of hundreds of thousands of people. So fun! Yay!" Her endearing mock enthusiasm elicited a sympathetic laugh. "So I'm going to go first, because you know what? I'm not going to ask you to do something that I'm not willing to do."[47] The anticipation was almost palpable as the silent question is asked: what will she reveal?

"When I asked God what to share, you know, there's *so* many. Which one?" she asked sardonically. "I hated the one, not because it's the worst one. I've got worse ones! I could shock and awe you." The audience laughed with her. "But this is the one that makes me cry."

She was having dinner with a friend, she explained, and they were talking about the IF:Gathering. "We were saying things like, 'It's so humble, it's so broken, it's so real. You know, things that y'all just *are*.'" And then her friend said: "You know, Jennie, if God were going to build something that wasn't *fake*, that wasn't *pretend* humble, and that was actually really messy and broken, He would have to take a leader that actually believed she wasn't worthy. That actually believed she wasn't enough." The room filled with a deep silence. It sounded as if she had just admitted that she was not the humble, broken, and real leader that everyone thought she was.

Tears welled up in Jennie's eyes at the memory. She wiped her nose and tried to keep going: "But the sin is that I *try* to be. The sin is that I don't let God just be awesome. I try to be awesome too." What sounded like a confession of being too proud was actually an admission of trying too hard. She believed God wants to restore her to true humility, and in revealing her failures, she hoped to open a door to her audience to join her in vulnerability.

"I just want to be done with this right now, ok?" she told the audience. "I mean, we've got nothing to prove. And I know some of you are in living rooms with your mom," she said jokingly, referring to the roughly half a million people who are streaming this event live from their homes or churches. "But we just wanted to give you some space,

Jennie Allen (third from the left) founded the IF:Gathering as a space for the spiritual renewal of women. Image courtesy of IF:Gathering.

and Jeanne is going to lead it. To connect with God . . . and to receive His cleansing."

Pastor Jeanne Stevens joined Jennie on stage, ready to lead the crowd in a communal confession. Jeanne was the co-pastor of a young Chicago megachurch, Soul City Church, and a friend to many of the women who appeared at this event, and, before she began, she turned to Jennie and looked straight into her eyes. "Thank you for being the woman that goes first. And letting us *see*." The audience started to clap. "For letting us see the fullness of you. I'm so humbled. And a little nervous." They shared a sheepish smile. Then she turned back to the crowd.

A soft sustaining piano melody began, signaling the invitation for participants to allow their emotions to bleed through. Jeanne continued: "The sacred act of confession . . . is that beautiful practice of letting ourselves be seen . . . . As the Psalmist says, 'He wants to search us. He literally wants to examine us . . . and to know our heart . . . . He wants us to be *honest*. He wants us to be *authentic* . . . . This is what our good God does, to take what has been living in the dark and lead it into the light . . . and to confess, to fully confess, we have to be willing to be seen."[48]

Jeanne asked everyone to take out their cell phone and let the home screen shine. She began to list sins they have kept "in the dark" and the women should lift their glowing phones and bring their offenses "into the Light."

"I confess that I have clung to the opinion of others . . ."

The women around me were a little hesitant, looking around a bit before holding their phones in the air. Later we joked about how we were worried that people would infer all manner of sin by our answers, but for now a hush held the auditorium still.

"I confess that I lie . . ."

"I confess that there is an ongoing pattern of sin, an addiction . . ."

"I confess that I use blame and shame to emotionally hurt others . . ."

"I confess that I mask my pain with anger, humor . . ."

"I confess that I have kept the scales over my eyes when it comes to the injustices of this world . . ."

"I confess that I am living way beyond my limits . . ."

The darkened auditorium looked like a constellation of stars, blinking on and off as hundreds of phones rose toward the dark ceiling. It was a modern take on coming to the altar. Women in the crowded theatre and around the country, watching in simulcast, exposed their sins before the watching crowd. It was intensely private, as women looked inward, but this was a communal act of seeing and being seen as people silently nudged each other toward contrition.

From the earliest days of the Christian church, the act of confession has been an integral part of a believer's spiritual life. The acknowledgment of sinful behavior was deemed necessary for forgiveness, but it also served a crucial didactic function. For as the Apostle Paul claimed he could "gladly boast of my weakness," which drew attention to the power of God, the Christian tradition maintained a long tradition of confessor-teachers.[49] St. Augustine's *Confessions*, the Western world's first autobiography, was his book-length recitation of his missteps on his path to God, which served also as an exhortation to all Christians to examine their own hearts.[50] The power in both giving and receiving confession held throughout the centuries. In time, the Catholic Church came to treat it as a sacrament that only a priest could perform, and, though the Protestant Reformation rejected such a view, many denominations still insisted on the necessity of publicly recognizing one's shortcomings and receiving absolution. Even nonliturgical churches found that confession was essential to maintaining church discipline, requiring it as part of admission to membership. As believers told their stories of transformation, these "testimonies" of being saved became their greatest teaching tool. As sin turned to repentance, a believer's "testimony" or "witness" became a source of authority.[51] It was, as one theorist has argued, "a ritual that unfolds within a power relationship."[52]

As we have seen, by the 1990s it was expected that women's testimonies were also somehow revelations of their secrets. Lysa TerKeurst, founder of Proverbs 31 Ministries, unveiled her new book as a dark exploration of her own abandonment by her father.[53] Sarah Jakes, the daughter of America's most famous black preacher, T. D. Jakes, burst onto the national scene with her tell-all book revealing her pregnancy at thirteen and her new status as a twenty-five-year-old single mom and divorcée.[54] It was a world that demanded that nothing be hidden. "I spent humid nights cutting up the thin skin of my wrists, bleeding out of pain I could no longer contain," wrote another bestselling author about her childhood.[55] Every facet and angle of a woman's tragedy was explored like a newly hewn gemstone held up to the light.

THE PROFESSIONAL

As we have seen, the Christian therapeutic woman found room to operate in a male-dominated culture of pulpiteers for a number of reasons. She exploited the gap in the "culture of professionalization" that caused ministers to cede expertise to psychologists and counselors in the first place.[56] Church members sought out the advice of psychologists or the opinion of doctors for issues that once had been the domain of clergy. In this shrinking space for pastors, women counselors stepped into the void as popular experts in the interior world. But they did so without competing with the pastor, whose role they often mirrored. The typical Christian celebrity woman was a speaker, author, counselor, and mentor. In her guise as therapist, counselor, and friend, she would never be accused of trying to usurp the pulpit. Just the limelight.

Women attempting to gain public recognition typically borrowed openly from both psychological and ministerial categories to earn recognition as mental experts with a variety of accredited and claimed titles. A counseling degree offered women in evangelical contexts a large measure of freedom. These degrees, or corresponding degrees in social work, qualified them for work in a variety of roles, from religious schools, private practice, children and family services, hospitals, and funeral homes to homeless shelters. In a congregational setting, the work of counseling did not seem to trigger the same concerns around authority and oversight. After all, in the sacred walls of the church, the titles like "pastor" and "counselor" did not compete with one another. They were apples and oranges, electric guitars and bell choirs—they lived in separate spaces with different audiences. Female counselors could then take on a variety of ecclesial roles; they could be directors of family ministries, directors of children's ministry, or serve in a variety of support staff positions.

Outside of traditional seminaries, there was a wide array of counseling certification processes, ranging from the rigorously accredited to those available to anyone with a little money in their pocket. Light University, for instance, offered certified continuing education in online courses and DVD sets based, in part, on the teaching of Christian celebrity psychologists. Dr. James Dobson, parenting guru of the 1980s and founder of the multi-million-dollar organization Focus on the Family, was the figurehead of the "The James C. Dobson School of Marriage and Family" program. The American Association of Christian Counselors marketed the "Extraordinary Women" thirty-lesson box set ("Regular Tuition: $800. However, call [this number] to receive a $300 scholarship") with video lessons by a medley of professionals and popular women's speakers like Beth Moore. The topics were wide-ranging, including diet and beauty, menopause, spiritual devotion, spousal abuse, depression, female sexuality, and mothering.

Further, the counseling woman was easily tolerated when the work itself was private, one-on-one, mentoring to groups, or to groups of women. In this way, the job of counseling often kept the spheres of inside vs. outside and private vs. public intact, the longstanding sense that respectable work for women was best done *inside* the home and *privately.*[57] Much of the therapeutic language of women's ministry to women hit those domestic notes. Take, for instance, the popular therapeutic manual for women entitled: *Kitchen Table Counseling: A Practical and Bible Guide for Women Helping Others.* In wedding the home and work, women did not stray from the domestic sphere.

Seminary training in counseling, however, did not necessarily help a woman climb her way to celebrity or even significantly improve her chances for a position in the most recognized churches. In examining 2016 megachurch employment postings, it was clear that advertisements focused on personality and strategic vision, with seminary education as a preference but not a prerequisite.[58] Kasey Van Norman, for example, was a licensed counselor, but did not include that credential or her educational background in her author and speaker biography.[59] While, to be sure, many applicants had a seminary degree, the emphasis was on more intangible spiritual and personal qualities. Likewise, once hired, a woman's educational credentials would rarely become a prominent part of her public persona.

Celebrity women often found it difficult to incorporate their education or titles into their public role, despite the fact that many went to respected schools. While men were introduced by degree or titles—like Dr. James Dobson or Pastor Craig Groeschel—women, no matter their age, were usually introduced by their first name.[60] Like Miss America contestants, they learned to hide their frustration and ambition with assurances like "I'm just happy to be here." Their accomplishments were buried in their online biographies under a host of softening flourishes:

> "Hello! Thanks for stopping by. If we met over coffee, I suspect in minutes we'd be laugh-crying over sea-salted dark chocolate or inhaling pumpkin scones."—Rebekah Lyons[61]

> "Here's what I'm passionate about: God's Word, flowers, the church, coffee, color, seeing other women worship, laughing with my kids, reading fiction, running, juicing, kissing my man, binge watching Gilmore Girls on Netflix, cuddling, dancing and laughing."—Jess Connolly[62]

> "Priscilla Shirer is a wife and a mom first. But put a Bible in her hand and a message in her heart and you'll see why thousands flock to her conferences and dive into her Bible study series each year."—Priscilla Shirer[63]

The wise spun this straw into marketing gold. Many used these breezy introductions to their advantage as memorable brands and accessible invitations to follow their ministry, usually summarized in friendly identifiers like these Twitter handles:

Priscilla Shirer, daughter of megachurch pastor Tony Evans, is a bible teacher and star of Christian inspirational films. Photo by David Lowe. Image courtesy of LifeWay, www.lifeway.com.

"Wife to the Farmer: Mama to 7: Author of NYTimes Bestsellers: The Broken Way, One Thousand Gifts, & The Greatest Gift. Seeking to follow One alone."—Ann Voskamp[64]

"wife to Matt. mother to audrey, reid + norah. lover of God. singer of songs. writer of stuff."—Lauren Chandler[65]

"Author. Speaker. Novice tortilla maker."—Margaret Feinberg[66]

Women in evangelical and pentecostal circles who could not claim "pastor" reached for other titles. For those looking for a foothold into public ministry, many women choose the title "life coach," drawn from the murky world of psychological credentialing. The lines between life coaching and counseling differed at the level of professional services they offered, and there were a host of "certified" types. With varying degrees of legitimacy—ranging from certification from established entities like the International Coach Federation to fly-by-night certificate mills—the label "life coach" was available to a wide range of people looking to be a professional encourager.

Life coaching was once a man's game. The wider American culture had fallen in love with the winning figure of the life coach in the 1980s when boardroom executives began to hire male athletes and coaches with crossover advice for office culture. One of the household names in professional motivation and selling success was Zig Ziglar, who inspired Christian speakers to trademark their work.[67] Christian speaker Liz Curtis Higgs became "Liz Curtis Higgs, The Encourager™." The retiree-favorite Mary Sutherland became "The Stress Buster." By the 1990s, popular talk shows kept life coaches like Oprah-favorite Iyanla Vanzant[68] and *The Steve Harvey Show*'s fixture Lisa Nichols on staff for ready counsel.[69] The life coach had become a natural career path for aspirational women inside and outside the church.

American churches of all denominations seemed to find a role for the life coach. Whether for pulpit ministry, motivational speaking, publishing, or blogging, women in the church reached for this label to describe their ability to reorient listeners and direct them to their goals. McLean Bible Church provided its 16,500 members with a counseling center staffed with men and women licensed as psychologists, counselors, social works, and life coaches.[70] Even the United Methodist Church, with all its mainline gravitas, officially recognized life coaching in 2008 as "an important new pastoral discipline" to help parishioners move into the "'fullness of life' which Jesus offers (John 10:10)."[71]

Women might add an extra theological flourish to the title— "Christian life coach" or "Bible life coach" or even "Shepherd-Coach"— to attempt to re-brand life coaching as inherently evangelical rather than metaphysical. They were right to worry. The archetype of the life coach was a blurry hodgepodge of metaphysical, corporate, and psychological origin. A popular life coach resource website, for instance, reserved an entire section for "The Law of Attraction," a common New Thought principle that the mind attracts or repels good fortune.[72] Unsurprisingly, the most common use of the term "life coach" arose among those from a prosperity gospel tradition, whose own blend of pentecostalism and New Thought leaned heavily on metaphysical arguments that a positive mindset is the most powerful tool in the Christian life. Prosperity preaching televangelists and megachurch pastors such as Paula White, Juanita Bynum, and Taffi Dollar described themselves as motivational speakers and life coaches with an expertise in creating the conditions of a better life.

Life coaching quickly became a woman's game. Banking on common assumptions about women's innate emotional intuitiveness, it was natural to market women as professional encouragers. Life coach websites began to feature sections exclusively for men in an industry increasingly dominated by women. Though its culture of self-promotion ran against the grain of typically female forms of marketing (friendly and indirect about both personal credentials and approach), women had to be quick to toot their own horns in the crowded world of life coaching. Rachael Miller, for instance, began her profile with her educational and life coaching credentials and ended with fanfare: "To the hundreds of women she now serves they affectionately call her Sis. Rachael along with scores of titles; such as: mentor, pastor, prophetess, spiritual mother, God's handmaiden, life coach, spiritual sergeant, spiritual midwife and spiritual Harriet Tubman."[73]

In the end, women used their credentials only as much as they needed them in a Christian world that was substantially less interested in their titles than their hearts. Denied direct access to the pulpit, the women of megaministry found ways to use what had been discarded—expertise in matters of the mind—and stepped into the ancient role of counselor and advisor. And once a woman found her place in power, her educational titles, like other unused things, found themselves in the dustbins of history.

THE INDUSTRY OF DISCLOSURE

In ceding the world of the mind to women, a range of topics under the banner of "Religion and Spirituality" became coded as female topics; in becoming experts on themselves, they became leaders in a range of areas related to emotional well-being. Take, for instance, the focus of the women's ministry organization "Girlfriends in God." Girlfriends in God was co-founded by three well-known leaders in women's ministry: Gwen Smith, songwriter and author of *Broken into Beautiful*; Mary Southerland, author of *Hope in the Midst of Depression* and *Escaping the Stress Trap*; and Sharon Jaynes, former vice president of Proverbs 31 Ministries, author of sixteen books including *Your Scars Are Beautiful to God*. Their parachurch ministry was a hub for their individual and collective brands, an online store for their co-written books, an advertisement for events like their "Girlfriends in God Caribbean Cruise," a live feed for their Facebook, Instagram, and Twitter activity, and a daily devotional that went out to eight hundred thousand women.[74] Their shared language was of wounded healers. They were amateur advisors in the five common themes that fell under the guise of "Christian Counseling and Recovery" in online and retail Christian bookselling: anxiety, depression, self-esteem, grief, and mental illness.

Of these, the most common interventions into mental health treated symptoms of anxiety, self-hatred, or depression as theological and mental errors. Women who felt anxious needed to remember that God held their futures. Women who loathed their bodies must be told that they were created by God as good and beautiful. Light interventions into these problems were staged at almost every women's event, either through a spoken word performance of a woman confronting her own demons of low self-worth or a testimony, usually by a seemingly perfect person with relatable problems.[75]

A turning point in the depth and specificity of women's interventions into mental health came in 2013 with the suicide of the son of the most famous pastoral couple in America, Rick and Kay Warren.[76] Over the years Kay had played quieter roles while it was her husband, Rick, who was the evangelical darling whose book, *The Purpose Driven Life*, had made him an international sensation with thirty million copies sold. In 2007, she articulated her own sense of a call to be "gloriously ruined" for international orphan care in the wake of the HIV/AIDS crisis.[77] Kay became the beating heart of the twenty-two-thousand-member Saddleback empire. As the founder of their new HIV & AIDS Initiative, she threw herself into her new role as an advocate, traveling abroad widely while meeting with relief organizations, medical experts, church leaders, and even the Rwandan president as she helped to facilitate Rwanda's attempt to become the world's first "Purpose Driven Nation." Though at Saddleback's 2014 inaugural conference on mental health, a little over a year after her son's death, Kay was a different woman. "My life was ruined again on April 5, 2013," she said, "but this time there was nothing glorious about being ruined. This time it felt like we had been wounded in a way that

Kay Warren became the public face of grief when her son, Matthew, ended his own life after years of struggling with mental illness. Reprinted with permission from *Christianity Today*, www .christianitytoday.com.

could never be repaired or mended or fixed as we were devastated by the suicide of our 27-year-old son Matthew."[78] Her eyes crinkled into half-moons when she smiled sadly, and her strong voice broke during the tender spots of the story of her altered life. "There have been moments when I couldn't take the next breath," she paused, seeming a little winded. "Moments in which I said, *I am ruined. Forever.*"[79]

Kay's public grief stirred a national conversation about mental illness in Christian communities. A recent poll had shown 48 percent of evangelicals to believe that mental illness should be righted with purely spiritual means: biblical study, prayer, exorcism, and repentance.[80] Meanwhile, as Rick and Kay wrote in their op-ed for *Time* magazine, the National Alliance on Mental Illness reported that sixty million Americans, one in four adults, suffered from a mental health condition.[81] Regardless, Saddleback received a wave of criticism from Southern Baptists about their positive stance on the role of medication can play, in particular, in the care of the mentally ill.[82] Though former Southern Baptist Convention (SBC) president Frank Page revealed the news of his own daughter's suicide, and Ed Stetzer, former president of the SBC research arm, LifeWay Research, argued for the acceptance of medication, the Warrens' own denomination was conflicted.[83]

In the last decade, it has been much more common for famous pastors' wives to admit—even under the microscope of church life—their own struggles with mental illness. Kay Warren speaks frankly about her lifelong struggling with depression.[84] Some fought their battles spiritually while others dealt with their illness through therapy and medication. In 1999, Juanita Rasmus was the co-pastor of a ground-breaking Houston megachurch that was winning awards and thanks for its incredible success with the city's homeless. She and her husband had two small children and a thriving ministry. Then she experienced a sudden manic-depressive episode that was so overwhelming that she announced to her church that she was "taking a sabbatical."[85] She was not sure she was coming back. She was exhausted, panicked, and disinterested with all the things she once cherished, but her husband and her church stood by her. Looking back at that season, she marveled that he told the congregation what she was going through: "He *named* my illness. . . . And while for some people that really blew them away—'Oh my God! She's so faithful! She's so spiritual! How could she be experiencing depression?!'—the only thing they forgot in that equation is that 'She's so human.' Mental illness can happen to anyone."[86] Now she spoke freely about the stigma of therapy and medicine, as well as efforts the church can make to support those suffering from depression and bipolar disorders.

For the women under the heat of the spotlight, public ministry might mean public illness. Spiritual deliverance would always be the deepest hope and, often, the unspoken expectation. Despite living in a culture increasingly open to understanding the sometimes fractured nature of the human mind, the women of megaministry would bear the brunt of facing down the stigma of wounded minds in a spiritualized world more accustomed to tending to wounded hearts.

Perhaps one of the most successful sustained interventions into mental solace came with the topic of grief and child loss. Though fathers, too, had grief to bear, it was women who bore the public acts of grieving for children, born and unborn. With more than 750,000 books sold, Pam Vredevelt was one of the most popular authorities on the subject of child loss. She was a licensed counselor with a master's degree in psychology. She introduced herself to audiences as married to her best friend, John, and the mother to four children—"two reside in the United States, two are in heaven."[87] Angie Smith, wife of a singer in the contemporary Christian band Selah, stumbled into her own career as a Christian author and speaker. Or rather, she fell headlong into it in a season of catastrophic grief. Her blog, *Bring the Rain*, drew enormous readership as it pored through the tender details of her pregnancy with baby Audrey who, Angie knew, would live only a few hours after birth.[88] The blog would become her first book, *I Will Carry You*, filled with painful hope and dreams deferred. In this entry written a few days before her delivery, she gave voice to the frantic love of interrupted motherhood:

> April 1, 2008
> I wanted to try and fit a lifetime of love into a few short months, and as we approach the end of the road, it occurs to me that there isn't enough time to tell her everything. And so now I have to trust a different side of God the Father. Will You tell her all about me and what I would have been to her? Will You show her glimpses of how we would have lived life together?[89]

As bearers of children, women's bodies are gatekeepers of life and death. In a culture largely reluctant to make news of miscarriage and stillbirth public, women's ministries became a sanctuary for the enormous range of emotions that arise when some lives begin and others end. Some efforts were frank and practical. The Lutheran Women's Missionary League sold clothing patterns for burial outfits, templates for blankets, bonnets, dresses, and trousers easily dressed on stiff, small dead bodies.[90] Titles like *What Was Lost* filled up the shelves.[91] Most publications were artful, marketed with allusion and spare symbols: a bright seed pod is cracked open, seeds spilling out; a knitted pink bootie is coming unraveled; a flower weighed down by the rain droops toward earth. The separate sphere of women's ministry was opened to reveal a place of holy sorrow.

PITFALLS OF REVELATION

In the double language of psychology and Christianity—and, in this case, a form of therapeutic evangelicalism—women's conferences could be powerful sites of liberation as individuals experienced freedom from past experiences that, consciously or unconsciously, steered their lives. Perhaps one of the most cathartic facilitators of women's megaministry came in the role of the comedian. Female comedians were a staple of the largest women's ministry tours and women like Anita Renfroe knew its fine art. Now a household name in Christian circles, Anita got her start in megaministry playing the melodramatic musical backdrop to women's mass confessions. "When I first began in the 1980s," Anita told me, "women's conferences, by and large, consisted of a deep Bible teacher speaking, followed by a tragic testimony, followed by another Bible teacher building up to an altar call and a mournful song. I played the song."[92] We laughed at the memory of so many events we have seen like it. "I would be doing these musical segments in these deep, dark moments and I would think *I'm drowning*. If we don't exhale here, I don't know if these women can receive what comes next." The "what comes next" is the confession, the radical openness that is the necessary first step to forgiveness, but, as Anita observed, these events could feel "so deep and dark." So she began to make jokes at the piano, breaking up the intensity with a little commentary on "something ridiculous and universal" and, gradually, conference organizers started to pay her for it.

She began to see the advantages of bringing women into a place of vulnerability with laughter: "I believe strongly that laughter causes you to lose self-consciousness. It's a very democratic experience, and it causes those emotional walls to fall away a little bit. And that puts you in a position where your arms are uncrossed. It's really hard to laugh and stay closed up physically. You can still be shut down while listening, nodding and writing things down. There is so much that opens our spirits. If the room feels good and open to me, I can deliver a little truth bomb. I can say to women, 'We are a mess but God loved us before we knew that.' These women are all dealing with shame. But I believe that if you can laugh about it, you can survive it."

Women's conferences themselves existed in that push-pull between self-improvement and self-acceptance. They wanted to emphasize transformation, and yet so much of what women longed to hear is that they were loved as they were. The comedic woman was able to speak a little more freely and make comments that were a little risqué, earning the audience's trust as someone who "tells it like it is." In a recent conference, Lisa Harper, a seasoned speaker in her fifties, opened her talk with the story of driving her adopted daughter to school in her pajamas without a bra.[93] Once she realized she was blocked from the carpool lane, she began her walk of shame into the school on foot, which Lisa told with mournful detail about body parts that "shouldn't be swinging" and would require on-lookers to receive counseling. It was almost too hard to hear her over the sound of side-splitting laughter from the crowd. Lisa managed to find a way to incorporate the moral seriousness of the lesson coupled with enough self-deprecating humor to let audiences see her humanity. Or, as the speaker Jo Saxton quoted at a recent conference, her Nigerian-English accent punctuating every word:

> If I ever believed in reincarnation, though I admire these people
>   greatly, I wouldn't want to come back as an American woman.
> They have to be beautiful, but not *too* beautiful.
> They have to be smart, but they can't be *too* smart.
> They haven't got to have it down at home, they've got to be perfect
>   and all together, but they've got to lean in to their careers . . .
> They can't be too much and they've got to be *enough*.[94]

The audience murmured as she diagnosed American culture as one of impossible perfection for women,[95] and I saw tears in people's eyes as Jo next led them through God's imagined delight at looking at them. Before God, they were assured, they are beloved.

At times, however, the orchestration of mass vulnerability could also stir feelings or memories with damaging results. One Christian celebrity recalled the experience of watching a fellow speaker elicit raw vulnerability from hundreds of women without the skills or experience to bring them any resolution. They were left with their own wounds without sutures. "It was like terrible therapy," she recalled.[96] The dangers of this sort of exposure had been learned earlier by tabloid television, where participants were sometimes driven to violence or psychological damage by their experience on these programs. An experienced woman in the conference circuit must know how to tap into deep emotional wells without letting audiences be drowned in what surfaces.[97] Particularly in the post-1990s heyday of confession, when speakers were encouraged to package and repackage stories of their worst moments for consumption, there was also the lingering concern among speakers about whether these confessional entrepreneurs were properly motivated to rebuild their audiences completely. After all, if every audience member was completely freed from shame, self-doubt, and emotional turmoil, the therapeutic industry of megaministry women would come to a sudden halt.

Pentecostal evangelist Christine Caine, one of the biggest stars of women's ministry, summarized the problem perfectly: "I never wanted to graduate to women's ministry because it is always women's *miseries*, the repetition of the same, sad story again and again: 'I was never loved. I was never whole. I was never . . .' Look, I want women to get *free*. I want women to be saved and renewed and transformed by the power of the Holy Spirit. But is that really what we are positioned to do? If these women are completely set free, will they come back to buy our books? We give them little bits and pieces of truths, but always leave them coming back. We need them to keep coming back."[98]

In fact, the therapeutic industry created an endless market for disclosure within a difficult constellation of constraints. The therapeutic celebrity must give something away, but not too much. Audiences must feel like she has been *seen*, and yet she cannot give away everything, for she is still a role model, an example, and something of a marvel. Jennie Allen, for instance, was an example of someone who tried to move against the grain by attempting to rub away some of the polish of her own conference, describing it as "messy" and "broken." And yet, as she described in her confession, there was almost insurmountable temptation—and likely pressure—to be as impossibly perfect as the event itself. For this reason, women usually "confessed" to almost nothing at all, offering the appearance of vulnerability without the substance. A woman who was a "slave" to eating too much bread or "convicted" of sniping at her husband had surrendered little and gained much.

Those women who found that they were not seen as a Christian Mary Poppins, practically perfect in every way, found themselves without an audience. These women, thrown out on the open market and typically institutionally vulnerable, they could not afford to give away too much. I asked Jeanne, who led the IF:Gathering's public moment of confession, about what it was like to stand in front of hundreds of thousands of people in that moment and choose what to reveal.[99]

"I tried to write from within. I did a personal, private confession time and said, 'Okay, God, I'm going to show all of me, open up, and unzip this. I won't hold anything back.' I could have held my light up for every single one of them, depending on where I was in any given day. I also know that I am at my best when I let others see me and when I choose vulnerability and to go into that place that I want to keep hidden," she said, thoughtfully.

"It must be a hard balance. The confession can't be all that terrible, can it? You can't say: 'I am currently cheating on my husband and you will all be the first to know,'" I replied.

"It's a tricky thing. You don't want to make it too light, because then people will have a false sense that [they] confessed the fullness of their sin and got right with the Lord." The thinness of these women's public confessions threatened to lead others into theological error by allowing them the appearance of confession without the substance of repentance.

"But that is usually the way speakers go," I answered. "They confess to having yelled at their kids in a bank or been too swayed by the opinions of others. I imagine there are a lot of people out there with serious problems who shake their heads at the paltry 'sins' being confessed."

She laughed. "I know! As a communicator, preacher, and teacher, I am always walking the line. I ask myself: 'Just because it's true, is it necessary?' I think it's a helpful question because there's a lot of things I *could* talk about which are true, but they might not be necessary for me to talk about in a sermon."

"Have you ever said too much?" I asked.

"I remember once, in a sermon, I was confessing the depth of my shame around body image. But after the service I had probably three or four women come up to me afterwards and say, 'I would love to help you with some personal training,' or 'I'd love to be your dietician.' And I thought, 'No, no, no. Overshare!' I said too much. I created a situation where the congregation felt like they had to take care of me. The last thing that a leader needs to do is create a sense of responsibility in the audience and make the sheep feel like they need to take care of the shepherd."

"So how do you be vulnerable without being too vulnerable?"

"I could take it one way and never reveal my humanity. Or be the neediest person on the planet and make everyone feel like they need to hear me, fix me, and take care of me. I aim for twenty percent of the story. It's still honest, but I don't always need to tell one hundred percent of everything."

Women must pay for this kind of privacy. Since men typically had their own institution—a church or a parachurch bearing their name—they had multiple staff members who acted as secretaries, assistant pastors, communication directors, and any number of go-betweens. Women, on the other hand, usually had to hire their own lines of defense. In fact, a number of businesses specialized in new female celebrities who could not afford to have full-time staff. They answered E-mail, tweeted, created social media content, organized travel, accompanied the celebrity to events, and acted as event managers so that the talent was not overwhelmed by direct interaction with the criticism and emotional unburdening of the public. There were also professional social media companies to take their content (bible studies, books, and blogs) to create a series of personalized social media posts (on Twitter, Instagram, Facebook) that allowed the woman to seem public without excessive exposure.

Jeanne had chosen to have layers, but layers were difficult to maintain. In the pietistic tradition, the minister hears confession with the mandate to offer comfort and bring about absolution. A full accounting of one's sin must be made to God or perhaps the pastor, but not the church. Communications scholar Mimi White argues that when therapeutic language began to be popular on television, confession became not only a popular topic on television shows, but it also redefined what people expected from a confession. A new series of relationships were forged on television between the one confessing (usually a guest on the program) and his or her listeners. The guest was expected to be an open book, willing to confess to a television audience, and viewers, in turn, became used to watching and weighing in while someone bared their soul.[100] People in the spotlight were deemed to be "trustworthy" and "authentic," simply by these acts of revelation. When the person at the microphone fails to tell all, the question lingers: are they real?

This question became a significant crisis for those balancing the multiple expectations of celebrity—evangelical and therapeutic—with the rise of Christian stars of reality programming. In the last ten years, one of the major pipelines for spiritual superstardom was not exactly the glamor of the silver screen, but the shaky footage of cable networks experimenting with various concepts for reality shows.[101] Some shows, like home renovation programs, expected that the renovations themselves provide enough fodder for drama that the actors themselves did not need to be inherently controversial. But most reality programs, based on the template of *The Real Housewives* franchise, needed the cast to become characters, providing storylines and cliffhangers that garnered ratings and controversy. The creation of reality shows like *Preachers of L.A., Preachers of Atlanta,* and *Preachers of Detroit* demonstrated not only the remarkable parallelism between the high-roller lifestyle of megachurch (usually prosperity) preachers and nouveaux-riche housewives, but the natural friction created by television genres predicated on exposure. The television medium required them to bare all, and yet preachers, by profession, could not come down from every pedestal. Christian leaders, at a very basic level, must be admired to be followed.[102]

The most common pattern of confession centered on tragedies in which the heroine remained the heroine. Megachurch senior pastor (and spiritual advisor to Donald Trump) Paula White trumpeted her transformation from a "messed-up Mississippi girl" in her book, *Deal With It!,* which begins with the calamities that set it all in motion; her childhood had been marred by sexual and physical abuse and her father's suicide.[103] But the premise of her book, her ministry, and her brand is of second chances and new tomorrows. As the dust jacket of her book reads, "Real issues demand real answers. No one understands this better than evangelist and national Christian television host Paula White. In *Deal With It!* Paula shows you how to turn obstacles into stepping stones that lead you to your God-given purpose."[104] Her setbacks can mean your gains.

Paula White Ministries *presents*
2006 Annual Conference
PURSUE THE
Passion

April 13 - April 15, 2006
Tampa, Florida
Register Today: $39.00
www.paulawhite.org

Conference Speakers Include:

PAULA WHITE
JOYCE MEYER
BISHOP NOEL JONES
DARLENE BISHOP
STORMIE OMARTIAN
JUDY JACOBS

...and many more

USF Sun Dome
4202 E. Fowler Ave
Tampa, FL 33620
1.866.99PAULA

Paula

Limited Seating · Don't miss your MOMENT!

Paula White was one of the brightest stars of televangelism in the early 2000s before she and her husband (and co-pastor) Randy divorced. Reprinted with permission from Charisma Media, www.charismamedia.com.

A woman without a platform needs a story. I was teasing a well-known Christian author before an event about all the women in the audience who hoped to be famous. She is an older woman and has seen much of the inner workings of the industry, so I knew she would know a thing or two about the internal competition. "Oh man," she said with a laugh, "these women are just *wishing* they could get a life-threatening disease right now and write about it."[105] She was joking, no question. Nevertheless, she had aptly summarized the economic relationship between heartbreak and success in this industry. Almost every popular Christian speaker, at some point in her life, had a story of walking through fire. The death of a child. An abusive childhood. A critical illness. Unless someone had found fame by relation (a pastor's wife or daughter), it was otherwise nearly impossible to find a niche in the crowded industry of women's ministry. Classic educational qualifications mattered little in a world in which a woman's authority was found by turning her insides out.

Faithfulness, unfortunately, made for boring television, but too much vulnerability threatened to erode what little authority they had accrued. Take, for instance, the allegations of alleged domestic violence in the ministries of "Real Talk Kim," the blonde preacher always seen in a tutu and high heels on *Preachers of Atlanta*, and Juanita Bynum, one of the most popular pentecostal ministers of the early 2000s. Both were beautiful, confident women in the public eye, whose abuse by each of their husbands shocked audiences. But while photos of Juanita's bruised body appeared on the nightly news, Kim publicized her own horrors, weaving it into her own story of rescue and redemption. Juanita would never again be restored to stardom as the untouchable celebrity of black pentecostalism. She had been laid low by her husband, a bishop in his own right and ostensibly her pastor, a tragic end to the multi-million-dollar television event that had been their wedding. Audiences had seen too much. As Marla Frederick observed in *Colored Television*, the difference in fate of white women and their black counterparts, both laying bare their lives, held a racial subtext.[106] The power of African American women in their local churches, as "First Ladies" or "Mothers of the Church," was built on irreproachable respectability as models of black Christian womanhood.[107] There, weakness and vulnerability were not seen as assets but as failures; confessions of failures led to an erosion of their positions. Those who can afford to tarnish their image a little are women who can afford to gamble with their privilege.

As cultural studies scholar Sarah Hagelin observed in her study of vulnerability and femininity in popular culture, vulnerability was an ambivalent category. "Popular culture consistently and relentlessly

Juanita Bynum was famous for her story of sexual brokenness redeemed by a star-studded wedding, until her abuse led to her downfall. Reprinted with permission from Charisma Media, www.charismamedia.com.

imagines vulnerability as female . . . but we don't *just* construct vulnerability as female; we construct it as white and female."[108] As the case of Juanita Bynum shows us, black women first have to be understood as vulnerable, rather than sexually deviant, for the category if they are to successfully solicit protection and sympathy.[109] This was the case for one African American speaker I interviewed who had been invited to speak on Christian television but had been left stranded at the airport by male television staffers who did not think it appropriate to be alone in the car with her. For all the rhetoric of women needing to be protected and sheltered by men, ultimately these policies protected the reputations of white men over the dangers of a single black woman getting into a stranger's car.[110] When the separation of men and women into separate spheres charged each situation with a sexual connotation, suspicions about the true nature of women, especially black women, surfaced. The use of power-through-weakness raised questions about the implicit and explicit racial dynamics that such rhetoric upheld.

LEADING FROM BELOW

As we have seen, the language of vulnerability in Christian megaministry was both a powerful tool for women and a weapon used against them. It could win them tremendous goodwill as it bolstered a sense of likable authenticity, or it could risk making women look deviant. It might look like strength in baring all or a confirmation that women were unfit to lead. Women who relied a great deal on the power of vulnerability often found that it was difficult to always lead from a position of abasement.

Any professional confessor knew she was striking a bargain that would cost her, for she lived in an echo chamber of her own heartbreak. Her platform was built on her own experiences, the stories of tragedy that brought her spiritual lessons to share. No matter how traumatic and exhausting, she would have to become accustomed to her own voice saying the words: "I was afraid for my life"; "I held him until his breath slowed and stopped"; "I never thought I would ever feel love again." She must live in the moment that made her famous.

That moment, however painful, could also be incredibly lucrative. The most successful careers capitalized on those rhythms of want and plenty, transforming the course of a human life into a long string of revelations. I once joked with an ambitious young speaker about how many tragedies she could hope for in her career, and she answered quickly, without irony: "Four."

I repeated that story a number of times in interviews with women who specialized in this kind of tell-all genre, and they shared a common reaction: they winced and then laughed as they started to agree with the math. A popular pentecostal evangelist, who asked not to be named, offered the most helpful analysis: "Well, the first book can talk about a wild life before conversion. Then there is the initial crisis book where something has gone terribly wrong. Then there is a deepening in faith book where the problem is pretty small by comparison, but it serves as a teaching tool. And then, if you are still in ministry by mid-life, there is always a curveball that you can write about. Like an illness or a marital problem. That amounts to a crisis in your 20s, 30s, 40s, and 50s."[111]

Sixty-year-old Sheila Walsh had enjoyed a golden career of revelations. She was once a co-host for *The 700 Club*, host of *Heart to Heart with Sheila Walsh* on the Family Channel, and a well-known contemporary Christian music singer, but she was better known to audiences for what she had suffered. In 1996, Sheila's book *Honestly* told the story of her battle against depression and her institutionalization in a psychiatric hospital, an account that became popular again a decade later with Saddleback's renewal of the church's interest in mental health. In each subsequent book, a new revelation appeared with an equally therapeutic justification. In 2016, she unveiled her new book, *The Longing in Me*, about her divorce twenty-five years earlier, telling her interviewer that "unless you understand your history, you're destined to repeat it."[112] The book became a way to break her own patterns, but it is also sold as a way for readers to break theirs. As the promotional preface reads: "You vowed you'd never repeat the same mistakes—yet you find yourself right where you started . . . *The Longing in Me* will help you understand that your cravings are not the problem. It's where they lead you that makes all the difference."[113] The book was sold in a hardcover, E-book, audiobook, and a DVD and paperback study guide format for large group use. That confessional exchange—those blurry lines between Sheila's own healing and the reader's own—was best explained by historian Kathryn Lofton, who shows how the confessor "receives blessings only after she has exposed the extremity of her need to a viewing audience."[114] The mass confessions of women's ministry were spectacles of vulnerability disguised as uncomplicated transformations.

The act of revelation could be costly indeed. I recently spoke with September Vaudrey, an author and teacher for Willow Creek Community Church, whose book, *The Colors of Goodbye*, was a meditation on grief after the death of her daughter. Over the course of her career in ministry, she had been both the confessor and the counselor, telling and hearing painful stories of both loss and shame, and she found there was a marked difference between pain and shame: "I can talk about losing Katie now, and while it is always painful to recall the death of my daughter, it doesn't cost me too much personally because I had nothing to do with her death. She died of natural causes and I am more or less the good guy in that story. I have other stories where I am not the good guy. I've hurt those I love, and those stories are physically exhausting to tell. Afterward, I could come home and sleep for 12 hours."[115] And while September had done the difficult work of therapy and healing in the wake of her grief, those speakers who fail to do that work often find their story lives in the eternal present. I spoke briefly with a well-known expert on child loss who, because of her own experience of loss, simply did not feel emotionally well enough to be interviewed, even about stories she had told again and again. She struggled to create enough time between events to allow the past to be the past.

For others, perhaps only for a time, the act of public confession could be freeing. "It's the only way I know how to process," said one speaker to me. "I just have to get it out there and not let it take over my life."[116] She made her confession into a reminder that she was liberated from her past. Whether costly to the teller or not, the story was a portal. It transported readers into the hearts and minds of those willing to lay things bare. In her first book, Kay Warren revealed secrets of her own molestation and her subsequent sexual experimentation. The stories were painful, layered, and difficult to tidy up for delicate audiences. "Why am I telling you all of this?" she asked her readers, anticipating their shock. "Because acknowledging secrets—not just the secret sins done *to me* but the secret sins done *by me*—allows me to identify with others who have fallen into the same traps."[117] In other words, she had built a bridge. And thousands upon thousands would use it to cross over.

Chapter Five

THE BEAUTY

You are altogether beautiful, my darling; there is no flaw in you.
—Song of Songs 4:7[1]

When Karen Clark filled in at the last minute as the guest on her sister Dorinda's weekly television show, the two women couldn't help joking about all the effort it took to make them camera ready.[2] Now in their late fifties, they had been performing together since they were girls as part of the legendary gospel group "The Clark Sisters" before embarking on solo careers that had brought them a lifetime of fame and seven Grammy Awards between them.

"She got all made up and everything," exclaimed Dorinda admiringly. "You all want to do all this, you want to be in the limelight, but you don't know what it takes . . ."

"They don't know," echoed Karen.

"You got to get the right makeup on!"

"I didn't want to call my makeup artist at the last minute, so I tried to remember how he does it," said Karen with a smile, "I didn't do a bad job, did I?" She patted her makeup lightly, batting her fake eyelashes and pretending to primp her long strawberry hair. Karen and Dorinda shared a long laugh as they pointed at each other's flawless makeup.

"We thank God for our makeup artists," said Dorinda. "They keep us looking good, right?"

"People say we have natural beauty, but that's all because of my mom, Dr. Mattie Moss-Clark." Their mother had been a pioneering choir director in the largest African American denomination, and the founder of the vocal group that had launched her daughters' careers. "She was beautiful," continued Karen, "but it's her fault that vanity got a hold of us." The crowd laughed with them as Karen said with mock seriousness: "But we're representing *Jesus*."

"We do!" exclaimed Dorinda, rushing in to support Karen's joke with a Bible verse. "For it says that 'He will beautify the meek with salvation.'[3] So, thank you Father. And we thank God for our mom for teaching us the importance, in this industry, of keeping an image."

"That's so important now," said Karen, "When you hit that screen you don't forget who you're representing. You're representing Christ."

The two went on to discuss how Karen's fitted leather dress came from her gospel-singing daughter's plus-sized clothing line, Eleven60, inspired by Dorinda's own forays into fashion with her online collection of shiny wrap dresses, hitting modestly below the knee to satisfy any churchgoing audience. It was one of those rarefied conversations about success that audiences cheered but cannot have lived. They laughed about how they were in the same Grammy Award category that year with the ease of two middle-aged women who looked a decade younger with smooth skin and slim figures zipped into richly embellished dresses. As both singers and evangelists, they knew how to bring Hollywood to church.

It is important to consider why physical attractiveness should have become an issue in megaministry. As we will see, part of the answer lay in the evangelical subculture's slow decision to shed its notions of separation and rearguard resistance to the wider world's folkways and mores. No longer would its media personalities be easily identifiable by obsolete fashions and outdated signals of modesty in length of skirts and sleeves; no more would towering hairdos and brassy makeup be markers of coquettish righteousness. As the production value of Sunday worship, Christian music, and televangelism increased over the course of the 1980s and 1990s, evangelical leaders would come to closely resemble those of secular television.

But the change in visual signals applied much more to women in ministry than to men. For males, the shift came largely in the form of better-tailored suits than previous generations had worn: preposterous comb-overs and impressive bellies would never keep men from religious stardom. As the secular marketplace was allowed to dictate how women presented themselves, beauty would come to play a defining role both in the content of their messages and in how they were presented. A woman's body was more than a showpiece—we will see that it became a model of holy desire. Those who could comply with the new towering standards of beauty prospered, while those who could not, perhaps because of age, body shape, sexuality, or marital status, struggled to find a market for their unseen virtues.

THE SPECTER OF SECOND-WAVE FEMINISM

The late twentieth-century evangelical theological backlash against feminism had been swift and fierce, but what was perhaps as telling was how long it lingered. Years after second-wave feminism adopted a conciliatory tone toward women in the workplace *and* the home, the lessons about gendered presentation learned in the fight against the Equal Rights Amendment still seemed to be in effect. Media workshops showed women how to present themselves in front of a crowd, keeping a pleasant smile, upright posture, and covered knees with legs crossed at the ankle. If women were fortunate enough to represent anti-feminism on television, the advice was even more straightforward: "Reduce. Go on diet. TV adds 10 lbs."[4] The cause of the homemaker was entwined with a dainty femininity.

One of the primary evangelical objections to feminism was that it eroded the biological distinctions between men and women ("the male to call forth, to lead, initiate and rule, and the female to respond, follow, adapt and submit," summarized Elisabeth Elliot), and so conservative Christian leaders called on both sexes to advertise their differences.[5] At times, the accusatory gaze fell on men. The lingering influence of the American counterculture and its iconic long-haired hippies had made the length of men's hair into an obsession.[6] Chuck Smith built his little church of Calvary Chapel into one of southern California's most influential religious associations—with over a thousand churches, including three dozen megachurches[7]—and an early hub of the long-haired "Jesus People"; but he admitted that his first reaction was more in step with the prevailing Pentecostal opinion of the day: "My original thought was 'Why don't they cut their hair and get a job and live a decent life?'"[8] Conservative Christians liked to see their men with short hair and clean-shaven, which, as the 1970s wore on, translated into additional angst over creeping sideburns.

The range of critique for women was much more far reaching. There was always the matter of hair length, because, as 1 Corinthians 11:15

stated, "If a woman has long hair, it is a glory to her: for her hair is given her for a covering." And while uncut hair was typically a marker of by-gone Holiness standards, long hair was still implicitly preferred across denominational traditions. There were open attempts to police women's tresses in books like *Women's Hair: The Long and Short of It,*[9] but, in practice, these were delicate matters better suited to being modeled than preached. In the 2010s, evangelical and pentecostal speakers on the circuit rarely had short hair, in part because of the suggestion of lesbianism. "A woman with short hair is going to keep people guessing," said one speaker who asked not to be named.[10] Ambiguous sexuality was undoubtedly bad for business, so most women liked to leave little doubt that they were straight. Though lacking a scriptural prescription, hats were, in some circles, a weighty matter of theology, tradition, and decorum. Southern Baptist matriarch Dorothy Patterson gloried in her husband's authority by insisting on wearing hats in church as a sign of her deference, while neo-pentecostal black women in the 1990s removed theirs to show their church was casting off the strictures of denominationalism.[11]

Women's bodies were both canvases of self-expression and objects of critical projection. More traditional megachurches complained about their pastors' wives wearing pants (especially jeans) and sleeveless shirts. "I remember the first Sunday a man came up to me to complain about my pants," remembered Donna Miller, the pastor's wife of a Presbyterian megachurch. "I just smiled at him and said: 'Thanks! Don't you like them?'"[12] Cleavage and exposed legs were the primary targets of accusations of impropriety, followed by the tightness of clothing and precisely how it fit. A gaping button or a shifting slit in the side of a skirt could make all the difference in whether an outfit was deemed "decent." One California Baptist megachurch simply made it a rule that any woman on stage would need to ensure that her dress came down to her knees. Partially clothed women were Jezebels who made God's house into a "flesh show."[13] "If we don't have everything covered just right [men] aren't going to be thinking about the wonderful grace of Jesus. Some of you men want to help me with this tonight?" Pastor Paul Chappell said, cupping his hand to his ear to solicit a big "AMEN!" from men in the crowd.[14] However, even if their clothing was pitch perfect, women in megaministry often heard complaints about whether it was fashionable or even varied enough. The leader of the largest women's parachurch ministry in the country, Mandy Arioto, admitted that she received audience complaints if she happened to wear the same outfit for two events in a row.[15]

There was, of course, already a longstanding dress code in church tradition. Since the early church, robes have been used as the uniform of the ministerial class, their shapeless swaths diminishing the individuality and sexuality of the priest or pastor. These highly decorative clothes identified not only the Protestant, Catholic, or Orthodox tradition to which they belong, but the status of the person wearing them. Indeed, some early twentieth-century female leaders had dressed in wide, formless robes, for a "sexless" body evoked both purity and power.[16] A woman in robes may bow low to the church as a sexless figure but stands high on the platform in glory. The few women who lead megachurches as senior pastors almost universally buck the national trend of informal dress and slip on churchly vestments, sometimes in fitted preaching jackets or robes with embroidered stoles slung over their shoulders and swaying with each movement. Dr. Cynthia Hale, senior pastor and founder of the two-thousand-member Cathedral of Hope in Decatur, Georgia, was one of them. She cut an imposing figure at six feet fall, her short silver hair always as shiny as her sleek preaching jacket and matching skirt. She had the firm voice and smile of a woman accustomed to strength in leadership: as one of two African American women in the United States leading a megachurch she had founded (rather than inheriting it from her husband), she made her own rules. Her Sunday suits were not quite vestments, and yet they were usually a nod to the Disciples of Christ denomination she belonged to, with a feminine twist. However, a woman in a robe was still a rare sight. Even if a husband and wife co-pastor team had the same education, there has not yet been a famous pair who dared to wear matching clerical collars—it would imply equality. Women in robes intuited that their bodies had become representations of spiritual authority in flowing garments stitched with gleaming thread, an authority so uncommon that few would even recognize it outright on a woman. One associate pastor at an Episcopalian church relayed to me her chagrin at accidentally spilling wax on her outrageously expensive robe. She took it to the dry cleaner. When she went to pick it up, the worker at the cash register slid the robe back over the counter and looked deeply into her eyes. "Just so you know," said the cleaner, "this is *not* a pretty dress."[17]

The culture of display that developed in evangelical and pentecostal megachurches found expression on the bodies of its leading ladies. Standards of beauty, as a fragile construct of economy, theology, and media, were also declarations. But these declarations were not precisely the same as the cutting edge trends of broader American culture. Evangelicals and pentecostals saw themselves as a separated people, aware of (but not in thrall to) the larger society in which they were immersed. Aesthetic shibboleths—hair, jewelry, dress style—would remain a beat or two behind contemporary fashion, much as they lagged in imitating other cultural trends.[18] Instead of *The Tonight Show* there was *The 700 Club*, and there was a Christian crooner like Michael W. Smith for every soft rocker like Michael Bolton. The heavy costuming of Christian televangelism was a perfect barometer of trends that were new to Christians but dated to the mainstream. Tammy Faye Bakker's makeup was the stuff of *Saturday Night Live* parody; a marketer had manufactured T-shirts with a smeared face imprint—like a cosmetological Shroud of Turin— with the caption "I Just Ran Into Tammy Faye at the Mall." (For the vulnerability she embodied and her allegiance to massive fake eyelashes she would later become an unexpected icon in the gay community and a drag favorite.)[19] Jan Crouch at the Trinity Broadcasting Network was mercilessly mocked as a rather fragile figure under her towering blonde, pink, and purple wigs.[20] Trendiness was not nearly as important to the evangelical and pentecostal subcultures in the 1970s and 1980s as femininity, which was not only a fashion statement but an alternative sexual ethic.

These standards of beauty were also declarations of triumph: by putting outwardly beautiful women on stage, or in front of the camera, or on a magazine cover, evangelicals and pentecostals were asserting that theirs was a faith for successful people. A subtext of Jan and Tammy's celebration of materialism was also a parallel story of pentecostalism's rising economic status and newfound cultural capital. As other studies of pentecostalism and gender have concluded, middle-class identity was closely tied to new beauty standards and a loosening of restrictions on women's dress.[21] The gorgeous wives of megachurch pastors were not simply trophy wives, they were trophies that the entire movement proudly put on display. Little wonder, then, that megaministries made celebrities out of people who could teach young girls how to use their beauty as a "witness" and that this theologically distinct beauty culture became a significant part of the "family values" debate.[22]

MISS AMERICA

Beauty had long been a ticket into Christian ministry for American women. The first Miss America contestant to ever evangelize from the platform, Vonda Kay Van Dyke, became an immediate star with her sweet and proper advice for Christian teens in books like *Dear Vonda Kay* (1967). She was named Outstanding Christian Witness of the Year by Youth for Christ and even appeared at Billy Graham crusades, with and without her signature comedy sidekick, ventriloquist dummy Kurly Q. Her book *That Girl in Your Mirror* sold a million copies for its combination of beauty tips and scriptural tidbits with lessons encouraging girls that "with God's light and His guiding hand" girls would climb to new "heights of beauty . . . she'll possess that inner sparkle that only Christ can give."[23] It was a mixed message, but a powerful one: true beauty was found on the inside, but it needed to be polished from the outside.

Most celebrity-driven beauty manuals did not veer far from the tropes of the 1978 classic *The Inside-Out Beauty Book*, which promised that "every woman can be a lovely, lovable, and loving person and thereby, give genuine glory to the Creator."[24] Perhaps the most famous champion for beauty during the formative years of women's ministries was Joanne Wallace, the fashion editor for *Virtue* magazine. The former Mrs. Oregon titleholder founded her own company, Image Improvement Inc., and hosted her own syndicated television program to help Christian women choose between styles like "The Enchantress" and "The All-American Natural."[25] Forays into fashion became such a standard part of women's ministries that a specialty market for teenage girls developed. Focus on the Family's magazine for teenage girls, *BRIO*, had its own Miss Oklahoma runner-up as their beauty editor, who also trademarked workshops called B.A.B.E.: Beautiful, Accepted, Blessed, Eternally Significant®.[26]

Miss America 1965, Vonda Kay Van Dyke, was famous for her ventriloquism and her Christian advice manuals. Image courtesy of Tempe History Museum.

Today's Christian

W╱man

July/August 1995

Miss America
**Heather
Whitestone's**
Dream Come True
page 26

**What Your
Husband
Really Wants**

**Why Being Busy
Isn't So Bad**

One Woman's Story:
**"My Sexual Past
Plagued My
Marriage"**

**TCW Readers'
Very Best
Vacations!**

$3.50

Heather Whitestone, Miss America 1995, became the first deaf
winner of the pageant and a popular Christian evangelist.
Reprinted with permission from *Christianity Today*, www
.christianitytoday.com.

Beauty queens became a constant fixture behind Christian television's
news anchor desks. Miss America Cheryl Prewitt was the first pentecostal winner of the pageant in 1980, touring the country with her story of
her miraculous recovery from a car accident. She and her sister-in-law
Lindsay Roberts (the raven-haired daughter-in-law of Oral Roberts)
made a gorgeous duo as co-hosts of their own television program and
founders of their own women's ministry.[27] Women were only reluctantly
being welcomed to mainstream news broadcasting by the late 1970s, but
Christian television networks quickly understood the importance of a

well-placed beauty reciting the headlines. Miss Wisconsin Terry Meewsen, who won the crown in 1973, soon became a regular co-host on *The 700 Club*, offering, as she put it, "a softer, more sensitive view of the issues. And as a mother of four children, I will bring a 'mom's' perspective that I think many in our audience will appreciate."[28] Because Dede Robertson, Pat's wife, had largely remained in administrative roles behind the scenes at the Christian Broadcasting Network, the role of co-host stayed open to many a woman with a pretty face and a quick wit. The warm presence of Danuta Soderman, the former co-host of *Sun Up San Diego,* was an audience favorite, but she left suddenly when Pat Robertson's run for the American presidency in 1988 made the show's political agenda overwhelming for her.[29] The Scottish songbird Sheila Walsh, whom Pat called his "naughty daughter" for her spitfire personality, would later take her place as co-host.[30]

Even as beauty pageants fell in and out of fashion over the decades, beauty queens with a Christian message could almost always find their place on the women's circuit as flawless faces and trained speakers with an eclectic set of skills. Jessica Haas received top billing at "PINK IMPACT," one of largest women's conferences of 2017, as "the first speed painter in the history of the Miss Tennessee to ever win the talent portion of a beauty contest by painting the face of Jesus Christ in only 90 seconds upside down."[31] In reality, women on the circuit were more likely to relate to Saddleback's Kay Warren's frank assessment of her own assets: "I held out hope for a while that I would turn into a gorgeous Miss America type . . . . While no one has told me I'm ugly, I've never walked into a room and heard audible gasps from those present who are stunned by my beauty! I'm just average."[32] Those who had the raw material put it to their advantage, and those who didn't still knew its power. Beauty was its own currency.

ON POINT

Another church might have found it difficult to top the explosion of confetti on the megachurch mainstage that concluded the 2016 Divine Women's Conference, but with $41 million in annual revenue, Free Chapel in Gainesville, Georgia, could afford to try.[33] The next year's

conference adopted the theme "All Things Beautiful" in keeping with
Senior Pastor Jentezen Franklin's soft prosperity theology that reflected
an unselfconscious ease with the American fashion industry.[34] The
advertisement showed only a model's taut, unsmiling face. The promotional video was filmed like an advertisement for a teen clothing label
like Abercrombie and Fitch, with young women capering about on a
southern California beach or staring at the camera as if daring to be
defied. In one shot, a willowy woman with platinum blonde hair stands
under a light shower of white feathers, her nose crinkled in delight,
before she pretends to notice the camera for the first time and strikes a
girlish pose. The conference was social media gold, a perfect cluster of
pre-packaged flawless images to share online with friends, as well as
staged mini-backdrops at the event itself, set up to ensure an impeccable selfie. Women attending the conference could linger at the boutique
in the lobby to try on samples or even ask a conference speaker herself
for fashion tips since, last year, style guru and pastor's wife Taylor Madu
had addressed the crowd.[35] Every detail from the black cotton T-shirts
reading "Simply Divine" to the personal styling of organizers Cherise
and Caressa Franklin, the wife and daughter of the megachurch's senior
pastor, was perfectly in tune with American consumer culture. One
look at the women of megaministry and audiences might conclude that
popular Christianity was mainstream at last.

By the 2010s, the largest women's ministries were dazzling displays
of commercial beauty. From the quality of the social media marketing
to the decorations in the lobby to the pricy dress and statement necklace of the megachurch wife on stage, beauty was one of the most
important markers of success. There was the clean, modern styling of
the Propel Women organization, which targeted audiences of young professionals to rethink their careers as a spiritual vocation with a brand
similar to the unfussy cool of a Madewell clothing line. The Propel
Conversation Series Curriculum about women in leadership came in a
magazine format dominated by large, lush photographs of models
headed to work, their long hair partially obscuring their faces and their
artsy vibe drawing the reader's eye to their apparel.[36] Part of the stunning success of the IF:Gathering was its ability to seamlessly integrate
their aesthetic and products with the trends of the educated, affluent
women who felt most at home with bohemian lifestyle brands like An-

thropologie (or even the Christian look-alike store called "Altar'd State").[37] At their annual conferences there were little flourishes here and there that made the attendees feel as if they were being invited into an experience that had been "curated," one of the great marketing buzz-words of the era. Instead of a bare lobby at the IF:Gathering or MOM-CON, there were white peonies in mason jars on little tables set out for women to gather around as they set down their coffees, and slabs of wood with gorgeous cursive that advertised a new product line or brought a little smile with a *bon mot*.

Even the Abundance Conference put on by LifeWay was the peak of Southern Baptist women's chic with thirty-five hundred middle-aged women sporting crisp bobs, floral shirts, and white jeans and lugging highlighted Bibles around in their oversized Vera Bradley handbags. The 2016 Abundance Conference had all the staples of a typical women's ministry event: a lobby decorated like a delicate English garden with florals splashed on every handout and product; hand-drawn Bible verses on large signs covered in faint gold leaf; a rough brown paper on a table for attendees to write their prayers on; a staged photo area with a colossal photo frame for participants to stick their heads through and take a photograph; and a jumbotron scrolling through the glossy promotional photos of the event speakers, Lisa Harper, Lysa TerKeurst, Annie Downs, and music by Natalie Grant and Christy Nockels.[38] The conference program left room for participants to scribble down the takeaways from each session, read though little excerpts of upcoming books, consider a Caribbean cruise with LifeWay authors, purchase at-home access to the upcoming Beth Moore and Priscilla Shirer simulcasts, or tear off the attached bookmark that doubled as an advertisement for Lisa Harper's bible study series on the Gospel of Mark. It was a marketplace of delights.

Men's conferences, by comparison, were bare by design. Long after the men's movements of the mid-1990s like Promise Keepers had swept through American auditoriums, the men's megachurch conferences of the new millennium seemed a little tired, alternately corporate or athletic or military in tone.[39] When men stormed the stage of LifeWay's Annual Conference in 2016, it was called THE MAIN EVENT. Its promotional video was a highlight reel of thick-necked males in suits and sports jerseys—athletes, entrepreneurs, leadership consultants, and senior pastors—and a loud voiceover calling above a strong bass beat for the "masculine heart" to "charge after the mission of advancing the Kingdom of God."[40] The year before had featured Tony Evans (Priscilla Shirer's dad and megachurch pastor), former Clemson football coach Tommy Bowden, and the author of *The Dude's Guide to Manhood*. The women's event had chosen instead to advertise the faces of its speakers as Polaroids clipped to a laundry line and flapping in the breeze. The soft beauty of Christian women's "new domestic"[41] atmosphere placed them much more squarely in line with American popular culture and its burgeoning market for Christian lifestyle products.

During the downturn of the Great Recession, the marketplace became dominated by the maker-culture of millennials, a move toward craftsmanship and art that could be seen in everything from the rise of home breweries to the omnipresence of fedoras and lumberjack beards on male twenty- and thirty-somethings. The hipster was now one of the fashion industry's most coveted consumers, and, with independent online crafting sites like Etsy, the words "handmade" and "vintage" suddenly had economic traction. This (typically white) cultural love affair with producer lifestyles like farming and woodworking, as we discussed in Chapter Two, made the homemaker and her domestic craftsmanship into a lauded figure. Women like Lisa Leonard, Emily Ley, and Jessica Honneger were craftswomen-turned-gurus with spiritual insights interwoven with elaborate product lines of jewelry, planners, and clothing.[42]

The home was a place of re-enchantment once more. Readers identified with Ann Voskamp, for instance, because she was known as a homeschooling mother and farmer's wife from Ontario—"My name's plain & simple Ann, without even the fanciful 'e.'"[43] There were photos of plates heaped with food at a farm table or a hand skimming over the top of golden grain. These Christian blogs were an important stepping stone for many to gain a wider audience (a phenomenon that has since tapered) because the format was ideal for the commercialization of homespun beauty—a well-photographed house and kids could do the trick. HGTV's *My Big Family Renovation* made evangelical Jen Hatmaker into a reality show favorite,[44] forging the connection between home remodeling, evangelical family values, and reality television that would later make Chip and Joanna Gaines into stars for renovating small town America homes on HGTV's *Fixer Upper*. It was only a matter of time before Jen

Jen Hatmaker in her trademark oversized earrings became a popular evangelical author and speaker, known for her dry humor and approachable evangelism. Copyright© 2018 Religion News Service LLC. Republished with permission of Religion News Service LLC, all rights reserved.

launched her own line of fashion and home décor products through the Christian company Glory Haus, which included her characteristic massive earrings, a distressed baseball cap that read "Bless This Mess," and a print reading "Love God, Love People, The End."[45] Meanwhile, Chip and Joanna opened a vast store in the heart of downtown Waco called Magnolia Market and an exclusive line of "mini-shops" inside Target stores across the country, both peddling their line of home goods.[46] There was money to be made in embodying the Christian home.

Social media and new technology were revolutionizing the ways that everyday people visually narrated their everyday lives, producing not only a "selfie" generation but also eager entrepreneurs who knew how to put these tools to use in building their own brands. It was easier than ever to flood the media with manipulated images of blemish-free faces, carefully angled bodies, leisurely experiences in a domestic setting.

Though the disconnect between reality and depictions of reality only grew, the expectation of perfection in women in megaministry was growing too. Every blog post or newsletter had to have an accompanying inspirational photo with stylized script or a sweet moment first captured and then captioned. A peek at author Ann Voskamp's popular weekly blog and E-newsletter shows the dominance of high-definition photography in capturing the essence of her brand.[47] Tragedy and inspiration alike were displayed for maximal emotional impact. The staged nature of their homes and lives was ripe for YouTube satires like "Christian Girl Instagram: 101 Tips & Tricks to Get More Likes on Your Devotional Photos," which gained a million views for faux-helpful recommendations on how to photograph a Bible, coffee cup, and prayer journal while showing off a purity ring. "Do you spend hours framing the perfect picture without the payoff of people knowing how spiritual you are on the Internet?" asked the narrator.[48]

Finding authors and speakers who were not too caught up in what it took to become famous was the kind of problem that kept Phil and Debbie Waldrep on their toes. The husband and wife team behind the Women of Joy tour, among others, knew how difficult it was for all parties involved to stay commercially viable without becoming superficial. Their conferences had hosted everyone from President George W. Bush to television commentator Gretchen Carlson, as well as the brightest stars of the evangelical circuit, and what they concluded was simple: in a contest between the business side and the spiritual side of the conference industry, the spiritual side must win. It was, however, a complicated calculus. They worked hard to ensure that the "wow" factor of a celebrity face could be matched by content focused on the pressing needs of the audience.

"We feel like we know our audiences," Debbie told me while we sat backstage at a Women of Joy conference.[49] "We read the prayer cards that come in and make support counselors available, and what they are going through is heartbreaking. Broken marriages. Spousal abuse. Drug addiction. Struggling children. This is an important weekend for them, and we need to find speakers who can really connect with their issues."

"Sometimes we can find a speaker with an amazing faith," added Phil, "but everything about her life seems too perfect. She has a perfect husband, a perfect marriage, and she . . ." He paused tactfully.

"She's a supermodel," I piped in.

"Exactly," he said. "Frankly, people don't want to hear from someone who seems perfect."

It was a double-edged sword. The hyperfemininity of modern Christian women's culture had created an appetite for the impeccable staging of private lives. But for women, perfection would always come at the cost of that most precious commodity: the common touch.

PERFECTION

Victoria Osteen's Fall Fashion Extravaganza was a star-studded annual event. Gone were the days of amateur fashion shows with church ladies, pinking at the ears, filing up and down an aisle between folding chairs filled with friends and acquaintances. Instead there were stylists and producers, bright lights and fashion bloggers scribbling their reviews. Local celebrities—news anchors, socialites, and even Victoria's daughter Alexandra—joined professional models on the runway in clothing provided by Dillard's department store, and attendees shopped for fashions they saw at the pop-up marketplace of clothing, shoes, and handbags, outside the sanctuary. The parade of dipping necklines and bare legs exposed by flirty fall dresses and sequined gowns remade the Lakewood Church's hallowed spaces into a lightly sanctified equivalent of New York Fashion Week catering to churchgoing women looking for a little glamour. And as Victoria hosted the event in a splashy black dress and stiletto boots, she looked every bit as effortlessly stylish and willowy as the models stalking the catwalk.

Pentecostal success stories used to begin with a tale of hardship. Oral Roberts, A. A. Allen, Jack Coe, Gordon Lindsay, and even Jim and Tammy Faye Bakker had childhood tales of poverty and sometimes illness that brought a teary smile from audiences. Foursquare founder Aimee Semple McPherson liked to remind the crowds how she had slept in tents on the side of the road with her two children to support her fledgling ministry. However, Joel and Victoria Osteen, second-generation megachurch leaders and inheritors of their spiritual kingdom, were the picture of comfort. Almost always pictured tucked into the crook of her husband Joel's arm, Victoria had no dramatic story of healing, nor did she (like her mother-in-law) boast that she had facilitated the healing of others. There was barely tamed ambition stirring under her stories of asking Joel to envision living in a bigger house or learning to speak in front of the Lakewood crowds.[50] She and Joel toyed with the theme of Victoria's appetite for the finer things in their multi-city tours, "A Night of Hope." Joel regularly told the story of their chance meeting, her sophistication and beauty as a young woman working in her father's luxury watch shop, and his attempts to impress her by taking her to a Houston Rockets game at the very arena that their church now called home. His descriptions of her always included a bit of a nod to her Hollywood looks, her own "Victoria's Secret" after the red-hot lingerie company, and then the lights faded fast on the audience laughing at Joel's final punchline: "And she's been taking my money ever since."[51] While she may be touted as a co-pastor, partner, and spiritual powerhouse, audiences also knew her as the desirable belle with an eye on his wallet.

It was a tribute to Victoria's prosperity theology that she demanded more and refused to admit failure, for the movement had sharp words for those who failed to master their minds. The theological tradition with the greatest emphasis on physical beauty was undoubtedly the prosperity gospel, and its strong influence on 40 percent of megachurches with over ten thousand members gave megaministry much of its reputation for setting the entertainment industry's standards of beauty. Joyce Meyer, its most famous televangelist, did not mind admitting to ABC News that she had had a facelift, and men like Ron Carpenter and the late Eddie Long loved to show off their bulging muscles built at their megachurches' own gyms.[52] It was a faith meant to be read onto a believer's perfect body and life. As a result, Victoria's book, *Love Your Life,* had none of the harried qualities of women's Christian everyday-fulfillment literature. There were stories of letting go of a cup of tea to hug her nephew or being frustrated when her children changed out their Easter clothes before the official photo was taken, but, overall, her authorial voice was distant and observational.[53] She chose to be the never-breathless encourager who pointed the way, refusing to master the great juggling act of female celebrity—that double act of perfection and relatability.

Despite the power of the vulnerability narrative we discussed in the previous chapter, the women of megaministry rarely allowed the calls for "authenticity" to filter down to their physical appearance. Its importance was written into the titles of women's ministries with a long list of

It's Time to Change Your Mind

Based on the One-Million-Copy Bestseller

Battlefield of the mind

DEVOTIONAL
100 Insights That Will Change the Way You Think

JOYCE MEYER

In *Battlefield of the Mind,* Joyce Meyer encourages you to **take control of your negative thoughts** and live a more empowered and fruitful life in God. Now, in this 100-day devotional filled with Scripture and prayers, she gives you a **day-to-day guide to achieve your goals.**

"Meyer's messages cross all boundaries and attract people from all denominations, genders, races and income levels."

—Kimberly Hayes Taylor, *Detroit News*

Available in hardcover
Visit our Web site at www.twbookmark.com

WARNER *Faith*
Time Warner Book Group

Joyce Meyer has been open about having a facelift, saying "I want to look my best for God." Reprinted with permission from Charisma Media, www .charismamedia.com.

acronyms like B.A.B.E. or the endless stream of Sunday morning Twitter hashtags like #churchfashion, #Sundayfashion, and #churchflow to showcase the sanctuary aisles as the new catwalks. Shoes were a constant source of empowering metaphors, from Seattle co-pastor Wendy Treat's *Shoes Wisely: Choosing the Right Shoe For Every Occasion* to a star of *Preachers of Atlanta* ministry's, *Conquering Hell in High Heels.*[54] The sartorial choices of megaministry wives were even deemed newsworthy. The city of Charlotte's local media gushed about how First Lady Kimberly Alexander's style was "current, classy, conservative, yet creative," with advice about how a great pair of boots completed a look. She was shown in a white wrap coat, the collar popped around her smiling face.[55] Others tucked beauty into their own biographies. Lady Kimberly McKissick, billed as a "beauty enthusiast," penned her provocatively titled first book, *The Joy Spot*, promising to assist fellow first ladies in learning their "wifely role" with lessons drawn from her experiences motivating women at the Mary Kay cosmetics company.

Lady Crisette Ellis, whose husband Charles was both a megachurch pastor and the presiding prelate of the Pentecostal Assemblies of the World (PAW) denomination, set the standard for other beauty moguls. She was the mother to his daughter Kiera and his namesake, Charles IV, and dutiful director of their women's ministry called "Powerful Women of Purpose" at their eight-thousand-member church. But she made beauty into a commercial specialty too as a much-lauded Mary Kay cosmetics saleswoman who had already won five of their iconic pink Cadillacs and founded her own lifestyle brand, "Affirmations by Crisette."[56] Her blog published her monthly fitness goals, so readers were informed that she wanted to lose five pounds; she also promoted her own products with positive declarations emblazoned on them.[57] As her website explained, "She is a true believer that life and death are in the power of the tongue and what you say will either enable you to be victorious or will hinder you from reaching your full potential." Or, as one of her T-shirts summarized it: "Speak It. Believe It. Work It. Become It."[58] Her brand expanded to include children's books centered on practicing positive speech, much like Victoria Osteen, each orbiting as living proof of the prosperity gospel's premium on gorgeous, camera-ready lives.

The annual First Ladies High Tea was the epitome of black megaministry's ultra-chic aesthetic. Founded in 1997 by the gospel music editor at *Billboard* magazine, the star-studded afternoon hosted roughly one thousand church ladies from the Los Angeles area for a gospel concert, awards ceremony, and fashion show held at the posh Beverly Hills Hilton Hotel. But the excitement was in the mix and mingle of African American Hollywood celebrities and megachurch first ladies, black

This 1996 advertisement for Total Woman Ministries promises "dramatic makeovers done by our team of professionals . . . designed to give women a greater level of effectiveness as ambassadors of Jesus Christ." Reprinted with permission from Charisma Media, www.charismamedia.com.

church royalty like Togetta Ulmer from the eight-thousand-member Faithful Central Bible Church.[59] During her red-carpet interview, First Lady Togetta expressed her gratitude at being celebrated and deflected the attention to her church's upcoming Habitat for Humanity projects, but the gala was as much about the clothes as it was about the charity work. She and other first ladies were dazzling displays of black church fashion. There were, of course, the church hats with spiraling ribbons or wide brims loaded down with netting or cloth flowers—the sort of hat whose height might make her seatmates repeat the old joke that a woman like that should have the decency to sit in the back.[60] These hats were typically a point of generational difference, the crowns of older women, since black women had largely moved away from church hats since the 1990s, but at these high fashion moments hats made a resplendent comeback as theatrical showpieces. Dresses were rich and sparkling, perfectly modest with necklines that only grazed the collarbone, and complemented by long gloves and heavy jewel earrings, necklaces, bracelets, and brooches. A first lady was no longer simply a pastor's wife but a woman who could stand beside Yolanda Adams, Erica and Tina Campbell, Omarosa, Cedric the Entertainer, and other standouts in the entertainment industry in a lightning storm of camera flashes.

SLIM FOR HIM

As women's ministry matured, it never shed its emphasis on the ornamental body. Women's conferences, if they offered food at all, were typically stocked with diet go-tos such as light popcorn, bananas, bottled water, and coffee with aspartame. Barbara O'Chester, pioneer of Southern Baptist women's ministries, frankly told women in her seminars to write down their weight and then subtract the weight they were when they got married. That number should be ten pounds or less because *that* was the woman her husband married.[61] Even casual advice about self-care suggested that audiences should keep an eye on their waistlines, like Victoria Osteen's chatty counsel to "kick back under a tree and enjoy an ice cream cone (fat free, of course!)."[62]

As Marie Griffith has shown, "born again bodies" captured the religious imagination of conservatives and became a seamless theology of

the sanctification of the flesh, a tandem physical and a spiritual examination.[63] The Christian weight-loss industry mushroomed from the
1970s onward with bestsellers like Patricia Kreml's *Slim for Him* (1978)
and Marie Chapian and Neva Coyle's *Free to Be Thin* (1979).[64] In the
1980s the spectacularly coiffed Gwen Shamblin began her Weigh Down
Ministries, which combined an anti-Trinitarian message with a biblically based slimming program,[65] while in the next decade T. D. Jakes
made a small franchise out of his *Lay Aside the Weight*, an account of
how when he and his wife, Serita, lost 110 pounds and 40 pounds, respectively. Later it would be Don Colbert's *What Would Jesus Eat?* It
was an expansive genre: Shirley Cook's *Diary of a Fat Housewife* led to
her *Diary of a Jogging Housewife* and then her *The Exodus Diet Plan*, a
devotional series about how to move from a "heavyweight to a light-
weight" as one learned about God's sustenance.[66] Since credibility was
earned primarily through physical credentials—a trim body and a successful weight-loss experience—it was a genre instinctively open to a
breakthrough star. However, an existing celebrity who unleashed his or
her own secrets to healthy living always made a huge splash.

In the 1970s, readers loved to see their favorite celebrities join the lei-
sure craze, setting aside the lapels for a sweatband and velour jogging
ensemble. Activist and beauty queen Anita Bryant's *Running the Good
Race* (1976) promoted her family's "dual program of physical fitness and
Christian fellowship" to help "lazy Christians get off the starting line."[67]
The Christian Broadcasting Network hired its own professional nutri-
tionist, Yvonne Turnbull, whose "Shape Up, America" seminars and *Free
to Be Fit* bestseller made her a living model of Christian health. The prosperity gospel's teaching about divine health continued to make many
of their teachers into embodiments of fit faith. Pat Robertson promoted
an "Age-Defying Shake," while Paula White not only released a fitness
guide with her trainer but starred in her own workout video to model
the techniques.[68] Even the world's most-watched female televangelist,
Joyce Meyer, penned *Eat & Stay Thin* to urge believers to follow her path
to being freed from "bondage to weight loss."[69]

Most women in the spotlight, however, were already "free" to be thin.
One of the most visually striking features of my examination of the websites of the one hundred largest megachurches in the country was the
weight of its leading ladies—they were significantly thinner than the

Marie Chapian's *Free to Be Thin* fad made her body into a
primary theological argument. Reprinted with permission from
Christianity Today, www.christianitytoday.com.

average American woman and, as a close accounting of church website
photos revealed, slimmer even than women featured in smaller megachurches. (See Appendix II for more on the appearance of pastors' wives.)
There are a few explanations for the thin frames of these celebrity wives.
First, the image of the pastor and his wife was often used as a brand to
unify a large church population, often scattered across multiple campuses. As a result, there was likely more effort paid to the staging and
production of the images of her, which not only makes her appear more
attractive (through makeup, Photoshop, and airbrushing) but subtly or
overtly caused her to intensely focus on her own appearance. Second,
the scale of megachurch architecture and a revolution in sound and

lighting equipment (discussed in Chapter Three) led many churches to dim the house lights and focus greater attention onstage. When Hillsong Church, Australia's largest megachurch, underwent this transformation, singers went from wearing longer modest skirts and clothes from home to treating their outfits as costumes on par with the importance of set lists. Third, large megachurches frequently tapped their pastors' wives for some public leadership role, but even when the title was purely ceremonial they were always present. A woman who is not pictured in any promotional photos with her husband is often hidden, by choice or by design. "It is one thing to see yourself on a television screen," quipped Bible teacher Lisa Harper. "But it is quite another to see yourself on a jumbotron."[70]

When it came to hiding weight, Christian celebrities used the same grab bag of tricks that made Instagram a museum of perfect profile pictures. There was the tell-tale angled shot from above, a decorative scarf wrapped around the neck, or, most commonly, a larger white woman hidden behind her children and her husband as she peeked over their shoulders. It was hard to imagine someone like Frances Hunter, the jolly celebrity of pentecostal healing ministries in the 1970s and 1980s, in this social media universe, her dyed auburn hair in a puffy halo around her head and her wide body in loose floral dresses. Even her own weight loss book, *God's Answer to Fat*, showed the beaming grandmotherly figure holding up a pair of oversized pants she could once fit into in a way that showed little polish or even superiority.[71]

There were a few exceptions to the rule that a megaministry woman ought to be thin. Comedians, as a rule, could be any weight because their role was that of the jester, part entertainer and part subverter of expectations. Anita Renfroe's parodies of women who should not wear spandex pants ("Those Ain't Pants") or push-up bras ("You Raise Me Up") brought a body-positive message to both her audiences and her brand.[72] The black megachurch was more forgiving about women's proportions, even celebrating the rounder curves of its first ladies (except prosperity and neo-pentecostal churches that liked to see black women made up and slim). Megachurch wives from churches with more formal dress codes benefited from the greater level of decorum around their ministers' wives and, though confined to stiff Sunday dresses, were usually allowed to be as plump as they pleased. Overall, if the pastor was overweight and dressed in a suit, the pastor's wife could look her age. However, if the pastor was overweight and dressed in jeans and a T-shirt, she would still be required to channel her inner Cindy Crawford. The come-as-you-are informality popularized by Willow Creek's "seeker-sensitive" model had led to a generation of churches that encouraged their parishioners to wear jeans, sneakers, and T-shirts, but did little to lower the expectations megachurches had for the polish and perfection of their first ladies.

Author and speaker Liz Curtis Higgs had been touring since the early 1990s as one of the few large women in popular ministry, a reality that she embraced with characteristic good humor. "I gave up on the idea of being perfect a long time ago," she told me. It started with realistic promotional photos which informed clients and audiences "that I'm a 'large and lovely' speaker . . . and from the platform I call myself, accurately, a size 22 Tinkerbell."[73] Then she began to see (and market) her weight as a competitive advantage, an opportunity to be memorable and to relate with audiences. "I no longer apologize for my size, nor do I dress in big, black, shapeless dresses," she told *Today's Christian Woman* in her 1994 cover story.[74] Her book, *One Size Fits All and Other Fables*, was one of thirty-six books she published over the years, with 4.6 million copies in print, though her gospel of body positivity was never without unbelievers. Up-and-coming women in ministry knew, directly or indirectly, that their weight would be an issue. There were some bodies that would never live up to white American ideals of perfection, and Neva Coyle, cofounder of Overeaters Victorious, was living proof. Her book *Free to Be Thin* had become a full-blown Christian phenomenon with five hundred thousand copies sold by the early 1980s with an accompanying cookbook and even an aerobics video set to praise music. She and her business partner, Marie, were inspirational figures with a booming national weight-loss organization and national media coverage of their message of "living for Him and eating for Him."[75] But when Neva regained her weight, she lost her platform. Her subsequent book, *Loved on a Grander Scale*, tried to retract her self-described "simplistic and self-righteous" former ways. "I remember being thin. I remember the accolades that came with thinness. Not for my spiritual gifts of teach-

TODAY'S CHRISTIAN WOMAN

January/February 1994 $2.95

Author and Humorist **Liz Curtis Higgs** on:

Being a Big, Beautiful Woman in a Narrow, Nervous World

In a Spiritual Slump? How to Get Out

GREAT HUSBANDS— What You Told Us About Yours

WHY WE LOVE GOSSIP— and How We Can Learn to Hate It

ONE WOMAN'S STORY: "My Daughter Is a Lesbian"

Liz Curtis Higgs won audiences with her humor and honesty around Christian discussions of weight and beauty. Reprinted with permission from Charisma Media, www.charismamedia.com.

ing, insight, wisdom, writing and music but for being thin," she remembered.[76] But her new teaching and body would not put her back in the spotlight.

REALITY STARS

In the early 2010s, reality shows catering to churched women were discovering the commercial possibilities in black megaministry's first ladies as symbols of beauty, fashion, and sexuality. In the first episode of TLC's reality program *The Sisterhood*, following the lives of preacher's wives in Atlanta, audiences are introduced to Tara in a canary yellow bra top at the gym.[77] "I love the fact that I can have this long Barbie-doll weave, these eyelashes, this fit body, be glamorous and yet still love God with all my heart," exclaimed the First Lady of Phenomenal Life Church, pushing through her next weightlifting set with a loud "Oooh Jesus!"[78] She explained how she met her pastor-husband at the gym, and how she loved to be his "poster chick." First Lady Christina was caricatured as the stereotypical fiery Latina. Introduced on the show as "straight Dominican," she had to restrain herself from injuring churchwomen who threw themselves at her husband. As another cast member, Domonique, explained: "The first lady has to appear perfect because she sets the standard for the congregation," and she made certain that her church fashion boutique "The Queen Maker" was featured heavily on the program.[79]

The distortive nature of reality show television magnified the comparison between megaministry wives and other famously kept women. The wildly successful *Real Housewives* television franchise on Bravo followed women with wealthy husbands who created their own plotlines by gossiping, brawling, weeping, and mostly brunching, and had already made the ex-wife of one megachurch pastor into a breakout star. Former First Lady Gizelle Bryant headlined *The Real Housewives of Potomac* as the "vibrant socialite" and single mother of three who busied herself with philanthropic projects and her own makeup line after her divorce from Jamal Bryant, the famous son of an African Methodist Episcopal bishop.[80] Gossip magazines were happy to dish about how the former model had lived a glamorous lifestyle of Bentleys and million-dollar condos as the First Lady of the Empowerment Temple in Baltimore, only to reinvent herself on the show after she discovered he was allegedly cheating.[81]

The near-comfortable fit between megaministry wives and a genre fueled by betrayal, plastic surgery, and obscene spending was rendered commonplace when a new series based on the *Real Housewives* franchise, hit the airwaves. *Preachers of LA*, *Preachers of Detroit*, and *Preachers of Atlanta* tapped mostly black megachurch pastors and their wives as their stars. The shows followed their lives as high-rolling ministers (since almost all were neo-pentecostal prosperity preachers) willing to air their behind-the-scenes drama. As cultural critics of reality television observed, black women's storylines were dominated by a myth of self-actualization when, in fact, their identities were constantly filtered through racial caricatures, particularly of the hyper-sexual Jezebel or the overbearing Sapphire (the "angry black woman").[82] Instead of the unvarnished icon of the First Lady, audiences saw the unmarried Bishop Noel Jones, pastor of the one of the largest churches in California, argue with his leading lady about whether she was allowed to be called his girlfriend, and the pregnant fiancée of gospel star Deitrick Haddon squeal over sexy new lingerie. With footage of women pressed up against Noel's limo as he pulled away from his Sunday service, these programs both inflamed stereotypes of the oversexed preacher-pimp and conceded speculation about megaministry that filled gossip sites like "Lipstick Alley"—rumors of infidelity and breast augmentations, Botox injections, and unacknowledged children.[83] With female cast members billed as everything from pastors' wives and co-pastors to girlfriends and "special friends," the figure of the black megachurch wife stirred up a vast popular imagination about powerful men and the women by their sides and in their bedrooms. Such lifestyle fantasies were glamorized in reality shows like *Basketball Wives* and even novelized in an entire subgenre of African American romance fiction like *Even the Preacher Got a Side Chick* and *Undercover Deacon*.[84] There was always an audience for the build-up and take-down nature of reality television and the cast members willing to risk a little scandal to gain a large following.[85]

SATISFIED

"I've been married to the beautiful Myesha Chaney for nine years. We have three children. My wife is intelligent, sophisticated, my wife is spiritual, but that girl is *fine* too."[86] Wayne Chaney of the thirty-five-hundred-member Antioch Church in Long Beach, California, is introducing his wife to the cameras of *Preachers of LA* and recapitulating one of the most common plotlines for preachers' wives on reality television: that of the sexually satisfied and satisfying woman. It was a common boast among a cast of outspoken preachers that sexuality, purity, and sexual excitement went hand in hand, and they were more than happy to point to the women responsible. First Lady Myesha was shown waiting for her husband to come home from work in her leopard print robe;

First Lady Ivy Couch of *The Sisterhood* was first introduced to audiences when her husband gave her a pair of handcuffs for some marital recreation; and Pastor Ben Tankard, whose prosperity-preaching family ministry was featured on the reality show *Thicker Than Water*, loved to joke about his sexy wife, Jewel, swinging from the chandeliers.[87] The phenomenon of talking about a wife's spicy side became so common that *Relevant* magazine published the plea, "OK, Let's Stop With All the Talk About 'Smokin' Hot' Wives,'" when even the pastor giving the opening prayer for the NASCAR Nationwide series race thanked his wife for being so hot.[88]

There had always been an endless appetite for the love stories of famous pastors. As we discussed in Chapter Two, most female leaders tried their hand at writing their own love stories as a defense of Christian marriage. Even Derek Prince, the intense scholar-preacher who typically applied his mind to the study of demons and exorcism, penned *God Is a Match-Maker* to tell of the divine interventions that led from his first marriage and subsequent widowhood to this second marriage. (While the book's cover drips with hearts, the cerebral Prince could never approximate effusiveness. In contemplating marriage he confessed: "Though I could build philosophical theories about humanity, I knew very little about dealing with real human beings.")[89] The most powerful symbol of the culture wars against feminism was the satisfied housewife, the woman who knew her place in the kitchen and the bedroom. And no one advertised that contentment better than Marabel Morgan in *The Total Woman*, a runaway hit that earned national press coverage and a spot on the *New York Times* bestsellers list. Her famous advice to spice a marriage up by wearing nothing but Saran Wrap was echoed by a generation of other conservative women who, by innuendo or proclamation, communicated that they practiced what they preached. "Jim never knows if I'm going to be a redhead, a blonde, or a brunette," said Tammy Faye Bakker brazenly.[90]

As Amy DeRogatis has argued, conservative Christians' tireless promotion of married sex reflected their perennial worry that unfettered sexuality was a danger to the soul.[91] In youth, girls could slip on a purity ring, attend a father-daughter purity ball, or re-read one of many pink fairy-tales penned for little princesses learning not to give their first kiss to just any prince. Teenagers could read modesty blogs, kiss dating goodbye, and enlist their fathers to help them find suitable future hus-

A REVELL PUBLICATION

Today's
Christian

Woman

JULY/AUGUST 1985 $3.95

Marabel Morgan
She Made
Marriages Sizzle...
Now She Tells How To
ADD SPARKLE
TO HUMDRUM
DAYS

When Hospitality
Takes Its Toll

...For Raising
...ive Kids

...ssions Of
...fectionist

...s With
...zz

Marabel Morgan was most famous for bringing playful sexuality
into Christian marriages. Reprinted with permission from
Christianity Today, www.christianitytoday.com.

bands. After saying "I do," the happy couple could flip open detailed instructions for the wedding night written by husband-and-wife teams like Tim and Beverly LaHaye, whose step-by-step instructions glory in the biblical foundations of Christian lovemaking. Even after abuse, sexual freedom could be found in spiritual breakthroughs coached by celebrity preachers like T. D. Jakes with his bestselling franchise on women's empowerment dubbed *Woman, Thou Art Loosed.*

Megachurch wives, in particular, became the indispensable sources of the "female perspective" as their husbands launched their own sermon series and books on the topic of sex and marriage. There was Mark and Grace Driscoll's *Real Marriage,* Chris and Kerry Shook's *Love at Last Sight*, and even stalwart Presbyterian Tim and Kathy Keller's *The Meaning of Marriage.* This his-and-her approach was particularly common when couples adopted an official or unofficial co-pastor model, effectively rendering themselves professionally married. Ed and Lisa Young made national headlines for their co-authored book, *Sexperiment,*[92] which found the couple in a bed on the roof of their Texas church for twenty-four live-streamed hours to chat mostly with other famous megachurch spouses about "tantalizing truths about sex as God intended." Though Ed was temporarily treated for an eye injury sustained from the camera lights reflecting off the white bedsheets, the stunt was a rousing success. When they challenged married couples in their twenty-five-thousand-member congregation to have sex for seven days in a row, "the guys gave us a standing ovation," said Ed Young in his CNN interview, while Lisa chimed in that "God is the author and creator of sex."[93] She sat beside her husband in a leopard-print dress, her long straight hair framing her carefully made-up face; and while she spoke a pop-up caption on the television under her read: "Married to Ed for more than 26 years. They have four children."[94] In advertisements, she appeared in yet another leopard-print dress, pulling her husband suggestively by the tie toward her on the couch.[95] Sexual prowess became another bit of expected expertise in a megachurch wife's grab bag of tricks.

There was an accepted cruelty toward famous women in ministry who failed to meet these standards. In the era of "militant feminism," Ruth Peale begged feminists to stop warring against male exploitation and realize that the "real enemy" was their own lack of femininity.[96] Women who didn't want to be sexualized, she worried, might make "downright frigid" sexual partners.[97] Likewise, Beverly LaHaye initially felt sorry for a woman being berated by her husband for looking tired on a date, but then sympathized with the husband for not having a wife with a little more pride in herself. "What a pity to see a Christian woman who has developed her inner beauty but has done nothing to the frame she must house it in," she fretted.[98] The common argument given was that men were visual creatures, which made women's appearance a part of her wifely duties. Her beauty and her sexuality were not her own. When Ted Haggard, megachurch pastor and leader of the National Association of Evangelicals, was caught with a gay prostitute, fellow megachurch pastor Mark Driscoll publicly aired his concerns about "a wife who lets herself go and is not sexually available to her husband."[99] Mark had already made headlines on his own accord for having instructed a woman in his church to give her husband a blow job as an apology for not "serving" him.[100] There was always a woman to blame for a man who strayed.

Even the matronly Terrie Chappell, who described herself as a "meek-spirited woman of God" who serves "joyfully and faithfully" by the side of her husband, confessed her enduring wish to meet megaministry's unrealistic standards.[101] That perfect woman, she wrote, looks "fresh and attractive all the time. Her hair always does what she wants it to do and it's never flat. Her fingernails are never broken." [102] This ideal woman also doubled as a domestic expert who, with a submissive and cheerful spirit, "bakes everything from scratch" and always sticks to her diet.[103] Terrie's online ministry painted a much more realistic picture of her life as a grandmother who was never far from a prim pearl necklace and a crockpot recipe, who often helped lead an old-fashioned "Ladies Ministry" with classes called "Kindred Hearts," "Ladies of Today," and "H.O.M.E." (Helping Our Mothers Excel). Her book, covered in images of cupcakes, lingered on the trials of putting up floral wallpaper and learning to be patient. In 2017, the average megachurch wife was around Terrie's age, wrestling with approaching retirement, and lightly out of step with American culture. She was hardly the sexpot that dominated the marketing of the women in the highest rungs of megaministry, strutting across the mainstage, but audiences still seemed to want her to try.

THE ADULTERESS

Hope Carpenter looked tired, which was a good thing.[104] She and her husband, Ron, had once led their own megachurch in Greenville, South Carolina, together and had seen it grow into a ten-thousand-person Goliath, one of the largest churches in the Southeast. They had been the pride and joy of their little Holy Ghost denomination, the International Pentecostal Holiness Church. She was a deacon's daughter and a beauty pageant contestant, and he was the son of the denomination's general superintendent, and together they were the golden couple with an ultramodern take on charismatic faith.[105] They had even been the advertisements for a fitness lifestyle brand, side-by-side blondes with toned bodies, giving their testimony about their new diets and gym schedules.[106]

But now she was the woman who had been sent away for rehabilitation after her multiple sexual affairs went public. She was returning to face her home congregation for the very first time.

"I knew this day would come," she said to her congregation at an evening service, sitting down on a stool beside her husband, who hung his head as she spoke.[107] "We don't have enough time for me to really adequately tell you my journey, tell you what God has done for me. That'll be in a book, maybe," she joked. The crowd was silent.

"But I did want to come to you today and apologize to you. That's my sole purpose." She ran her tongue over her teeth nervously, pressing her lips together at every pause and dabbing her eyes with a handkerchief as tears started to trickle down. The more she cried the warmer the audience seemed to become, a smattering of applause that gained momentum as she began to praise them ("You're just so special. You're a rare breed!"). But Ron's large frame stayed hunched over and his eyes downcast, heaving deep breaths visible even to the cameras as if anticipating the moment to come.

Hope could not quite look at him until she said the words: "I hurt my husband. Who is your pastor." She paused as her jaw trembled. "You have no idea the pain that we have walked through. I jeopardized everything that we have built, our time, our energy, our money, our resources, our family, our church, our retirement, and I know that trust takes a long time to be regained. And I'm willing to walk through it to take the time to get his trust back." Ron put his large hands over his eyes for a moment and wiped away tears.

"My children . . . ," she sobbed. "I left you. I left you through those selfish years. I'm so sorry. I'm so sorry. You are the most important thing that God has ever given me. Ever. And nothing in my life is more important than you. Nothing. If I never preach, I am content. If I never get a new car, I am content. If I never go on another trip or have another girlfriend, I am content. I am content being in my house with my pajamas and my family, cooking for you, being with you." The crowd erupted into pounding applause. The prodigal daughter had returned home.

Hope turned to the crowd, sitting a little taller now and a smile on her lips. "To the women of this church, I love you. I know you are who I'm called to. I've known since I was a little girl. Many of you call me mama, pastor, apostle, friend, girlfriend, all those things. To some of you

Once the venerated co-pastor of their shared megachurch, Hope Carpenter stepped down from public ministry after news of her infidelity became public. Photo by Josh Morgan. Reprinted with permission from *USA Today*, usatoday.com.

I was your only role model and you looked to me and I let you down . . . And I'm sorry. I pray that you can look today and get some hope renewed . . ." Hope faltered for a moment, having exchanged looks with her husband and quickly explained that Ron warned her not to preach ("though I am anointed"), but to apologize. She looked back at the auditorium and swore not to stand in front of them again until her "covering," her spiritual overseer and husband, agreed that she had become "like a tree planted before the waters" (Jeremiah 17:8). But the more she explained, the more she picked up steam. She praised the church, asked for prayer, and threw in a few jabs about how Ron had made mistakes too. ("See, he ain't perfect, y'all!") The time for apologizing was over. The couple ended the segment with a careful hug while the audience snapped pictures and clapped in approval. It had been announced that T. D. Jakes himself was helping the couple with their reconciliation, and so there was little left for the church to do but pray and accept Hope's apology. To speed that process along, Ron declared that the Lord had instructed the congregation to lift their hands in the air and, in sixty seconds, let go of any anger and forgive.[108] The church obliged, and Ron was ready to move on.

What scholar Susan Wise Bauer has called "the art of the public grovel" was perfected by Jimmy Swaggart at the height of the 1980s televangelism scandals. "I have sinned against you," Swaggart publicly confessed to his congregation, denomination, and the Lord. His model would be imitated by many famous politicians and ministers after him.[109] In 2013, three famous pastors in the Orlando area alone resigned over sexual affairs: David Loveless (founder of the four-thousand-member Discovery Church), Isaac Hunter (pastor of the forty-three-hundred-member Summit Church), and televangelist Sam Hinn (brother of the even more famous TV preacher Benny Hinn).[110] The following year it was marriage expert and Senior Pastor Bob Coy of the twenty-thousand-member Calvary Chapel in Fort Lauderdale, and then megachurch pastor Tullian Tchividjian, Billy Graham's grandson.[111] Like politicians, church leaders preferred to keep these revelations as vague and tidy as possible with an obvious redemption narrative: the sin is discovered, exposed, and repented, at which time the sinner is temporarily exiled.[112] This was a sentence typically endured by the entire family of the senior pastor, who often, for their own sake, found it too difficult to return to normal life. Internet message boards dedicated to keeping curious audiences updated on the whereabouts of their missing pastor and his family were common.[113] As highly skilled, highly valued assets, and usually founders of their own communities, many megachurch pastors were eventually redeemed by a "restoration" process. Prosperity preachers were notorious for restoring themselves after a temporary hiatus, since there was typically little independent oversight to prevent it. Only eight months after the scandal of his four-year sexual affair led Sam Hinn to step away from the pulpit, he was "re-ordained" against the advice of the pastor assigned to oversee his restoration process.[114]

Women in ministry, on the other hand, rarely survived the hint of sexual impropriety. When the photographs of already-married televangelists Paula White and Benny Hinn holding hands hit the cover of the *National Enquirer*, Benny Hinn immediately ended his association with her while protesting that there was "no immorality whatsoever."[115] With Paula recently divorced from her second husband and co-pastor, Randy, and Benny estranged from his wife, he could not afford the disgrace of innuendo, and as a single woman she was no longer deemed innocent. With women as the appointed models of safe sexuality, their virtue was a precious commodity that once lost was almost impossible to regain. In her explanation of her call to ministry, Pastor Elaine Fisher felt she had to explain how "the Lord restored my purity" after having misspent her teenage years being a "fake" and "tease."[116] It was a genre of female writing rife with suggestion and fueled by the need to explain *why,* why the daughter of Robert and Debbie Morris, co-pastors of the fourth-largest church in the country, needed to be supervised while she was dating, and why her fiancé waited until proposing to kiss her. Her virginity needed explanation in ways that any son's would not.

On a more basic level, these concerns about dangerous sexuality made it difficult for women to operate in ministry without fear of the "appearance of evil," a commonly used extra-biblical phrase to indict unsupervised male-female interaction. Though women were lauded as keepers of the home, they were often treated as temptresses. Take, for instance, the common practice of refusing to allow a man and a woman to be unchaperoned. Billy Graham famously made it a policy that he would never be alone with a woman other than his wife. His institution of the rule (agreed upon by his close ministerial team in what was called the "Modesto Manifesto") was an effort to avoid even the appearance of impropriety.[117] However, in practice, it had two significant effects. First, the consequence of sex-segregated spaces was that women would find it very different to gain powerful mentors. Most power lay within the hands of nationally known male megachurch pastors, and without reasonably easy means to interact, it was increasingly difficult for women (especially unmarried women) to participate in the lifeblood of celebrity—networking. There were few sustained encounters—a car ride, a quick lunch, let alone a golf game—between men and women who were not already closely acquainted. Secondly, it sexualized interactions between the genders.

Jenni Catron, one of the most high-level women to work in executive leadership at a megachurch (not married to the pastor), told me how difficult it has been for her to find and maintain mentoring relationships with male leaders in the highly charged world of evangelicalism. As a pretty

Ruth Bell Graham was the esteemed wife of Billy Graham, whose fidelity to her was famous and envied. But the "Billy Graham Rule" also prevented other women from finding male mentors without the risk of impropriety. Reprinted with permission from *Christianity Today*, www.christianitytoday.com.

young woman, she had to devote significant attention to the constant accusation of overstepping or flirting. It was a constant conundrum:

> One of the challenging things for me as a woman in church leadership is mustering up the confidence and the resilience for every environment I enter. As the founder and CEO of a company that consults churches, I am working with senior leaders who are predominantly men. As I reach out to network, I am continually afraid that they will misinterpret my interest. Will they be offended that I ask to meet with them? Do I need to clarify that a co-worker will come with me? Do I need to ask

their wife to join us? There are so many layers that feel absurd. If I were a man doing the same work, I would confidently reach out to a church leader that I hope to work with. I would have the resilience to continue to network. I am often afraid that my motives will be misunderstood. I have to constantly push through this.

She kept her brand clean and polished, without feminine flourishes, and her manner a little tougher to communicate a professionalism that some might find hard to believe.[118] Beauty could as easily be a gift as a curse.[119]

TRANS-GRESSIONS

Paula Williams travelled in a different circuit than she used to. We sat down to chat on the grass at the 2016 Wild Goose Festival, one of the few events for progressive liberal Christians who wanted to hear stories like Paula's. For over three decades, she was a golden boy of the vast Christian Churches/Churches of Christ megachurch network. She had been the chairman and CEO of the Orchard Group, growing the church-planting organization into a $4 million a year enterprise, and she had become a trusted advisor for the scores of megachurches affiliated with the tradition. When a megachurch was on shaky ground, she was brought in to chair the board. When a pastor had a breakdown, she was the listening ear and personal coach. For twelve years she served as the editor-at-large for the denomination's flagship magazine, *Christian Standard*, and regularly served as a teaching pastor when a senior pastor needed a break. She had preached in many of the top twenty megachurches and often taught in seminaries around the country. She even facilitated conversations at the megachurch pastors' annual retreat and regularly facilitated a retreat of leaders of rapidly growing new churches—both tightknit groups of their most powerful men—in part because she was one of the only leaders with the personal connections and bravado to tell big personalities when to sit down and stop talking. Or at least she used to.

"When did that life end?" I asked.[120]

"I started transitioning [from Paul to Paula] four years ago. . . . If you ask me I would say that I was *called* to it. But if you ask my daughters and my wife they would say that I would have died if I hadn't changed. . . .

Pastor Paula Williams was cut off from her evangelical community when she transitioned from Paul to Paula. Image courtesy of Paula Williams.

I had never felt that experience of calling before. I went into church planting because it was strategic. I went into ministry because my father was a minister. So when I experienced this sense of call . . . I sobbed. I screamed. I knew . . . I was going to lose everything, and thought 'I can't do this.' But I had this strong sense from God that I needed to."

It had been an especially difficult decision because Paula Stone Williams had come from old religious stock. She had been named after Barton Stone, her great-great-great grandfather and one of the most famous preachers of the Second Great Awakening, whose revivals helped give birth to the Christian Churches and Churches of Christ of the Restorationist tradition. It was an austere movement most famous for its general opposition to women in public ministry. A trans-woman was not only out of the question, it was unthinkable. There had been only two known lesbian megachurch pastors in American history (Jo Hudson's story was addressed in Chapter One) but she had been, like many progressive megachurch pastors, more of a community leader than a figure in the popular marketplace.[121] As an expert in church branding, Paula knew with excruciating certainty her transition would bring an end to her career. There were no transgender Christian leaders with a national profile, much less leaders from more conservative denominations. Q Ideas, an evangelical forum for hot-button topics, hosted a symposium on "the transgender conversation."[122] But for the most part the national religious conversation on the issue was framed by Christian conservatives concerned more generally about the erosion of *their* religious liberty in favor of state LGBTQ+ protections, or who worried about people using public restrooms that did not correspond with their sex as indicated on their birth certificate (leading to the conservative introduction and support of restrictive "bathroom bills" in states like North Carolina).[123] Few conservative churches would grant transgender people pulpit access or entry into church leadership roles. Evangelist Franklin Graham was one of the most outspoken critics of accommodations and broader cultural sympathy for transgender people. "God is the one who gave the rainbow," posted the evangelist, "and it was associated with His judgment."[124]

Rhetoric like this had consequences. "I was horribly treated by evangelical churches," Paula said. She resigned from her positions of authority and, in an instant, lost almost every high-powered Christian friend she had made over decades of shared service to the church. "I understood why they didn't reach out to me. But why did my punishment extend to my wife? Why would no one reach out to her?" she agonized. The silence was the beginning of a long exile.

"What aspect of service do you miss most from your old life?" I asked.

"Leadership," she said immediately. "That's a capacity I've always had, to hold many parts together." Paula had delicately folded her tall frame onto the small picnic blanket beside me, but had the presence of someone accustomed to commanding a large room. However, for the most part, there were few large organizations for her to lead. By 2016, a few liberal Christian denominations had become vocal about welcoming transgender Christians, like the United Church of Christ and the Metropolitan Community Church, but as a "a good ol' evangelical with mainline theology" the exiled pastor found her new theological place uncomfortable. Paula joined the board of the Q Christian Fellowship (formerly Gay Christian Network, and of no connection to Gabe Lyons's Q Ideas forum),[125] whose annual conference had become one of the most important LGBTQ+ Christian hubs in the country, but, as a matter of scale, progressive causes had nowhere near the budgets and organizational breadth of the evangelical bodies Paula had once led. Megaministry was dominated by conservative giants with empires to run, while the world of progressive theology found its energy in smaller (and often shrinking) denominations with few megachurches or thriving parachurch ministries. According to a 2015 Pew survey, most American Christians were accepting of same-sex relationships, but support among evangelicals remained low at 36 percent.[126] As a result, the most resource-heavy churches in American Christianity, drawn overwhelmingly from these Christian conservatives, remained closed to leaders like Paula despite her resumé. The pragmatism of American megachurches made them able to forgive a multitude of sins in their leaders, from emotional abuse to sexual wantonness, but a transgender woman who was faithful to her wife was not the kind of person to be forgiven.

"Do you notice that, simply as a woman, Christians expect different qualities from you?" I wondered.

"I noticed immediately how much more vulnerable and empathetic people expected me to be. And I was happy to cultivate that safe and nurturing space. It is incredible the things that people will tell me now that they never did before," she marveled before her face twisted into a sardonic smile. "But it's also incredible how stupid I apparently became overnight. Now, when I speak, it's hard to get anyone to listen."

ALONE

Annie F. Downs had wide eyes and a huge smile that audiences could see from the back row. As a featured speaker of LifeWay and the author of several popular books like *100 Days to Brave*, the thirty-five-year-old

Annie Downs built a national reputation for her chatty and accessible brand of evangelicalism. Image courtesy of Annie Downs.

had built her reputation on being everyone's friend they haven't met. "I want people to feel like they *know* me. I never want to be untouchable. Please come tell me and possibly punch me if that happens," she laughed loudly.[127] It suited her. Her ministry tagline read: "Author. Speaker. Loud laugher."

"Every time I see you speak, you seem to have to explain why you're single," I said. We were drinking chai lattes in her green room as we waited for the next speaker to finish. All the other women hitting the stage that weekend were married, and Annie's humorous preamble to her talk had included references to how she was "obviously" single and how sometimes "not all your dreams come true." She had deftly moved from her own foibles to the purpose of her talk, but it was a glaring bit of self-deprecation in comparison with most women's chatty references to their husbands and children.

"It's one of those things that I feel God has called me to be really open about. I want people to listen to me and say: 'Me too.' So I need to find a way to connect to the roughly forty percent of my audience that *is* single. And I need to communicate to everyone else that we all have things in our lives that we really want and have to live without."

Annie was one of only a handful of well-known speakers who were single, a problem that the magazine *Christian Single* understood all too well. With such a large percentage of single readers and such a small percentage of single celebrities, it was hard to find someone to put on the cover that anyone could recognize.[128] Christian publishing had plenty of guidebooks for modern singles with suggestive or clever titles like *Stripped* or *Singled Out*, but the stigma of singleness lingered.[129] Though conservatives ostensibly understood that Jesus himself was a single man, evangelicals and pentecostals had more in common with Mormon speakers when it came to their rhetoric of marriage and family. "The only relationship on planet earth that's analogous to His relationship to His people is marriage," argued Ed Young. It was the family-first theology memorialized by Focus on the Family and lauded by the Religious Right under the banner of "family values."[130] God's true purpose was best expressed then through the bonds of marriage. But what of those whose Twitter bio did not include "doting wife"? "Sometimes being a single woman in vocational ministry feels like being a soybean burger at a cattlemen's convention. I'm not always viewed as a complementary or valuable component," said Lisa Harper. "I bump up against what's probably a subconscious assumption that my lack of a husband equates to a lack of spiritual efficacy."[131]

Singleness was also a fragile career, both economically and topically. Financially, singleness meant that a speaker like Annie was responsible for hiring her entire staff. A megachurch wife could typically rely on the resources of her megachurch for administration, storage, and office space. Further, singleness was a narrow platform on which to build a career, changing with age and situation. If she found her mate, she lost her credibility as the single gal who "gets it," and if she never found someone, she ran the risk of appearing rejected. Single women like Lisa and Annie must allow audiences to wonder whether their favorite speaker minded going home alone.

FOREVER YOUNG

In the late 1990s, the Women of Faith tour had put a bevy of silver-haired ladies on stage who could spin a yarn—women like Patsy Clairmont. She

Lisa Harper has built a long and successful ministerial career as a bible teacher in the spotlight after years working behind the scenes. Reprinted with permission from *Christianity Today*, www .christianitytoday.com.

and a gaggle of retirees loved to play with the tropes of the unshackled older woman, advertised cruising around in an open-top convertible to bring the gospel to the highways and byways. However, for the most part, women's ministry was a difficult beat for an older woman. Women well into their sixties rarely went gray, sticking to a tight regime of coloring, and if they did not they ran the risk of advertisers doing it for them. Liz Curtis Higgs once found that her white hair had been touched up in yellow by event producers, even though her brand depended on unvarnished honesty about her appearance. There were books about *The Super Years* and "developing the ageless attitude" but it was a young woman's game.[132] The average megachurch pastor was well into his fifties, and pastors and their wives, on television and on stage, struggled against time.

The Christian tradition customarily held that Jesus himself was not terribly attractive, and that the words of Isaiah the prophet describe him well by saying: "He had no beauty or majesty to attract us to him, nothing in his appearance that we should desire him."[133] Nonetheless, as the scale of megaministry continued to grow, the industry's expectations for women swelled with it. The brightest stars would have to set aside their comfortable flats for heels and pull on their slimming Spanx. After all, they knew the rules better than anyone. Hair and eyelash extensions, slimming clothes, the right makeup, and tall heels were the uniform of popular ministry. There were market advantages to being slim but not skinny, curvy but not voluptuous, trendy but not avant-garde. While trumpeting the value of true righteousness, they learned to make the most of their youth, their marriage, their looks, and their charms. While the men at their sides would be subjected to theological and moral scrutiny, the women of megaministry learned to live as if their bodies possessed the keys to their character. They had become embodied arguments for God's perfect plans for the holy femininity that would have to be seen to be believed.

Conclusion

A few words on influence. This is woman's power. That
distinctively belongs to man, and is exercised by authority.
Law and penalty grow out of it. It regulates actions, it
punishes crime. Influence, on the other hand, awakens
feeling, generates opinions, implants sentiments in the soul,
silently yet emphatically; and thus it crushes vice, promotes
virtue, and avoids the necessity of penal infliction. Now, this
is pre-eminently the potent lever in the hands of woman for
regenerating and reforming the political and moral world.
—John Holmes Agnew, Address Before the Monroe Female Seminary, 1851[1]

Jennifer Crow has perfected the fine art of co-pastoring. She had once
been a singer for Oral Roberts's wildly popular 1980s television specials
and even recorded with Aretha Franklin, and, over the years, she made
certain that her many talents were her husband's gain. She worked full-
time to put her husband through seminary and led every worship ministry and youth choir in every church where he paid his dues as a young
pastor. When he began his own career as an itinerant minister, she took
over all administrative duties as his personal secretary. She responded
to his decision to jog across America to publicly protest abortion by pa-
tiently driving behind him with their three children in a motorhome.[2]
They co-founded a church in 1994, and, while homeschooling their now
five children and keeping house, she oversaw all worship and media production for the five-thousand-member congregation's five services,
usually while singing lead. Even when she struggled, she turned her story
into a self-help book and a publicity tour. She was golden.

When her husband's alleged affair became national news in 2014, it
was reported that the married father of five had admitted to infidelity
and would be stepping down from one of the largest churches in the
country.[3] What was less apparent was that it would spell the end for both
husband and wife. The church called one of their local campus pastors
to replace the disgraced pastor and suddenly the role of "co-pastor" was
also filled—by another man's wife. If Mark had simply died, it would be

quite natural for a church like theirs to tap Jennifer as the successor. But like her husband retreating in scandal, Jennifer had to master her own disappearing act.[4]

In almost every spiritual empire, there was a she. She could be shuttled off-stage when her husband's misconduct forced her to defend or abandon him; or she might be smiling genuinely at the crowds while assuring them that her man was still her best friend. She might be quietly walking the aisles before a service taking note of new faces before she found her seat, or waiting in the greenroom for a spotlight she hated to share. She might be the headliner for a sold-out crowd or the reality show star whose range of home goods was always available online, or the anonymous wife only trotted out for church billboards and Christmas cards. She might be the famous mother, daughter, sister, or wife of a pastor whose name was always appended to her introduction. She could be known for her new song, her latest book, her worst tragedy, her bubbly personality, or simply her presence as the rock on which the ministry was built. "There is something about her presence," commented one megachurch staffer, "that makes the event feel legitimate."[5]

If she had gifts, they were used. As we have seen, the creation of a women's program in the largest churches was directly tied to the public profile of the pastor's wife. Entire ministries might be created to express her interests and her passions. In fact, her role was so important that if she were missing, another woman had to be called up in her place. (Even the openly gay pastor of a popular black LGBTQ+ church in Atlanta asked his ex-wife to come back to lead as co-pastor because the congregation would not follow him without her.[6]) And if she were somehow unfit or ill-equipped, she might even be re-invented. There were always ghostwriters with anecdotes about a famous woman who needed a book but lacked the talent or the insight. She was a story waiting to be told.

For most Protestant women of all theological backgrounds, the road to formal power in the largest churches had long been barred. No matter how intelligent a woman might be, education did not ensure her a smooth path to leadership. Seminaries often funneled them into alternative careers and denominations struggled to find first appointments that would accept female ordinands after graduation.[7] Despite the existence of dozens of mainline megachurches, only a handful were led by women. And while progressive denominations had proven their willingness to elevate women to the highest ranks of the administration, their careers were largely marked by quiet service. For most liberal denominations, the marketplace and the church's headquarters were worlds apart and women who succeeded in one rarely conquered the other. It was almost impossible for a woman to gain the kind of equivalent celebrity that was within reach of almost any male megachurch pastor through traditional means.

It was in the market that women soared. They had conquered the small screen and dominated many of the most-watched Christian programs in America. By the 2010s, the nation had been watching female televangelists like Gloria Copeland and Marilyn Hickey for almost thirty years on networks that women like Jan Crouch, Tammy Faye Bakker, Joni Lamb, and Mother Angelica had founded. Almost anyone on the planet could tune in to watch Joyce Meyer's *Enjoying Everyday Life* and her quizzical brow arch as she made wry observations between bits of biblical commentary. When it came to the largest churches in the country, megachurches had always been known not only for their charismatic pulpiteers but for their talented wives. Ruth Peale had been the administrative arm of Norman Vincent Peale; Arvella Schuller was her televangelist husband Robert's best producer; Victoria Osteen bookended Joel's folksy talks with a hard pitch for the financial offering; and Lisa Young gave her husband's reputation enough of a sexy sheen to co-write their own intimacy guide. And if audiences came to hear a celebrity, the Christian conference circuit was a woman's game. Arenas around the country were the new sites of old-fashioned revivalism, filled with singing, teaching, and comedy that pulled audiences to the altar. On social media, authors like Glennon Doyle kept the spokesmen of the Southern Baptist Convention on their toes. Bedside (and poolside) paperbacks were the essence of Christian women's celebrity with dozens of *New York Times* bestselling authors to choose from. Famous women usually had men by their sides, but they were also fully capable of outshining them altogether. Some got the last laugh, brought the house down, or had that star quality that kept the camera trained on them alone. And sometimes they were simply so beautiful that their presence seemed to still the crowd. Theirs was a groundswell of remarkable gifts.

The women of megaministry claimed not to have power: they had influence. Dozens of conferences, women's ministries, networks, events, and even Caribbean cruises were devoted to cultivating the elusive "woman of influence," the one who made an impact in both her family and her world. But influence was a slippery word. Was this authority from above or below? Was she a leader or a follower? How far beyond her home could her reach extend? Was she, as leadership gurus like to say, a "change maker" or was her influence so diffuse that it could not be measured?

Let us consider two examples of how women are broadly considered in relationship to the category of leadership. Before the allegations of megachurch pastor Bill Hybels's inappropriate behavior toward his female staffers made national headlines, the most dazzling Christian leadership conferences had been held annually by his Willow Creek Church. It was a grand affair. In 2016, its live telecast was seen by 305,000 people in hundreds of locations throughout the world, and viewers watched CEOs, politicians, Ivy League powerhouses, and Christian leaders mix it up and strategize about leadership. Eager audiences might catch a glimpse of Tony Blair or Bono with the biggest names in ministry. In its fifteen-year history, the conference has not featured a single female pastor.[8] It was not because Hybels was opposed to women in ministry. Far from it: the church tapped a woman named Heather Larson as co-pastor at Hybels's retirement.[9] But for the conference to find women with significant institutional leadership experience, they chose to (or perhaps had to) look outside of the church. The Willow Creek Global Leadership Summit selected women from a deep pool of famous businesswomen, politicians, bestselling authors, and Wall Street sharks. In the end, it was the careers of male megachurch pastors that received the most significant boost by sharing the platform with headline-making women drawn from all sectors of American culture. People flocked to hear Melinda Gates speak, only to find her made the equal of a senior pastor with a large suburban church. The era of women's leadership had arrived, but the era of women's theological leadership had not.

Or let us look at a well-known ministry called Leading & Loving It specializing in "equipping women in ministry and leadership."[10] In 2017, the organization was spearheaded by two megachurch wives, Lori Wilhite and Brandi Wilson, whose husbands led the twenty-one-thousand-member Central Church (Las Vegas) and the five-thousand-member Cross Point Church (Nashville), respectively.[11] The pair hosted a series of retreats in sunny Las Vegas for women who, like themselves, were in full-time ministry. Though billed as an event for leaders, the registration form asked women to choose between the following options to describe themselves:

- Senior Pastor's Wife
- Church Planter's Wife
- Executive Pastor's Wife
- Associate Pastor's Wife
- Campus Pastor's Wife[12]

Further down the list, when the titles "pastor" or "director" appeared, they were affixed to women's ministry, family ministry, student ministry, counseling, and administration. When I asked Lori about how they put together the categories, I could practically hear her flinching over the phone.

"It's nailing spaghetti to the wall!" she exclaimed. "Every time we update the website we have to change the categories. All I want to say is, are *you* the person in ministry or are you married to the one who is?" The website, she explained, was not meant to be prescriptive but rather descriptive of the kinds of ministerial careers to which most women belonged. "We're not here for the theological argument [about women in ministry]. We focus on what unifies us, which is the call that God has on our lives."

Lori had effectively run a ministry that granted her access to the heartaches and concerns of ministry wives across the country for almost a decade, and so I asked her, "What are the biggest disadvantages of having women in ministry who don't feel that call?"

"Loneliness. Depression. Bitterness. Pain," she said frankly.[13] Lori wanted women to find language of joyful meaning and true calling for careers they had not necessarily chosen. What they chose to do with those opportunities was to their credit, but the fact remained that most conservative women's careers rested on authority that was associational and, as such, contingent. They could not rule, but they were indispensable.

That a woman's place is under her husband's authority has been one of the longest held and least challenged tenets in Christian history. Virgin. Wife. Widow. Under those three banners, most women lived out their lives. In modern America, patriarchy remained both a theological argument about the divine order of churches and families as well as a practice of custodianship over sacred speech and spaces. Women in megaministry lived perpetually in its shadow. Almost everything about a woman's career could be interpreted as a gesture of overreaching or her ill-advised independence: the length and volume of her speech, her nearness to the pulpit, whether she stayed alone in a hotel or with the pastor's family, or how she narrated her relationship to her home pastor. It was a career in which appearances mattered and quiet gestures could speak volumes. The keen attention paid to small detail freighted relationships between the sexes, making it difficult for women—especially single females—to build relationships with pastors and other industry professionals that would enhance their careers.

In this business, patriarchy did not simply mean an overweening male presence, but the reality of unequal remuneration. Despite complementarian claims of the equal spiritual worth of men and women, there was no complementarity of financial treatment. Almost none of the megaministry wives I interviewed made as much as their husbands—if anything at all, as the role of pastor's wife is often an unpaid position with a hefty job description. As early as the STOP ERA movement, conservative Christian women generally agreed that women deserved equal pay for equal work, but they clearly did not apply these standards to their own labor. Even at the height of the Praise the Lord television network's financial mismanagement, when Jim Bakker asked the board for a bonus of $200,000, Tammy Faye would get only $50,000.[14]

Male "spiritual covering" remained an essential part of how women articulated their validated authority. Submission to a celebrity male ecclesial figure was still an essential part of the pageantry of success. When Paula White was a rising star, even as a married adult woman she made references to her well-known mentor T. D. Jakes as her "spiritual daddy."[15] Likewise, when T. D. Jakes's other protégé, Juanita Bynum, made public amends with him after a falling out, she shuffled across the stage on her knees to prostrate herself at his feet and call him her father to whose authority she submitted.[16] Male patronage was essential in shielding women from the accusation of transgressing by overstepping set boundaries. Even Joyce Meyer, undisputedly the most powerful female figure in popular ministry, needed a husband to remind audiences that her first ministry was to her family. When the hundreds of thousands of newsletters from Joyce Meyer ministries were mailed out every year—each painstakingly prepared and frequently personalized with a hand-written note from a volunteer—there was often an image deemed so central to Joyce's reputation that it covered the entire envelope. It was a portrait of Joyce and her husband, Dave. She sat tall on her chair as the brightest star of the pentecostal universe and he stood over her, an otherwise invisible patriarch with his hands on her shoulders.

As we have seen in each chapter, the heights to which Christian celebrity women could rise depended on their ability to master the rules of complementarianism and capitalism, finding financial stability without appearing to be theologically overreaching. Women found a public voice in credentialing themselves as wives, mothers, and homemakers. From Elisabeth Elliot to Joanna Gaines, audiences rewarded those who opened the door to let them into their famously Christian homes. The title of "wife and mom" was so powerful that even the popular writer Rachel Held Evans was rejected by a Christian publisher on the grounds that, since she was not yet a mother, she could not write authoritatively about Christian womanhood.[17] Performing women earned tremendous power on their own, but instead of power by association (through marriage) they found themselves working on a borrowed stage. Though they gained independence as they soared up the charts, many found their careers were perpetually brokered by those with their own theological and financial agendas. Women who tendered their own lives for theological and therapeutic purposes, in memoirs, revelations, and confessions, found themselves with a potent but easily exhausted authority. The act of disclosure ran the risk of saying too much or rubbing away the shine of a polished career. And, likewise, managing beauty and sexuality in public life created tremendous market advantages but as many pitfalls, for women in conservative culture never fully managed to escape the suspicions reserved for the heirs of Eve.

Women who made it to the limelight understood how difficult it was to get there. Aspiring women in ministry without connections typically scratched out their niche in obscurity for years. Christena Cleveland learned the trade doing weekly talks for Campus Crusade, and Annie F. Downs volunteered at her megachurch's youth group until she built a reputation in nearby churches. Compensation for women was paltry.

There were always stories of those who slept on church pews or were billeted with church members. Angie Hong, former creative director at a Willow Creek satellite church, recalled how she worked her way up in music ministry singing for every local church until her vocal talents were finally noticed.[18] Those who wanted to make it knew that they had to beat their own drum for years, so when an online debate erupted between the industry's stars about their own relentless self-promotion—with Beth Moore boldly crying "Crucify it!"—small-time bloggers protested that they had little choice.[19] Breaks were few and far between.

But these women were not simply kept in place by the men in their lives. It was more complicated than that. Operating inside a tight-knit economy, these women learned to value conformity and agreement, avoiding controversial subjects and controversial people by extension. Silence rather than disagreement characterized public rhetoric, and hot topics were reserved for the banter of a select few leaders who could afford to keep Twitter abuzz. But not many could risk alienating potential audiences and endorsers when their profits hung in the balance. The Christian industry was simply too small—and too quick to punish—to sustain the careers of thorny brands. Over coffee and in private messages on social media, they fretted about Faustian bargains that might be made to keep their ministries afloat. Theirs was a fragile enterprise with careers that hung like a spider web on thousands of filaments. Without many powerful institutions under their complete control or even undisputed spiritual titles to claim, every step of their rise had to be carefully planned and perilously maintained. And when they succeeded they had had to create their own niche, curate their own story, and secure platforms without directly challenging the practices of male headship that ruled the boisterous market.

The market brought these women certain kinds of freedom, but it had its own cruelties. Take, for instance, the career of Jen Hatmaker. She had been evangelicalism's golden girl who enjoyed the great freedoms of the market, from starring in her own Target commercial to flogging organic cleaning products on her Facebook page.[20] But when she strayed from the flock by supporting LGBTQ+ relationships, she was sharply criticized by other female evangelical celebrities[21] and dropped by LifeWay Christian Resources, who pulled her books from their shelves. Hatmaker received death threats, her books were burned, and formerly supportive readers mailed their books back to her—after having mutilated them in some fashion.[22] "A lot of the faith community, and the public sphere, is predicated on group consensus and sort of, behaving, if you will," she reflected. "Making a break from any of them still carries the consequence of rejection. It's financially punitive. There's a real cost to breaking from party lines across a variety of issues."[23]

In the mid-2010s, a new era of protest began to make it unfeasible (or at least more difficult) for Christian women celebrities to maintain a polite silence about political issues that directly related to their brand: godly femininity. American society was stirred by a heated debate about inequity in the American Dream, seen most clearly in the rise of a decentralized African American justice movement called Black Lives Matter and the feminist resurgence which crystallized in the 2017 Women's March. The political sphere was roiled by the presidency of Donald Trump, the businessman and reality show star who had become a flawed hero for the evangelical base of the Republican party. As he gained traction with the religious right's Washington powerbrokers and a wide network of politically oriented pastors, Trump proclaimed a deeply evangelical theology of self-made men, small government, and a Christian America that galvanized voters tried in the fires of past culture wars. But it was Trump's championing of certain hot-button issues that tested the political quiescence of celebrity Christian women. To hear a serial adulterer fighting for "traditional families" and a sexual braggart at the helm of a purity-obsessed culture, women in the spotlight found themselves having to choose between defending or decrying a president on topics that lay directly in their area of expertise.

For stars like Beth Moore, the Trump presidency proved to be a bruising examination of the internal coherence of the movement's moral claims about the worth of women. After an extremely lewd *Access Hollywood* recording of Trump surfaced, Beth abandoned her practice of not speaking publicly about political matters. To her 880,000 Twitter followers, she wrote: "Try to absorb how acceptable the disesteem and objectifying of women has been when some Christian leaders don't think it's that big a deal. I'm one among many women sexually abused, misused, stared down, heckled, talked naughty to. Like we liked it. We didn't. We're tired of it."[24] While still an ardent complementarian, Beth argued that sexism was "no longer about a role in a church. It becomes an attitude

Beth Moore's incredible success is nonetheless fragile, as her livelihood depends on not alienating her evangelical and deeply Republican audience. David Lowe Photography–davidlowephotos.

of gender superiority. And that has to be dealt with." Christian men should not treat women "any less than Jesus treated women in the Gospels: always with dignity, always with esteem, never as secondary citizens." For her boldness, she was asked by male evangelical leaders to repent, and she was deserted by some of her female supporters. Attendance at her events dropped, and some women swore they would never buy another of her bible studies again.[25]

A number of observers have seen the treatment of Beth Moore and women like her as a demonstration of the patriarchy in action, a clear signal that complementarianism punishes women who speak up on political issues, thus violating a sphere properly belonging to men. Zakiya Jackson, an executive with the Expectations Project, a faith-based nonprofit addressing public education, claimed: "White evangelical women do as much as they are allowed to do . . . in terms of the cultural norms and cultural acceptability of what it means to be good Christian women. . . . There are times some women speak up more, but it would violate their primary role as being someone who shines a light on what their husband is doing or what their pastor is doing." In Jackson's opinion, Beth Moore's error was over-stepping her bounds and neglecting the role mandated for evangelical women: "to be loving Jesus and taking care of their families."[26] This view, however, forgets the many evangelical women who are active in politics but who have not suffered the negative consequences. Take, for example, Cissie Graham Lynch, granddaughter of Billy Graham and involved with both the Samaritan's Purse and the Billy Graham Evangelical Association. She penned the pre-election blog post entitled "Unapologetically Voting for Trump" and a subsequent foray "President Trump's First Year—We Survived!" which expressed dismay that evangelicals were critical of the president. She said:

> Don't you remember the crossroads we stood on the eve of November 8, 2016? It was a race for America's future. Two candidates. Two visions. Two different kind of Americas.
>
> One was a vision of progressive secularists who hate God, hate His followers and hate anything of Biblical Christianity. The other was a vision friendly to religious liberty and the sanctity of human life.
>
> Instead of complaining, evangelicals should be thanking God for President Trump. Even those who did not vote for him. Yes, I said it. You should be thanking God for him. Because no president in recent history has done as much for the evangelicals as President Trump has.

Chonda Pierce, the award-winning Christian comedienne known as "The Queen of Clean," performed at Trump's inaugural and received abuse from those who despised him. She joked about her car being vandalized and noted: "Ever since I have been talking about Donald Trump and liking him I haven't had to buy toilet paper—not one time. I go out into the yard and get it off the tree."[27] But her career had not suffered defections from her base audience—she was still the bestselling female comedian of all time.[28]

As leaders in the evangelical movement wrestled with the political dimensions of their public ministries, the aftershocks of the #MeToo movement had only began to be felt in the world of ministry. The complementarian framework of most large churches and ministries required

Chonda Pierce's popularity with the evangelicals who voted for Donald Trump made her a natural choice to perform at his inauguration. Reprinted with permission from *Christianity Today*, www.christianitytoday.com.

an implicit public trust that men could lead with a benevolent authority, a mirror of Christ's love for his Church. But as a renewed conversation about sexual abuse and "toxic masculinity" more broadly rippled through the church and social media, #ChurchToo and #SilenceIsNotSpiritual hashtags began a flood of stories of victimization by Christian male leaders. In short order, prominent church leaders such as megachurch pastors Andy Savage and Bill Hybels, evangelist Acton Bowen, and Frank Page, the president of the Southern Baptist Convention Executive Committee, were brought down by accusations of misconduct.[29] It was an uncomfortable reckoning with masculine authorities that put some megaministry wives on the defensive. Rebekah Lyons, wife of Q Ideas founder Gabe Lyons, reacted to the public airing of mistreatment in the church by asking women not to make it a "megaphone for bitterness. Confront privately. Winsome wins in the end."[30] She was met with a tremendous swell of anger for asking that meetings held to deal with problems that were structural or long term should be held in private. Not everyone was married to the boss.

In the #MeToo era of women's empowerment, it was easier to see that the borrowed power that sustained the careers of most celebrity women was fragile indeed. Influence gained through proximity to a man in ministry did not easily translate into lasting gains, particularly when it came to succession. By the late 2010s the average megachurch pastor was teetering on the edge of retirement, and the future was an open question. To whom would he bequeath the empire? One child might have all the markers of a divine calling while another might be a spiritual dullard. With few exceptions, every major televangelist and minister tapped a son over a daughter.[31] The most famous evangelist of the twentieth century, Billy Graham, used to say that it was his daughter, Anne Graham Lotz, who was the best preacher in the family.[32] Though early on he had not supported her in her ministry, seeing her preaching as an affront to her primary calling as a wife and mother, he eventually conceded that she had been called to teach the Bible. And yet Billy chose his son, Franklin, to receive his mantle. He would become the public face of the Graham name, taking up leadership of the Billy Graham Evangelistic Association and, according to some accounts, directing his elderly father's controversial public engagement in the waning years of his life.[33] Though Anne had a thriving ministry of her own (and the daughter of evangelical royalty), she would still encounter hostility on account of her sex. Prominent Baptist leaders kept her from their pulpits, and some even literally turned their backs on her as she addressed the crowd.[34] Even at her father's funeral, the presiding pastor thanked God for all the Graham children but singled out a pure line of male heirs as the true bearers of Graham's legacy.[35]

Even the most stratospheric successes for women in ministry could be undone and forgotten. Because women were often relegated to itinerant ministry or parachurch leadership, they rarely led substantive

Though she never claimed to have spiritual authority over men, Anne Graham Lotz faced many challenges to her authority to lead at all. Reprinted with permission from *Christianity Today*, www.christianitytoday.com.

Christian institutions that could carry on their work after their deaths. This is perhaps best seen in the collapse of Kathryn Kuhlman's preaching and healing foundation after her death in 1976. Her ministry had been a one-woman show, the product of her dominant personality, until late in her life when, suffering severe health problems, she made a series of unfortunate personnel decisions. On her demise it was discovered that her foundation was not to be her beneficiary, but that most of her property and money had been diverted to her unreliable business manager. With no one groomed to take her place, and few resources to carry on, her ministry imploded, leaving Kuhlman with no institutional legacy.[36]

Likewise, Mother Angelica's famous Catholic television network had no obvious charismatic successor. In 2019, the sudden death of author Rachel Held Evans, 37, met with a massive outpouring of grief and questions about the afterlife of her efforts. She had been one of the leading voices in the ex-evangelical movement and a fierce advocate of sexual and racial minorities in church leadership. As her spiritual following was largely online, what structures were in place to preserve her memory and further her work? The ability to preserve legacy was a privilege reserved almost exclusively for those men at the helm of powerful religious organizations. Since most women of all theological persuasions lacked the prerequisite institutional backing, memory itself was in peril.

Most women's power in modern megaministry was contingent and noninstitutional. The only way that women in ministry were going to achieve a lasting influence was if institutions changed. But transformation was so often precipitated only by crisis. If we return to the example of Nancy Wilson, the only openly lesbian woman ever to lead an American denomination, we recall that she believed that her path to power was based on two factors: the first was a charismatic predecessor who knew when to let go of his control, and the second was the AIDS crisis. "Gay men had more power, more education, and often more resources," she recalled, "and those men in the early days had to be challenged by lesbians to make room. The AIDS crisis radically changed the gender dynamic after we lost so many leaders, and women had to step in to those positions."[37]

The problem remained that contingency limited the imagination around women in leadership—but there were glimmers of change on the horizon. Jeanne Stevens of Soul City Church in Chicago was one of the few evangelical megachurch co-pastors with equal authority to her husband. She and her husband were sure to set equal salaries and operate with their own chains of commands with staff. "I decided a long time ago that I wanted to be a great pastor. I didn't want to be a great female pastor because I've never heard a man say, 'I'm a great male pastor,'" Jeanne said firmly.[38] It was the sort of confidence in one's own abilities that women had to borrow for a moment as they set out to assume pastoral duties and titles that were usually intended for someone else. Could she do it? What if she allowed herself to try?

Amy Butler had spent long hours wondering what the price of leadership might be. As one of the only solo women in megachurch leadership, she had assumed control of the historic Riverside Church in Manhattan in a flurry of controversy over the last pastor's departure. Hers was a national platform and an opportunity to lead one of the great American liberal pulpits that Rev. Henry Fosdick had made famous a generation before with his fiery prose. One day, she was wandering around the archives and found herself staring into the glass case in which Henry Fosdick's preaching robes were immaculately preserved. After a moment of doubt, she shook off her nerves and opened the case, carefully lifting the robes off the dress form and slipping them on.

"I didn't think they would fit," she said, laughing. "But wouldn't you know. They did. Perfectly."[39]

MEGACHURCHES IN THE UNITED STATES

To become familiar with the wives of megachurch pastors and gain insight into larger patterns, researcher Joshua Young and I surveyed all the megachurches in the United States as of July 2014. We began with the list of megachurches compiled by the Hartford Institute for Religion Research.[1] Based on the accepted definition of a megachurch as a Protestant congregation with more than two thousand regular attendees, including both adults and children at its weekly worship services, we identified 1,551 congregations that can be classified as "megachurches." Armed with this list, we created profiles of each congregation's Internet presence as well as the social media imprint of the wife of the senior pastor. Appendix I introduces readers to the broader landscape of American megachurches which varies widely in size, location, and theological persuasion.

TOP TEN LARGEST PROTESTANT MEGACHURCHES

e.g., Megachurch (Location)—membership

1) Lakewood Church (Houston, TX)—43,500
2) North Point Community Church (Alpharetta, GA)—30,629
3) LifeChurch.TV (Edmond, OK)—30,000
4) Gateway Church (Southlake, TX)—28,000
5) Willow Creek Community Church (South Barrington, IL)—25,743
6) Fellowship Church (Grapevine, TX)—24,162
7) Christ's Church of the Valley (Phoenix, AZ)—23,395
8) NewSpring Church (Anderson, SC)—23,055
9) Elevation Church (Matthews, NC)—22,200
10) Church of the Highlands (Birmingham, AL)—22,184

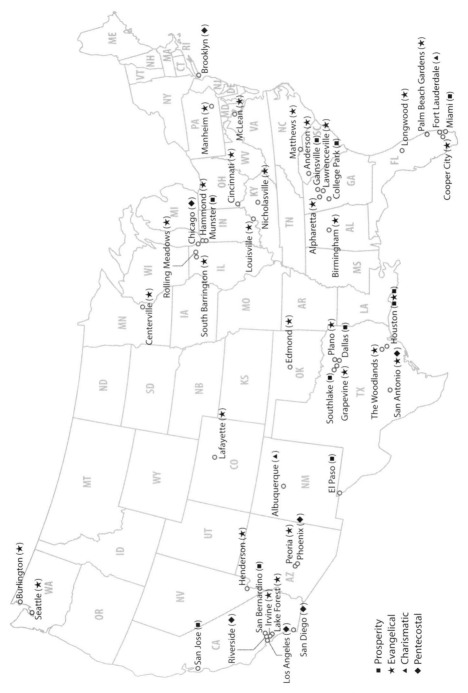

Figure 3. Illustrated map of top fifty megachurch locations.

THE LARGEST MEGACHURCH FOR THE TWENTY LARGEST PROTESTANT DENOMINATIONS

e.g., Denomination: Largest Megachurch within Denomination (Location of Megachurch)—Membership Size of Megachurch (Ranking of Megachurch in The Hartford Institute List)

1) Southern Baptist Convention: Fellowship Church (Grapevine, TX)—24,162 (No. 6)
2) United Methodist Church: Church of the Resurrection (Leawood, KS)—10,137 (No. 76)
3) Church of God in Christ: West Angeles Church of God in Christ (Los Angeles, CA)—13,000 (No. 41)
4) National Baptist Convention: Eastern Star Church (Indianapolis, IN)—10,000 (No. 91)
5) Evangelical Lutheran Church in America: Lutheran Church of Hope (West Des Moines, IA)—10,578 (No. 71)
6) National Baptist Convention of America: Wheeler Avenue Baptist Church (Houston, TX)—6,000 (No. 228)
7) Assemblies of God: Dream City Church (Phoenix, AZ)—21,000 (No. 12)
8) Presbyterian Church, USA: University Presbyterian Church (Seattle, WA)—3,896 (No. 478)
9) African Methodist Episcopal Church (AME): First AME Church of L.A. (Los Angeles, CA)—10,000 (No. 88)
10) National Missionary Baptist Convention of America: New Birth Missionary Bapt. Church (Lithonia, GA)—12,000 (No. 52)
11) Lutheran Church—Missouri Synod: None
12) Episcopal Church: St. Michael and All Angels Episcopal (Dallas, TX)—5,000 (No. 297)
13) Churches of Christ: Oak Hills Church (San Antonio, TX)—8,663 (No. 116)
14) Pentecostal Assemblies of the World: Apostolic Church of God (Chicago, IL)—10,500 (No. 73)
15) African Methodist Episcopal Zion Church: None
16) American Baptist Church, USA: Friendship-West Baptist Church (Dallas, TX)—9,000 (No. 108)
17) Evangelical Covenant: LifeChurch.TV (Edmond, OK)—30,000 (No. 3)
18) Calvary Chapel: Calvary Chapel (Fort Lauderdale, FL)—18,521 (No. 16)
19) Foursquare Gospel: New Hope Christian Fellowship (Honolulu, HI)—11,000 (No. 67)
20) The Wesleyan Church: 12 Stone Church (Lawrenceville, GA)—13,563 (No. 36)

THE LARGEST MEGACHURCH FOR EACH THEOLOGICAL TYPE

Megachurches tend to associate with other churches of their theological type, rather than strict denominational or regional associations. In the Glossary on pages xv–xvii, I defined various theological subtypes of megachurches. The following are the largest instances of each of these kinds of churches.

Prosperity: Lakewood Church (Houston, TX)—43,500 (No. 1)

Evangelical: North Point Community Church (Alpharetta, GA)—30,629 (No. 2)

Pentecostal: Dream City Church (Phoenix, AZ)—21,000 (No. 12)

Charismatic: Calvary Chapel (Fort Lauderdale, FL)—18,521 (No. 16)

Pentecostalized Historic Black: New Birth Missionary Baptist Church (Lithonia, GA)—12,000 (No. 52)

Mainline: Lutheran Church of Hope (West Des Moines, IA)—10,578 (No. 71)

Historic Black: First AME Church of L.A. (Los Angeles, CA)—10,000 (No. 88)

RESEARCHING MEGACHURCH PASTORS' WIVES

When researcher Joshua Young and I created profiles of the largest 1,551 congregations classified as "megachurches," we undertook an examination of the role of women's public roles. We sought to identify the following characteristics of either the congregation or the pastor's wife:

- Congregation's Size
  ○ The number of weekly participants as determined by The Hartford Institute
  ○ This dimension was largely straightforward, but we did adjust numbers that were drastically out of line with other data. In these instances, we alerted The Hartford Institute of the discrepancy to allow them to update their information. An example of this type of situation is Elevation Church based in Matthews, NC. Elevation had experienced considerable growth since the data was compiled by The Hartford Institute, leading to the data they provided being inaccurate.

- Congregation's Location
  ○ The geographic location of the congregation's main campus
  ○ While straightforward, this dimension raised the interesting question of what to do with satellite sites. We eventually settled on treating satellite sites as part of the larger whole for numerical purposes, and the location as anchored in the main campus. The question of satellite sites and how to treat them promises to be an important piece of future research on the subject of megaministries.

- Congregation's Denomination
  ○ The official denominational affiliation of a congregation
  ○ For the most part, this category was straightforward with only a few caveats to consider: 1) often "non-denominational" congregations

actually maintained important links to established denominations, which led us to categorize them as said denomination; 2) a few congregations we looked at changed denominations in the course of our study (see Newhope Church in Durham, NC, as an example of switching).

- Congregation's Denominational Type
  - Groupings of denominations that share a family resemblance in terms of theology, ecclesiology, and general approach to ministry.
  - The types we identified were: Prosperity, Evangelical, Pentecostal, Charismatic, Historic Black, Pentecostalized Historic Black, and Mainline.
  - Congregations have more in common with churches of their same type than they do with those outside of it. By grouping similar congregations together, regardless of official denominational affiliation, we achieved two important aims: 1) we created more meaningful categories to determine overarching patterns and trends; and 2) we were able to distinguish between "non-denominational" congregations without any official alignment, which make up the majority of megachurches but actually vary a great deal within that label of non-denominational.

- Senior Pastor's Name
  - The name of the senior/lead pastor of the main campus congregation
  - This dimension was very straightforward except for one or two congregations that changed pastors during the examination. The most prominent example of such a departure/change was Mark Driscoll and Mars Hill Church in Seattle, WA.

- Senior Pastor's Wife's Name
  - The name of the senior/lead pastor's current wife
  - For the overwhelming majority of the megachurches we looked at, this information was readily available from the church website. As congregation size decreased, however, examples surfaced that required greater digging and sources outside of the church website. Eventually, this reality was factored into the coding of "Pastor's Wife's Internet Presence," which will be discussed elsewhere.

- Wife's Title
  - Title provided on the church website for the Pastor's Wife, if a title is provided
  - Title categories captured: Dr., First Lady, Pastor, Co-Pastor, and Other Title
  - The vast majority of the women examined had no official title at all. That said, where titles were used and what they were correlated to other factors, such as age, race, and denominational type. It is worth noting that we only captured official titles promoted on church materials, not more informal ones.

- Wife's Age
  - The approximate decade age-range of the senior/lead pastor's wife
  - The decade categories were 20s (20–29 years old), 30s (30–39 years old), 40s (40–49 years old), 50s (50–59 years old), 60s (60–69 years old), 70s (70–79 years old), and 80s+ (80 years old and older).
  - The determination of age proved surprisingly difficult. Most pastors did not present their age on any of the official materials for the church. Many appeared considerably younger than they actually were. Both of these realities were exponentially truer when it came to their wives. Consequently, we had to look elsewhere to get such information. Social media proved helpful in this process, and the source of many age determinations was graduation dates and autobiographical stories about how the couple met and got married.
  - Given these limitations, we decided to group age by approximate decade rather than attempt to obtain to precise age. The result of said choice produced a normal distribution centered on the 50s.

- Wife's Education
  - The highest level of education obtained by the senior/lead pastor's wife
  - Levels included: High School diploma, Bible College, Bachelor's degree, MA/MDiv/MTS, Ph.D/Th.D./MD, Other Education, and No Education Available
  - Education proved to be one of the more challenging categories to capture. In almost all cases, we had to look elsewhere to obtain the necessary information, as it was not generally presented on the church website. Those instances where the church promoted the

wife's education proved enlightening as they generally accompanied other markers such as race, denomination, or area of specialization.

o As with age, social media and autobiographical snippets proved invaluable in determining level of education.

o There were numerous instances in which level of education could not be determined. This lack of data was itself useful and an important pattern.

- Wife's Specialization
  o The area of expertise/interest held by the senior/lead pastor's wife
  o This dimension frequently included such topics as women, parenting, marriage, homemaking, evangelism, foster care, human trafficking, social justice, Bible study, and global missions.
  o As opposed to constructing categories, we simply cataloged what categories the women claimed for themselves. This resulted in a large assortment of categories, but also a pattern of the most frequent ones.

- Wife's Race
  o The race of the senior/lead pastor's wife.
  o The racial categories we used were: White, Black, Latina, Asian, and Other.
  o This category was straightforward but proved very consequential. In almost all instances, the wife's race aligned with the senior/lead pastor and the congregation at large, but there were a few examples of the wife being of a different race.
  o Race proved an important predictor of other dimensions.

- Is the Senior Pastor's wife from a Christian dynasty?
  o This dimension categorizes if the wife come from a famous/established Christian celebrity family either through birth, marriage, or transmission of authority. In almost all instances, such connections were mentioned on the church website or other media platforms. In those instances where such connections were not explicit, we relied on our wider knowledge of the landscape of American Protestantism in the United States to locate these women within the informal network of famous families.

- Are the Senior Pastor's children involved in the ministry?
  ○ This category gauges the level of involvement of the couple's children in ministry. This was directly related to theological categories. For instance, most churches categorized as "prosperity," hired their children as successors.
  ○ In some instances, children were actively involved in ministry and were celebrities in their own right. Other times, children were simply mentioned or pictured as part of the senior/lead pastor's bio on the church website. There were also numerous instances in which there either were no children, or the children were not publicly involved in the ministry to the point their names were not available.

- Does the wife maintain a public ministry? If so, what is it focused on?
  ○ This category sought to capture the public activities of the senior/ lead pastor's wife.
  ○ What this activity included varied widely from woman to woman, and most of the wives we examined maintained no real public ministry aside from being the pastor's wife. The higher a woman fell on the Internet Presence scale we developed, though, the more likely she was to have several active public ministries.

- Wife's Internet Presence
  ○ Early on, we realized that the women in question maintained differing Internet presences. In response to this realization and the belief that said differences were significant, we established the coding system shown in Table 1 to rank pastors' wives' Internet presence.
  ○ This coding system in turn gave us a quantifiable means of identifying where along the spectrum of celebrity we could locate each woman.

This process produced a digital card for each megachurch pastor's wife. The following is an example of said card:

0024.—Serita Jakes—The Potter's House—16,141

Title: First Lady
Age: 50s
Education: No Ed Listed (Education is mentioned, but not specified in any way)
Profile: Own profile on church website

Table 1: Internet Presence Rating System

	Qualities
0.0	No discernable Internet presence
0.5	Only a mention of her on the church / ministry website
1.0	Slightly more than a mention (typically a paragraph or picture) on the church / ministry website
1.5	Joint profile on the church / ministry website
2.0	Own profile on the church / ministry website
2.5	Own inactive website / blog (irregular updates, some outdated information, static)
3.0	Own active website / blog (regularly updated, up-to-date information, dynamic, interactive)
3.5	Niche ministry with its own website
4.0	Multiple inactive / passive websites / blogs
4.5	Multiple active websites / blogs
5.0	Appears in numerous places on the internet, numerous results come up on an internet search; information about her is available apart from the church / ministry
+0.5 bump	Book(s) or curriculum
	Radio or television ministry in addition to central church / ministry

Area of Specialty: Women
Racial Identity: Black
Dynasty: No Dynasty
Children: Absent Children (none pictured; mere mention) (Daughter achieved fame during study)
Public Ministry: Author, Social Media (Twitter & Facebook)

Each answer was tagged and cataloged such that the entire database could be searched for specific qualities. This searchability quality allowed us to see and track overarching patterns and characteristics as well as identify outliers and exceptions.

Similarly, we generated a spreadsheet from our cards that contained some of the pertinent information for each congregation and woman. Figure 4 shows the spreadsheet entries for the top ten megachurches at the time of the research. We then used the master spreadsheet to generate more targeted sheets for dimensions of note or importance.

Rank	Church Name	Av. Atten.	Pastor Name	Wife Name	Geographic Location	Denomination	Type	Race	Age	Web
1	Lakewood Church	43500	Joel Osteen	Victoria	Houston, TX	NONDEN	Prosperity	White	40	5
2	North Point Community Church	30629	Andy Stanley	Sandra	Alpharetta, GA	NONDEN	Evangelical	White	50	3.5
3	LifeChurch.TV	30000	Graig Groeschel	Amy	Edmond, OK	EC	Evangelical	White	30	5
4	Gateway Church	28000	Robert Morris	Debbie	Southlake, TX	NONDEN	Prosperity	White	40	5
5	Willow Creek Community Church	25743	Bill Hybels	Lynne	South Barrington, IL	NONDEN	Evangelical	White	60	5
6	Fellowship Church	24162	Ed Young	Lisa	Grapevine, TX	SBC	Evangelical	White	40	4
7	NewSpring Church	23055	Perry Noble	Lucretia	Anderson, SC	BAPT	Evangelical	White	40	4
8	Church of the Highlands	22184	Chris Hodges	Tammy	Birmingham, AL	NONDEN	Evangelical	White	50	3.5
9	Saddleback Church	22055	Rick Warren	Kay	Lake Forest, CA	SBC	Evnagelical	White	50	5
10	Southwest Christian Church	21764	Dave Stone	Beth	Louisville, KY	CHRIST	Evangelical	White	50	3.5

Figure 4. Top ten megachurches at the time of the survey.

As we progressed through the process, though, it became apparent that some dimensions were no longer providing useful information. When we reached these points, we found a logical place to stop, continued to examine the congregation up to that point, and captured information about the women in question. Regardless, we went through all 1,551 of the megachurch congregations identified by The Hartford Institute, even if they were below the cutoff point. Also, we fully captured complete information on any congregation that was the largest of any category. Finally, we fully captured all congregations for specific groups, such as the Southern Baptist Convention and the Mainline, as the complete picture for these groups was important to the overall argument of the book or a specific chapter.

In addition to the concrete aspects of the study, we routinely met to discuss our impressions and compare notes that we each made for each woman in addition to the data points we were collecting. These conversations tapped into our historical knowledge, familiarity with the congregations, previous interactions with the woman in question and others.

SOME DEMOGRAPHICS FROM THE PROFILES

As we conducted the examination described in Appendix II, we collected a great deal of demographic data on megachurches. This data simultaneously demonstrates the diversity of the phenomenon and confirms many commonly held understandings of it. Several key areas were particularly important to the story of women in megaministry: age, race, congregation type, and Internet presence. As such, each of these areas warrant a closer look.

AGE

We captured age by decade (e.g., 20s, 30s, 40s, 50s, 60s, 70s), since in general finding the exact age of the people in question was extremely difficult. This difficulty was exacerbated by the fact that the American cult of youth means that most public figures obscure their age to appear younger. Due to this reality, we had to rely on several factors to determine the approximate decade within which each person's age fell. Things such as graduation dates, historical clues in biographic profiles, birthday celebration events on social media, and the age they were when they assumed leadership of their church were considered in such determinations. In those instances in which a determination could not confidently be made, age was cataloged as "Unknown." The result of these considerations led to the following decade breakdown for the top 275 megachurch pastors.

Since we captured the decade rather than actual age, calculations concerning age were more complicated than other demographics. The result was a range rather than a concrete number. For example, the

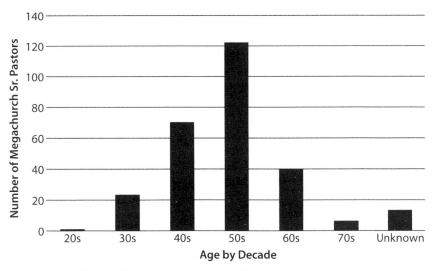

Figure 5. Age by decade for top 275 megachurch senior pastors.

mean age of the pastors of the top 275 megachurches was between 47.44 and 56.44. If one averages the two ends of the spectrum, the mean age of the top 275 megachurch pastors was 51.94. The median was between 50 and 59, and the average median within the spectrum was 54.5. Since the majority of these numbers were collected in 2014 and 2015 as part of the initial examination, three and a half years needs to be added to them to arrive at a realistic approximation for 2018. The resulting figures would be a mean age spectrum from 50.94 to 59.94, with an average within this range being 55.44. The median range would then become 53 to 62 with an average median of 58. Assuming a normal distribution for the means of the unknowns would strengthen these figures. Given the low level of retirements, deaths, or other reasons for exiting ministry by megachurch pastors, as well as the age floor for adulthood, the relatively small number of new megachurches founded by younger pastors since the examination was conducted would have a relatively minor influence on these numbers. As a result, our data suggests that the average megachurch pastor in 2018 is in their fifties with half or more in their late fifties or early sixties. Due to this age breakdown, the question of succession has become even more pressing.

Many megachurches have begun to consider what life and ministry will look like for their organization without their founder and senior pastor. Further research will need to be conducted over the next several years to determine how these congregations address this potential problem and how successful their choices prove to be.

RACE

To determine the race of a congregation, we used the commonly held understanding that a congregation is classified according to a given race if 80 percent or more of its members belong to a single race. Congregations with more than 20 percent of congregants from a race different than the predominant race are classified as mixed race. As with age, this determination was made through a combination of factors including self-identification, photographs of the congregation, online descriptions, the race of the senior pastor and other staff, and tradition affiliation. Of these factors, self-identification was weighted

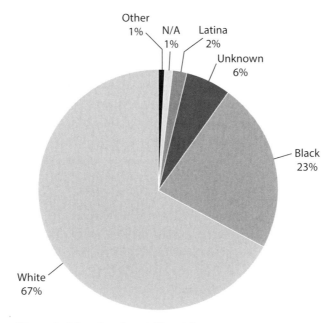

Figure 6. Megachurch racial breakdown.

highest in the determination. If unable to make a solid determination based on these factors, the congregation was designated as "unknown" for racial composition. Further research is needed on the subject of the "unknown" category as well as the "other" (primarily, Asian and Hawaiian).

Based on these factors, we found the racial breakdown of the megachurches we profiled to be as follows:

Megachurch Racial Breakdown

> White—67%
> Black—23%
> Latina—2%
> Other—1%
> Mixed—1%
> Unknown—6%

CONGREGATION TYPE

Building on my earlier work, researcher Joshua Young and I broke the megachurches we examined into seven types: Evangelical, Pentecostal, Prosperity, Charismatic, Historic Black, Pentecostalized Historic Black, and Mainline (definitions available in the Glossary on pages xv–xvii). The designation of type was based on theology, ecclesiology, associations, and brand. The assignment of type allowed us to transcend the rise of non-denominational affiliations as well as the complicated relationships between megachurches and formal denominational structures. It also brought patterns into focus that denominational affiliation, or lack thereof, obscured or minimized.

Type Breakdown

> Evangelical—52%
> Pentecostal—14%
> Prosperity—14%
> Charismatic—6%
> Historic Black—6%
> Pentecostalized Historic Black—5%
> Mainline—3%

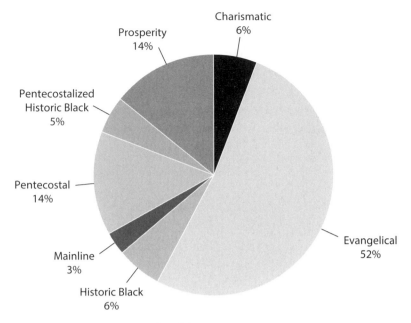

Figure 7. Congregation type breakdown.

INTERNET PRESENCE

As discussed in Appendix II, we created a coding system to gauge the Internet presence of megachurch pastors' wives. The results gave us a numerical way of understanding the different levels of presence these women maintained online.

As you can see from Figure 8, roughly a third of the women we examined maintained a very minimal Internet presence, but few maintained no presence at all.

For those women who maintained an Internet presence beyond their husbands' profile, the most common presence was their own profile or ministry website.

The bump received for a book, curriculum, or radio or television ministry boosted several women, but it did little to move a woman from the minimal (0–2.5) to significant (3–5) category.

In addition to the Internet presence scale, we also captured the social media platforms used by those women whose presence was deemed

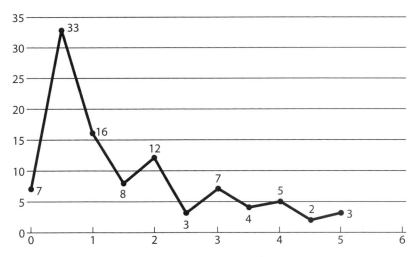

Figure 8. Internet presence of megachurch pastors' wives.

significant. The platforms we considered were Twitter, Facebook, Pinterest, Instagram, LinkedIn, and Other (platforms like YouTube or Christian social media platforms). Of those women with a 3+ Internet presence, approximately 13 percent did not maintain any form of social media presence and 3 percent only used one of the considered platforms. The rest of the women had a presence on multiple platforms. The most widely used platform was Twitter with roughly 74 percent of these women. Facebook was used by 63 percent; Pinterest was used by 50 percent; Instagram was used by 28 percent; LinkedIn was used by 32 percent; and 3 percent of these women used another form of social media. The higher a woman's Internet presence score, the more likely she was to maintain numerous, if not all, social media platforms. At the same time, the larger the woman's congregation, the more likely she was to maintain multiple platforms. For those women with a significant Internet presence, there was no racial difference with regard to which platforms they used or the number they maintained, and the Internet presence score for racial breakdown mirrored the composition of the broader megachurch landscape.

WOMEN IN CONSERVATIVE SEMINARIES

In order to assess the employment opportunities that various theological degrees make possible, we wanted to gauge the presence of women at conservative seminaries. We wanted to examine the presence of women on faculty as well as their specialties; in addition, we researched the options available to female students and programming and courses aimed at women. To accomplish all of these tasks, we identified the thirteen top conservative seminaries in the United States.[1] Once we had compiled the list of seminaries, we examined their websites and other publications to get a sense of the place of women attending and working at the institutions. We paid attention to female faculty members, courses, and programs concerning women, and the overall portrayal of women in a seminary's materials. This examination resulted in some quantifiable numbers about women at conservative seminaries and some general impressions about the opportunities available to women at these institutions.

The seminaries we studied were:

- Dallas Theological Seminary (Dallas, TX)
- Fuller Theological Seminary (Pasadena, CA)
- Golden Gate Baptist Theological Seminary (Mill Valley, CA)
- Gordon Conwell Theological Seminary (Charlotte, NC)
- Liberty University School of Divinity (Lynchburg, VA)
- Midwestern Baptist Theological Seminary (Kansas City, MO)
- New Orleans Baptist Theological Seminary (New Orleans, LA)
- Oral Roberts University (Tulsa, OK)
- Regent University School of Divinity (Virginia Beach, VA)
- Southeastern Baptist Theological Seminary (Wake Forest, NC)
- Southern Baptist Theological Seminary (Louisville, KY)
- Southwestern Baptist Theological Seminary (Fort Worth, TX)
- Trinity Evangelical Divinity School (Deerfield, IL)

Table 2: Southern Baptist Convention (SBC) v. Non-SBC

Southern Baptist Convention	Non-SBC
Golden Gate Baptist Theological Seminary	Fuller Theological Seminary
Midwestern Baptist Theological Seminary	Gordon Conwell Theological Seminary
New Orleans Baptist Theological Seminary	Dallas Theological Seminary
Southeastern Baptist Theological Seminary	Liberty University School of Divinity
Southern Baptist Theological Seminary	Oral Roberts University
Southwestern Baptist Theological Seminary	Regent University School of Divinity
	Trinity Evangelical Divinity School

Noticing patterns and trends, we further broke the list down into Southern Baptist Convention (SBC) and non-SBC-affiliated seminaries. The breakdown is shown in Table 2.

Seminaries shared greater similarities with the institutions within their same theological family than the other. For example, women's ministry as a professional category supported by courses and programs is prominent at SBC-affiliated seminaries, but only appears at two non-SBC seminaries, Liberty and Regent. Similarly, areas of specialty broke down differently depending on theological family. An example of this difference can be seen in the fact that SBC seminaries do not have any women specializing in history, Bible, or theology, but non-SBC seminaries do. Finally, SBC schools tend to draw faculty from themselves and other SBC institutions, while non-SBC schools tend to have a much greater diversity in terms of faculty training. Through all of these factors, though, Liberty University School of Divinity remains an outlier in that it more closely resembles the SBC schools than the non-SBC seminaries for a number of markers. Given its lack of official affiliation with the SBC, we chose to group it with the non-SBC seminaries despite these differences.

With the seminaries selected and sorted, we collected data on the following three topics (shown in Tables 3 through 7):

- Number of Women on Faculty
- Titles of Women on Faculty
- Areas of Expertise of Women on Faculty

Table 3: Faculty Gender Breakdown at SBC Seminaries

	Faculty Gender Breakdown at SBC Seminaries		
	Total Faculty	Male Faculty	Female Faculty
Golden Gate	27	24 (89%)	3 (11%)
Midwestern	36	35 (97%)	1 (3%)
New Orleans	78	67 (86%)	11 (14%)
Southeastern	64	62 (97%)	2 (3%)
Southern	68	66 (97%)	2 (3%)
Southwestern	109	97 (89%)	12 (11%)
	382	351 (92%)	31 (8%)

Table 4: Faculty Gender Breakdown at Non-SBC Seminaries

	Faculty Gender Breakdown at Non-SBC Seminaries		
	Total Faculty	Male Faculty	Female Faculty
Dallas	108	94 (87%)	14 (13%)
Fuller	62	51 (82%)	11 (18%)
Gordon Conwel	65	56 (86%)	9 (14%)
Liberty	57	55 (96%)	2 (4%)
Oral Roberts	24	21 (88%)	3 (12%)
Regent	37	33 (89%)	4 (11%)
Trinity	51	45 (88%)	6 (12%)
	404	355 (88%)	49 (12%)

Table 5: Average Gender Breakdown at Conservative Seminaries

	Average Gender Breakdown at Conservative Seminaries		
	SBC	Non-SBC	Combined
Mean Faculty	63.67	57.71	60.46
Mean Male Faculty	58.5 (92%)	50.71 (88%)	54.31 (90%)
Mean Female Faculty	5.17 (8%)	7 (12%)	6.15 (10%)

Table 6: Female Faculty Title Breakdown

	Female Faculty Title Breakdown		
	SBC	*Non-SBC*	*Combined*
Adjunct	2 (6%)	10 (13%)	12 (11%)
Assistant	6 (19%)	17 (22%)	23 (21%)
Associate	8 (26%)	23 (30%)	31 (29%)
Full Professor	13 (42%)	22 (29%)	35 (33%)
Other	2 (6%)	4 (5%)	6 (6%)
	31 (29%)	76 (71%)	107

Table 7: Female Faculty Expertise Breakdown

	Female Faculty Expertise Breakdown		
	SBC	*Non-SBC*	*Combined*
Bible	-	12 (16%)	12 (11%)
Communication	-	8 (12%)	8 (7%)
Counseling	3 (10%)	10 (13%)	13 (12%)
Education	9 (29%)	15 (20%)	24 (22%)
English/Writing	3 (10%)	-	3 (3%)
History	-	2 (3%)	2 (2%)
Intercultural	1 (3%)	4 (5%)	5 (5%)
Library	2 (6%)	-	2 (2%)
Music	4 (13%)	7 (9%)	11 (10%)
Pastoral Studies	-	3 (4%)	3 (3%)
Preaching	-	4 (5%)	4 (4%)
Social Work	2 (6%)	-	2 (2%)
Sports Ministry	-	2 (3%)	2 (2%)
Women	7 (23%)	2 (3%)	9 (8%)
Other	-	7 (9%)	7 (7%)
	31 (29%)	76 (71%)	107

To assess these numbers, we reviewed both the faculty directory and the faculty pages for the school in question. For the most part, gender was easy to determine based on faculty biographies provided and pronouns used. In the handful of instances in which it was difficult to determine gender from these sources, further research was conducted to verify any questionable genders. We also paid attention to how easy or difficult it was to determine.

While gender was relatively easy to determine, it was more difficult to determine faculty rank for women at several of the institutions in question. As such, faculty members whose rank was indeterminable were excluded from calculations to minimize error. We gauged expertise only for those whose title was clear.

WOMEN ON STAFF AT MEGACHURCHES

Next, we turned our attention to women on staff at megachurches. Returning to our original list of megachurches from our general examination of pastors' wives, we cataloged whether a congregation had a female pastor or a female staff member with high enough rank to warrant inclusion on the church website. We also captured the title of the highest-ranking female on staff and how female staff members were presented compared to male staff members. In all instances, presentation was critical. While it is highly likely that all of the churches we considered had at least one woman on staff in some capacity, we were interested in the women the congregations were putting forth as part of their public face, as well as those women who achieved a level of success or celebrity that there were benefits for the church to include. In those instances in which we could find no information on staff, we directly contacted the congregations with inquiries about the makeup of the staff. Some congregations were responsive to our inquiries, others were not. In instances in which an answer could not be definitively determined, it was marked as "unknown."

The female pastors and staff members breakdown for the top twenty-five congregations is shown in Table 8.

Even within the top twelve, several things stand out about these results.

- None of the top twelve congregations were led by a female senior pastor; this reality held until number eighty-five, Greater Saint Stephen Full Gospel Baptist, where Debra Morton serves as the senior pastor.
- The fact that Southern Baptist Convention congregations do not have a female pastor is not surprising. What was surprising, though, was how much they obscure their entire staff other than the male ordained clergy. SBC congregations were especially difficult to determine if they

Table 8: Female Staff at Top Twenty-Five Churches

Congregation	Sr. Pastor	Pastor	Staff	Title
Lakewood Church	No	Yes	Yes	Co-Pastor / Associate Pastor
North Point Community Church	No	Yes	Yes	Associate Pastor
Lifechurch.TV	No	No	Unknown	-
Gateway Church	No	Yes	Yes	Associate Sr. Pastor
Willow Creek Community Church	No	Yes	Yes	Executive Pastor
Fellowship Church	No	No	Unknown	-
NewSpring Church	No	No	No	-
Church of the Highlands	No	No	Yes	-
Saddleback Church	No	No	Unknown	-
Southeast Christian Church	No	No	Unknown	-
Central Christian Church Henderson	No	No	Unknown	-
Dream City Church	No	No	Yes	Director of Women's Ministry

had women on staff, much less the titles held by these women. The overwhelming majority of them did not respond to inquiries for information about their staffs.

- The first congregation in which the highest woman on staff was the director of women's ministry was Dream City Church.
- Overall, titles were far more difficult to determine than we originally anticipated. While pictures and biographies were often presented for both men and women, these items often stood alone, absent a title. The exceptions to this rule were ordained clergy, who almost always carried a title in all of their presentations.
- The only congregation in the top twelve for which we could find staff directories and other online listings but could not identify a single woman on staff was NewSpring Church.

This kind of cataloging and analysis was done for all of the megachurches we profiled for the pastors' wives described in Appendix II.

Table 9: Senior Pastors

Congregation	Attend.	Sr. Pastor	Type	Race
Willow Creek Community Church[a]	25,743	~~Heather Larson~~	Evangelical	White
Greater St. Stephen Full Gospel Baptist[b]	10,000	Debra Morton	Pentecostalized Historic Black	Black
Victory Christian Center[c]	9,500	~~Sharon Daugherty~~	Prosperity	White
Victory Church[d]	8,000	~~Jennifer Crow~~	Prosperity	White
Christian Faith Center[e]	5,000	~~Brenda Timberlake~~	Prosperity	White
Glide Memorial United Methodist[f]	3,000	~~Karen Oliveto~~	Mainline	White
Without Walls International[g]	3,000	Paula White	Prosperity	White
Christ Gospel Church[h]	2,500	Berniece Hicks	Pentecostal	White
Riverside Church	2,500	Amy Butler	Mainline	White
The Rock Church International[i]	2,225	~~Anne Gimenez~~	Pentecostal	White
Ray of Hope Christian Church	2,000	Cynthia Hale	Pentecostalized Historic Black	Black
Faith Deliverance Christian Center	2,000	Sharon Riley	Pentecostal	Black
City of Life Church[j]	2,000	Amy Smith	Prosperity	White
Cathedral of Hope	1,800	~~Jo Hudson~~	Mainline	White
Marilyn Hickey Ministries[k]		Marilyn Hickey	Prosperity	White

[a]Having served less than a year in the position, Heather Larson and her co-lead pastor Steve Carter resigned along with the entire Board of Elders in the wake of a scandal surrounding founding pastor, Bill Hybels.

[b]She is listed as pastor, but her husband is listed as bishop and included in all presentations.

[c]The church has been turned over to Sharon's son and his wife, Paul and Ashley Daugherty.

[d]After Mark Crow was accused of infidelity, co-founder Jennifer Crow turned to a separate parachurch ministry. The church they founded now has all male pastors.

[e]The church was led by Brenda Timberlake who gave the ministry to her son and his wife. The church website lists both Jennifer and her husband as the lead pastors.

[f]Karen Oliveto has been elected bishop, and she no longer serves at Glide Memorial.

[g]Though Paula is the senior pastor and nationally known, it is difficult to find any mention of her on the church website. Instead, her husband is presented as the bishop.

[h]Given her age, it is unclear what her actual role is in the day-to-day operations of the church, but she is heavily promoted as the founder of the tradition and the leader of the church.

[i]The church was founded by John and Anne Gimenez, and led by John. Anne was widowed into the position of leadership.

[j]Amy and her husband, Jeff, are listed as the current senior pastors. If one drills down, it is clear that she is in charge of the women's ministry and he is in charge of everything else. They inherited the church from his parents, who are now listed as founding pastors.

[k]Marilyn and her husband, Wally, used to lead a megachurch known as "The Happy Church" in Denver, Colorado. Marilyn has been largely outside of congregational ministry for the last two decades. Her daughter, Sarah Bowling, is now heavily involved and appears to have stepped into the role previously occupied by her mother. Marilyn, however, remains the public face of the ministry.

In addition to women on staff, we also cataloged those congregations that had a female senior pastor. During the course of the research for this book (2013–2018), we identified fourteen megachurches that were led by a woman. These congregations represent 0.84 percent of the total megachurch population. Yet, even in the small amount of time that has transpired, many of them have left their positions, and many of those who remain are not presented as the true leaders of their congregations. We also included in Table 9 Marilyn Hickey as an instance of mega-ministry (television, Internet, and previously a megachurch pastor in her own rite).

HIGHLIGHTS OF THE TIMELINE OF WOMEN'S ORDINATION

1815 Clarissa Danforth was ordained by the Free Will Baptist denomination in New England, becoming the first woman ordained by a denomination in the United States.

1842 Emma Hale Smith became first president of the Female Relief Society of Nauvoo of the Church of Jesus Christ of Latter Day Saints.

1853 Antoinette Brown Blackwell was ordained by a Congregationalist church, but her ordination was not recognized by the denomination, so she joined the Unitarian denomination, which recognized her ordination in 1878.

1876 Anna Oliver was the first woman to receive a Bachelor of Divinity degree from a seminary in the United States, Boston University School of Theology.

1879 Mary Baker Eddy founded The Church of Christ, Scientist.

1898 The African Methodist Episcopal Zion Church began ordaining women as pastors with a rule change.

1923 Aimee Semple McPherson founded the historic (megachurch) Angelus Temple, marking the beginning of the International Church of the Foursquare Gospel.

1956 Margaret Towner was ordained by the Presbyterian Church (USA); another woman had been ordained by a congregation from one of the parent denominations in 1930, but Towner was the first woman officially ordained by the new, collective denomination.
Maud K. Jensen became the first woman to receive full clergy rights within the General Conference of the United Methodist Church.

1964 Addie Davis became the first woman ordained within the Southern Baptist Convention. The denomination officially stopped ordaining women in 2000, but women ordained prior to this point were allowed to continue in their jobs.

1965 Rachel Henderlite became the first woman ordained by the Presbyterian Church in the United States.

1970 Elizabeth Alvina Platz became the first woman ordained by the Lutheran Church in America on November 22.
Barbara Andrews became the first woman ordained by the American Lutheran Church in December.

1974 Eleven women were irregularly ordained priests in the Episcopal Church in Philadelphia on July 29. Prior to the Episcopal Church permitting women's ordination on September 16, 1976, these women were known as the "Philadelphia 11."

1980 Marjorie Matthews became the first woman bishop in the United Methodist Church.

1988 Barbara Harris became the first woman bishop in the Episcopal Church.

2000 Vashti Murphy McKenzie was elected the first female bishop of the African Methodist Episcopal Church.

2002 Sharon Brown Christopher became the first female bishop to serve as the president of the Council of Bishops within the United Methodist Church.

2013 Elizabeth Eaton was elected the first female presiding bishop of the Evangelical Lutheran Church in America.

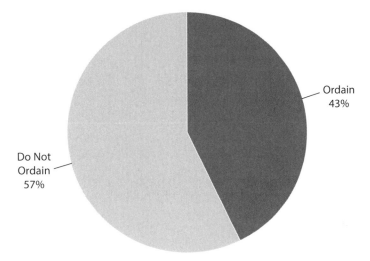

Figure 9. Ordain v. Do Not Ordain based on membership.

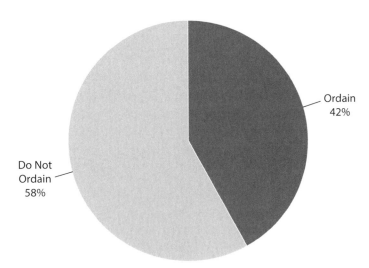

Figure 10. Ordain v. Do Not Ordain based on number of megachurches.

Ordain Women	Do Not Ordain Women
The United Methodist Church	The Southern Baptist Convention
The Evangelical Lutheran Church, USA	The Church of God in Christ
The Assemblies of God	The National Baptist Convention
The Presbyterian Church, USA	The National Baptist Convention of America
The African Methodist Episcopal Church	The National Missionary Baptist Convention of America
The Episcopal Church	The Lutheran Church Missouri Synod
Pentecostal Assemblies of the World	The Churches of Christ
The African Methodist Episcopal Zion Church	Calvary Chapel*
American Baptist Church, USA	
Evangelical Covenant	
Foursquare Gospel	
The Wesleyan Church	
Vineyard*	

*These traditions are not officially denominations.

As seen in the left-hand column, there are many denominations that ordain women. There are, however, more churchgoers represented in the denominations in the right-hand column.

NOTES

A PERSONAL NOTE

1. Ruth Behar, *The Vulnerable Observer* (Boston: Beacon Press, 1997).
2. The phrase "familiar stranger" was coined by Todd Gitlin in *Media Unlimited: How the Torrent of Images and Sounds Overwhelms Our Lives* (New York: Henry Holt and Company, 2002); Larry Z. Leslie, *Celebrity in the 21st Century: A Reference Handbook* (Santa Barbara, CA: ABC-CLIO, 2011), 11.
3. Chris Rojek, *Celebrity* (London: Reaktion Books, 2004), 9–11.

INTRODUCTION

1. Samuel Miller, *Letters on Clerical Manners and Habits: Addressed to a Student in the Theological Seminary at Princeton, N.J.* (New York: G. & C. Carvill, 1827), 339.
2. Genesis 2:18, NIV.
3. According to Scott Thumma and Davis Travis, in 1970 the number of megachurches was fifty, but by 2016, the number had grown to 1,551. See *Beyond Megachurch Myths: What We Can Learn from America's Largest Churches* (San Francisco: Jossey-Bass, 2007), 7.
4. Joyce Meyer Ministries, https://www.joycemeyer.org/about/board-of-directors/joyce-meyer (accessed May 3, 2017).
5. Take, for instance, HarperCollin's acquisition of Zondervan in 1988. Founded in 1931, Zondervan made a name for itself in the evangelical community for publishing Bibles and other evangelical nonfiction. After their acquisition by HarperCollins, Zondervan expanded and now includes four presses (Zondervan, Zondervan Academic, Zondervan Kids, and Editorial Vida) under HarperCollins's Christian Publishing. Recent titles written by celebrity women they have published include Christine Caine's *Unexpected*, *Wild and Free* by Jess Connolly, and Hayley Morgan and Alli Worthington's *The Year of Living Happy*.
6. See Kimberly Karnes, Wayne McIntosh, Irwin Morris, and Shanna Pearson-Merkowitz, "Mighty Fortress: Explaining the Spatial Distribution of American Megachurches," *Journal for the Scientific Study of Religion* 46.2 (2007): 261–68; and Barney Warf and Morton Winsberg, "Geographies of Megachurches in the United States," *Journal of Cultural Geography* 27.1 (2010): 33–51, for discussions of the geographic distribution of megachurches across the United States.
7. Belinda Luscombe, "Jen Hatmaker Talks Faith, Family and the Church's Battles," *Time*, August 17, 2017, http://time.com/4904287/jen-hatmaker-of-mess-and-moxie/ (accessed July 5, 2018).
8. Ibid.; Emma Green, "What Obligation Do White Christian Women Have to Speak Out About Politics?," *The Atlantic*, August 20, 2017, https://www.theatlantic.com/politics/archive/2017/08/jen-hat-maker-of-mess-and-moxie-politics/536808/ (accessed July 5, 2018); Kate Shellnut, "The Bigger Story Behind Jen Hatmaker," *Christianity*

Today, November 15, 2016, https://www.christianitytoday.com/ct/2016/november-web
-only/bigger-story-behind-jen-hatmaker.html (accessed July 5, 2018).

9. The areas of women's activism were not initially explicit. As Joshua Young and I
examined the web presence of megachurch pastors' wives, we took note of the areas of
specialty and activism undertaken by these women. Over time, similarities and patterns began to emerge around the most common topics. In almost all instances, the
most predictive element of what topic for which a woman would advocate was how well
said topic aligned with her brand. At the same time, certain topics were clearly defined
as women's issues, however informal such identification seemed. This list here is an abbreviated one of the most common topics. For a more robust discussion of activism
and our finds regarding it, please see Appendix II.

10. Jesse Bogan, "America's Biggest Megachurches," *Forbes,* June 26, 2009, http://
www.forbes.com/2009/06/26/americas-biggest-megachurches-business
-megachurches.html (accessed June 11, 2015).

11. See Heather Alex, "Critics Assail Recent Sermon by Lakewood Co-Pastor Victoria Osteen," *Houston Chronicle,* September 6 2014, http://www.houstonchronicle.com
/news/houston-texas/houston/article/Critics-assail-recent-sermon-by-Lakewood
-5738922.php (accessed June 11, 2015); Brian Rogers, "Jurors: Attendant 'Exaggerated'
Osteen Conflict," *Houston Chronicle,* August 14, 2008, http://www.chron.com/life
/houston-belief/article/Jurors-Attendant-exaggerated-Osteen-conflict-1777790.php
(accessed June 11, 2015.); "Joel and Victoria Osteen's Vision for Their Ministry," Oprah
.com, January 8, 2012, http://www.oprah.com/own-oprahs-next-chapter/Joel-and
-Victoria-Osteen-Share-the-Vision-for-Their-Ministry (accessed June 11, 2015). In reference to Lakewood Church (Houston) being the largest church in America, it is possible that, by 2017 North Point Community Church (Atlanta) and Life Church (Edmond) had matched or eclipsed its numbers (I am relying on self-reported numbers
that change as quickly as churches perform audits).

12. For a discussion of the incident and resulting trial, see James C. McKinley, Jr.,
"Jury Finds Pastor Did Not Assault a Flight Attendant," *The New York Times,* Au-
gust 14, 2008, https://www.nytimes.com/2008/08/15/us/15houston.html (accessed
June 27, 2018).

13. For an example of Joel and Victoria with Oprah, see "Joel and Victoria Osteen's
Vision for Their Ministry/Oprah's Next Chapter/Oprah Winfrey/Network with Oprah,"
YouTube, January 8, https://www.youtube.com/watch?v=uC8gaUQyZn8 (accessed
May 5, 2017).

14. See The Pew Center on Religion and Public Life, "Fifteen Largest Protestant Denominations," May 7, 2015, http://www.pewforum.org/2015/05/12/chapter-1-the
-changing-religious-composition-of-the-u-s/pr_15-05-12_rls_chapter1-03/ (accessed
May 2, 2017).

15. See Hartford Institute for Religion Research, "Megachurch Database," n.d.,
http://hirr.hartsem.edu/cgi-bin/mega/db.pl?db=default&uid=default&view_records
=1&ID=*&sb=3&so=descend (accessed May 2, 2017) for a current list of megachurches
in the United States as well as their pastor, location, and average weekly attendance.

16. As is explained at greater length in Appendixes I and II, the women selected
for this study were drawn from the largest ministries across denominations. And most
hailed from what I am calling here "conservative" traditions. This term is both too broad
and too evocative for elegant use, but I use it nonetheless to describe those who hold a

complementarian position on women in ministry. This describes many, though not all, evangelical and pentecostal traditions, despite the fact that—as we shall see—pentecostalism's emphasis on spiritual gifts often gave women far greater freedoms. Though I often use the word "conservative" simply to refer to a theological conclusion about traditional views of women's subordinated status, the term really suggests much more. It is better imagined as one side of a theological spectrum that is typically pietistic, experiential, scripturally inerrantist, and politically right-leaning. (See also "conservative" in the Glossary.)

17. Catherine Brekus explores the idea of female evangelists in her book *Strangers and Pilgrims: Female Preaching in America, 1740–1845*. Describing the difficulties faced by Anne Rexford even as she routinely preached at a chapel built specifically for her in Camptown, NJ, Brekus asserts that "because of her 'natural' subordination to men, she could never hope to be a local pastor, but only a traveling evangelist" (Brekus 255). Previously, Brekus established that evangelists were often broken down into formal and informal categories. During the colonial period, women were limited to the informal evangelist, or exhorter category, which "publicly admonished or encouraged others to repent," but had no institutional authority (Brekus 48). By the nineteenth century, the options available to women expanded such that they were able to serve as traveling evangelists in some contexts. This expansion, however, was not without its critics, and many socially conservative clergy and laity contended that such preaching was too close to the formal power of the local pastor. For more information, see Catherine Brekus, *Strangers and Pilgrims: Female Preaching in America, 1740–1845* (Chapel Hill: The University of North Carolina Press, 1998).

18. See, for instance, Moore's awards for her 2010 book, *So Long, Insecurity*, from the Christian Book Expo, http://christianbookexpo.com/bestseller/bestof2010/ (accessed June 29, 2018).

19. I do not mean to suggest that Beth Moore is not utterly sincere in her complementarian views, but only that her popularity makes tight boundaries around her authority to be pragmatically impossible.

20. For an example of Beth Moore's stadium teaching, see "Passion 2014 Beth Moore," YouTube, February 28, 2014, https://www.youtube.com/watch?v=g8QkuRL5ikg (accessed May 30, 2017).

21. See, for instance, the 2016–2017 LifeWay Women Catalog, which begins with pages and pages of strictly Beth Moore products before cramming all other authors toward the end, https://issuu.com/biblicalsolutionsforlife/docs/2015cat_singles (accessed May 6, 2017).

22. I define a "parachurch" as a ministerial organization with evangelistic aims (which might include relief and justice work) but is not primarily defined by liturgical functions. It does not typically serve communion, baptize believers, or keep membership as its primary goals. Examples include Focus on the Family and InterVarsity Christian Fellowship. See Wesley K. Willmer, J. David Schmidt, and Martin Smith, *The Prospering Parachurch: Enlarging the Boundaries of God's Kingdom* (San Francisco: Jossey-Bass, 1998) for a discussion of the potential in parachurch organizations within evangelicalism.

23. See Mark Chaves, "All Creatures Great and Small: Megachurches in Context," *Review of Religious Research* 47.4 (2006): 329–46 for a discussion of the 1970s and the origins of megachurches.

24. See Pink Impact, the women's ministry for Debbie Morris's Gateway Church, https://pinkimpact.com/ (accessed May 6, 2017).

25. Take, for instance, Ana Maldonado of the thirteen-thousand-member El Ray Jesús (King Jesus Ministry), Maria Garcia's seven-thousand-member Segadores de Vida (Harvesters of Life), and Eva Higueros's twenty-five-hundred-member Ministerieos Bethania USA (Bethany Ministries USA). Kate Bowler, "Looking Up: Latino Megachurches and the Politics of Social Mobility," unpublished paper.

26. Kathy Khang, *Raise Your Voice: Why We Stay Silent and How to Speak Up* (Downers Grove, IL: IVP Books, 2018).

27. Kathy Khang, interview with Kate Bowler, October 15, 2018.

28. Take, for example, Templo Calvario was one of the country's largest Latino megachurches with its vast congregation of eleven thousand, but also one of the oldest with a rich legacy of social engagement.

29. Grace Ji-Sun Kim, interview by Kate Bowler, October 15, 2018.

30. Gail Song Bantum, interview by Kate Bowler, October 18, 2018.

31. It is commonly assumed by people who affirm women in ministry and people who reject women in ministry that the issue of women's ordination defines the terms "liberal" and "conservative." This is, of course, too simplistic: though every mainline denomination supports the ordination of women, not every evangelical denomination opposes it (the Evangelical Covenant Church does not).

32. The first woman ordained in the United States was Clarissa Danforth in 1815 by the Free Will Baptist denomination. She served primarily as an itinerant preacher until she was married to the Rev. Danford Richmond, a Baptist minister from Pomfret, CT. After her marriage, she only occasionally preached. For more information on Clarissa Danforth, see I. D. Stewart, *The History of the Freewill Baptists for Half a Century: With an Introductory Chapter; from the Year 1780 to 1830*, vol. 1 (Dover, NH: Freewill Baptist Printing Establishment, 1862), 335–90.

33. For a discussion of this loose coupling, see Mark Chaves, *Ordaining Women: Culture and Conflict in Religious Organizations* (Cambridge, MA: Harvard University Press, 1997). I will address the topic in greater depth in Chapter One.

34. Fellowship Church, https://fellowshipchurch.com/ (accessed March 25, 2017).

35. See Fellowship Church, "A Gathering of Women," https://fellowshipchurch.com/flavour/ (accessed May 2, 2017).

36. Christopher Wynn, "Dear God: Is Dallas society ready for Fellowship Church's sex-loving, million-dollar minister?" *The Dallas Morning News*, December 12, 2013, http://res.dallasnews.com/interactives/2013_December/pastored/ (accessed May 21, 2017).

37. For an archive of Ed Young's sermons at Fellowship Church, see http://edyoungsermons.com/series (accessed May 6, 2017).

38. For a listing of New Life Church's staff, see https://www.newlifechurch.tv/about#our-staff (accessed July 2, 2018).

39. Lysa TerKeurst, "My Story," http://lysaterkeurst.com/lysas_story/ (accessed March 25, 2017).

40. Lysa TerKeurst, "Rejection, Heartache, and a Faithful God," https://lysaterkeurst.com/2017/06/rejection-heartache-and-a-faithful-god/ (accessed July 5, 2018).

41. Lysa TerKeurst, "My Story," http://lysaterkeurst.com/lysas_story/ (accessed March 25, 2017).

42. "Leon & Sally Fontaine," https://www.springschurch.com/about-us/leon-and -sally-fontaine (accessed October 1, 2018).

43. See Sheryl Sandberg, *Lean In: Women, Work and the Will to Lead* (New York: Knopf Doubleday, 2013).

44. Elizabeth Dias, interview by Kate Bowler, March 15, 2017.

45. Elizabeth Dias, "Barbara Brown Taylor Faces the Darkness," *Time*, April 17, 2014, http://time.com/66260/barbara-brown-taylor-new-book-faces-the-darkness/ (accessed May 21, 2017).

46. See Mark Chaves, *Congregations in America* (Cambridge, MA: Harvard University Press, 2004), 23–26, and 208, for a discussion of Roman Catholic congregations and their place within the broader landscape.

47. Robert Maclean, "Mother Mary Angelica, nun who built Catholic media network, dies at 92," *CNNMoney*, March 28, 2016, http://money.cnn.com/2016/03/28 /media/ewtn-mother-angelica-death/ (accessed May 21, 2017). There are hundreds of large Catholic churches that would meet the criteria for the size of a Protestant megachurch. But Catholic parishes are so radically different in ecclesiology and leadership that scholars of megachurches excluded them from comparison. However, Catholic women's forays into parachurches and televangelism (both included under the banner of "megaministry") were remarkably similar to the efforts of Protestant women.

48. Betty Peebles, Sharon Daugherty, and Brenda Timberlake were famous megachurch widows.

49. John Burnett, "Can a Television Network Be a Church? The IRS Says Yes," *npr .org*, http://www.npr.org/2014/04/01/282496855/can-a-television-network-be-a-church -the-irs-says-yes (accessed March 25, 2017).

50. Daisy Osborn, "Women Who Win," recording housed at the Holy Spirit Research Center in Tulsa, Oklahoma, n.d.

51. For information about Proverbs 31 Ministries, see http://proverbs31.org/about /about-us (accessed July 6, 2018).

52. For a list of endorsed speakers, see http://proverbs31.org/speakers/ (accessed April 30, 2017).

53. See Robert B. Shoemaker, *Gender in English Society, 1650–1850: The Emergence of Separate Spheres?* (New York: Longman, 1998) for a discussion of gendered separate spheres.

54. See 1 Timothy 2:9–10 as an example of this type of instruction.

CHAPTER ONE: THE PREACHER

1. King James version.

2. @BethMooreLPM, Beth Moore Twitter feed, https://twitter.com/BethMooreLPM (accessed July 6, 2018).

3. Author visit, Living Proof Live, Norfolk, VA, April 29, 2016.

4. Mark 6:5–6, ESV.

5. Beth Moore, "A Quick Word with Beth Moore," B&H Publishing Group, http:// www.bhpublishinggroup.com/PDF/9780805432794_A_Quick_Word-Breaking_Free _tips.pdf (accessed May 21, 2017).

6. "King Jesus International Ministry's History," El Rey Jesús Global, www .elreyjesus.org/us (accessed April 13, 2017). According to the Hartford Institute for

Religion Research Megachurch Database, Ministerio Internacional El Ray Jesus is the 45th largest church in the United States with 12,540 regular weekly participants. Among Latino megachurches, it is second only to New Life Covenant Ministries in Chicago, which has 12,994 weekly participants and just ahead of Templo Calvario Assembly of God in Santa Ana, CA, which has eleven thousand weekly participants.

7. Ana Maldonado, "CAP 2009 Profeta Ana Maldonado," YouTube, posted on November 2, 2009, https://www.youtube.com/watch?v=VbS1fl7mbAU (accessed April 13, 2015). I am indebted here to Tito Madrazo for his analysis of Ana Maldonado. See Tito Madrazo, "Profeta Ana Maldonado: Pushing the Boundaries of Paradoxical Domesticity," *Perspectivas*, Spring 2017, 140–53.

8. Ibid.

9. Matthew Hibbard, "Joyce Meyer convention boosts area business," *St. Louis Business Journal,* September 21, 2012, http://www.bizjournals.com/stlouis/blog/2012 /09/joyce-meyer-convention-boosts-area.html (accessed May 5, 2017).

10. Joyce Meyer Ministries, "At-A-Glance," March 2017, http://www.joycemeyer.org /MediaRelations/AtAGlance.aspx (accessed May 5, 2017).

11. @JoyceMeyer Twitter, https://twitter.com/JoyceMeyer (accessed September 19, 2018).

12. For a list of Joyce Meyer's books, see https://www.amazon.com/Joyce-Meyer/e /B001H6NG9I.

13. Lois A. Boyd and R. Douglas Brackenridge, *Presbyterian Women in America: Two Centuries of a Quest for Status* (Westport, CT: Greenwood Press, 1996), 97.

14. Mark Chaves was not the originator of the idea of loose coupling, but his application of it to women's ordination is unique. The term appears in works as early as the 1950s, but the most frequently cited uses are in Robert B. Glassman, "Persistence and Loose Coupling in Living Systems," *Behavioral Science*, March 1973, https://doi .org/10.1002/bs.3830180202 (accessed October 30, 2018); and Karl E. Weick, "Educational Organizations as Loosely Coupled Systems," *Administrative Science Quarterly* 21, March 1976, https://www.jstor.org/stable/2391875?seq=1#page_scan_tab_contents (accessed October 30, 2018).

15. Mark Chaves, *Ordaining Women: Culture and Conflict in Religious Organizations* (Cambridge, MA: Harvard University Press, 1997), 14–37.

16. 1 Corinthians 14:34–35; 1 Timothy 2:11–15, KJV. There have been recent attempts to disassociate the apostle from these passages. Jerome Murphy-O'Connor makes the argument that the Corinthian injunction is a post-Pauline interpolation; see "The First Letter to the Corinthians," in *The New Jerome Biblical Commentary,* ed. Raymond E. Brown, S.S., Joseph A. Fitzmyer, S.J, and Roland E. Murphy, O.Carm. (Englewood Cliffs, NJ: Prentice Hall, 1990), 811–12. See also Elaine H. Pagels, *The Gnostic Paul: Gnostic Exegesis of the Pauline Letters* (London: Trinity Press International, 1992).

17. See Kevin Madigan and Carolyn Osiek, *Ordained Women in the Early Church: A Documentary History* (Baltimore, MD: Johns Hopkins University Press, 2005); Ute Eisen, *Women Officeholders in Early Christianity: Epigraphical and Literary Studies* (Collegeville, MN: Liturgical Press, 2000); Patricia Cox Miller, ed., *Women in Early Christianity* (Washington, DC: Catholic University of America Press, 2005); Deborah F. Sawyer, *Women and Religion in the First Christian Centuries* (New York: Routledge, 1996); and Gary Macy, *The Hidden History of Women's Ordination* (New York: Oxford University Press, 2007).

18. Charles Butler, *The American Lady* (Philadelphia: Hogan and Thompson, 1836), viii.

19. Horace Bushnell, *Women's Suffrage: The Reform against Nature* (New York: Charles Scribner, 1869), 112.

20. Mary Hershberger, "Mobilizing Women, Anticipating Abolition: The Struggle against Indian Removal in the 1830s," *The Journal of American History* 86.1 (June, 1999): 15.

21. The phrase "republican motherhood" seems to have been coined by Linda K. Kerber, *Women of the Republic: Intellect and Ideals in Revolutionary America* (Chapel Hill: University of North Carolina Press, 1980).

22. See Gerda Lerner, *The Grimké Sisters from South Carolina: Pioneers for Women's Rights and Abolition* (Chapel Hill: University of North Carolina Press, 2004); Stephen Howard Browne, *Angelina Grimké: Rhetoric, Identity and the Radical Imagination* (East Lansing: Michigan State University Press, 1999); and Carol Berkin, *Civil War Wives: The Lives and Times of Angelina Grimké Weld, Varina Howle Davis, and Julia Dent Grant* (New York: Alfred A. Knopf, 2009) for discussions of the Grimké sisters, specifically Angelina Grimké.

23. For a more in-depth examination of Lucretia Mott, see Carol Faulkner, *Lucretia Mott's Heresy: Abolition and Women's Rights in Nineteenth-Century America* (Philadelphia: University of Pennsylvania Press, 2011).

24. Blanche Glassman Hersh, "'Am I Not a Woman and a Sister?' Abolitionist Beginnings of Nineteenth-Century Feminism," in *Antislavery Reconsidered: New Perspectives on the Abolitionist*, ed. Lewis Perry and Michael Fellman (Baton Rouge: Louisiana State University Press, 1979), 252.

25. Elizabeth Cady Stanton, Susan B. Anthony, and M. J. Cage, *A History of Women's Suffrage* (Rochester, NY: Fowler and Wells, 1889). A pdf of the declaration taken from this source can be found at https://www.womenshistory.org/sites/default/files/document/2017-11/Taking%20a%20Stand%20Woman%20Suffrage%20and%20Protest%20at%20the%20White%20House%20Post-Field%20Trip%20Activity%20High%20School.pdf (accessed September 19, 2018).

26. Barbara Leslie Epstein, *The Politics of Domesticity: Women, Evangelism, and Temperance in Nineteenth-Century America* (Middletown, CT: Wesleyan University Press, 1981), 2–3. For more on class identity and female reform, see Lori Ginzberg, *Women and the Work of Benevolence: Morality, Politics, and Class in the Nineteenth-Century United States* (New Haven, CT: Yale University Press, 1992).

27. Anne Braude, *Sisters and Saints: Women and American Religion* (Oxford: Oxford University Press, 2007), 83–84.

28. Estelle Freeman, "Separatism as Strategy: Female Institution Building and American Feminism, 1870–1930," *Feminist Studies* 5 (1979): 512–29.

29. Susan Tank Lesser, "Paradigms Gained: Further Readings in the History of Women in the Progressive Era," in *Gender, Class, Race, and Reform in the Progressive Era*, ed. Noralee Frankel and Nancy S. Dye (Lexington: University of Kentucky Press, 1991), 180–93.

30. Epstein, *Politics of Domesticity,* 90.

31. Braude, *Sisters and Saints,* 78.

32. Ibid.; and Kathi Kern, *Mrs. Stanton's Bible* (Ithaca, NY: Cornell University Press, 2001), 83.

33. Susan E. Marshall, *Splintered Sisterhood: Gender and Class in the Campaign against Woman Suffrage* (Madison: University of Wisconsin Press, 1997), 20–22. Elizabeth Cady Stanton was a fierce opponent of Christianity and Judaism and the author of *The Women's Bible*; Woodhull was notorious for her advocacy of free love.

34. Freeman, "Separatism as Strategy," 512–29.

35. See Lee's biography, *Religious Experience and Journal of Mrs. Jarena Lee, Giving an Account of Her Call to Preach the Gospel* (Philadelphia: 1849) and Jocelyn Moody, "Sin-Sick Souls: Jarena Lee and Zilpha Elaw," in *Sentimental Confessions: Spiritual Narratives of Nineteenth-Century African American Women* (Athens: University of Georgia Press, 2003).

36. Dana L. Robert, *American Women in Mission: A Social History of Their Thought and Practice* (Macon, GA: Mercer University Press, 1997).

37. Nancy Hardesty, *Women Called to Witness: Evangelical Feminism in the Nineteenth Century* (Knoxville: University of Tennessee Press, 1999), 107.

38. Jane Hunter, *The Gospel of Gentility: American Women Missionaries in Turn-of-the-Century China* (New Haven, CT: Yale University Press, 1984), 53.

39. Beverly Ann Zink-Sawyer, *From Preachers to Suffragists: Woman's Rights and Religious Conviction in the Lives of Three Nineteenth-Century American Clergywomen* (Louisville, KY: Westminster John Knox Press, 2003), 80.

40. Ibid., 192.

41. Ibid., 159.

42. Unmarried women were also accepted on a denominational basis.

43. Robert, *American Women in Mission,* 129.

44. Ibid.

45. Dana L. Robert, "Protestant Women Missionaries: Foreign and Home," in *Encyclopedia of Women and Religion in North America*, ed. Rosemary Skinner Keller, Rosemary Radford Ruether, and Marie Cantlon (Bloomington: Indiana University Press, 2006), 837.

46. Joseph A. Conforti, *Jonathan Edwards, Religious Tradition and American Culture* (Chapel Hill: University of North Carolina Press, 1995), 104.

47. Boyd and Brackenridge, *Presbyterian Women in America*, ix–x.

48. Amanda Smith, *An Autobiography: The Story of the Lord's Dealings with Mrs. Amanda Smith, The Colored Evangelist* (Chicago: Meyer & Brother, Publishers, 1893), 204.

49. Stephen Ward Angell and Anthony B. Pinn, *Social Protest Thought in the African Methodist Episcopal Church, 1862–1939* (Knoxville: University of Tennessee Press, 2000), 282; and Zink-Sawyer, *From Preachers to Suffragists*, 99.

50. As Dana Roberts points out, this statement applies to women pietists and thus the bulk of Protestants, but not to Catholics or to earlier Protestant chaplains. Personal correspondence, October 4, 2018.

51. Priscilla Pope-Levison, *Building the Old-Time Religion: Women Evangelists in the Progressive Era* (New York: New York University Press, 2016), 1.

52. Robert, "Protestant Women Missionaries: Foreign and Home," 834–43.

53. Robyn Muncy, *Creating a Female Dominion in American Reform, 1890–1935* (New York: Oxford University Press, 1991).

54. Robert, *American Women in Mission,* 26.

55. Dawn Sangrey, "The Feminization of the Unitarian Universalist Clergy: Impacts, Speculations and Longings," *Journal of Liberal Religion* 2.1 (2000): 5; Barbara Zikmund, Adair Lummis, and Patricia Chang, *Clergy Women: An Uphill Calling* (Louisville, KY: Westminster John Knox Press, 1998), 5.

56. For a complete timeline of denominations' ordination of women, see Chaves, *Ordaining Women,* fig. 2.1, pp. 16–17. See Appendix VI for a discussion of women's ordination and an abbreviated timeline.

57. Zikmund, Lummis, and Chang, *Clergy Women*, 13.

58. James A. Beckford and Jay Demerath, *The SAGE Handbook of the Sociology of Religion* (London: SAGE, 2007), 303.

59. "Ordination of Women," The Episcopal Dictionary of the Church, https://www.episcopalchurch.org/library/glossary/ordination-women (accessed July 7, 2018).

60. See Elizabeth H. Flowers, *Into the Pulpit: Southern Baptist Women and Power since World War II* (Chapel Hill: University of North Carolina Press, 2014).

61. Ibid., 102–13.

62. See also Derek Prince, "Fatherhood," *New Wine*, April 1974, 4–6, https://www.csmpublishing.org/wp-content/plugins/pdf-viewer-for-wordpress/web/viewer.php?file=https://www.csmpublishing.org/wp-content/NewWineArchives/Full_Issues/1974/NewWineMagazine_Issue_04–1974.pdf (accessed May 23, 2017), in which he argues that fatherhood is an "office in God's government."

63. S. D. Moore, *The Shepherding Movement: Controversy and Charismatic Ecclesiology* (London: T & T Clark, 2003), 111.

64. Matthew Avery Sutton, *Aimee Semple McPherson and the Resurrection of Christian America* (Cambridge, MA: Harvard University Press, 2007).

65. Zikmund, Lummis, and Chang, *Clergy Women*, 64.

66. E. Brooks Holifield, *God's Ambassador: A History of the Christian Clergy in America* (Grand Rapids, MI: Eerdmans, 2007), 323.

67. See Sally B. Purvis, *The Stained Glass Ceiling: Churches and Their Women Pastors* (Louisville, KY: Westminster John Knox Press, 1995).

68. Mark Chaves and Alison Eagle, *Religious Congregations in 21ˢᵗ Century America: A Report from the National Congregations Study* (Durham, NC: Department of Sociology, Duke University, 2015), 16, http://www.soc.duke.edu/natcong/Docs/NCSIII_report_final.pdf (accessed May 25, 2017).

69. Beckford and Demerath, *SAGE Handbook of the Sociology of Religion*, 303–7; and Barbara Finlay, *Facing the Stained Glass Ceiling: Gender in a Protestant Seminary* (Lanham, MD: University Press of America, 2003), 127.

70. Data collected from Tracy Sukraw, "25 years after consecration of Bishop Barbara C. Harris," Episcopal News Service, February 21, 2014, http://episcopaldigitalnetwork.com/ens/2014/02/21/25-years-after-consecration-of-bishop-barbara-c-harris/ (accessed September 19, 2018); and via personal correspondence with the United Methodist Church offices on July 30, 2018.

71. Todd W. Ferguson, "Failing to Master Divinity: How Institutional Type, Financial Debt, Community Acceptance, and Gender Affect Seminary Graduates' Career Choices," *The Review of Religious Research* 57.3 (2015): 357.

72. Ibid., 357, 342.

73. Finlay, *Facing the Stained Glass Ceiling,* 125.

74. Ferguson, "Failing to Master Divinity," 357.

75. In addition to Mark Chaves's work, see Jackson W. Carroll's *God's Potters: Pastoral Leadership and the Shaping of Congregations* (Grand Rapids, MI: Eerdmans, 2006); Jackson W. Carroll, Barbara Hargrove, and Adair T. Lummis, *Women of the Cloth: A New Opportunity for the Churches* (New York: Harper & Row, 1983); and Edward Lehman, Jr., "Placement of Men and Women in the Ministry," *Review of Religious Research* 22.1 (1980): 18–40, for a cross-section of the broader conversation about women's ordination in both theory and practice.

76. Zikmund, Lummis, and Chang, *Clergy Women*, 105.

77. Ibid. See also Paula D. Nesbitt, *Feminization of the Clergy in America* (New York: Oxford University Press, 1997).

78. Finlay, *Facing the Stained Glass Ceiling*, 6, 61–77; and Sue E. S. Crawford, Melissa M. Deckman, and Christi J. Braun, "Gender and the Political Choices of Women Clergy," in *Christian Clergy in American Politics*, ed. Sue E. S. Crawford and Laura R. Olson (Baltimore, MD: Johns Hopkins University Press, 2001), 47.

79. See "Statement Commemorating the 40th anniversary of the Philadelphia 11 ordinations," issued by the Executive Council of the Episcopal Church, July 14, 2014, http://www.episcopalchurch.org/library/document/statement-commemorating-40th -anniversary-philadelphia-11-ordinations (accessed May 25, 2017).

80. See "AME Zion Welcomes First Female Bishop," *Los Angeles Sentinel,* July 24, 2008, https://lasentinel.net/A.M.E.-Zion-Welcomes-First-Female-Bishop.html (accessed May 5, 2017); Usher's Temple C.E.E. Church, "The Rev. Dr. Theresa Snorton Is Elected First Female Bishop of the Christian Methodist Episcopal (C.M.E.) Church," http://www.c-m-e.org/Announcements/bishopteresasnortonrelease.htm (accessed May 25, 2017).

81. Adelle M. Banks, "US Assemblies of God elects first woman executive in more than a century," *Religion News Service*, April 24, 2018, https://religionnews.com/2018 /04/24/us-assemblies-of-god-elects-first-woman-executive-in-more-than-a-century (accessed September 18, 2018).

82. Mark Chaves discusses the idea of women's ordination as symbolic in "Chapter 2: The Symbolic Significance of Women's Ordination" of his book *Ordaining Women: Culture and Conflict in Religious Organizations* (Cambridge, MA: Harvard University Press, 1997), 14–37. Here he contends that formal rules about women's ordination signaled the denomination's environment more so than changes to actual practices. The idea of tokenism builds on this concept to its next level and concerns instances in which women are elected or appointed to prominent positions while little change occurs on the local or policy level. For example, Elizabeth Eaton was elected Presiding Bishop of the ELCA in 2013, but the level of female clergy and the denomination's position on women's issues remained largely unchanged. Critics have therefore asserted that Eaton's election was an instance of tokenism.

83. See, for instance, the stark look of denominational initiatives and the debates over LGBTQ+ ordination in chapter three of R. W. Holmen's *Queer Clergy: A History of Gay and Lesbian Ministry in American Protestantism* (Cleveland, OH: Pilgrim Press, 2014). Some Quakers also allowed openly gay leadership, but as they do not ordain a clerical class, they are not listed above. The Metropolitan Community Church ordained the first transgender Christian minister in 1979, with some more liberal Protestant denominations following more recently. The UCC, for example, passed a resolution in

2003 that affirmed the ministry and participation of transgender people. However, ordination of transgender people remains controversial in other mainline denominations, like United Methodism. Duncan Dormor, "'Like Gender, Organised Religion Is a Complex Matter': The Growing Acceptance of Transgender people in Protestant Christianity," *Modern Believing* 58.4 (2017): 373–92; Julie Zauzmer, "The United Methodist Church has appointed a transgender deacon," *The Washington Post*, June 7, 2017, https://www.washingtonpost.com/news/acts-of-faith/wp/2017/06/07/the-united -methodist-church-just-appointed-a-transgender-deacon (accessed July 7, 2018).

84. Patty Fitzpatrick, interview by Kate Bowler, July 19, 2016.

85. Mandy Sloan McDow on Twitter: https://twitter.com/RevMama (accessed July 9, 2018). See also Mandy Sloan McDow, *Reverend Mama,* July 17, 2016, https://mandymcdow.com/ (accessed May 23, 2017).

86. John Bingham, "'Clergy couture' range launched for fashion-conscious female priests," *The Telegraph*, May 21, 2016, http://www.telegraph.co.uk/news/2016/05/21 /clergy-couture-range-launched-for-fashion-conscious-female-pries/ (accessed September 18, 2018).

87. Stephen Fendler, interview by Kate Bowler, June 29, 2016.

88. Susan Gillies, interview by Kate Bowler, December 16, 2016.

89. American Baptist Churches USA, "10 Facts You Should Know About American Baptists," http://www.abc-usa.org/10facts/ (accessed May 5, 2017).

90. American Baptist Churches USA, "Women in Ministry," http://www.abc-usa .org/women-in-ministry/ (accessed May 5, 2017).

91. Helen Barrett Montgomery was the first woman president of the National Baptist Convention and a leader of many talents. She was a well-known activist for women's education nationally and internationally and the first woman to publish a translation of the New Testament from Greek, a wildly successful fundraiser for the American Baptist Foreign Missionary Society. C. Douglas Weaver, *In Search of the New Testament Church: The Baptist Story* (Macon, GA: Mercer University Press, 2008), 143; Laceye C. Warner, *Saving Women: Retrieving Evangelistic Theology and Practice* (Waco, TX: Baylor University Press, 2007), 183–22; Helen Barrett Montgomery, "The New Opportunity for Baptist Women," Third Baptist World Congress Stockholm, July 21–27, 1923, ed. W. T. Whitley (London: Kingsgate Press, 1923), 100.

92. See Andrew Abbott, *The System of Professions: An Essay on the Division of Expert Labor* (Chicago: University of Chicago Press, 1988), and Merle Jacobs and Stephen E. Bosanac, *The Professionalization of Work* (Whitby, ON: De Sitter, 2006) for discussions of professionalization.

93. Holifield, *God's Ambassador,* 346.

94. Rachel Held Evans, personal correspondence with Kate Bowler, October 16, 2018.

95. Laceye Warner, interview by Kate Bowler, March 15, 2017.

96. Susan Gillies, interview by Kate Bowler, December 16, 2016.

97. For a discussion of televangelism and the effects of the FCC rule change, see Jeffrey K. Hadden and Charles E. Swann, *Prime Time Preachers: The Rising Power of Televangelism* (Reading, MA: Addison-Wesley, 1981); Steve Bruce, *Pray TV: Televangelism in America* (New York: Routledge, 1990); and Jeffrey K. Hadden, "The Rise and Fall of American Televangelism," *The Annals of the American Academy of Political and Social Science* 527.1 (1993): 113–30.

98. *Women's Devotional Bible* (Zondervan: Grand Rapids, MI, 2012); *The Woman's Study Bible* (Nashville, TN: Thomas Nelson, 2017).

99. Susan Salley and Justin Coleman, interview by Kate Bowler, December 2, 2016.

100. Sociologist Mark Chaves identifies this reality as the catalyst for the exponential growth in the number of megachurches witnessed during the 1970s in his 2005 H. Paul Douglass Lecture, "All Creatures Great and Small: Megachurches in Context." Rejecting traditional explanations for megachurch growth, Chaves argues that efficiency was maximized as costs continued to rise. As a result, churches required greater and greater numbers of participants to maintain the staffing and resources necessary to ensure programing levels and quality. See Mark Chaves, "All Creatures Great and Small: Megachurches in Context," *Review of Religious Research* 47.4 (June 2006): 329–46.

101. American Baptist Churches USA, "Our History," http://www.abc-usa.org /what_we_believe/our-history/ (accessed May 5, 2017).

102. David A. Hollinger, *After Cloven Tongues of Fire: Protestant Liberalism in Modern American History* (Princeton, NJ: Princeton University Press, 2013).

103. HarperOne, "About HarperOne," http://harperone.hc.com/about/ (accessed May 5, 2017).

104. NRSV, "About the NRSV," http://www.nrsv.net/about/about-nrsv/ (accessed May 5, 2017).

105. Barna, "Is Evangelism Going Out of Style?" December 17, 2013, https://www .barna.com/research/is-evangelism-going-out-of-style/ (accessed May 5, 2017).

106. On the simultaneous "cultural victory" and "organizational defeat" of liberal Protestantism, see N. J. Demerath III, "Cultural Victory and Organizational Defeat in the Paradoxical Decline of Liberal Protestantism," *Journal for the Scientific Study of Religion* 34. 4 (December 1995): 458–69, and chapter one of Hollinger, *After Cloven Tongues of Fire.*

107. Sam Hodges, "Dallas' Cathedral of Hope, World's Largest Predominantly Gay Church Celebrates 40 Years," *Dallas Morning News*, July 24, 2010, https://www .dallasnews.com/news/news/2010/07/24/dallas_cathedral-of-hope-world_s-largest -predominantly-gay-church-celebrates-40-years (accessed May 5, 2017).

108. Jeffrey Weiss, "Cathedral of Hope in Dallas Rocked by Loss of Senior Pastor, Other Key Staff," *Dallas Morning News*, May 2013, https://www.dallasnews.com/news /news/2013/05/03/cathedral-of-hope-in-dallas-rocked-by-loss-of-senior-pastor-other -key-staffers (accessed May 5, 2017).

109. Jo Hudson, interview by Kate Bowler, November 28, 2016.

110. Weiss, "Cathedral of Hope."

111. Garrison Keillor, *Life Among the Lutherans* (Minneapolis, MN: Augsburg Fortress, 2009).

112. Terry Gross, "Lutheran Minister Preaches a Gospel of Love to Junkies, Drag Queens and Outsiders," *Fresh Air,* September 17, 2015, http://www.npr.org/2015/09/17 /441139500/lutheran-minister-preaches-a-gospel-of-love-to-junkies-drag-queens -and-outsiders (accessed May 23, 2017).

113. Nadia Bolz-Weber, interview by Kate Bowler, April 4, 2017.

114. Ibid.

115. Ibid.

116. Two of Nadia's mentors were emerging church movement leaders Phyllis Tickle and Tony Jones. For more on the importance of emerging church networks, beliefs, and practices, see Gerardo Marti and Gladys Ganiel, *The Deconstructed Church: Understanding Emerging Christianity* (New York: Oxford University Press, 2014).

117. Nadia Bolz-Weber, interview by Kate Bowler, April 4, 2017.

118. Ibid.

119. Gross, "Lutheran Minister Preaches a Gospel of Love."

120. See *Why Christian?* "WX2016," http://www.whychristian.net/ (accessed May 3, 2017) for information about the *Why Christian Conference.*

121. Denise O'Donoghue, interview by Kate Bowler, December 12, 2015.

122. Mark Chaves, *National Congregations Study.*

123. Ibid.

124. The thirteen seminaries that Joshua Young and I examined included: Fuller Seminary, Gordon Conwell Theological Seminary, Dallas Theological Seminary, Trinity Evangelical Divinity School, Liberty University Rawlings School of Divinity, Regent University School of Divinity, Oral Roberts College of Theology and Ministry, Gateway Seminary, Southern Baptist Theological Seminary, New Orleans Baptist Theological Seminary, Midwestern Baptist Theological Seminary, Southwestern Baptist Theological Seminary, and Southeastern Baptist Theological Seminary.

125. John Piper, "Is There a Place for Female Professors at Seminary?" "Ask Pastor John" podcast transcript, January 22, 2018, https://www.desiringgod.org/interviews/is-there-a-place-for-female-professors-at-seminary (accessed July 11, 2018).

126. Barbara Brown Taylor, "The Bad News about Christian Celebrity," personal correspondence with Kate Bowler, May 6, 2018.

CHAPTER TWO: THE HOMEMAKER

1. Chapter 31 of the Book of Proverbs outlines the attributes of a virtuous woman and ideal wife. The second section of the chapter (vv. 10–31) is called the Woman of Valor and describes the perfect woman as the personification of wisdom, industrious and fearing of the Lord. In recent years, it has been emphasized by the biblical womanhood movement.

2. See https://swbts.edu/events/art-homemaking-conference/ for information about Southwestern Baptist Theological Seminary's *The Art of Homemaking* annual conference.

3. At the time, Paige Patterson was the president of Southwestern Baptist Theological Seminary, before being fired in 2018.

4. See Elizabeth H. Flowers, *Into the Pulpit: Southern Baptist Women and Power Since World War II* (Chapel Hill: University of North Carolina Press, 2014) for a discussion of how the divide within evangelical associations shifted from questions of inerrancy to questions of women's roles, rights, and responsibilities.

5. Rick Patrick, "Stuffed Baboon Reading Darwin," *SBC Voices*, December 3, 2012, http://sbcvoices.com/stuffed-baboon-reading-darwin/ (accessed May 5, 2017).

6. Ephesians 5:22 (NRSV).

7. Simone de Beauvoir was a French writer, philosopher, political activist, and social theorist most known for her influence on feminist existentialism and feminist theory. Her 1949 book, *The Second Sex*, which detailed women's oppression, is viewed by many as a foundational text of contemporary feminism in the West. Betty Friedan was an American feminist, writer, and activist who co-founded the National Organization for Women (NOW) and wrote the famous *The Feminine Mystique* that describes a depressed suburban housewife who abdicated her own career and dreams in favor of getting married at nineteen and raising a family. Both of these women were giants in the feminist movements of the 1960s, 70s, and 80s, and the focus of the ire of the conservative backlash.

8. Elisabeth Elliot, *Through the Gates of Splendor*, 2nd ed. (Peabody, MA: Hendrickson, 2010), 267–78.

9. Elisabeth Elliot's story became the first of the Harper Missionary classics series, published from 1956 to 1966 in mainstream publishing. See Kathryn Long, "In the Modern World, but Not of It: The 'Auca Martyrs,' Evangelicalism, and Postwar American Culture," in *The Foreign Missionary Enterprise at Home*, ed. Daniel H. Bays and Grant Wacker (Tuscaloosa: University of Alabama Press, 2003), 223–36.

10. Philip Delves Broughton, "How the Fish Found Her Bicycle; Pioneering Feminist Gloria Steinem's Marriage Stunned Her Devotees and Thrilled Her Opponents . . . ," *The Daily Telegraph*, July 11, 2001. Steinem was rather famous for this quip but it was a feminist mantra first used by Irina Dunn.

11. Author and poet Alice Walker was the first to use the term "womanist." For an account of womanism and Christian theology, which includes critiques of white feminists and male black liberation theologians, see Delores S. Williams, *Sisters in the Wilderness: The Challenge of Womanist God-Talk* (Maryknoll, NY: Orbis Books, 1993).

12. *Eisenstadt v. Baird*, 405 U.S. 438 (1972) established the right of unmarried people to possess contraception on the same basis as married couples. In *Roe v. Wade*, 410 U.S. 113 (1973), the Court found that a right to privacy under the Due Process Clause of the 14th Amendment covered a woman's choice to have an abortion, but that said right must be balanced with the state's interest in protecting both a woman's health and the potential for life, leading to a balancing test that permitted state regulation of abortion during the third trimester. Both cases drew on *Griswold v. Connecticut*, 381 U.S. 479 (1965), which was another conception case that established the right to privacy with regard to intimate acts and one's own body. Initially, these cases were only opposed by Catholic religious groups, but they became a litmus test within the evangelical community with the rise of the religious right, particularly the Moral Majority in 1978.

13. Betty Rollin, "Motherhood, Who Needs It?" *Look*, September 22, 1970, 15–17.

14. David Frum has noted that the protagonists of the most popular shows were all without children: *Mary Tyler Moore, Rhoda, Three's Company, The Bob Newhart Show, The Jeffersons*. The eponymous heroine of Maude had a grown-up daughter but compensated by getting an abortion. See David Frum, *How We Got Here: The 70s: The Decade that Brought You Modern Life—For Better or Worse* (New York: Basic Books, 2000), 106.

15. Sonny Curtis, "Love Is All Around," YouTube, October 22, 2010, https://www.youtube.com/watch?v=kuuYvQsN-ak.

16. Robin Morgan, *Sisterhood Is Powerful: An Anthology of Writings from the Woman's Liberation Movement* (New York: Random House, 1970), 534.

17. Mary Daly, *Beyond God the Father: Toward a Philosophy of Women's Liberation* (Boston: Beacon Press, 1973).

18. Rosemary Radford Ruether, "The Emergence of Christian Feminist Theology," in *The Cambridge Companion to Feminist Theology*, ed. Susan Frank Parsons (Cambridge: Cambridge University Press, 2002), 3–22.

19. For a reflection on the Lutheran Church, under the leadership of then presiding Bishop Rev. Elizabeth Eaton, beginning the practice of ordaining women, see Evangelical Lutheran Church of America, "ELCA celebrates 45 Years of ordaining women," November 19, 2015, https://www.elca.org/News-and-Events/7798 (accessed May 24, 2017).

20. For a discussion of the ordination of women by the Episcopal Church as reported by the *National Catholic Reporter*, see Bill Tammeus, "Episcopal church celebrates 40 years of women in the priesthood," July 28, 2014, https://www.ncronline.org/news/faith-parish/episcopal-church-celebrates-40-years-women-priesthood (accessed May 24, 2017).

21. See the Reformed Church in America's article, "Women in the RCA," https://www.rca.org/women/women-rca (accessed May 24, 2017) for more information on the ordination of women within the RCA.

22. Letha Dawson Scanzoni and Nancy A. Hardesty, *All We're Meant to Be: A Biblical Approach to Women's Liberation* (Waco, TX: Word Books, 1974). This quote comes from Pamela D. H. Cochran, *Evangelical Feminism: A History* (New York: New York University Press, 2005), 12.

23. See Cochran, *Evangelical Feminism*, 12–13, and Scanzoni and Hardesty, *All We're Meant to Be*.

24. Jack Balswick and Judith Balswick, *The Dual-Earner Marriage: The Elaborate Balancing Act* (Old Tappan, NJ: F. H. Revell, 1995). Quotes drawn from Baker Books' promotional advertisement in their 1995 catalogue.

25. Sybil Stanton, *The 25-Hour Woman: Managing Your Time and Life* (Old Tappan, NJ: F. H. Revell, 1986). Quotes drawn from Revell's advertisement for the book in their 1986 catalogue.

26. Joanne Wallace, *The Working Woman* (Old Tappan, NJ: F. H. Revell, 1985). Quotes drawn from Revell's advertisement for the book in their 1985 catalogue.

27. Seth Dowland, *Family Values and the Rise of the Christian Right* (Philadelphia: University of Pennsylvania Press, 2015), 152.

28. Rebecca Klatch, *Women of the New Right* (Philadelphia: Temple University Press, 1987), 134.

29. Donald T. Critchlow, *Phyllis Schlafly and Grassroots Conservatism: A Woman's Crusade* (Princeton, NJ: Princeton University Press, 2005), 221.

30. Betty Cuniberti, "Other Voices Crying Out Against the Feminists: Concerned Women for America at 2nd Convention Join Other Conservatives," *LA Times*, October 2, 1985, http://articles.latimes.com/1985-10-02/news/vw-16246_1_conservative-women/2.

31. Daniel Vaca, *Commercial Religion: Media, Markets, and the Spirit of Evangelicalism* (Cambridge, MA: Harvard University Press, forthcoming 2019).

32. James Ruark, *The House of Zondervan: Celebrating 75 Years* (Grand Rapids, MI: Zondervan, 2006), 144.

33. Helene Ashker, "Women's Lib: A Biblical View," 1976. Recording housed at the Holy Spirit Research Center at Oral Roberts University, Tulsa, Oklahoma.

34. Ibid.

35. *Aglow* magazine had already been in circulation since the late 1950s, the product of the pentecostal organization called Women's Aglow Fellowship. For an in-depth look at Women's Aglow, see Ruth Marie Griffith, *God's Daughters: Evangelical Women and the Power of Submission* (Berkeley: University of California Press, 2000).

36. Janet Taylor Addison, *A History of Today's Christian Woman: 1978-1988* (master's thesis, University of Mississippi, 1989), 9.

37. Ibid.

38. John Naisbitt, *Megatrends: Ten New Directions Transforming Our Lives* (New York: Warner Books, 1982), 240.

39. Emily Suzanne Johnson, *This Is Our Message: Women's Leadership in the New Christian Right* (New York: Oxford University Press, 2019).

40. See Jeffrey Hadden and Charles E. Swann, *Prime Time Preachers: The Rising Power of Televangelism* (Reading, MA: Addison-Wesley, 1981); Jeffrey Hadden and Anson Shupe, *Televangelism, Power and Politics on God's Frontier* (New York: Henry Holt, 1988); Bobby C. Alexander, *Televangelism Reconsidered: Ritual in the Search for Human Community* (Atlanta, GA: Scholars Press, 1994); and Steve Bruce, *Pray TV: Televangelism in America* (New York: Routledge, 1990) for discussions of televangelism in the United States.

41. The 1985 National Leadership Conference, featuring James Robison, Gerald Derstine, and Charles Green, was held in the Ridgecrest Conference Center, Ridgecrest, North Carolina, May 20–23, 1985, and advertised in *Charisma* magazine in the months leading up to it.

42. Daisy Osborn, *5 Choices for Women Who Win* (Tulsa, OK: Harrison House, 1986).

43. Focus on the Family, "Our Vision," http://www.focusonthefamily.com/about /foundational-values (accessed August 11, 2018).

44. Seth Dowland, "'Family Values' and the Formation of a Christian Right Agenda," *Church History* 78.3 (2009): 614. Furthermore, Dowland offers an account of the evolution of evangelical thinking on the family in the 1970s.

45. Shuly Rubin Schwartz, *The Rabbi's Wife: The Rebbetzin in American Jewish Life* (New York: New York University Press, 2006), 184–85.

46. Marilyn Brown Oden, *The Minister's Wife: Person of Position?* (Nashville, TN: Abingdon, 1966), 15–16.

47. Ibid., 17.

48. Golda Maude Elam Bader, *I Married a Minister* (New York: Abingdon-Cokesbury Press, 1942), 29–32.

49. Ruth Truman, *Underground Manual for Ministers' Wives* (Nashville, TN: Abingdon, 1974), 149.

50. There had always been a market for the story of "Mrs. Man of God." Readers earlier in the century had wanted to know about revivalist Dwight Moody's wife, Emma, or the woman who managed the fast-talking Billy Sunday and found their answers in Emma Moody Powell's *Heavenly Destiny: The Life Story of Mrs. D. L. Moody* and Mrs. William Ashley Sunday's *Ma Sunday Still Speaks*.

51. Catherine Marshall's millions of readers knew her as the biographer of her husband, chaplain of the United States Senate, in *A Man Called Peter*, but her fame quickly eclipsed her widowhood with bestsellers *Christy, Beyond Our Selves*, and *Something*

More, giving her one of the largest readerships in the evangelical marketplace. The earliest stars were, like Catherine Marshall, women with ties to historic denominational pulpits and storied institutions.

52. Morrow C. Graham, *They Call Me Mother Graham* (Old Tappan, NJ: F.H. Revell [Baker], 1977). Morrow Graham and her daughter, "the first family of the Christian church," even penned *Mothers Together* about the universal struggles of motherhood.

53. Sheila Schuller, *Robert Schuller: My Father & My Friend* (Milwaukee, WI: Ideals Publishing Corporation, 1980), and Sheila Schuller, *Between Mother and Daughter* (Old Tappan, NJ: F. H. Revell [Baker], 1982).

54. Helen Kooiman Hosier, *Living Cameos* (Old Tappan, NJ: F. H. Revell [Baker], 1984).

55. Rita Bennett, *I'm Glad You Asked That: Timely Questions Women Ask about the Christian Life* (Edmonds, WA: Aglow/Logos Publications, 1974). Her husband, Dennis Bennett, had sparked a renewed interest in the gifts of the Holy Spirit when, as an Episcopalian minister in 1960, he announced that he had received the Baptism of the Holy Ghost that allowed him to speak in tongues and prophecy. The ensuing (and controversial) charismatic movement is the subject of Vinson Synan, ed., *The Century of the Holy Spirit: 100 Years of Pentecostal and Charismatic Renewal, 1901-2001* (Nashville, TN: Thomas Nelson, 2012).

56. Elisabeth Elliot, *The Mark of a Man: Following Christ's Example of Masculinity* (Grand Rapids, MI: Fleming H. Revell, 2006), 5.

57. Shirley Boone, *One Woman's Liberation* (Carol Stream, IL: Creation House, 1972), 222.

58. Ibid., 222–23.

59. In their 2005 book, *Century of Difference: How America Changed in the Last One Hundred Years*, Claude Fischer and Michael Hout explore changes that took place within American society throughout the twentieth century. One of the shifts they consider is the increased presence of women in the American workforce. They assert that "in 1900, 24 million men and 5 million women made up a workforce of 29 million people age fourteen and older," but by 2000, "the American labor force topped 135 million, and the number of women approached the number of men" (Fischer & Hout, 101). This increase meant that while roughly 20 percent of women participated in the workforce at the dawn of the twentieth century, approximately 60 percent did so by the early years of the twenty-first century. Prior to the 1970s, women tended to participate in the workforce up until their first child was born and after their youngest child reached their teens. During the 1970s and 1980s, however, women began to stay on "the job after they got pregnant and returned right away after they had their babies" (Fischer & Hout, 103). Many evangelicals found this increased presence of women in the workforce a threat to the family and God's ordained order for the world. Yet, Robert Putnam and David Campbell demonstrate how from "1973 to 2008, highly religious women (those who attend church almost every week) and secular women (those who almost never attend) entered the workforce in increasing numbers and at virtually the identical pace" (Putnam & Campbell, 237). Despite, or potentially because of, this similarity, evangelicals came to view women's increased role in the American workforce as a sign of how the nation had gone astray. In turn, "many Americans were deeply unhappy about the direction the country had taken during the long Sixties, and they expressed themselves both religiously and politically over the next several decades"

(Putnam & Campbell, 100). In the process, age-old debates became reframed around the questions surrounding women, chief among them, their place in the working world that they found themselves increasingly forced to participate in. See Claude Fischer and Michael Hout, *Century of Difference: How America Changed in the Last One Hundred Years* (New York: Russell Sage Foundation, 2006); and Robert Putnam and David Campbell, *American Grace: How Religion Divides and Unites Us* (New York: Simon & Schuster, 2010).

60. Constance Grady, "The Waves of Feminism, and Why People Keep Fighting over Them, Explained," July 20, 2018, https://www.vox.com/2018/3/20/16955588 /feminism-waves-explained-first-second-third-fourth (accessed August 11, 2018); Laura Brunell and Elinor Burkett, "The Third Wave of Feminism," *Encyclopædia Britannica*, July 6, 2018, https://www.britannica.com/topic/feminism/The-third-wave-of-feminism (accessed August 11, 2018); and Gabriele Griffin, "Third-wave Feminism," in *A Dictionary of Gender Studies* (Oxford: Oxford University Press, 2017).

61. Dana L. Robert, *Christian Mission: How Christianity Became a World Religion* (Malden: Wiley-Blackwell, 2011), 128.

62. Word of Faith Family Worship Cathedral, "About Us—Dr. Nina D. Bronner," http://www.woffamily.org/about-us/dr-nina-d-bronner/ (accessed May 5, 2017).

63. Mildred Grace Brown, *The Top of the World: The Story of Ken and Sarah Gaetz, Dan and Grace Priest and Many Other Missionaries in the Northwest Territories* (Saskatoon, SK: Modern Press, 1977).

64. See, for instance, the portrayals of missionary women in books like Elly Hansen and Mary Wallace's *Elly: Following Jesus All the Way* (Hazelwood, MO: Word Aflame Press, 1987) and Mollie Thompson's *When You're In, You're Out* (Hazelwood, MO: Word Aflame Press, 1986).

65. Elizabeth Flowers, *Into the Pulpit: Southern Baptist Women and Power* (Chapel Hill: University of North Carolina Press, 2012), 136.

66. Barbara O'Chester, interview by Kate Bowler, October 27, 2017.

67. Alex Comfort, *The Joy of Sex: A Cordon Bleu Guide to Lovemaking* (New York: Simon & Schuster, 1972).

68. Susie Hawkins, interview by Kate Bowler, January 24, 2017.

69. For a discussion of evangelical sex manuals, see Amy DeRogatis, *Saving Sex: Sexuality and Salvation in American Evangelicalism* (New York: Oxford University Press, 2014).

70. Barbara O'Chester, interview by Kate Bowler, October 27, 2017.

71. Susie Hawkins, interview by Kate Bowler, January 24, 2017.

72. Flowers, *Into the Pulpit*, 180.

73. Ibid., 77.

74. Anthea D. Butler, *Women in the Church of God in Christ: Making a Sanctified World* (Chapel Hill: University of North Carolina Press, 2007).

75. "First Lady Lavette Gibson Biography," Life Church of God in Christ, http:// www.lifechurchriverside.org/first-lady-lavette-gibson.html (accessed October 10, 2018).

76. Susie Hawkins, interview by Kate Bowler, January 24, 2017.

77. Flowers, *Into the Pulpit*, 118.

78. For a discussion of the prosperity gospel, see Kate Bowler, *Blessed: A History of the American Prosperity Gospel* (New York: Oxford University Press, 2013).

79. Wendy Treat, *The Fulfilled Woman: You Can Live a Happy Christian Life* (Seattle, WA: Casey Treat Ministries, 1989).

80. Kenneth Hagin, *The Woman Question* (Tulsa, OK: Faith Library Publications, 1978), 52.

81. Don Basham, "Women in Ministry," *New Wine* 6.9 (October 1974): 19.

82. James Schaffer and Colleen Todd, *Christian Wives: Women Behind Evangelists Reveal Their Faith in Modern Marriage* (Garden City, NY: Doubleday, 1987), 41–48.

83. Bowler, *Blessed*, 107–10.

84. Mia K. Wright, "Bio," http://miawright.com/about-mia/bio/ (accessed May 5, 2017).

85. Lakewood Church, "Victoria Osteen," https://www.lakewoodchurch.com/pages/new-here/victoria-osteen.aspx (accessed May 5, 2017); Phillip Luke Sinitiere, *Salvation with a Smile: Joel Osteen, Lakewood Church and American Christianity* (New York: New York University Press, 2015), 149.

86. From the Heart Church Ministries, "Our Pastor's Wife," http://www.fthcm.org/our-pastors-wife (accessed May 5, 2017).

87. Warren Bird of Leadership Network, personal correspondence with Kate Bowler, November 11, 2016 http://leadnet.org/megachurch/.

88. The National Baptist Convention, USA, "Pastor and Other Clergy Frequently Asked Questions," http://www.nationalbaptist.com/resources/church-faqs/pastor-clergy-faqs.html (accessed May 5, 2017).

89. Voices of Faith Baton Rouge, "Lady Hawkins," http://voicesfaith.org/batonrouge/about-us/lady-hawkins/ (accessed August 16, 2018).

90. Mrs. Norman Vincent Peale, *The Adventure of Being a Wife* (Englewood Cliffs, NJ: Prentice-Hall, 1971), 231.

91. See Bowler, *Blessed*, 55–58, for numbers on Peale's success.

92. Peale, *The Adventure of Being a Wife*, 230.

93. Theodore Thomas Frankenberg, *The Spectacular Career of Rev. Billy Sunday, Famous Baseball Evangelist* (Columbus, OH: McClelland & Company, 1913), 178.

94. Schaffer and Todd, *Christian Wives*, 70.

95. Oden, *The Minister's Wife*, 23.

96. Kelsey Menehan, "Life in the Spotlight," *Today's Christian Woman*, January–February, 1984, 18–21, 72–78; and Patti Roberts and Sherry Andrews, *Ashes to Gold* (Waco, TX: Word, 1983).

97. Oden, *The Minister's Wife*, 22.

98. Schaffer and Todd, *Christian Wives*, 142.

99. Peale, *The Adventure of Being a Wife*, 31.

100. See Addison, *History of Today's Christian Woman*, 43.

101. Susan Friend Harding, *The Book of Jerry Falwell: Fundamentalist Language and Politics* (Princeton: NJ: Princeton University Press, 2001), 169.

102. Harry Salem and Cheryl Salem, *Being #1 at Being #2: Success through Servanthood* (Tulsa, OK: Harrison House, 1998), 210.

103. C. S. Lovett, *Unequally Yoked Wives* (Baldwin Park, CA: Personal Christianity, 1968), 59.

104. Ibid., 33.

105. "Seminary Prof a Homemaker First," *Billings Gazette*, November 7, 2003, https://billingsgazette.com/lifestyles/seminary-prof-a-homemaker-first/article_7076e781–6e7d-53e7-bd18–6663cd2c8250.html (accessed July 25, 2018).

106. Jean Brand, *A Woman's Privilege* (London: Triangle, 1985).

107. John Gimenez and Anne Gimenez, *Upon this Rock: The Remarkable Story of John & Anne Gimenez: The Miracle of Rock Church* (n.p.: Souls Books, 1979), photo insert.

108. Harding does a wonderful analysis of this dynamic in the rhetoric of Jerry Falwell, whose speeches are "full of ribald cross-currents of meaning, hierarchy, humor, and (feigned?) hostility" (Harding, *Book of Jerry Falwell,* 167).

109. Dale Evans Rogers and Carole Carlson, *Woman: Be All You Can Be* (Old Tappan, NJ: F. H. Revell, 1980), 63.

110. Harding, *Book of Jerry Falwell,* 168.

111. Schaffer and Todd, *Christian Wives,* 47.

112. Morning Star Women, mstarwomen on Instagram, https://www.instagram.com/mstarwomen/ (accessed May 5, 2017).

113. Living Proof Live, Norfolk, Virginia, April 29, 2016.

114. Susie Hawkins, interview by Kate Bowler, January, 24, 2017.

115. Wes Granberg-Michaelson, interview by Kate Bowler, December 16, 2016.

116. Richard W. Dortch, *Integrity: How I Lost It, and My Journey Back* (Green Forest, AR: New Leaf Press, 1992), 142–43. For an overview of the Bakkers' complicated relationship with Falwell and the Swaggarts, see chapters 13 and 14 of John Wigger, *PTL: The Rise and Fall of Jim and Tammy Faye Bakker's Evangelical Empire* (New York: Oxford University Press, 2017). For background on Graham's controversial decision to speak at Oral Roberts University's dedication, see David Edwin Harrell, Jr., *Oral Roberts: An American Life* (Bloomington: Indiana University Press, 1985), 229–30.

117. Donna Miller, interview by Kate Bowler, November 9, 2016.

118. Donna J. Miller, *Growing Little Women: Capturing Teachable Moments with Your Daughter* (Chicago: Moody Publishers, 1997); *Growing Little Women for Younger Girls: Capturing Teachable Moments with Your Daughter* (Chicago: Moody Publishers, 2000).

119. Sandra Stanley, interview by Kate Bowler, November 15, 2015.

120. Patsy Willimon, interview by Kate Bowler, February 10, 2017.

121. Monique Moultrie, interview by Kate Bowler, March 9, 2017.

122. This should not have been true for white mainline megachurches, where the prominence of the pastor's wife was significantly diminished by the premium placed on ministerial education and credentials.

123. Grace Ji-Sun Kim, interview by Kate Bowler, June 2, 2018.

124. National Episcopal Health Ministries, "United Presbyterian Church in the USA Bill of Rights for Ministers' Spouses," January 2011, http://www.episcopalhealthministries.org/files/resources_attachments/diocesan-staff.pdf (accessed August 27, 2018).

125. NewSpring Church, "Man vs Wife," Q&A with Perry and Lucretia Noble, November 28, 2010, https://newspring.cc/sermons/man-vs-wife/qa-with-perry-and-lucretia-noble (accessed May 5, 2017).

126. Joseph Walker and Stephaine Walker Hale, *Becoming a Couple of Destiny* (Nashville, TN: Abingdon, 2011).

127. Ibid., n.p.

128. Much as *The Cross and the Switchblade* book and subsequent movie (featuring the young Pat Boone) had made churches aware of the gritty realities of teen life, Raul's life also demonstrated Calvary Chapel's pentecostalized inheritance in trying to stay relevant to young people.

129. Sharon Ries, *My Husband, My Maker* (Eugene, OR: Harvest House, 1989), 139.

130. Battered wife syndrome (or battered person syndrome as it is now known) is a physical and psychological condition of those who have suffered emotional, physical, and/or sexual abuse at the hands of another over a period of time. It is a legally recognized condition. More information can be found at FindLaw, "Battered Women's Syndrome," http://family.findlaw.com/domestic-violence/battered-women-s-syndrome.html (accessed May 24, 2017). For a powerful treatment of the relationship between spiritual submission and sexual and physical abuse, see R. Marie Griffith's *God's Daughters: Evangelical Women and the Power of Submission* (Berkeley: University of California Press, 1997), 113–21.

131. Holly Green, "The Darker Side of Submission," *Today's Christian Woman*, January–February, 1985, 93.

132. Feminists have argued that "socially structured gender inequality is a primary reason for the high rate of violence against women." Natalie J. Sokoloff and Christina Pratt, *Domestic Violence at the Margins: Readings on Race, Class, Gender, and Culture* (New Brunswick, NJ: Rutgers University Press, 2005), 2. Christians for Biblical Equality hosted a conference entitled "Women, Abuse, and the Bible" to explore how teachings on headship and submission had been used to justify violence. See Catherine Clark Kroeger and James R. Beck, *Women, Abuse, and the Bible: How Scripture Can Be Used to Hurt or Heal* (Grand Rapids, MI: Baker, 1996).

133. Ries, *My Husband, My Maker*, 146–47.

134. Stephen Paul Walker, "Million Man March" in Tiffany K. Wayne, ed., *Women's Rights in the United States: A Comprehensive Encyclopedia of Issues, Events, and People* (Santa Barbara, CA: ABC-CLIO, 2014), 170.

135. Name withheld, interview by Kate Bowler, October 21, 2018.

136. Ibid., 141.

137. Ibid., 134.

138. Sarah Pulliam Bailey, "Isaac Hunter Dead: Summit Church Pastor and Son of Obama Adviser Joel Hunter Dies in Apparent Suicide," *The Huffington Post*, January 23, 2014, https://www.huffingtonpost.com/2013/12/11/isaac-hunter-dead_n_4427371.html (accessed August 27, 2018).

139. Leonardo Blair, "Zachery Tims' Ex-Wife Riva Explains Why Churches Fail at Restoring Fallen Pastors," *The Christian Post*, February 3, 2017, http://www.christianpost.com/news/zachery-tims-ex-wife-riva-explains-why-churches-fail-at-restoring-fallen-pastors-174088/print.html (accessed March 9, 2017). He later died of a heroin overdose.

140. Peale, *The Adventure of Being a Wife*, 142.

141. See Set Apart Girl (founded 2015), https://braveheartedstore.com/magazines (accessed May 24, 2017).

CHAPTER THREE: THE TALENT

1. English Standard Version.

2. *The Tammy Faye Show*, 1978, produced by Praise the Lord and performed by Tammy Faye.

3. Ibid.

4. John H. Wigger, *PTL: The Rise and Fall of Jim and Tammy Faye Bakker's Evangelical Empire* (Oxford: Oxford University Press, 2017), 114–16.

5. James Schaffer and Colleen Todd, *Christian Wives: Women Behind Evangelists Reveal Their Faith in Modern Marriage* (Garden City, NY: Doubleday, 1987), 5.

6. David Edwin Harrell, *Oral Roberts: An American Life* (San Francisco: Harper-Collins, 1987), 46.

7. Paul Crouch, *Hello World! A Personal Letter to the Body of Christ* (Nashville, TN: Thomas Nelson, 2003), 25.

8. William Lobdell and Mitchell Landsberg, "Rev. Robert H Schuller, who built Crystal Cathedral, dies at 88," *Los Angeles Times*, April 2, 2015, http://www.latimes.com /local/obituaries/la-me-robert-schuller-20150403-story.html.

9. Schaffer and Todd, *Christian Wives*, 123.

10. Ibid., 122.

11. Ibid., 122–23.

12. Wes Granberg-Michaelson, interview by Kate Bowler, December 16, 2016.

13. Ibid.

14. Nicole Santa Cruz, "Arvella Schuller dies at 84; wife of Crystal Cathedral founder Robert Schuller," *Los Angeles Times*, February 11, 2014, http://articles.latimes .com/2014/feb/11/local/la-me-arvella-schuller-20140212.

15. Randall Balmer, "Rex Humbard," *Encyclopedia of Evangelicalism* (Waco, TX: Baylor University Press, 2004), 347; Schaffer and Todd, *Christian Wives*, 67–89; and Colette M. Jenkins, "Televangelist Rex Humbard's wife Maude Aimee Humbard dies at age 89," *Akron Beacon Journal*, May 15, 2012, http://www.ohio.com/news/local /televangelist-rex-humbard-s-wife-maude-aimee-humbard-dies-at-age-89–1.307290.

16. Kate Bowler, *Blessed: A History of the American Prosperity Gospel* (New York: Oxford University Press, 2013), 74.

17. Schaffer and Todd, *Christian Wives*, 70.

18. Ibid., 70.

19. Jamie Buckingham, *Daughter of Destiny: The Authorized Biography of Kathryn Kuhlman* (Alachua, FL: Bridge-Logos, 1999), 165; Amy Collier Artman, *The Miracle Lady: Kathryn Kuhlman and the Transformation of Charismatic Christianity* (Grand Rapids, MI: Eerdmans, 2019).

20. Raymond Arroyo, *Mother Angelica: The Remarkable Story of a Nun, Her Nerve and a Network of Miracles* (New York: Doubleday, 2005).

21. Ibid.

22. Ibid., 149.

23. Ibid., 132.

24. Ibid., 133

25. Ibid., 147.

26. Ibid., 162.

27. Ibid., 187.

28. Crouch, *Hello World!*, 44. A solitary person talking to a screen is often an ineffective communication method because people miss the collective cues which indicate how to respond. Thus, the need for a laugh track, crowd, or a wife who helps send the appropriate message to the audience. See Randall Collins, *Interaction Ritual Chains* (Princeton, NJ: Princeton University Press, 2005).

29. Some churches like the Crystal Cathedral and the Cathedral of Tomorrow proved that simply televising church services could be dynamic. But the variety show format was capable of filling much more airtime and was the preferred format of the 1980s.

30. Steven C. Tracy, "Black Twice: Performance Conditions for Blues and Gospel Artists," in *The Cambridge Companion to Blues and Gospel Music*, ed. Allan Moore (Cambridge: Cambridge University Press, 2003), 89–101. For more on the history, see Bob Darden, *People Get Ready! A New History of Black Gospel Music* (New York: Bloomsbury Academic, 2004).

31. Wen Reagan, *A Beautiful Noise: A History of Contemporary Worship Music in Modern America* (PhD diss., Duke University, 2013); Julie C. Dunbar, "Rosetta Tharpe," in *Women, Music, Culture: An Introduction* (New York: Routledge, 2015), 193–195.

32. "Mahalia Jackson: A Millionairess' Legacy to Blacks," *Jet*, February 17, 1972. Joshua Young and I looked at all copies of *Jet* magazine from 1951–2000. We noted all mentions of gospel music, the singers the magazine choose to cover, and any images that accompanied articles on the topic. The February 1972 cover of *Jet* was one of the most prominent examples of the magazine's continual coverage of gospel music, the gospel music scene, and the leading role that woman played within it.

33. Emmett Price, Tammy L. Kernodle, and Horace Joseph Maxile, *Encyclopedia of African American Music* (Santa Barbara, CA: ABC-CLIO, 2011), 69.

34. See entry on "Gospel Periodicals," in *Encyclopedia of American Gospel Music*, ed. W. K. McNeil (New York: Routledge, 2010), 153.

35. The industry categories of "Southern Gospel," "Christian Worship Music," and "Contemporary Christian Music" are dominated by Euro-Americans.

36. "Happy 46th Birthday, CeCe Winans," *Essence*, October 8, 2010, http://www.essence.com/2010/10/08/happy-birthday-cece-winans (accessed August 20, 2018).

37. Jon Pareles, "Marion Williams Is Dead at 66; Influential Pioneer of Gospel," *The New York Times*, July 4, 1994, http://www.nytimes.com/1994/07/04/obituaries/marion-williams-is-dead-at-66-influential-pioneer-of-gospel.html.

38. Glen Hinson, *Fire in My Bones: Transcendence and the Holy Spirit in African American Gospel* (Philadelphia: University of Pennsylvania Press, 1999), 136.

39. Ibid., 105.

40. Jewly Hight, "'At This Age, This Is Who I Am': The Gospel According to CeCe Winans," *The Record: Music from NPR*, February 2, 2017, http://www.npr.org/sections/therecord/2017/02/02/512850020/at-this-age-this-is-who-i-am-the-gospel-according-to-cece-winans (accessed May 6, 2017).

41. "Tramaine Hawkins: 'People Get Ready' for a gospel superstar," *Cross Rhythms*, June 1, 1991, http://www.crossrhythms.co.uk/articles/music/Tramaine_Hawkins_People_Get_Ready_for_a_gospel_superstar/33229/p1/ (accessed September 12, 2018).

42. "Mary Mary 'God In Me' Controversey [sic]," *The Gospel Blog*, http://thegospelblog.com/mary-mary-god-in-me-controversey/ (accessed August 27, 2018).

43. Angela Wilson, "Trap Gospel Flow: Erica Campbell Dishes on Controversial Song 'I Luh God,'" *Vibe*, April 8, 2015, http://www.vibe.com/2015/04/trap-gospel-flow -erica-campbell-dishes-on-controversial-song-i-luh-god/ (accessed September 12, 2018).

44. Associated Press, "Mary Mary's Erica Campbell on Going Solo, Grammys Nods and Her Controversial Skintight Dress," *Billboard*, March 13, 2014, https://www .billboard.com/articles/columns/the-juice/5930508/mary-marys-erica-campbell-on -going-sologrammys-nods-and-her (accessed September 12, 2018).

45. For more information on *Get Up! Mornings with Erica Campbell*, see Interactive One, LLC, https://getuperica.com/ (accessed May 8, 2017).

46. Bossip Staff Writer, "Fix It, Jesus: Yolanda Adams Booted from Her Religious Radio Show & Replaced by Erica Campbell," *Bossip,* April 28, 2016, https://bossip.com /1308646/fix-it-jesus-yolanda-adams-booted-from-her-religious-radio-show -replaced-by-erica-campbell/ (accessed May 26, 2017).

47. She not only brought great fame to her own COGIC congregation and its bishop, but she became one of the editors of the denomination's hymnal and served as president of their National Music Department; see Greg Prato, "Mattie Moss Clark, Artist Biography," *AllMusic,* http://www.allmusic.com/artist/mattie-moss-clark-mn0000 170806 (accessed May 24, 2017).

48. For more information on Unsung and their television show, see "The Clark Sisters," *TV One*, https://tvone.tv/5720/clark-sisters/ (accessed September 12, 2018).

49. "The Elect Lady—Dr. Dorinda Clark-Cole," Church of God in Christ, Inc., http://www.cogic.org/evangelismdepartment/about-us/elect-lady/ (accessed May 7, 2017).

50. *Preachers of Detroit*, Oxygen Network, http://www.oxygen.com/preachers-of -detroit (accessed May 8, 2017).

51. Gladys L. Knight, "Shirley Caesar," in *Encyclopedia of African American Popular Culture*, vol. 1, ed. Jessie Carney Smith (Santa Barbara, CA: ABC-CLIO, 2010), 225–27.

52. Congregational visit to Mount Calvary Word of Faith Church, June 10, 2007.

53. Pannellctp Traditional Gospel Music, "Hold My Mule," YouTube, December 5, 2010, https://www.youtube.com/watch?v=ZyutFBpelGE (accessed September 12, 2018).

54. Jay Howard and John Streck, *Apostles of Rock: The Splintered World of Contemporary Christian Music* (Lexington: University Press of Kentucky, 1999), 199.

55. Randall Balmer ed., "Amy Grant," *Encyclopedia of Evangelicalism* (Louisville, KY: Westminster John Knox, 2002), 303–4.

56. See Holly Meyer, "Amy Grant says she accepts LifeWay's decision not to sell new album," *WBIR.com*, November 2, 2016, http://www.wbir.com/news/local/lifeway-stores -say-no-to-amy-grants-christmas-album/346276386 (accessed September 12, 2018); Melissa Riddle, The Story of Us: Gary Chapman," *Today's Christian Music/TCM*, April 7, 2001, http://www.todayschristianmusic.com/artists/gary-chapman/features /the-story-of-us/; Bill Milkowski, "Amy Grant: No Ego-Tripping Here," *Christian Science Monitor*, December 19, 1986, http://www.csmonitor.com/1986/1219/lamy-f.html (accessed September 12, 2018); and Amy Grant and Vince Gill, "Interview with Amy Grant and Vince Gill," *Primetime,* ABC News, October 3, 2002, http://abcnews.go.com /Primetime/story?id=131919&page=1 (accessed May 25, 2017).

57. Meyer, "Amy Grant says she accepts LifeWay's decision."

58. Michael Goldberg, "Grant Brings Gospel into the '80s," *Sun Sentinel*, June 7, 1985, http://articles.sun-sentinel.com/1985-06-07/features/8501230021_1_amy-grant -gospel-music-christian-music/2 (accessed September 12, 2018).

59. Adam McGill, "Jessica Simpson: Gospel Girl Gone Bad," *D Magazine*, March 2002, https://www.dmagazine.com/publications/d-magazine/2002/march /jessica-simpson-gospel-girl-gone-bad/ (accessed March 19, 2017).

60. Rebecca St. James, *40 Days with God: A Devotional Journey* (Cincinnati, OH: Standard, 1996).

61. Dave Geisler, "Grammy Winner Rebecca St. James 'True Love Waits,'" *lovematters.com,* http://lovematters.com (accessed March 19, 2017).

62. Rebecca St. James, "Wait for Me," YouTube, May 5, 2006, https://www.youtube .com/watch?v=ooAi3KJ5I-s (accessed May 8, 2017); Rebecca St. James, *Wait for Me Journal: Thoughts for My Future Husband* (Nashville, TN: Thomas Nelson, 2003); and Rebecca St. James, *Wait for Me Study Guide: Discover the Power of Purity* (Nashville, TN: Thomas Nelson, 2005).

63. Rebecca St. James and Lynda Hunter Bjorklund, *SHE: The Woman You're Made to Be* (Carol Stream, IL: Tyndale House, 2004).

64. Camerin Courtney, "Balancing Act," *Today's Christian Woman*, March/April, 2005, 31–34.

65. Tony Cummings, "Jaci Velasquez: The Tex/Mex 16 Year Old Pop Singer—Jaci Velasquez," *Cross Rhythms*, August 1, 1996, http://www.crossrhythms.co.uk/articles /music/Jaci_Velasquez_The_TexMex_16_year_old_pop_singer/40547/p1 (accessed March 19, 2017).

66. See, for instance, Urban Youth Workers Institute, "Interview with Jaci Velasquez," January 22, 2010, http://uywi.org/interview-with-jaci-velasquez/ (accessed March 19, 2017).

67. Mark Moring, "Jaci Velasquez Divorced," *Crosswalk.com*, August 22, 2005, http://www.crosswalk.com/culture/music/jaci-velasquez-divorced-11617517.html (accessed March 19, 2017).

68. Mark Moring, "Jaci Velasquez: A 'Diamond' Refined," *Christianity Today*, February 7, 2012, https://www.christianitytoday.com/ct/2012/februaryweb-only /jacivelasquez-february7.html (accessed September 12, 2018).

69. Wen Reagan, "Contemporary Christian Music," in *Encyclopedia of Christianity in the United States*, ed. George Thomas Kurian and Mark. A. Lamport (Lanham, MD: Rowman & Littlefield, 2016), 629.

70. See https://www.amazon.com/Kansas-Jennifer-Knapp/dp/B000005OJE for an image of Jennifer Knapp's *Kansas* album cover (accessed May 8, 2017).

71. Jennifer Knapp, interview by Kate Bowler, December 31, 2016.

72. *LifeWay: True Love Waits,* http://www.lifeway.com/n/Product-Family/True -Love-Waits (accessed May 8, 2017).

73. Jennifer Knapp, *Facing the Music: My Story* (New York: Howard Books, 2014), 180.

74. Ibid., 188.

75. Jennifer Knapp, personal correspondence with Kate Bowler, October 1, 2018.

76. Lakewood Church, "Leadership Team," https://www.lakewoodchurch.com /pages/new-here/leadership-team.aspx (accessed May 8, 2017); Kate Bowler and Wen

Reagan, "Bigger, Better, Louder: The Prosperity Gospel's Impact on Contemporary Christian Worship," *Religion and American Culture: A Journal of Interpretation* 24.2 (2014): 186–230.

77. See Cindy Cruse Ratcliff, "Cindy Cruse Ratcliff-Majesty," YouTube, November 22, 2010, https://www.youtube.com/watch?v=VfE2st8XdII for an instance of the video of the performance cover (accessed May 8, 2017).

78. Ibid.

79. Sheila Marikar, "Los Angeles Churches Make Worship . . . Hip?" *The New York Times*, December 12, 2015, https://www.nytimes.com/2015/12/13/fashion/mosaic-oasis -hillsong-churches-los-angeles.html (accessed May 8, 2017).

80. Passion Conferences, https://268generation.com/ (accessed May 8, 2017).

81. W Publishing Group, "My Anything Stories: Shelley Giglio #AnythingProject," YouTube, June 15, 2015, https://www.youtube.com/watch?v=T11JXmyCKIk (accessed May 25, 2017).

82. Reagan, *A Beautiful Noise*.

83. Christy Nockels, interview by Kate Bowler, March 12, 2016.

84. For an example of "My Anchor," see "Christy Nockels—My Anchor," YouTube, February 23, 2015, https://www.youtube.com/watch?v=JzqhUYaAI78 (accessed May 8, 2017).

85. GMA Dove Awards, "Past Winners," http://doveawards.com/awards/past -winners/ (accessed May 8, 2017).

86. Leonardo Blair, "Church Bans Fat People from Worship Team Because They Would Interrupt Flow of Anointing," *The Christian Post,* October 14, 2016, http://www .christianpost.com/news/church-bans-fat-people-from-worship-team-because-they -would-interrupt-flow-of-anointing-170814/ (accessed May 8, 2017).

87. Geoff Surratt, "Should 'Fat' People Lead Worship?" ChurchLeaders.com, March 30, 2014, http://churchleaders.com/worship/worship-articles/173605-geoff -surratt-should-fat-people-lead-worship.html (accessed May 8, 2017).

88. See chapter two of John H. Wigger's *PTL: The Rise and Fall of Jim and Tammy Bakker's Evangelical Empire* (New York: Oxford University Press, 2017).

89. Extraordinary Women, Women of Faith, Women of Joy, and Lisa Harper's Renewing the Heart conferences.

90. 1 Corinthians 12:6, NIV.

CHAPTER FOUR: THE COUNSELOR

1. New International Version.

2. Randy Robison, "Kasey Van Norman: Staring Down Death (Randy Robison/ LIFE Today)," YouTube, July 31, 2014 https://www.youtube.com/watch?v=aE7-ivAoHYA (accessed May 26, 2017).

3. See Kasey Van Norman's YouTube postings at https://www.youtube.com/user /BeautifulAdventure/videos for examples of this usage as well as her testimony (accessed September 13, 2018).

4. William Cowper, "There Is a Fountain Filled with Blood," (1771) Hymn 622 in *The United Methodist Hymnal*, available at http://hymnary.org/hymn/UMH/622.

5. See chapter four of Kate Bowler, *Blessed: A History of the American Prosperity Gospel* (New York: Oxford University Press, 2013).

6. Kasey Van Norman, *Named by God: Overcoming Your Past, Transforming Your Present, Embracing Your Future* (Carol Stream, IL: Tyndale House, 2012), 63.

7. For a stunning account of this dynamic, see Kathryn Lofton, *Oprah: The Gospel of an Icon* (Berkeley: University of California Press, 2011), 85.

8. Carolyn Kitch, "Women in Journalism," in *American Journalism: History, Principles, and Practices,* ed. W. David Sloan and Lisa Mullikin Parcell (Jefferson, MO: McFarland, 2002), 87–88.

9. Kimberly Wilmot Voss, *The Social History of the American Family: An Encyclopedia,* vol. 1, *Advice Columnist,* ed. Marilyn J. Coleman and Lawrence H. Ganon (Los Angeles: SAGE, 2014), 41.

10. Rush Ashmore, "Side-Talk with Girls," *The Ladies Home Journal,* December 1893, 35.

11. C. E. Humphry, *Manners for Women* (London: James Bowden, 1898), 19.

12. Lynne Olson, "Dear Beatrice Fairfax," *American Heritage* 43.3 (May-June 1992): 90, http://www.americanheritage.com/content/%E2%80%9Cdear-beatrice-fairfax%E2%80%A6%E2%80%9C (accessed May 30, 2016).

13. Kitch, "Women in Journalism," 90.

14. Scott Coltrane and Michele Adams, *Gender and Families,* 2nd ed. (Lanham, MD: Rowman and Littlefield, 2008), 35.

15. Olson, "Dear Beatrice Fairfax," 90.

16. Some have suggested that certain forms of mass media—such as soap opera and melodrama with their open-endedness and repetition—are more naturally appealing to women. See Robert Clyde Allen, *Speaking of Soap Operas* (Chapel Hill: University of North Carolina Press, 1985), and Mimi White, *Tele-Advising: Therapeutic Discourse in American Television* (Chapel Hill: University of North Carolina Press, 1992), 16.

17. E. Brooks Holifield, *A History of Pastoral Care in America: From Salvation to Self-Realization* (Nashville, TN: Abingdon, 1983), 226–27.

18. Steven C. Ward, *Modernizing the Mind: Psychological Knowledge and the Remaking of Society* (Westport, CT: Praeger, 2002), 147.

19. Bowler, *Blessed,* 11–40.

20. See Anthony Babington, *Shell Shock: A History of the Changing Attitudes to War Neurosis* (London: Leo Cooper, 1997); War Office, *Report of the War Office Committee of Enquiry into 'Shell-Shock'* (1922), https://wellcomelibrary.org/item/b18295496#?c =0&m=0&s=0&cv=0&z=-0.815%2C-0.0826%2C2.6301%2C1.6521, accessed 3 October, 2018; Anton Kaes, *Shell Shock Cinema: Weimer Culture and the Wounds of War* (Princeton, NJ: Princeton University Press, 2009); and Jonathan H. Ebel, *G.I. Messiahs: Soldiering, War, and American Civil Religion* (New Haven, CT: Yale University Press, 2015) for discussions of war, soldiers, shell shock, the therapeutic, and post-traumatic stress disorder (PTSD).

21. See Eva Moskowitz, *In Therapy We Trust: America's Obsession with Self-Fulfillment* (Baltimore, MD: Johns Hopkins University Press, 2001); Susan E. Myers-Shirk, *Helping the Good Shepherd: Pastoral Counselors in a Psychotherapeutic Culture, 1925–1975* (Baltimore, MD: Johns Hopkins University Press, 2009), for discussions of ministry and the therapeutic.

22. For a broader discussion of the history of psychology in the United States and its role in schools and workplaces, see Thomas Good, ed., *American Education:*

Yesterday, Today and Tomorrow (Chicago: University of Chicago Press, 2000); Morton M. Hunt, *The Story of Psychology* (New York: Anchor Books, 2007); and Joseph M. Notterman, ed., *The Evolution of Psychology: Fifty Years of American Psychology* (Washington, DC: American Psychological Association, 1997).

23. Simone de Beauvoir's *The Second Sex* first appeared in 1949 and Betty Friedan's *The Feminine Mystique* was first published in 1963. In one of the era's most popular movies, *Miracle on 34th Street*, the heroine, played by Margaret O'Hara, is employed as a department store psychologist.

24. For a basic overview of Freud and his use of these terms, see C. R. Badcock, *Essential Freud* (Cambridge, MA: Blackwell, 1988); and Sharon Heller, *Freud A to Z* (Hoboken, NJ: Wiley, 2005).

25. See Holifield, *History of Pastoral Care in America,* 226–27; and Charles T. Holman, *The Cure of Souls: A Socio-Psychological Approach* (Chicago: University of Chicago Press, 1932), 29.

26. Holifield, *History of Pastoral Care in America,* 231.

27. Stephen Ministries was founded in 1975 by Dr. Kenneth Haugk and his wife, Joan, with the mission of training, equipping, and deploying lay people to provide quality pastoral care within their congregations as well as train others to do the same. According to the organization's website, there are Stephen Ministries programs in over thirteen thousand congregations that span 170 denominations in all fifty states. For more information on Stephen Ministries, see the organization's website at https://www.stephenministries.org/, as well as Kenneth C. Haugk, *When and How to Use Mental Health Resources: A Guide for Stephen Ministers, Stephen Leaders and Church Staff* (St. Louis, MO: Stephen Ministries, 2000).

28. See http://fuller.edu/school-of-psychology/ and http://www.rosemead.edu/ for more information on Fuller Theological Seminary's School of Psychology and Rosemead School of Psychology, respectively.

29. Agnes Sanford, *The Healing Light* (Watchung, NJ: Macalester Park, 1947).

30. James Stuart Olson, *Historical Dictionary of the 1950s* (Westport, CT: Greenwood, 2000), 124, 286. In the last half of the twentieth century, television became the dominant medium by which information was conveyed and attitudes were shaped. It eclipsed radio, films, and the printed word in the 1950s and, before the diffusion of audiences brought about by the proliferation of cable, the three dominant networks could expect viewers for their programs to number in the tens of millions.

31. Lee Bollinger and Carole O'Neil's *Women in Media Careers: Success Despite the Odds* (Lanham, MD: University Press of America, 2008), 38, charts Brothers' success on television and radio, in movies and newspapers, and on the bestselling book lists.

32. For an example of Brothers on the *Johnny Carson Show*, see a clip from the show from Time Life, "Time Life Presents Johnny and Friends—Burt Reynolds, Dom DeLuise and Dr. Joyce Brothers," YouTube, https://www.youtube.com/watch?v=9A_AUwvOX28 (accessed September 13, 2018), and on Hollywood Squares, "Hollywood Squares-Week of February 20, 1978 (George vs. Carolyn)," YouTube, https://www.youtube.com/watch?v=NvPc7ouVJSk (accessed September 14, 2018).

33. White, *Tele-Advising*, 28, 178, and 183.

34. The names of Jerry Springer, Ricki Lake, Phil Donahue, Montel Williams, Maury Povich, Jenny Jones, and Sally Jesse Raphael will live in television infamy for

their contributions to mental health. See Kevin Glynn, *Tabloid Culture: Trash Taste, Popular Power, and the Transformation of American Television* (Durham, NC: Duke University Press, 2000), and Andrew Tolson, *Television Talk Shows: Discourse, Performance, Spectacle* (New York: Routledge, 2001).

35. Ward, *Modernizing the Mind*, 154.

36. Ibid., 154. Here Ward is quoting Robert Sklar, "Prime-Time Psychology," *American Film* (March 1979): 63.

37. Eva Moskowitz, *In Therapy We Trust: America's Obsession with Self-Fulfillment* (Baltimore, MD: Johns Hopkins University Press, 2001), 224.

38. Philip Rieff, *The Triumph of the Therapeutic: Uses of Faith after Freud* (New York: Harper & Row Publishers, 1966), 15–25.

39. R. Marie Griffith, *God's Daughters: Evangelical Women and the Power of Submission* (Berkeley: University of California Press, 1997), 29. As historian Griffith observed about the participants in Women's Aglow, the pentecostal women's parachurch ministry, the concepts of "submission and surrender . . . contain an unmistakable potential for subjugation [but] may also offer what feminist theologian Sarah Coakley has approvingly termed 'power in vulnerability,' that is, 'the willed effacement to a gentle omnipotence which, far from 'complementing' masculinism, acts as its undoing'" (185).

40. In his work, *A Secular Age* (Cambridge, MA: Belknap, 2007), Canadian philosopher and ethicist, Charles Taylor, explores the idea that the current moment is best understood as the "Age of Authenticity." For a further discussion of authenticity and its implications for modern society, see Ulla Haselstein, Andrew Gross, and Maryann Snyder-Korber, *The Pathos of Authenticity: American Passions of the Real* (Heidelberg: Universitätsverlag, 2012); Charles Taylor, *Sources of the Self: The Making of the Modern Identity* (Cambridge, MA: Harvard University Press, 1992); Charles Taylor, *The Ethics of Authenticity* (Cambridge, MA: Harvard University Press, 1992); and Robert D. Putnam, *Bowling Alone: The Collapse and Revival of American Community* (New York: Simon & Schuster, 2001).

41. Sheila Walsh, *Honestly* (Grand Rapids, MI: Zondervan, 1996), 150. For a discussion of Alcoholics Anonymous and its Twelve Steps, see the organization's website at http://www.recovery.org/topics/alcoholics-anonymous-12-step/. For a cultural history of the broader recovery movement in the United States, see Trysh Travis, *The Language of the Heart: A Cultural History of the Recovery Movement from Alcoholics Anonymous to Oprah Winfrey* (Chapel Hill: University of North Carolina Press, 2009).

42. Katie Wright, *The Rise of the Therapeutic Society: Psychological Knowledge & The Contradictions of Cultural Change* (Washington, DC: New Academia Publishing, 2011), 3.

43. For more information on the IF:Gathering, see the organization's website at https://ifgathering.com/ (accessed September 13, 2018).

44. See Michael J. McClymond, ed., *Embodying the Spirit: New Perspectives on North American Revivalism* (Baltimore, MD: Johns Hopkins University Press, 2004), for a discussion of revivalism in the United States, both historically and in its contemporary manifestations.

45. IF:Gathering, February 5, 2016, Austin, TX.

46. See Brené Brown's website at https://brenebrown.com/videos/ for a video of this talk, as well as Brown's other TED talk on "The Power of Vulnerability" (accessed September 13, 2018).

47. The following series of quotes come from the IF:Gathering, February 5, 2016, Austin, TX.

48. Paraphrase of Psalm 139.

49. 2 Corinthians 12:9 (NRSV): "but he said to me, 'My grace is sufficient for you, for power is made perfect in weakness.' So, I will boast all the more gladly of my weaknesses, so that the power of Christ may dwell in me."

50. See Peter Kreeft, *I Burned for Your Peace: Augustine's Confessions Unpacked* (San Francisco: Ignatius, 2016), and William E. Mann, ed., *Augustine's Confessions: Philosophy in Autobiography* (New York: Oxford University Press, 2014), for a discussion of Augustine's *Confessions* and its uses over time.

51. Some churches in eighteenth- and nineteenth-century America deemed confession so important that they demanded congregants publicly make regular confession of sexual and other misdeeds—an often embarrassing and unpopular part of the drive for a purified church. In the Second Great Awakening some have detected a different sort of confession made by men and by women. Young unmarried middle-class women seem to have focused on emotional content—the anxiety and shame connected with their sinful desire to rebel against God. Confession brought relief from self-condemnation and assurance about the future. Males of the same class phrased their confessions in terms of the practical rewards of being saved, and relief from the pressures to convert exerted by female family members. For a more in-depth discussion of this point, see D. Bruce Hindmarsh, *The Evangelical Conversion Narrative: Spiritual Autobiography in Early Modern England* (New York: Oxford University Press, 2008); Kelly A. Ryan, *Regulating Passion: Sexuality and Patriarchal Rule in Massachusetts, 1700–1830* (New York: Oxford University Press, 2014), 141.

52. Michel Foucault, *The History of Sexuality*, vol. 1, *An Introduction*, trans. Robert Hurley, reissue ed. (New York: Pantheon Books, 1978). In the first of his three volumes on sexuality, Michel Foucault argues that "since the Middle Ages, at least, Western societies have established the confession as one of the main rituals we rely on for the production of truth," which has given it a "central role in the order of civil and religious powers" (58). He goes on to contend that "confession frees, but power reduces one to silence; truth does not belong to the order of power, but shares an original affinity with freedom . . . [truth's] production is thoroughly imbued with relations of power" and confession is an example of said process (60). Based on these points, he concludes, that "confession is a ritual of discourse in which the speaking subject is also the subject of the statement; it is also a ritual that unfolds within a power relationship, for one does not confess without the presence (or virtual presence) of a partner who is not simply the interlocutor but the authority who requires the confession, prescribes and appreciates it and intervenes in order to judge, punish, forgive, console, and reconcile; a ritual in which the truth is corroborated by the obstacles and resistances it has had to surmount in order to be formulated; and finally, a ritual in which the expression alone, independently of its external consequences, produces intrinsic modifications in the person who articulates it: it exonerates, redeems, and purifies him; it unburdens him of his wrongs, liberates him and promises him salvation" (61–62). Put differently, confession becomes a means of simultaneously reinforcing and inverting power dynam-

ics and societal norms as it creates space for the individual, who gains a voice while permitting continued oppression within systems of power. Women in Christian megaministries often occupy this intersection and engage in the act of confession to leverage said position in much the way Foucault describes.

53. Lysa TerKeurst, *Becoming More Than a Good Bible Study Girl* (Nashville, TN: Thomas Nelson, 2009).

54. Sarah Jakes, *Lost and Found: Finding Hope in the Detours of Life* (Bloomington, MN: Bethany House, 2015).

55. Promotional blog for Ann Voskamp's book, *The Broken Way: A Daring Path into the Abundant Life,* August 11, 2016, http://annvoskamp.com/2016/08/my-new-book -a-new-dare-that-we-all-need-right-about-now/ (accessed February 9, 2017).

56. Holifield, *History of Pastoral Care in America*, 231.

57. See for example Catherine A. Brekus, *Strangers and Pilgrims: Female Preaching in America, 1740–1845* (Chapel Hill: University of North Carolina Press, 1998).

58. Alex Grahmann, personal correspondence with Kate Bowler, September 24, 2018.

59. Kasey Van Norman, "About," http://kaseyvannorman.org/about/ (accessed September 4, 2018).

60. Take, for example, the famous "Danvers Statement on Biblical Manhood and Womanhood" of 1987 that served as a manifesto for those advocating complementarian roles for the sexes—the males signing on to the creed used titles such as "Professor," "Director," or "President"; every female was listed first as "homemaker" or "pastor's wife," even though many had solid credential or careers. A copy of CBMW.ORG's (Coalition for Biblical Sexuality) "The Danvers Statement" can be found at http://cbmw .org/uncategorized/the-danvers-statement (accessed May 26, 2017).

61. See Rebekah Lyons's website, http://rebekahlyons.com/.

62. See Jess Connolly's website, http://jessconnolly.com/about/.

63. See "Get to Know Priscilla," Going Beyond Ministries, http://www.goingbeyond .com/ministry/biography/ (accessed May 26, 2017).

64. See Ann Voskamp's Twitter account: https://twitter.com/AnnVoskamp (accessed September 14, 2018).

65. See Lauren Chandler's Twitter account: https://twitter.com/laurenchandler (accessed September 14, 2018).

66. See Margaret Feinberg's Twitter account: https://twitter.com/mafeinberg (accessed January 7, 2018).

67. See https://www.amazon.com/Zig-Ziglar/e/B000AP7VIY for a list of Zig Ziglar's books and a brief biography.

68. See Lofton, *Oprah*, 78.

69. See "Rescue Yourself! Lisa Nichols on the Steve Harvey Show," YouTube, May 9, 2015, https://www.youtube.com/watch?v=Kcu92UlIQfs (accessed September 14, 2018).

70. McClean Bible Church, "Counseling," https://www.mcleanbible.org/care-and -support/counseling (accessed May 26, 2017).

71. United Methodist Church, "Eleven Clergy Endorsed by UMEA for the Ministry of Life Coaching," *Higher Education and Ministry,* May 19, 2010, http://www.gbhem .org/article/eleven-clergy-endorsed-umea-ministry-life-coaching (accessed May 26, 2017).

72. Life Coach Hub, https://www.lifecoachhub.com/coaching/law-of-attraction -coaching (accessed September 14, 2018).

73. Taken from Refining Women Worldwide website, http://colormeorganizedtour .com/press.html.

74. See Girlfriends In God on Facebook: https://www.facebook.com/Girlfriends InGod or on their website: http://girlfriendsingod.com (accessed September 14, 2018).

75. For an example of this, see Rebekah Lyons's bio: http://qideas.org/contributors /rebekah-lyons/ (accessed September 14, 2018).

76. See Carlos Lozano, "Grief, mourning at church after suicide of Rick Warren's son," *Los Angeles Times*, April 7, 2013, http://articles.latimes.com/2013/apr/07/local/la -me-ln-rick-warren-son-suicide-mourning-20130407 (accessed May 26, 2017), for local and national media coverage of the Warrens' son's death.

77. Kay Warren, *Dangerous Surrender: What Happens When You Say Yes to God* (Grand Rapids, MI: Zondervan, 2007).

78. Gathering on Mental Health and the Church, Saddleback Church, Lake Forest, CA, March 28, 2014. https://saddleback.com/watch/24-hours-of-hope/plenary-5 -standing-together-in-suffering.

79. Ibid.

80. Bob Smietana, "Half of Evangelicals believe prayer can heal mental illness," LifeWay—Newsroom, September 17, 2013, http://blog.lifeway.com/newsroom/2013/09 /17/half-of-evangelicals-believe-prayer-can-heal-mental-illness/ (accessed May 26, 2017).

81. Rick Warren and Kay Warren, "Rick Warren: Churches Must Do More to Address Mental Illness," *Time,* May 27, 2014, http://time.com/40071/rick-warren-churches -must-do-more-to-address-mental-illness/ (accessed May 26, 2017).

82. Kathryn Joyce, "The Rise of Biblical Counseling," *Pacific Standard,* September 2, 2014, http://www.psmag.com/health-and-behavior/evangelical-prayer-bible -religion-born-again-christianity-rise-biblical-counseling-89464 (accessed May 26, 2017).

83. Frank Page, *Melissa: A Father's Lessons from a Daughter's Suicide* (Nashville, TN: B&H Books, 2013); Ed Stetzer, "Mental Illness & Medication vs. Spiritual Struggles & Biblical Counseling," *Christianity Today*, April 23, 2013, https://www .christianitytoday.com/edstetzer/2013/april/mental-illness-medication-vs-spiritual -struggles.html (accessed September 14, 2018).

84. Warren, *Dangerous Surrender*, 182.

85. "Juanita's Depression," YouTube, posted March 10, 2007, https://www.youtube .com/watch?v=zZP6vWFARqo&list=PLeQyWm-4HA3JXemE253cwwhTsKQe _uZgQ&index=10 (accessed May 26, 2017).

86. Ibid.

87. Pam Vredevelt, "About," http://pamvredevelt.com/about-us/ (accessed May 26, 2017).

88. Angie Smith's blog is found at http://angiesmithonline.com. The story of the loss of her daughter can be found in an entry entitled "Audrey's Story," 2008, http:// angiesmithonline.com/audreys-story/ (accessed May 26, 2017). See Angie Smith, *I Will Carry You: The Sacred Dance of Grief and Joy* (Nashville, TN: B&H, 2010).

89. These lines are from Smith's blog entry entitled "4:7," http://angiesmithonline .com/2008/04/47/ (accessed May 26, 2017).

90. For an example of this ministry, see "Diana's Angels Project," http://www.lwml
.org/posts/mission-servants-activities/march-2016?month=4&year=2016 (accessed
September 14, 2018).

91. Elise Erikson Barrett, *What Was Lost: A Christian Journey through Miscarriage*
(Louisville, KY: Westminster John Knox, 2010).

92. Anita Renfroe, phone interview by Kate Bowler, January 25, 2017.

93. LifeWay's Abundance Conference, March 11–12, 2016, Asheville, NC.

94. IF:Gathering, February 5, 2016, Austin, TX.

95. The idea of unrealistic conceptualizations of female beauty is not limited to
Christian women. See Naomi Wolf, *The Beauty Myth: How Images of Beauty Are Used
Against Women*, rep. ed. (New York: Harper Perennial, 2002). The topic of beauty will
be considered in greater depth in Chapter Four.

96. Name withheld, phone interview by Kate Bowler, December 20, 2016.

97. The most infamous example occurred in 1995 on the *Jenny Jones Show*, where
a young man revealed that he had a crush on a male friend. The friend brooded on this
and, anxious that he not be perceived as gay, killed the man. Murder charges were
brought, together with a $25-million lawsuit. The prosecutor in the murder trial
claimed, "The *Jenny Jones Show* ambushed this defendant with humiliation. And in
retaliation the defendant ambushed the victim with a shotgun." See Howard Kurtz,
Hot Air: All Talk, All the Time (New York: Times Books, 1996), 67.

98. Christine Caine, interview by Kate Bowler, December 3, 2016.

99. Jeanne Stevens, phone interview by Kate Bowler, March 8, 2016.

100. White, *Tele-Advising*, 8–9.

101. See Aaron Duplantier, *Authenticity and How We Fake It: Belief and Subjectiv-
ity in Reality TV, Facebook and YouTube* (Jefferson, NC: McFarland & Company, 2016);
Annette Hill, *Reality TV: Factual Entertainment and Television Audiences* (New York:
Routledge, 2005); Misha Kavka, *Reality TV* (Edinburgh: Edinburgh University Press,
2012); and Jervette R. Ward, ed., *Real Sisters: Stereotypes, Respectability and Black
Women in Reality TV* (New Brunswick, NJ: Rutgers University Press, 2015), for a discussion of Reality TV, its connection to authenticity, respectability, race, and notions
of intimacy.

102. From soap opera to talk shows to daytime television, confessional television
is deemed "women's" television. See White, *Tele-Advising*, 16.

103. Paula White, *Deal With It! You Cannot Conquer What You Will Not Confront*
(Nashville, TN: Thomas Nelson, 2005), x.

104. Ibid.

105. Name withheld, phone interview by Kate Bowler, April 4, 2016.

106. See chapter four of Marla Faye Frederick's *Colored Television: American Religion Gone Global* (Stanford, CA: Stanford University Press, 2016), 87–114.

107. In her book *Private Lives, Proper Relations: Regulating Black Intimacy* (Minneapolis: University of Minnesota Press, 2007), Candice Jenkins argues that the privileged position of respectability within African American communities stems from re-
current ideologies about black sexuality and the unspoken connection between the
"intimate" and the political within black culture. She contends that in order to subvert
accusations of sexual and domestic deviance the black community embraced bourgeois
notions of respectability. These efforts, she argues, are grounded in a "double vulnerability" of the black subject that encapsulates an opposition between racial scrutiny and

human intimacy. Given the significant role played by the black church within the African American community, it becomes a primary locale for the development and maintenance of said respectability. See Eddie Glaude, Jr., *Exodus! Religion, Race and Nation in Early Nineteenth-Century Black America* (Chicago: University of Chicago Press, 2000); Evelyn Brooks Higgenbottom, "African-American Women's History and the Metalanguage of Race," *Signs* 17.2 (2002): 251–74; Jonathan L. Walton, *Watch This! The Ethics and Aesthetic of Black Televangelism* (New York: New York University Press, 2009); Ward, *Real Sisters;* and Calvin White, Jr., *The Rise of Respectability: Race, Religion, and the Church of God in Christ* (Fayetteville: University of Arkansas Press, 2015) for discussions of race, respectability, and the black church.

108. Sarah Hagelin, *Reel Vulnerability: Power, Pain, and Gender in Contemporary American Film and Television* (New Brunswick, NJ: Rutgers University Press, 2013), 15.

109. See chapter five of Amy DeRogatis, *Saving Sex: Sexuality and Salvation in American Evangelicalism* (New York: Oxford University Press, 2015), 129–49, for a discussion of Bynum, sexuality, and vulnerability.

110. Name withheld, interview by Kate Bowler, February 7, 2017.

111. Name withheld, interview by Kate Bowler, June 7, 2016.

112. LifeTodayTV, "Sheila Walsh: My Divorce (Randy Robison / LIFE Today)," YouTube, posted June 1, 2016, https://www.youtube.com/watch?v=EcKBVN5qg1U (accessed May 26, 2017).

113. Book description on Amazon.com https://www.amazon.com/Longing-Me-Everything-Crave-Leads/dp/1400204895 (accessed September 14, 2018).

114. Lofton, *Oprah*, 85.

115. September Vaudrey, phone interview by Kate Bowler, February 3, 2017.

116. Name withheld, interview by Kate Bowler, March 13, 2016.

117. Warren, *Dangerous Surrender*, 123.

CHAPTER FIVE: THE BEAUTY

1. New International Version.

2. "Karen Clark-Sheard—Interview," YouTube, May 31, 2016, https://www.youtube.com/watch?v=djhEaZ8k-gM (accessed May 8, 2017).

3. Psalm 149:4, KJV.

4. Robin M. Morris, *Goldwater Girls to Reagan Women: Gender, Georgia, and the Rise of the New Right* (unpublished manuscript).

5. Elisabeth Elliot, *Let Me Be a Woman: Notes to My Daughter on the Meaning of Womanhood* (Wheaton, IL: Tyndale House, 1976), 50.

6. Larry Eskridge, *God's Forever Family: The Jesus People Movement in America* (New York: Oxford University Press, 2013), 42–43.

7. See Hartford Institute for Religion Research, *Hartford Megachurch Database*, 2017, http://hirr.hartsem.edu/cgi-bin/mega/db.pl?db=default&uid=default&view_records=1&ID=*&sb=2 (accessed May 8, 2017).

8. Eskridge, *God's Forever Family*, 69.

9. Daniel L. Seagraves, *Women's Hair: The Long and Short of It* (Stockton, CA: The Good Word, 1979).

10. Name withheld, phone interview by Kate Bowler, March 15, 2016.

11. Dorothy Kelley Patterson, "Dear Dottie: What's All This about Head Coverings?!?" *Biblical Woman*, May 7, 2012, https://biblicalwoman.com/dear-dottie-whats-all-this-about-head-coverings/ (accessed September 14, 2018).

12. Donna Miller, interview by Kate Bowler, November 16, 2016.

13. Paul Chappell, "Chappell: Thoughts on Modesty," YouTube, posted on November 14, 2014, https://www.youtube.com/watch?v=W3KYgF4uMfk (accessed May 8, 2017).

14. Ibid.

15. Mandy Arioto, interview by Kate Bowler, October 21, 2016.

16. Anthea D. Butler, *Women in the Church of God in Christ: Making a Sanctified World* (Chapel Hill: University of North Carolina Press, 2007), 5.

17. Ginger Strickland, interview by Kate Bowler, September 5, 2016.

18. See Randall Balmer, *Mine Eyes Have Seen the Glory: A Journey into the Evangelical Subculture of America*, 25th anniversary ed. (New York: Oxford University Press, 2014), for an example of this argument.

19. Michelle Tsai, "Tammy Faye Messner, Gay Icon," *Slate*, July 23, 2007, http://www.slate.com/articles/news_and_politics/explainer/2007/07/tammy_faye_messner_gay_icon.html (accessed May 8, 2017).

20. Christian McLaughlin, "Why I Love Jan Crouch," *The Advocate*, July 5, 2005. Viewers complained about their "worldliness" and even fellow leaders admitted that it made them uncomfortable. See Jack Hayford's foreword to Paul Crouch, *Hello World! A Personal Letter to the Body of Christ* (Nashville, TN: Thomas Nelson, 2003), viii.

21. A set of guidelines from a pentecostal church sets out the traditional position: "The basic reason for modesty of dress is to subdue the lust of the flesh, the lust of the eye, and the pride of life. The exposed body tends to arouse improper thoughts in both wearer and onlooker. To implement the purpose behind modest dress, the body should basically be covered, except for those parts which we must use openly for normal living. This suggests that clothes should cover the torso and upper limbs. Reasonable guidelines, then, would be women's dresses over the knee and sleeves to the elbow. In addition, we should avoid low necklines, sleeveless dresses or shirts, very tight clothes, very thin clothes, and slacks on women because they immodestly reveal the feminine contours of upper leg, thigh, and hip. Likewise, swimming in mixed company is immodest. Since the primary effect of makeup is to highlight sex appeal, we reject makeup as immodest." "Holy Doctrine of the United Apostolic Holiness Assemblies International," https://voiceoftruthapostolic.weebly.com/holy-doctrine.html (accessed September 18, 2018). Margaret English de Alminana and Lois E. Elena, eds., *Women in Pentecostal and Charismatic Ministry: Informing a Dialogue on Gender, Church, and Ministry* (Leiden, Netherlands: Brill, 2016), contains a number of chapters examining the connection between middle-class values and expectations of pentecostal women.

22. See Seth Dowland, *Family Values and the Rise of the Christian Right* (Philadelphia: University of Pennsylvania Press, 2015), for a discussion of the place of "family values" within the Christian right.

23. Vonda Kay Van Dyke, "Preface," in *That Girl in Your Mirror* (Old Tappan, NJ: F. H. Revell, 1966).

24. Promotional advertisement in Baker Publishing Catalogue, 1978. Betty Lougaris Soldo and Mary Drahos, *The Inside-Out Beauty Book* (Old Tappan, NJ: F. H. Revell, 1978).

25. See Joanne Wallace, *Dress with Style* (Old Tappan, NJ: F. H. Revell, 1983).

26. Andrea Stephens, "Andrea Stephens Ministries/About Andrea/The B.A.B.E. Journey," http://www.andreastephens.com/about.html (accessed March 30, 2017).

27. Cathy Milam, "The Unsinkable Linsay [sic] Roberts," *Tulsa World*, March 12, 1989, http://www.tulsaworld.com/archives/the-unsinkable-linsay-roberts/article_6afb8783–33e5–5c21–858d-c2af74031730.html (accessed March 25, 2017).

28. David Edwin Harrell, *Pat Robertson: A Life and Legacy* (Grand Rapids, MI: Eerdmans, 2010), 194.

29. Ibid., 183. See also Danuta Soderman, *Dear Danuta* (Old Tappan, NJ: F. H. Revell, 1986).

30. Harrell, *Pat Robertson,* 193.

31. Pink Impact, "Jessica Haas," https://pinkimpact.com/speakers/jessica-haas (accessed May 8, 2017). See also "About," https://www.jessicakhaas.com/about-me (accessed September 13, 2018).

32. Kay Warren, *Dangerous Surrender: What Happens When You Say Yes to God* (Grand Rapids, MI: Zondervan, 2007), 26.

33. Evangelical Council for Financial Responsibility, "Free Chapel," http://www.ecfa.org/MemberProfile.aspx?ID=31976 (accessed September 14, 2018).

34. Ecclesiastes 3:11 (KJV).

35. See the Divine Conference on Twitter: https://twitter.com/DIVINE_Conf (accessed May 8, 2017), and Taylor Madu, *Taylor Madu,* http://taylormadu.com/ (accessed May 8, 2017).

36. Propel Women, "Conversation Series Curriculum," 2017, http://www.propelwomen.org/content/curriculum/gju60p (accessed May 8, 2017).

37. URBN, "Who We Are," 2017, http://www.urbn.com/who-we-are/history (accessed May 8, 2017).

38. Abundance Conference, Asheville, NC, March 11–12, 2016.

39. Johnny Hunt's Men's Conference, "Breakouts," 2016, http://www.johnnyhuntmensconference.com/breakouts (accessed May 8, 2017).

40. LifeWay Men, "The Main Event 2016 Promo," Vimeo, https://vimeo.com/164579460 (accessed May 8, 2017).

41. Emily Matchar's lovely book, *Homeward Bound: Why Women Are Embracing the New Domesticity* (New York: Simon & Schuster, 2013), uses this term to account for the variety of activities from homesteading to knitting that became repopularized in the 2000s.

42. For examples of this, see Lisa Leonard Designs at https://www.lisaleonard.com/, Emily Ley Paper at https://www.emilyley.com/, and Jessica Honneger at https://www.noondaycollection.com (accessed September 14, 2018).

43. Ann Voskamp, "Home," http://annvoskamp.com (accessed May 8, 2017).

44. HGTV, *My Big Family Renovation,* http://www.hgtv.com/shows/my-big-family-renovation (accessed May 8, 2017).

45. Glory Haus online store, https://www.gloryhaus.com/jen-hatmaker_1558 (accessed September 14, 2018).

46. For more on Chip and Joanna Gaines, see https://magnolia.com/silos/ (accessed September 14, 2018); Kara Driscoll, "Chip and Joanna Gaines will open 'little shops' at Target stores," *Dayton Daily News*, September 13, 2017, https://www.daytondailynews

.com/business/chip-and-joanna-gaines-will-open-little-shops-target-stores/IA7WuIvMKZSGiGN3bDKcXP/ (accessed September 14, 2018).

47. See Ann Voskamp's website, https://www.annvoskamp.com (accessed September 14, 2018).

48. John Crist, "Christian Girl Instagram," YouTube, November 18, 2014, https://www.youtube.com/watch?v=ANv1_teeb3s (accessed September 14, 2018).

49. Phil and Debbie Waldrep, interview by Kate Bowler, October 29, 2016.

50. For the story of Victoria Osteen encouraging Joel to want a much bigger house, see Joel Osteen, *Your Best Life Now: 7 Steps to Living at Your Full Potential* (New York: Warner Faith, 2004), 7; and on her fear of public speaking, see Victoria Osteen, *Love Your Life: Living Happy, Healthy, and Whole* (New York, NY: Free Press, 2008), 35–36.

51. Kate Shellnutt, "Osteen on unapologetic wealth and Victoria's Secret lingerie," *Chron*, January 27, 2011, http://blog.chron.com/believeitornot/2011/01/osteen-on-unapologetic-wealth-and-victorias-secret-lingerie/ (accessed May 25, 2017); Ernest Herndon, "How a BIG Church Grew Bigger," *Charisma Magazine*, May 31, 2004, https://www.charismamag.com/component/content/article/146-j15/covers/cover-story/1259-how-a-big-church-grew-bigger (accessed September 14, 2018).

52. Cynthia McFadden and Mary Marsh, "How Joyce Meyer Built a Worldwide Following," *ABC News*, April 13, 2010, http://abcnews.go.com/Nightline/joyce-meyer-transparent-evangelist/story?id=10355887 (accessed May 8, 2017).

53. Osteen, *Love Your Life*, 83.

54. Wendy Treat, *Shoes Wisely: Choosing the Right Shoe for Every Occasion* (Seattle, WA: Casey Treat Ministries, 2013); *Preachers of Atlanta*, "Pastor Kimberly Jones-Pothier," Oxygen Network, http://www.oxygen.com/people/pastor-kimberly-jones-pothier (accessed May 8, 2017). See also *Heels and Tiaras Ministries*, http://heelsandtiarasministries.com/sample-page/ (accessed May 8, 2017).

55. Austin, "Woman of Style," *QCity Metro*, January 5, 2010, http://qcitymetro.com/2010/01/05/woman_of_style12124962/ (accessed May 8, 2017).

56. "First Lady Crisette M. Ellis," *Greater Grace Temple*, http://greatergrace.org/who-we-are/first-lady-crisette-m-ellis/ (accessed September 14, 2018).

57. Crisette Ellis, "August Fitness Goals," July 23, 2013, https://crisetteellis.wordpress.com/2013/07/23/august-fitness-goals/ (accessed May 8, 2017).

58. Crisette Ellis, "Store-Shirts," http://www.crisetteellis.com/store/c2/Shirts.html (accessed May 8, 2017).

59. Stephanie Garrett, "Togetta Ulmer @BishopUlmer at the 15th Annual First Ladies High Tea," YouTube, October 17, 2012, https://www.youtube.com/watch?v=iL-vnWfG_N8 (accessed May 8, 2017).

60. Hannah Baldwin, "Church Hats an Expression of Faith, Identity," Thenewsstar.com, March 25, 2016, http://www.thenewsstar.com/story/news/2016/03/25/church-hats-expression-faith-identity/82141598/ (accessed March 28, 2017); Lena Williams, "In Defense of the Church Hat," *The New York Times*, May 12, 1996, http://www.nytimes.com/1996/05/12/nyregion/in-defense-of-the-church-hat.html (accessed September 13, 2018).

61. Barbara O'Chester, interview by Kate Bowler, October 27, 2017.

62. Victoria Osteen, "Put Yourself on the List," JoelOsteen.com, https://www.joelosteen.com/Pages/Article.aspx?articleid=6497 (accessed September 18, 2018).

63. Ruth Marie Griffith, *Born Again Bodies: Flesh and Spirit in American Christianity* (Berkeley: University of California Press, 2004).

64. Patricia Kreml, *Slim for Him* (Plainfield, NJ: Logos International, 1978); Marie Chapian and Neva Coyle, *Free to Be Thin* (Minneapolis, MN: Bethany House Publishers, 1979).

65. Weigh Down, "Weigh Down—The Solution to Permanent Weight Loss," http://www.weighdown.com/ (accessed May 8, 2017); Gwen Shamlin, *Rise Above: God Can Set You Free from Your Weight Problems Forever* (Nashville, TN: Thomas Nelson, 2000); John W. Kennedy and Todd Starnes, "Gwen Shamblin in the Balance," *Christianity Today,* October 23, 2000, https://www.christianitytoday.com/ct/2000/october23/14.15.html (accessed September 14, 2018); and Martin Rademacher, *Devotional Fitness: An Analysis of Contemporary Christian Dieting and Fitness Programs* (Cham, Switzerland: Springer, 2017), 115, 209–210.

66. T. D. Jakes, *Lay Aside the Weight: Taking Control of It Before It Takes Control of You!* (Minneapolis, MN: Bethany House Publishers, 1997); Don Colbert, *What Would Jesus Eat?* (Nashville, TN: Thomas Nelson, 2005); Shirley Cook, *Diary of a Fat Housewife* (Denver, CO: Accent Books, 1977), *Diary of a Jogging Housewife* (Denver, CO: Accent Books, 1978), and *The Exodus Diet Plan* (Old Tappan, NJ: F. H. Revell Co., 1987).

67. Anita Bryant and Bob Green, *Running the Good Race* (Old Tappan, NJ: F.H. Revell Co., 1976).

68. "Pat Robertson's Age-Defying Shake," CBN, http://www1.cbn.com/community/pat-robertson%27s-age-defying-shake (accessed September 14, 2018); Paula White with Dodd Romero, *The Ten Commandments of Health and Wellness* (Tampa, FL: Paula White Enterprises, 2008).

69. Joyce Meyer, *Eat and Stay Thin: Simple, Spiritual, Satisfying Weight Control* (New York: FaithWords, 2002), 12.

70. Lisa Harper, interview by Kate Bowler, December 3, 2016.

71. Frances Hunter, *God's Answer to Fat: Lose It!* (Houston, TX: Hunter Ministries, 1971).

72. Anita Renfroe, "Those Ain't Pants/Anita Renfroe," YouTube, January 5, 2015, https://www.youtube.com/watch?v=MDQ5-zIUbbE (accessed September 14, 2018); "Anita Renfroe—You Raise Me Up," YouTube, July 25, 2008, https://www.youtube.com/watch?v=MarNBaD6p9o (accessed September 14, 2018).

73. Liz Curtis Higgs, *"One Size Fits All" and Other Fables* (Nashville, TN: Thomas Nelson, 1993), 92–93.

74. Jane Johnson Struck, "Being a Big, Beautiful Woman in a Narrow, Nervous World," *Today's Christian Woman* (January–February 1994): 32–35.

75. Neva Coyle and Maria Chapian, *Free to Be Thin* (Minneapolis, MN: Bethany House, 1979), 10.

76. Neva Coyle, *Loved on a Grander Scale* (Ann Arbor, MI: Servant Publications, 1998), 62.

77. *The Sisterhood,* TLC, Season 1, Episode 1, "Thou Shalt Not Cross a First Lady."

78. Ibid.

79. Ibid.

80. Bravo, "The Real Housewives of Potomac—Gizelle Bryant," Bravo, November 11, 2015, http://www.bravotv.com/people/gizelle-bryant (accessed May 8, 2017).

81. Ben Ashford, "How the marriage of Real Housewives of Potomac's Gizelle Bryant to megachurch pastor husband crumbled amid allegations of his cheating and out-of-wedlock children," *Mail Online*, January 18, 2006, http://www.dailymail.co.uk/news/article-3401543/How-marriage-Real-Housewives-Potomac-s-Gizelle-Bryant-megachurch-pastor-husband-crumbled-amid-allegations-cheating-wedlock-children.html (accessed May 25, 2017).

82. Latoya Jefferson-James, "Selective Reuptake: Perpetuating Misleading Cultural Identities in the Reality Television World," in *Real Sister: Stereotypes, Respectability, and Black Women in Reality TV*, ed. Jervette R. Ward (New Brunswick, NJ: Rutgers University Press, 2015), 46–49.

83. Lipstick Alley, https://www.lipstickalley.com/ (accessed September 14, 2018).

84. *Basketball Wives*, VH1; Angie Hayes, *Even the Preacher Got a Side Chick* (Cachet Presents, 2016); Andre Ray, *Undercover Deacon* (Andre Ray, 2016).

85. See Monique Moultrie, "Black Female Sexual Agency and Racialized Holy Sex in Black Christian Reality TV Shows," *Religion and Reality TV: Faith in Late Capitalism*, ed. Mara Einstein, Diane Winston, and Katherine Madden (London and New York: Routledge, 2018).

86. *Preachers of L.A.*, Oxygen Network, Season 1, Episode 1, "Comeback."

87. "Somebody Come Get Him: Top 5 Most Inappropriate Ben Tankard Sex Quotes," *EEW Magazine—News from a Faith-Based Perspective,* November 25, 2013, http://buzz.eewmagazine.com/eew-magazine-buzz-blog/2013/11/25/somebody-come-get-him-top-5-most-inappropriate-ben-tankard-s.html (accessed May 15, 2017).

88. Ame Fuhlbruck, "OK, Let's Stop With All This Talk About 'Smokin' Hot' Wives," *Relevant Magazine*, June 22, 2016, https://relevantmagazine.com/life/relationships/ok-lets-stop-all-talk-about-smokin-hot-wives (accessed September 14, 2018); ESPN, "2011 NASCAR Nashville Nationwide Pre Race Invocation by Pastor Joe Nelms," YouTube, July 29, 2011, https://www.youtube.com/watch?v=QhKELP-7UD8 (accessed May 8, 2017).

89. Derek and Ruth Prince, *God Is a Matchmaker: Seven Biblical Principles for Finding Your Mate* (Grand Rapids, MI: Chosen, 2011), 29.

90. James Schaffer and Colleen Todd, *Christian Wives: Women Behind the Evangelists Reveal Their Faith in Modern Marriage* (Garden City, NY: Doubleday, 1987), 8.

91. Amy DeRogatis, *Saving Sex: Sexuality and Salvation in American Evangelicalism* (New York: Oxford University Press, 2014).

92. Ed and Lisa Young, *Sexperiment: 7 Days to Lasting Intimacy with Your Spouse* (New York: FaithWords, 2012).

93. Lindy Royce-Bartlett, "Pastor and Wife Preach Married Sex with 24-Hour 'Bed-In,'" *CNN: Belief Blog*, January 13, 2012, http://religion.blogs.cnn.com/2012/01/13/pastor-and-wife-preach-married-sex-with-24-hour-bed-in/ (accessed April 2, 2017).

94. Ibid.; Anugrah Kumar, "'Sexperiment:' Ed Young Suffers Eye Injury; Leaves Before 24 Hours Over," *The Christian Post,* January 15, 2012, http://www.christianpost.com/news/sexperiment-ed-young-suffers-eye-injury-leaves-before-24-hours-over-67182/ (accessed April 2, 2017); Christopher Wynn, "Dear God: Is Dallas society ready for Fellowship Church's sex-loving, million-dollar minister?" *Dallas News,* December 12, 2013, http://res.dallasnews.com/interactives/2013_December/pastored (accessed May 8, 2017).

95. David Gibson/RNS, "Why Are So Many Pastors Pulling Stunts?," *Charisma News,* January 14, 2014, https://www.charismanews.com/us/42419-why-are-so-many -pastors-pulling-stunts (accessed September 14, 2018).

96. Ruth Peale, *The Adventure of Being a Wife* (Englewood Cliffs, NJ: Prentice-Hall, 1971), 238.

97. Ibid., 238.

98. Beverly LaHaye, *The New Spirit-Controlled Woman* (Eugene, OR: Harvest House, 1982), 126.

99. Mark Driscoll, "Evangelical Leader Quits Amid Allegations of Sex and Drug Use," *Resurgence,* November 2006, https://web.archive.org/web/20070126175840 /http://theresurgence.com/md_blog_2006-11-03_evangelical_leader_quits (accessed May 26, 2017).

100. Valerie Tarico, "Christian right mega-church minister faces mega-mutiny for alleged abusive behavior," *Salon,* April 3, 2014, http://www.salon.com/2014/04/03 /christian_right_mega_church_minister_faces_mega_muntiny_for_abusive _behavior_partner/ (accessed May 8, 2017).

101. Terrie Chappell, "Striving Together Publications," https://strivingtogether .com/Authors/Terrie-Chappell/ (accessed May 25, 2017).

102. Terrie Chappell, *The Choice Is Yours* (Lancaster, CA: Striving Together Publications, 2011), 83, 123–24.

103. Ibid.

104. "Who Shepherds Me, Part 3," posted July 27, 2014, http://www.redemptioni churchod.com.php53–9.dfw1–2.websitetestlink.com/?video_uuid=keh1db5r (accessed September 14, 2015).

105. Cedric Harmon, "Breakthrough in the Bible Belt," *Charisma Magazine,* May 31, 2000, http://www.charismamag.com/blogs/162-j15/features/spiritual -renewal/46-breakthrough-in-the-bible-belt (accessed March 27, 2017).

106. K 180 Fitness, "Success Stories," http://k180fitness.com/why-k180/success -stories/ (accessed March 27, 2017).

107. Nicola Menzie, "Hope Carpenter Repents, Apologizes to SC Megachurch for First Time Since Husband Ron Carpenter Revealed Marital Woes," *The Christian Post,* July 30, 2014, http://www.christianpost.com/news/hope-carpenter-repents-apologizes -to-sc-megachurch-for-first-time-since-husband-ron-carpenter-revealed-marital -woes-124021/ (accessed March 27, 2017).

108. Nicola Menzie, "Pastor Ron Carpenter, After Revealing Wife's Adultery and 'Sickness,' Says Bishop TD Jakes to Help Reconcile Marriage," *The Christian Post,* January 6, 2014, http://www.christianpost.com/news/pastor-ron-carpenter-and-wife -hope-carpenter-to-reconcile-marriage-with-help-of-bishop-td-jakes-112056/ (accessed May 8, 2017).

109. As Bauer shows, Swaggart's confession was a marked departure from that of Jim Bakker a year earlier. Both were accused of sexual sin, but whereas Bakker refused to confess and spoke angrily of his accusers, Swaggart accepted responsibility and his church's disciplinary proceedings. However, Swaggart adopted a more defiant response following a scandal three years later, which ultimately led to the disintegration of his ministry. See chapter seven of Susan Wise Bauer, *The Art of the Public Grovel: Sexual Sin and Public Confession in America* (Princeton, NJ: Princeton University Press, 2008).

110. Jeff Kunerth, "Discovery Church pastor resigns after admitting to affair," *Orlando Sentinel*, May 6, 2013, http://articles.orlandosentinel.com/2013-05-06/features/os-discovery-church-pastor-admits-affair-20130506_1_isaac-hunter-summit-church-discovery-church (accessed May 8, 2017).

111. Tim Elfrink, "Founder of Florida's Biggest Megachurch Accused of Molesting a 4-Year-Old," *Miami New Times*, November 14, 2017, https://www.miaminewtimes.com/news/bob-coy-founder-of-calvary-chapel-fort-lauderdale-accused-of-molesting-child-9827948 (accessed September 14, 2018); Bob Smietana and Morgan Lee, "Tullian Tchividjian Resigns after Admitting 'Inappropriate Relationship,'" ChristianityToday.com/ Gleanings, July 30, 2015, http://www.christianitytoday.com/gleanings/2015/june/tullian-tchividjian-resigns-after-admitting-inappropiate-re.html (accessed March 27, 2017).

112. For more on the phenomenon, see Edwin L. Battistella, *Sorry About That: The Language of Public Apology* (Oxford: Oxford University Press, 2014).

113. See, for instance, the attention paid to the absence of Bob Coy and his family: "First Public Update on Bob Coy," Phoenix Preacher—An Online Community of Faith, August 6, 2014, http://michaelnewnham.com/?p=18878 (accessed May 8, 2017).

114. Jennifer Leclaire, "Sam Hinn Getting Re-Ordained 8 Months After Sexual Misconduct," *Charisma News,* August 9, 2013, http://www.charismanews.com/us/40579-sam-hinn-getting-re-ordained-8-months-after-sexual-misconduct (accessed March 27, 2017); and Melissa Stefan, "Was Benny Hinn's Brother Restored to Ministry Too Soon After Affair?" *Christianity Today*, August 16, 2013, http://www.christianitytoday.com/gleanings/2013/august/benny-hinn-brother-sam-reordained-after-affair.html (accessed March 27, 2017).

115. Adrienne S. Gaines, "Benny Hinn Admits 'Friendship' With Paula White But Tells TV Audience It's Over," *Charisma Magazine*, August 10, 2010, http://www.charismamag.com/site-archives/570-news/featured-news/11683-benny-hinn-admits-friendship-with-paula-white-but-tells-tv-audience-its-over (accessed March 27, 2017).

116. Elaine Fisher, "My Story," http://www.elainefisher.com/about/ (accessed April 2, 2017).

117. For an in-depth look at Billy Graham, see Grant Wacker, *America's Pastor: Billy Graham and the Shaping of a Nation* (Cambridge, MA: Belknap, 2014).

118. Jenni Catron, interview by Kate Bowler, March 2, 2016.

119. In the aftermath of high-profile Hollywood sexual assault and harassment allegations in 2017 and the revelation that Vice President Mike Pence held to his own version of "the Billy Graham rule," secular and Christian media outlets were awash with debates about the efficacy and theological propriety of the rule. See for example, Katelyn Beaty, "A Christian Case Against the Pence Rule," *The New York Times*, November 15, 2017, https://www.nytimes.com/2017/11/15/opinion/pence-rule-christian-graham.html (accessed September 14, 2018); and Tish Harrison Warren, "It's Not the Billy Graham Rule or Bust," *Christianity Today*, April 27, 2018, https://www.christianitytoday.com/ct/2018/april-web-only/its-not-billy-graham-rule-or-bust.html (accessed September 14, 2018).

120. Paula Williams, interview by Kate Bowler, July 12, 2016.

121. The second being Karen Oliveto who served as the pastor of Glide Memorial Church in San Fransisco, CA, from 2008 to 2016 when she was elected bishop of the Mountain Sky Area of the United Methodist Church. Information about her and her

role as bishop can be found at http://www.umc.org/bishops/bishop-karen-oliveto (accessed October 30, 2018). Glide Memorial is the twelfth largest United Methodist Church in the United States and the 668th largest congregation in the nation with three thousand weekly participants. Information about Glide Memorial can be found at https://www.glide.org/church (accessed October 30, 2018).

122. Mark Yarhouse, "How Can We Thoughtfully Engage the Transgender Conversation?" Q Ideas, http://qideas.org/videos/transgender-1/ (accessed September 14, 2018).

123. T. J. Raphael, "This election season, evangelicals are focused on 'religious liberty,'" Public Radio International, November 3, 2016, https://www.pri.org/stories/2016-11-03/election-season-evangelicals-are-focused-religious-liberty (accessed September 14, 2018).

124. Billy Hallowell, "Seven Well-Known Pastors Who Are Speaking Out Against Gay Marriage Legalization: 'Culture Will Get Increasingly Darker,'" The Blaze, June 29, 2015, http://www.theblaze.com/news/2015/06/29/seven-well-known-pastors-who-held-little-back-over-the-supreme-courts-gay-marriage-ruling-culture-will-get-increasingly-darker/ (accessed May 25, 2017); Katherine Peralta, "Franklin Graham Says People Should Boycott Target," The Charlotte Observer, July 15, 2016, https://www.charlotteobserver.com/news/business/article89804127.html (accessed September 13, 2018).

125. See Q Christian Fellowship, https://www.qchristian.org/about-us/ (accessed July 11, 2018).

126. Carlyle Murphy, "Most U.S. Christian groups grow more accepting of homosexuality," Pew Research Center, December 18, 2015, http://www.pewresearch.org/fact-tank/2015/12/18/most-u-s-christian-groups-grow-more-accepting-of-homosexuality/ (accessed May 25, 2017).

127. Annie Downs, interview by Kate Bowler, March 12, 2016.

128. There were attempts by authors such as Marion Jordan, Nancy DeMoss, Jennifer Marshall, Carolyn McCulley, and Mandy Hale.

129. See Camerin Courtney, "30 and Single? It's Your Own Fault," Christianity Today, June 21, 2006, http://www.christianitytoday.com/ct/2006/juneweb-only/125–32.0.html (accessed May 8, 2017); and Nancy DeMoss Wolgemuth, Singled Out for Him (Buchanan, MI: Life Action Ministries, 1998).

130. See Dowland, Family Values.

131. Lisa Harper, interview by Kate Bowler, October 2, 2018.

132. There were always the "It's Okay" books, like Poppy Smith, I'm Too Young to Be This Old (Eugene, OR: Harvest House, 1997).

133. Isaiah 53:2 (NIV).

CONCLUSION

1. John Holmes Agnew, Woman's Offices and Influence: An Address before the Monroe Female Seminary, delivered August 6, 1851 (New York: J. F. Trow, 1851), 14–15.

2. Jennifer Crow, Perfect Lies: Overcoming Nine Hidden Beliefs That Stand Between You and a Healthy Joy-Filled Life (Tulsa, OK: Tyndale Momentum, 2012), 3–4.

3. Carla Hinton, "Oklahoma megachurch leader resigns because of infidelity," *News OK*, May 1, 2014, https://newsok.com/article/4745068/oklahoma-megachurch -leader-resigns-because-of-infidelity (accessed October 30, 2018).

4. By 2018, Jennifer Crow had found new footing as a leader of her own nonprofit, https://www.victory.church/people/jennifer-crow (accessed October 30, 2018) which followed the trend of moving from institutional leadership to parachurch ministry where women's leadership was common.

5. Name withheld, Propel Conference, Orlando, FL, December 3, 2016.

6. Lydia Meredith, *The Gay Preacher's Wife: How My Gay Husband Deconstructed My Life and Reconstructed My Faith* (New York: Gallery Books, 2016), 213.

7. Todd W. Ferguson, "Failing to Master Divinity: How Institutional Type, Financial Debt, Community Acceptance, and Gender Affect Seminary Graduates' Career Choices," *Review of Religious Research* 57.3 (2015): 341–63.

8. The two female Christian leaders who have ever ascended the platform have been billed as "advocates." Christine Caine is billed as "The A21 Campaign and Director of Equip and Empower Ministries," and Danielle Strickland, "Officer in The Salvation Army; Advocate and Author." See "Faculty," The Global Leadership Summit Website, August 18, 2016, http://willowcreek.com/events/leadership/index.html#faculty (accessed May 22, 2017), and "The 2015 Global Leadership Summit Faculty Announcement," Follow the GLS website, http://www.followthegls.com/leadership-lessons/the -2015-global-leadership-summit-faculty-announcement/ (accessed May 22, 2017).

9. Heather Larson had previously served as executive pastor at Willow Creek. In the wake of Willow Creek founder Bill Hybels's anticipated retirement, Larson was named lead pastor and Steve Carter teaching pastor. See Manya Brachear Pashman, "Female church executive named lead pastor of Willow Creek," *Chicago Tribune*, October 15, 2017, http://www.chicagotribune.com/news/local/breaking/ct-met-willow -creek-pastor-20171015-story.html (accessed July 10, 2018). When more news of misconduct was revealed, Larson stepped down to allow her church a "fresh start." See Bob Smietana, "Willow Creek Elders and Pastor Heather Larson Resign over Bill Hybels," *Christianity Today,* August 8, 2018, https://www.christianitytoday.com/news/2018 /august/willow-creek-bill-hybels-heather-larson-elders-resign-inves.html (accessed October 3, 2018).

10. *Leading & Loving It,* http://leadingandlovingit.com/ (accessed May 9, 2017).

11. Brandi Wilson continues to co-lead Leading and Loving It after Pete Wilson resigned his post in 2017. See Holly Meyer, "Attendance, giving down at Cross Point Church 6 months after pastor resigns," *Tennessean*, March 23, 2017, https://www .tennessean.com/story/news/religion/2017/03/23/attendance-giving-down-cross -point-church-6-months-after-pastor-resigns/99488694/ (accessed October 30, 2018).

12. Leading and Loving It has since expanded their categories to: Senior Pastor/ Wife, Church Planter/Wife, Executive Pastor/Wife, Associate Pastor/Wife, Campus Pastor/Wife, Worship Pastor/Wife, Women's Ministry Pastor/Wife/Leader, Adult Ministry Pastor/Wife/Leader, Family and Student Ministries Pastor/Wife/Leader, Care and Counseling Pastor/Wife/Leader, Administrative Staff/Wife, Miscellaneous Church Leader, and Non-Profit Director/Wife/Leader. Lori Wilhite, E-mail correspondence with Kate Bowler, October 31, 2018.

13. Lori Wilhite, interview by Kate Bowler, January 24, 2017.

14. John H. Wigger, *PTL: The Rise and Fall of Jim and Tammy Faye Bakker's Evangelical Empire* (Oxford: Oxford University Press, 2017).

15. "Interview: Paula White on TD Jakes as Her 'Spiritual Daddy,'" *The Christian Post*, 2017, http://www.christianpost.tv/interview-paula-white-on-td-jakes-as-her-spiritual-daddy-3675/ (accessed May 9, 2017).

16. "Juanita Bynum: A Renewed Covenant," YouTube, March 19, 2015, https://www.youtube.com/watch?v=KsczhFGLK6Q (accessed October 30, 2018). "TD JAKES and Subtle Slithering Deceit on Juanita Bynum," YouTube, posted December 17, 2010, https://www.youtube.com/watch?v=mVz8qCNTwFs (accessed October 30, 2018).

17. Rachel Held Evans, E-mail correspondence with Kate Bowler, October 20, 2018.

18. Angie Hong, interview by Kate Bowler, March 25, 2017.

19. After posting comments on Twitter, Beth Moore followed up with an April 20, 2017, blog post, "About that personal branding conversation," Living Proof Ministries, https://blog.lproof.org/2017/04/personal-branding-conversation.html (accessed May 22, 2017).

20. Jen Hatmaker, Facebook page, "You are going to love Grove Collective if you don't already," https://www.facebook.com/jenhatmaker/videos/you-are-going-to-love-grove-collaborative-if-you-dont-already-fall-scents-plus-f/1955644871394809/ (accessed October 30, 2018).

21. Former lesbian Rosaria Butterfield chided Hatmaker for failing "to discern the true nature of the Christian doctrine of sin," while Jennie Allen of the IF:Gathering made it clear that while the subject was a difficult one, traditional biblical teaching on marriage had to be affirmed. See "Evangelical Women Challenge Jen Hatmaker's LGBT Comments," CBNNews, November 1, 2016, http://www1.cbn.com/cbnnews/us/2016/november/evangelical-women-challenge-jen-hatmakers-lgbt-comments (accessed October 30, 2018).

22. Tiffany Stanley, "This Evangelical Leader Denounced Trump. Then the Death Threats Started," *Politico*, December 17, 2017, https://www.politico.com/magazine/story/2017/12/17/is-jen-hatmaker-the-conscious-of-evangelical-christianity-216068 (accessed October 30, 2018); Tish Harrison Warren, "Who's In Charge of the Christian Blogosphere," *Christianity Today*, April 2017, https://www.christianitytoday.com/women/2017/april/whos-in-charge-of-christian-blogosphere.html (accessed October 30, 2018); Kate Shellnutt, "LifeWay Stops Selling Jen Hatmaker Books over LGBT Beliefs," *Christianity Today*, October 27, 2016, https://www.christianitytoday.com/news/2016/october/lifeway-stops-selling-jen-hatmaker-books-lgbt-beliefs-chris.html (accessed October 30, 2018). Others whose books have been denied space in LifeWay stores for doctrinal reasons include Joel Osteen and Joyce Meyer.

23. Catherine Woodiwiss, "A Religious Leader for the Resisterhood," *Medium*, October 15, 2018, https://medium.com/s/powertrip/the-religious-leader-of-the-resisterhood-aac86dc521c8 (accessed October 30, 2018).

24. Beth Moore on Twitter, @bethmooreLPM, October 9, 2017 (accessed October 30, 2018).

25. Emma Green, "The Tiny Blond Bible Teacher Taking on the Evangelical Political Machine," *The Atlantic*, October 2018, https://www.theatlantic.com/magazine/archive/2018/10/beth-moore-bible-study/568288/ (accessed October 30, 2018).

26. Katelyn Beatty, "Why Evangelical Women Leaders Don't Talk about Politics," *Religion and Politics*, December 19, 2017, https://religionandpolitics.org/2017/12

/19/why-evangelical-women-leaders-dont-talk-about-politics/ (accessed October 30, 2018).

27. "Comedian Chonda Pierce on Jesus and Facebook—Comedy Videos," God-Tube, https://www.godtube.com/watch/?v=YWKZ7PNX (accessed October 30, 2018).

28. Chonda Pierce, "RIAA* Certified Top-Selling Female Comedian–In History!" https://chonda.org/2015/07/24/riaa-certified-top-selling-female-comedian-in-history/ (accessed March 20, 2018).

29. Jonathan Merritt, "In a #Metoo moment, will Southern Baptists hold powerful men accountable?," *The Washington Post,* April 30, 2018, https://www.washingtonpost.com/news/acts-of-faith/wp/2018/04/30/in-a-metoo-moment-will-southern-baptists-hold-powerful-men-accountable/?noredirect=on&utm_term=.ea97781d415b (accessed October 30, 2018).

30. A good summary of the pushback can be found here: "Why #Winsome Doesn't Always Win—#ThingsOnlyChristianWomenHear," April 25, 2017, https://sierrawhite.com/2017/04/25/why-winsome-doesnt-always-win-thingsonlychristianwomenhear/ (accessed October 30, 2018).

31. The exception was televangelist Marilyn Hickey, who might have chosen her son but was grooming her daughter to replace her.

32. Anne Graham Lotz—Angel Ministries, "About Anne Graham Lotz," http://www.annegrahamlotz.org/about-anne-graham-lotz/about// (accessed May 25, 2017). Her brother Franklin echoed this praise, noting that Anne knew the Bible better than most since she would "spend 16 hours [preparing] for one hour of Bible study." See Tammi Reed Ledbetter, "'60 Minutes' segment on Anne Graham Lotz muddied SBC stance on women in ministry," Baptist Press, June 7, 2001, http://www.bpnews.net/11051/60-minutes-segment-on-anne-graham-lotz-muddied-sbc-stance-on-women-in-ministry (accessed October 30, 2018); "Divine Impulses: Anne Graham Lotz on 'breaking lots of glass ceilings,'" *The Washington Post*, December 15, 2009, http://www.washingtonpost.com/wp-dyn/content/video/2009/12/15/VI2009121504587.html (accessed October 30, 2018).

33. Tim Funk, "New Billy Graham book echoes hard-line preacher of '50s, not grandfatherly evangelist of love," *Charlotte Observer*, October 6, 2015, https://www.charlotteobserver.com/living/religion/article38008473.html (accessed October 30, 2018).

34. "Divine Impulses," *The Washington Post.*

35. "Honoring the Life of Billy Graham," March 2, 2018, https://memorial.billygraham.org/funeral-service-transcript/ (accessed October 30, 2018).

36. Amy Collier Artman, *The Miracle Lady: Kathryn Kuhlman and the Transformation of Charismatic Christianity* (Grand Rapids, MI: Eerdmans, 2019).

37. Nancy Wilson, interview by Kate Bowler, December 20, 2016.

38. Jeanne Stevens, interview by Kate Bowler, April 4, 2016.

39. Amy Butler, interview by Kate Bowler, December 6, 2016.

APPENDIX I: MEGACHURCHES IN THE UNITED STATES

1. The most up-to-date list from the Hartford Institute for Religion Research Database of Megachurches in the United States can be found at http://hirr.hartsem.edu/megachurch/database.html (accessed October 30, 2018).

APPENDIX IV: WOMEN IN CONSERVATIVE SEMINARIES

1. Originally, we included Moody Bible Institute in the list as well. Upon examining its website and other materials, we concluded that Moody was doing something significantly different enough that it was not helpful to include it in our calculations. In addition to being programmatically different, Moody also had considerably more people listed as faculty, but it was not clear the specialty or training for these individuals. We treated Moody as any other seminary for the purposes of data collection, but its information was omitted from calculations and/or trends.

INDEX

Page numbers in *italics* refer to illustrations.